THE COMPLETE

EQUINE

VETERINARY MANUAL

THE COMPLETE
EQUINE
VETERINARY MANUAL
New Edition

A comprehensive and instant guide
to equine health

TONY PAVORD
BVSc, MRCVS
& MARCY PAVORD

David & Charles

Contents

INTRODUCTION

Horse ownership, whether for business or recreation, can be a fascinating and a lifelong pleasure. At the same time, the horse is a creature of fast reactions, prone to sudden flight; it is also susceptible to injury induced by work, training and competition, and to myriad illnesses, common and uncommon: for these reasons it can also be a cause for worry and anxiety.

This book is written with the aim of relieving some of that uncertainty and anxiety by providing an easily accessible handbook to guide the horse owner towards taking the correct action and making the right decisions in case of illness or injury of the horse.

PART I of the book is divided into four sections, the first of which, 'Knowing your Horse' is to help you to understand your horse's anatomy and physiology, and to assess good health. The second section, 'Preventative Treatment', explains the basic routine care essential to guard against the most serious common ailments and to keep your horse in good condition and able to work. The third section, 'You and Your Vet', is a guide based on visible symptoms as to situations when immediate, urgent help is required; those where veterinary treatment is essential but less urgent; and those which may require treatment if they are persistent, unpleasant or uncomfortable for the horse. The fourth section, 'First Aid', describes what the horse owner should do in a crisis, or whilst waiting for the vet to arrive. It also explains how to treat minor injuries, and how to give prescribed medicines, by mouth or injection.

PART II of the book is an **anatomical index of diseases**, giving briefly the symptoms, cause and treatment, and also the geographical location of each disease, arranged by reference to the horse's anatomy.

For example, under 'Diseases affecting Movement', you will find listed: 'Conditions of the Foot'; 'Conditions of the Limbs'; 'Conditions of the Musculature'; and 'Conditions of the Skeleton'. If you do not know the name of the problem from which your horse is suffering, look under the appropriate anatomical section and you will find all the possible conditions, together with their symptoms.

PART III gives a more expanded description of each disease, using an **A to Z** encyclopaedic formula. This can be consulted directly, or for a fuller explanation once you have found the symptoms and name of the disease via the Anatomical Index.

Above The third section of Part 1 is a guide based on visible symptoms as to situations where veterinary treatment of some degree is required

USING THE BOOK

EXAMPLE 1:

Your horse pulls up from a gallop very lame. At first there are no obvious signs of injury, but gradually the tendons below the knee in his near fore show swelling and heat. You are able to lead him slowly home.

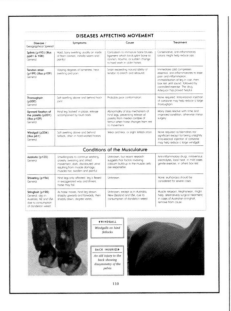

In the **Anatomical Index**, consult the section on 'Diseases Affecting Movement' and the sub-section 'Conditions of the Limbs'. Read the brief details of each condition to find the one with the most appropriate symptoms, in this case 'tendon strain'. Apply a cold compress to the injured leg immediately – a packet of frozen vegetables from your freezer will do – and call your veterinary surgeon who will come out straightaway and give anti-inflammatories and painkillers, and will immobilise the leg in a cast. (Notice the differences in the symptoms for 'tendon strain' and those for 'fractures'.)

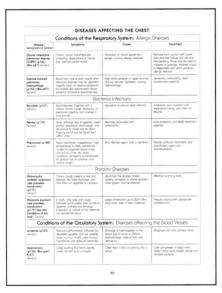

EXAMPLE 2: You are getting your horse fit to go team chasing: he has done his initial fittening work largely from the field, only stabled for part of the day, but for the last two weeks he has been stabled all the time. Unfortunately his breathing has become increasingly laboured, and he has started to cough. You give him a week's rest in the field, and he seems to improve. However, as soon as he is stabled again, the symptoms return.

Turn to the section of the **Anatomical Index** on 'Diseases Affecting the Chest' and the sub-section 'Conditions of the Respiratory System'. There are three which might fit the symptoms you observe in your horse: chronic obstructive pulmonary disease (now called recurrent airway obstruction), bronchitis and pneumonia.

However, you can analyse further and see that bronchitis is a constant condition, whereas your horse improves almost to normal when he is out in the field; and in pneumonia the horse loses his appetite and runs a high temperature, whereas yours is eating just as much and has no fever.

On consulting the entry for 'chronic obstructive pulmonary disease' in the **A to Z**, you will find that because COPD (RAO) is an allergic reaction, there is no reason why you should not be able to get your horse fit *as long as* you follow a rigorous clear-air regime; full details are given as to how to achieve this, also the drugs currently available to alleviate the condition.

Part I

KEEPING YOUR HORSE HEALTHY

KNOWING YOUR HORSE

ASSESSING CONFORMATION

Conformation is the word used to describe the physical structure of the horse and its attendant strengths and weaknesses. A horse that is well conformed has the physical potential to be trained for competition to a basic standard in any given sphere of equestrianism. Conformational variables render a horse either more or less suited to training for any given discipline, whereas actual faults of conformation pinpoint potential physical problems likely to occur when the horse is put under the stress of training.

The first requirement is that the various body parts should be in proportion, thus giving a balanced overall picture. Where proportions vary, counterbalancing points should have an equalising effect, an aspect most easily illustrated by reference to the head and neck.

In assessing conformation, look for a pleasing and well proportioned overall picture

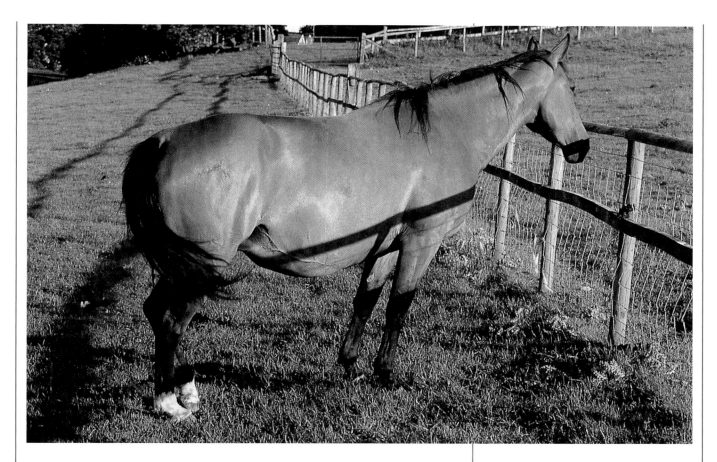

A Standardbred mare, showing the typically long head, short neck and powerful, muscular conformation

The Thoroughbred, showing long, clean limbs, small head and muscular but streamlined build

Head and neck: The head is ideally appropriate to the type of horse, for example a small, pretty head on an Arab or show pony, or a more workmanlike head on a cob. Smaller heads are generally preferred to larger ones, but this may be an aesthetic rather than a functional preference. Some breeds, such as the American Standardbred, characteristically carry a long head which is balanced by a comparatively short, muscular neck. The Thoroughbred, on the other hand, which is built for speed, typically has a comparatively small head and long neck.

The head and neck together, beyond the forelegs (or front pillars of support), represent a considerable proportion of the 60 per cent of weight which is carried on the horse's forehand. Clearly the neck must be sufficiently strongly conformed to carry the weight of the head easily, to enable the horse to stay well balanced. The neck should form a graceful curve from poll to withers, with a steeper curve from throat to chest and there should be room at the throat for flexion.

Facial features vary according to breed or type and there are no set parameters. However, it is generally accepted that the eye should be large, alert and have a kind expression. Breadth and shape of forehead is traditionally said to have a bearing on temperament and intelligence. An excessively dished face may restrict the free passage of air to the lungs; this is also influenced by the size and capacity for expansion of the nostrils. Conformation of the mouth is subject to considerable variation, and influences ease of acceptance of the bit as well as the ability to masticate food efficiently. 'Parrot mouth' is a conformation fault where the upper jaw overshoots the lower.

Withers and shoulders: The withers cover the spinal processes of the anterior thoracic vertebrae. They should be prominent to allow good attachment of ligaments and muscles, and well sloped back, in conjunction with a sloping shoulder, for good athletic performance. An upright shoulder with the minimum of angulation between scapula (shoulder blade) and humerus (linking the point of shoulder to the elbow) produces a shortened stride.

Chest and body: The space which is available for the heart, lungs and gut is determined by the depth of the chest and ribcage. The true ribs are ideally long and flat to allow the horse to carry a saddle and rider comfortably, while the remaining 'false' ribs are more rounded. The muscles of the ribcage and abdomen play a part in obtaining the round outline necessary for balance when carrying a rider.

Prominent withers and a long, sloping shoulder on this Thoroughbred horse

Back and loins: Medium length of back is most functional. A short back from withers to croup restricts the action and, if disproportionately short, can result in action faults or deviations. A long back is likely to have weaker loins and therefore reduced weight-carrying ability; it is often also associated with weak quarters.

Quarters: The quarters contain the heavy bones of the pelvic girdle and femur, connected by the hip joint and surrounded by large muscle masses. For athletic performance the quarters must be long, to allow for good angulation of the joints, and well muscled for propulsive power.

Limbs: Speed is related to length of forearm in the foreleg and gaskin in the hind leg. These should be strong and well muscled. The lower limbs, which are supported by tendons and ligaments, without muscles, should be short for strength and stability. The forelimbs, which bear the greater part of the horse's weight, are less angled than the hind limbs, which provide scope for forward propulsion.

Feet: Well conformed and well balanced feet are essential for long-term performance, and it should be remembered that the balance of the foot must be assessed in conjunction with the conformation of the limb above it, and taking into account the effects of the transference of bodyweight and forces of movement via the limb to the ground.

A Welsh Cob mare and her half-bred foal. This native breed contributes power, tough limbs and feet and native hardiness when crossed with the Thoroughbred

POINTS OF THE HORSE

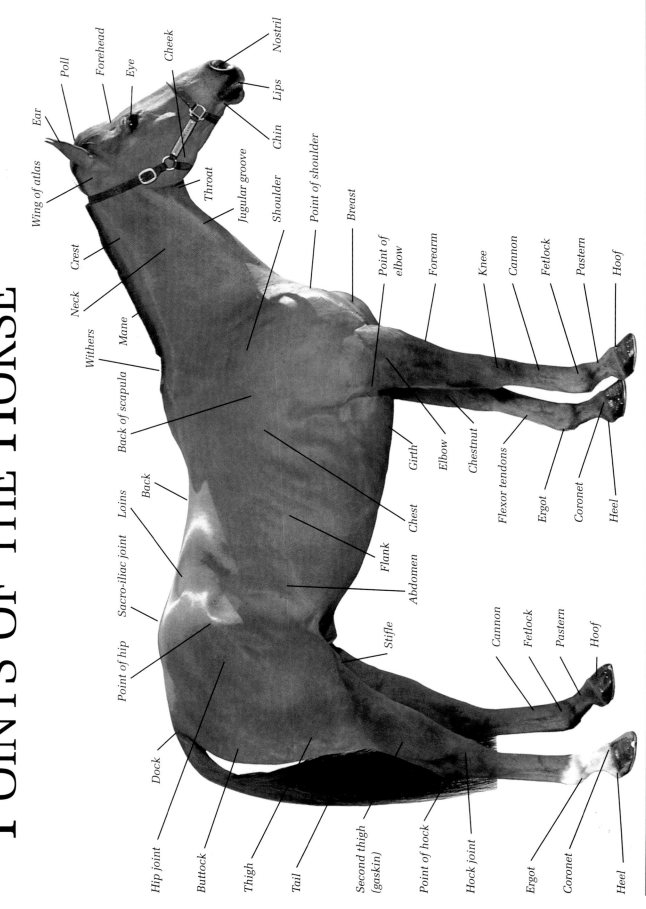

Forehead
Cheek
Poll
Eye
Nostril
Ear
Lips
Wing of atlas
Chin
Crest
Throat
Jugular groove
Shoulder
Point of shoulder
Breast
Neck
Point of shoulder
Mane
Point of elbow
Forearm
Knee
Cannon
Fetlock
Pastern
Hoof
Withers
Back of scapula
Girth
Elbow
Chestnut
Flexor tendons
Ergot
Coronet
Heel
Back
Loins
Chest
Sacro-iliac joint
Flank
Abdomen
Point of hip
Stifle
Cannon
Fetlock
Pastern
Hoof
Hip joint
Buttock
Thigh
Tail
Second thigh (gaskin)
Point of hock
Hock joint
Ergot
Coronet
Heel
Dock

Skeleton of the Horse

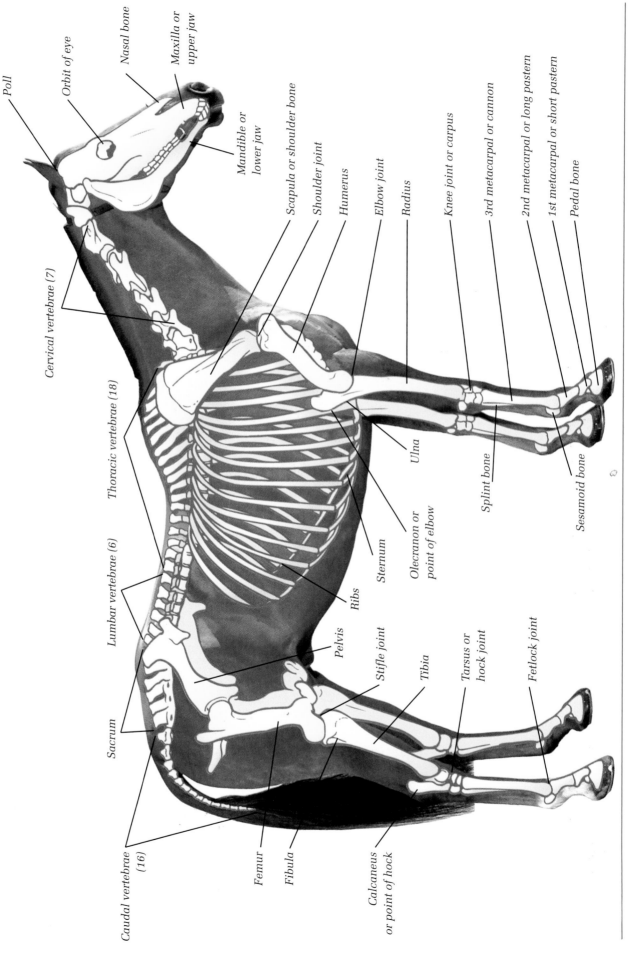

Poll

Orbit of eye

Nasal bone

Maxilla or upper jaw

Mandible or lower jaw

Scapula or shoulder bone

Shoulder joint

Humerus

Elbow joint

Radius

Knee joint or carpus

3rd metacarpal or cannon

2nd metacarpal or long pastern

1st metacarpal or short pastern

Pedal bone

Cervical vertebrae (7)

Thoracic vertebrae (18)

Lumbar vertebrae (6)

Sacrum

Caudal vertebrae (16)

Femur

Fibula

Calcaneus or point of hock

Pelvis

Stifle joint

Tibia

Tarsus or hock joint

Fetlock joint

Ribs

Sternum

Olecranon or point of elbow

Ulna

Splint bone

Sesamoid bone

THE SIGNS OF GOOD HEALTH

Horses are all individuals, and therefore it is beholden on you, the owner, to become familiar with the normal behaviour, vital signs and parameters of *your* horse or horses so that any variation can be investigated promptly and the effects of illness or injury minimised (see also tables on pp24–7).

APPETITE

Horses have evolved as grazing animals designed to eat more or less constantly, except when resting, moving on or socialising. They are adapted to a low-energy, high-fibre diet which keeps the gut working on a continuous basis. Insufficient fibre in the working horse's diet can increase the risk of colic and the likelihood of behavioural problems such as over-excitability. A contented, healthy horse should have a good appetite. The stress of training or competition can interfere with appetite: some horses, for example, will not eat their hard feed for twenty-four hours after a strenuous competition. It should also be remembered that lack of appetite or turning away from feed can be one of the first signs of illness.

Healthy youngsters enjoying mutual grooming

Turning the horse out can help resolve the former problem, since being able to move around helps the horse to relax and most horses will graze when the opportunity is available, thus keeping the gut working. Various additives are available to tempt 'fussy' feeders – for example herbal or vitamin products – but where there is an underlying reason for lack of interest in food, these are unlikely to solve the problem. Often, a few days' rest and giving smaller meals, also foods known to be palatable, appetite enhancers such as alfalfa (lucerne), or succulents such as carrots and apples, will work. Sometimes a particular ingredient in the diet is disliked and it may be necessary to experiment to see if this is the case. If inappetance is due to illness, however, the cause must be diagnosed and treated.

Clean, fresh water should be available to horses at all times. A sick horse may not move far or may find it difficult to reach down, so make sure that water is close at hand, and easy to reach, because it is vital to avoid dehydration.

The horse can sleep standing up, while resting a hind leg

ATTITUDE

The healthy horse is bright and alert, and quick to respond to outside stimuli; thus it will prick its ears at a sudden noise, or raise its head to look at something it has spotted in the distance. It has a calm, confident outlook and its movement is free, smooth and level with a spring in the stride. When standing still, the horse should be four square, taking its weight on all four limbs. Pointing a toe, or standing with the weight displaced backwards, indicates a problem; the well known 'laminitic stance' is a typical example. The free horse in the field carries 60 per cent of its weight on the forelimbs and 40 per cent on the hind limbs. This, plus the greater angulation of the hind limbs and muscular power of the quarters, enables the horse to be ready to explode into action instantly at a sign of danger.

At ease, the horse may alternately rest its hind legs. The 'stay' apparatus (a system of ligaments controlling movement of the joints) of the hind leg has a mechanism for locking the stifle joint, which also has the effect of fixing the other joints in place without the need for muscular tension; thus the horse can sleep, completely relaxed, while standing up.

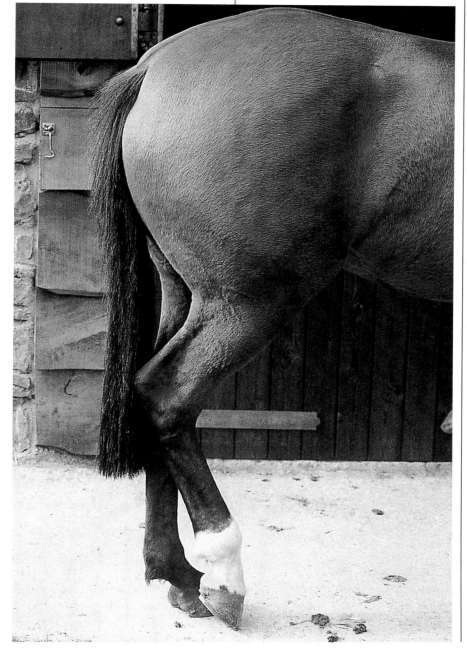

This emaciated pony was rescued by a horse and pony welfare society and made a full recovery

CONDITION

Bodily condition should be neither thin nor fat. The skeletal structure should be well covered with healthy, fit muscle, rounding the contours of the body. In a young horse the muscles will be soft, becoming harder and more clearly delineated as the horse grows older and begins to work. Rolls of fat indicating a horse that is overweight are easily identified. Conversely lack of condition is when the ribs become plainly visible and muscle wastage occurs along the back, over the loins and in the large muscles of the quarters. In winter a close check should be kept on all horses and ponies, particularly unclipped ones, as a thick coat can easily disguise loss of condition.

Coat: This should gleam with health and lie flat and smooth.

Skin: The skin should be elastic and supple.

Limbs: These should be clean, with the tendons well defined, cool and hard. Joints should be well defined and free from abnormal lumps, bumps, swellings or puffiness.

Feet: The feet should be well shaped and balanced, with resilient, sound horn, free from flaking, cracks or deformities. The heels should be clean, well formed and capable of adequate expansion. The sole should be slightly concave, with the frog well defined and rubbery in texture. Each foot should be a mirror image of its opposite partner.

Ears: The ears are alert and independently mobile, listening for sounds all around. The inner hair should not be removed from the ears because it helps to keep out dust and parasites; it is also thought to assist in the hearing process.

SEE ALSO PAGES **24–7** FOR TABLES OF

Normal Values, Haematology, Biochemistry and *Blood Mineral Levels.*

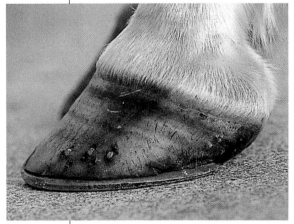

Flat feet, with long toes and insufficient support at the heel

16

Eyes: The eyes should be open (except when drowsing) and clear, with salmon-pink mucous membranes indicating a healthy blood supply. The horse lowers its head to see objects close at hand and raises it to see objects further away. The eyes are placed on either side of the head and this enables the horse to see almost all round it, but there are blind spots directly in front and behind. Thus if you approach a horse directly from the rear it will not be able to see you, and this may startle it and cause it to kick out; it is therefore one good reason always to let the horse know where you are.

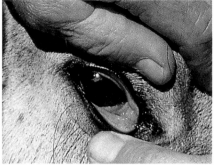

Healthy mucous membranes

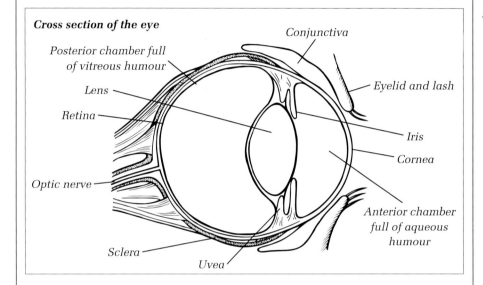

Cross section of the eye

Posterior chamber full of vitreous humour

Lens

Retina

Optic nerve

Sclera

Uvea

Conjunctiva

Eyelid and lash

Iris

Cornea

Anterior chamber full of aqueous humour

Nostrils, mouth and teeth: The nostrils should be dry and clean. The whiskers of the muzzle are used for sensory purposes and should *not* be trimmed or clipped. The gums should be salmon pink, with the teeth even and in good condition, appropriate to the age of the horse.

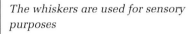

The whiskers are used for sensory purposes

The horse's teeth continue to grow throughout its life, and regular attention is necessary to keep them in good condition (*see* Ageing a Horse, overleaf; and routine care, p46).

Droppings: The droppings are a good indicator as to whether or not the horse is healthy. They can vary from the usual moist, slightly oval, mucus-covered balls, to soft, sloppy green cowpats when the horse is on spring grass, or hard, round bullets when it is stabled on a diet which is high in grain and relatively low in fibre. The cause of diarrhoea or bad-smelling droppings should always be investigated.

Urine: The urine is also an indicator of good health: often pale in colour and clear, it can also be darker or slightly cloudy. Red or black urine is not normal.

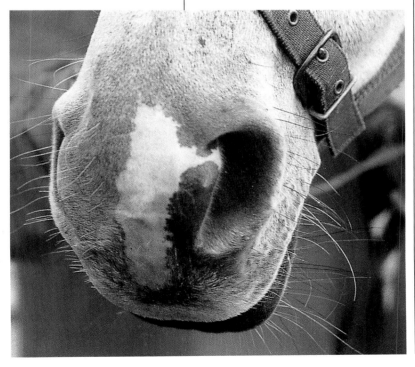

AGEING THE HORSE

There is no certain way to tell the exact age of a horse, if its date of birth is unknown. The traditional method of looking at the state of wear of the teeth in the older horse is, at best, an indication and, at worst, may be several years out either way. However, the teeth can give a better guide to the age of horses under six than to that of older horses. Tooth wear may vary with the breed of horse, the type of food it eats and the environment in which it is kept, also the individual conformation of the mouth, in addition to the progression of age. Nevertheless, careful examination of the mouth and teeth is still worthwhile when buying a horse, as their condition will indicate how well it can masticate its food and thereby maintain good bodily condition – or may warn you that it is a crib-biter. It should also be remembered that horses with chronic dental problems will require more frequent veterinary attention, and their nutrition will be more difficult to manage.

The theory of ageing a horse by reference to its teeth depends on the fact that the horse's teeth change throughout its life. The incisors, of which there are three pairs in each jaw, are the teeth normally considered when attempting to assess age. The young horse first grows temporary incisors, each pair of which is progressively shed, starting with the central pair at $2\frac{1}{2}$ years, the lateral pair at $3\frac{1}{2}$ years, and lastly the corner teeth by the time it is $4\frac{1}{2}$ years old. Between $3\frac{1}{2}$ and 4 years, tushes, or canine teeth, may erupt in the space between the incisors and molars in

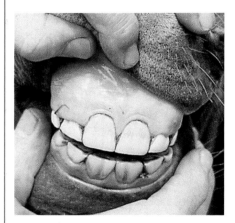

Teeth of a one-year-old horse

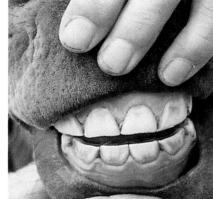

Teeth of a two-year-old horse

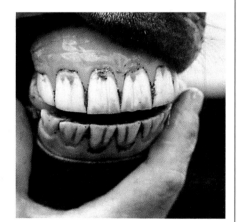

Teeth of a six-year-old horse

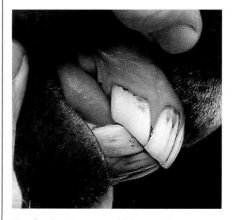

Teeth of a six-year-old horse showing beginning of seven-year hook

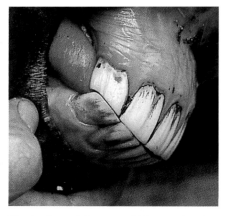

Teeth of an eight-year-old horse clearly showing seven-year hook

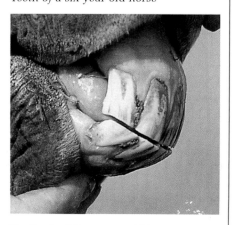

Teeth of a fifteen-year-old horse

the jaw of male horses (they do not usually appear in mares).

Several factors are considered to deduce the age of the horse by reference to the permanent incisors:

1. **The state of wear on the tables (biting surfaces) of the teeth:** A tooth which is recently erupted bears an infundibulum, which is an enamel ring, or cup, containing cement. As time passes, the table of the tooth wears until the cup, and finally the enamel ring disappear. With further wear the secondary dentine appears, showing as a brown stain called the 'dental star'. The shape of the dental star changes from a line, to oval and finally to round.

An eighteen-year-old brood mare in excellent condition. Her flea-bitten colouring is almost the only sign of age

2. **The shape of the tables:** Initially this is elliptical, progressing to round, then triangular and finally oval.

3. **The slope and angle of the incisors:** The angle that the upper and lower incisors make with each other is approximately 160°. This decreases with age, becoming about 80° at twenty years.

4. **The seven-year hook:** The presence of a 'hook' on the upper corner incisors, which is supposed to appear at seven and disappear at eight.

5. **Galvayne's groove:** A mark which appears also on the upper corner incisors around the age of ten, and grows down the tooth as the horse ages. It reaches the bottom at around the age of twenty.

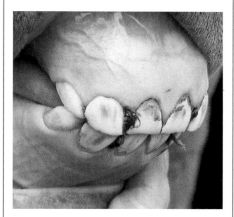

Teeth of a two-year-old horse with slightly overshot jaw

All these factors are affected by the rate at which the teeth grow, compared to the rate of wear.

Research in 1994 by Richardson, Lane and Waldron (*Veterinary Record 1994*, 135 31–34) using eighty horses of known age showed that although there was a good correlation between estimated and known ages up to five years, one horse known to be six years old was shedding its temporary corner incisors, in other words almost two years late. They also found that in older horses, there was much greater variability between dental age and actual age, and that the accuracy of the 'dental' age declined markedly after eleven years of age.

The ring of the infundibulum did not wear away at a consistent rate and was deemed to be of little value in estimating age. The dental star appeared sequentially in the central, lateral and corner incisors at relatively constant ages, but at one or two years earlier than previously found. The shape of the tables was a useful criterion, although again the study showed the changes occurring earlier than in previously documented work. The angle of the incisors and Galvayne's groove were both useful indicators of age, but the 'seven-year hook' was found in horses of practically any age over six years.

An examination of the teeth, coupled with the overall appearance of a horse, will help give a guide to approximate age and, perhaps more usefully, the horse's physical condition and potential for work. Other physical signs of ageing include wear and tear on the limbs; dipping of the back behind the withers; deepening of the hollows above the eyes; increase of white hairs in the coat, especially around the face in some breeds, and the change in coat colour to almost white or fleabitten in grey horses; stiffness in the joints; and ultimately, loss of bodily condition.

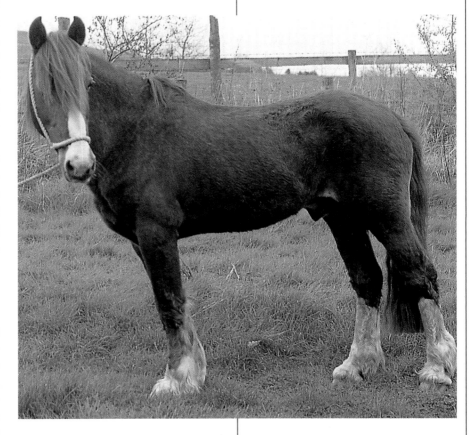

Where the age of a horse is uncertain, a pre-purchase veterinary examination will help provide an estimation of the horse's fitness for the proposed work, including an assessment of the heart, wind, eyes and soundness.

PSYCHOLOGICAL PROBLEMS

It seems extraordinary that the physical manifestations of psychological problems in the horse have traditionally been labelled 'vices', along with unco-operative behaviour generally, and have been dealt with by disciplinary measures or

Older horses lose condition easily. This one also shows a typically dipped back

physical restraint, rather than by trying to understand the animal's mental state and attempting to alleviate the initial cause of the problem. Whenever we consider why a horse behaves in a certain way, we should remember how it evolved: a free-ranging creature, at ease in wide open spaces, constantly eating low-energy, high-fibre food whilst on the move, with an instinct to flee from predators unless forced into a situation where to fight was the only option.

In domesticating the horse and using it as a beast of burden or transport, or as today for sporting and recreational purposes, people have totally altered its lifestyle. We have restricted its environment to the inside of a stable or, at best, the limited boundaries of a grazing paddock. Confinement reduces the open distant view which makes it feel safe, its ability to see danger from a distance and thus its chance to flee.

We have curtailed its choice of food, so that instead of a wide range of naturally growing herbage, it is offered only pasture grass with a limited number of plants and herbs, conserved forage, and concentrated foods which are much higher in energy and lower in fibre than nature intended it to eat. We have reduced the amount of time it can spend eating to times when food is made available; and, finally, we have limited the exercise it can take by shutting it in a stable for prolonged periods of time. No wonder the overall level of stress felt by horses kept under this so-called 'normal' routine increases.

The horse does not think or feel in the same way that a human being does, and it is dangerous for us to transpose human values whilst trying to understand equine problems; but if a horse is deprived of the stimuli which produce natural behaviour, we should not be surprised if it attempts to replace them with the closest available alternative and therefore indulges in what *we* presume to call 'stable vices'. Thus, crib-biting may represent the natural urge to graze continuously, whilst windsucking fills and empties the anterior oesophagus with air, and weaving or box-walking may be substitutes for the continual onward movement of the horse at liberty.

CRIB-BITING AND WINDSUCKING

In crib-biting, the horse grasps a fixed object such as the edge of a manger or fence post with its teeth, arches its neck, forcing open the soft palate, and gulps air, usually with a characteristic grunt. In time, the incisor teeth become excessively worn and may cause the horse difficulty in grazing. The windsucking horse achieves the same effect of gulping air, but without needing to grasp an object. It was always thought that cribbing and windsucking horses swallowed air which passed into the stomach and intestines causing indigestion and flatulence, together with an increased risk of colic and digestive disturbances. However, work done at Bristol University by McGreevy, Richardson, Nicol and Lane (E.V.J. Vol. 27 No. 2 page 92) has shown that air is taken in and expelled from the upper oesophagus only, and does not reach the stomach in any great quantity. It seems likely, therefore, that any unthriftiness or disease noticed in cribbing horses is due more to the underlying environmental conditions than to the condition itself.

A collar used to discourage crib-biting and windsucking

Collars are available which when fitted round the gullet cause pressure as the horse arches its neck and tries to swallow, and so reduce the amount of air passing through to the oesophagus; but these are unlikely to stop the horse from cribbing. Attempts can be made to deprive the horse of any convenient edge to grasp by adding split tubes to the top of stable doors or any edges, and by modifying stable design, but most cribbing horses will find some edge to crib on, or will learn to crib without the need to grasp. In extreme cases, surgery may be employed with varying degrees of success. However, this must be considered a final option, as the normal risks of any operation are likely to outweigh the benefits in most cases. Turning the horse out for longer periods may help, but is unlikely to eradicate the problem completely, as once learned, the habit becomes ingrained. Other measures may also help, such as increasing the amount of fibre provided in the diet, providing forage *ad lib*, or using haynets with small holes so that eating takes longer.

WEAVING

Weaving involves the horse standing, usually with its head over the stable door, shifting its weight rhythmically from one front foot to the other, and swaying the head and neck from side to side as if mesmerised. It is a

Grilles fitted to the stable door to discourage weaving

sign of frustration at being confined, and such behaviour is believed to give the horse a sense of comfort against its distress. The habit is also frequently found in zoo animals. A grille over the door may prevent a horse from starting to weave, but it will not discourage the confirmed weaver, which simply continues the habit behind the grille. Toys hung in the stable may also serve as a distraction. The real solution, however, is to turn the horse outside, thus removing the source of stress and enabling it to relax.

BOX-WALKING

Box-walking is related to weaving in that it has a similar cause: confinement. However, box-walking is also associated with the anticipation of competition in fit, highly conditioned horses, especially those of a more highly strung or sensitive disposition which may box-walk intermittently, for example during the night before an event, in a strange stable. An uncongenial horse next door, or in the case of mares, having a stallion close by, might also induce box-walking.

The horse is a social animal, and being confined in a stable where it cannot touch other horses, even if it can see them, may also contribute to weaving and box-walking.

All these behaviour patterns are well recognised to the extent that they may seriously reduce the sale value of the animal concerned, due to the difficulty of breaking the habits once they begin, even sometimes when the original cause is eradicated. For stabled horses, the remedy employed – such as the windsucker's collar or the anti-weaving grille – may often take the form of further misunderstanding and unkindness. These physical attempts to stop activities which are in themselves a displacement to relieve mental anxiety can have no curative effect, and the question should be asked whether keeping a horse continually in such a state is any more defensible than to neglect a physical injury or illness. Moreover the fact that these vices are so common is an indictment of the way in which people unthinkingly put convenience of management above the comfort and well-being of their horses.

A study by McGreevy, French and Nicol (*Veterinary Record 1995*, 137, 36–37) showed that endurance horses, which spend significantly more time out of their stables than horses competing in dressage and eventing, exhibited significantly less abnormal behaviour overall than horses in the other two groups. The percentages in each group were as follows:

endurance 19.5 per cent, eventing 30.8 per cent and dressage 32.5 per cent. The study considered data reported on 744 dressage horses, 796 event horses and 211 endurance horses. The only habit relatively common among endurance horses was box-walking, and the researchers hypothesised that either these horses were more motivated to keep moving because of some form of physiological reward, or they were more averse to being stabled than other horses because they were fed there less often, or were less habituated to being confined.

The effects of stable vices include loss of condition due to a combination of nervous tension, inappetance or fluctuating appetite; also horses may be depressed and dull, or alternatively highly strung, inattentive and difficult to handle. Stallions in particular may be gravely frustrated by an abnormal lifestyle and become increasingly unmanageable or even aggressive.

DEPRAVED APPETITE

A depraved appetite is yet another way in which a horse may react to an unnatural lifestyle, evidenced by eating his bedding or his own droppings, chewing the wood of his box, or eating other substances such as earth, or licking metal. There are several potential causes. Bedding may be eaten both because of boredom, or because fibre is lacking in the diet or is less palatable than the fibre in the bedding. Clean oat straw, for example, is often palatable and will do no harm in reasonable quantities. Young foals will eat their mothers' fresh droppings, and occasionally those of other older horses, and this is a natural course of behaviour for them. The reason is not completely researched, but is probably to do with the establishment of the correct balance of microflora in the foal's gut; it may also provide other substances. It is unnatural, however, for older animals to eat droppings, a phenomenon usually found to occur when a horse undergoes a sudden change of diet, or when fibre is lacking in the diet, for example if complete cubes are being fed instead of hay. The remedy is to remove droppings as soon as possible and to provide the horse with extra fibre.

WOOD-CHEWING

Wood-chewing in the stable may be attributable to lack of fibre, although boredom or lack of companionship may also be contributory factors. Horses at pasture often eat leaves, twigs and bark as well as chewing fences, and it may be that these things form a natural way of obtaining more fibre than is available from grass, particularly at certain times of the year, for example in winter when grass is sparse, or in the spring when the growth is soft and lush. Overeating of leaves and twigs may cause colic and it is advisable to see that the horse has sufficient digestible fibre available to prevent this.

EARTH-EATING

Eating earth or other substances usually indicates a mineral or salt deficiency and the diet should be checked. If there is no deficiency, the cause may be boredom, especially if the horse is confined in a small, bare paddock. More exercise and the increased provision of clean forage is indicated. Where the variety of plants in the horse's pasture or turnout area is limited, or for stabled horses, herbal supplements are often well received and improve appetite and condition.

A fence damaged by persistent wood chewing

NORMAL PARAMETERS OF GOOD HEALTH

Normal Values

NORMAL VALUES	RANGE		COMMENTS
Heart rate	/minute	38 ± 10	Can rise markedly during periods of stress
Respiration rate	/minute	12 ± 6	Hot weather can cause higher levels
Body temperature	°C °F	37.9 ± .5 100.5 ± 1	Has a slight diurnal rhythm
Total volume of blood	litres	35 ± 10	This varies according to bodyweight
Total amount of faeces production	kilograms	17.5 ± 3	As above
Total amount of urine production	litres	6 ± 3	As above
Onset of reproductive activity	months	18 ± 6	As above
Length of oestrus cycle	days	21 ± 2	Depends markedly upon body condition
Duration of oestrus period	days	6 ± 3	Varies according to time of year
Length of dioestrus period	days	15 ± 5	As above
Ovulation	hours	48 ± 12	Before the end of the oestrus period
Optimum covering period	hours	48 ± 24	In the period 48 hours before the end of oestrus up to the end of oestrus
Gestation period	months	11 ± 1	Varies considerably between mares, but each individual is generally much the same from year to year
Foal heat	starts	8 ± 3	Days post foaling. Not always evident but often causes diarrhoea in foal

ABBREVIATION USED
g/dl = grams per decilitre
pg = picograms
g/l = grams per litre
mm/hr = millimetres per hour
mmol/l = millimoles per litre
iu/l = International units per litre
U/ml = units per millilitre

Haematology

Test	Range		Use
Red blood cells (RBC) Thoroughbred in training Non-Thoroughbred	x10¹²/litre	**7–10** **6–10.5**	Use as an aid in determining the well-being of the horse. Low levels might suggest anaemia. Crude estimate of fitness – levels gradually increase with training
Haemoglobin (Hg) Thoroughbred in training Non-Thoroughbred	g/dl	**11.5–17** **9–15.5**	As above – used as an aid in determining the well-being of the horse. Low levels might suggest anaemia. Crude estimate of fitness – levels gradually increase with training
Packed cell volume (PCV)	% volume of red red blood cells to blood plasma	**35–50**	A rise is indicative of haemoconcentration, due to stress, dehydration or toxaemia. A fall could be due to anaemia
Mean corpuscular volume (MCV)	fl	**39–49**	Immature red blood cells are larger than mature ones so the MCV is helpful in determining the type of anaemia
Mean corpuscular haemoglobin (MCH)	pg	**12–19.2**	As above
Mean corpuscular haemoglobin concentration (MCHC)	g/dl	**34–38**	As above
White blood cells (WBC)	x10⁹/litre	**5.5–12**	Generally raised during bacterial infection or lowered after a virus infecton or in septicaemia
Neutrophils (segmented)	x10⁹/litre	**3–6.5**	Raised during inflammation
Neutrophils (banded)	x10⁹/litre	**0–0.2**	An increase in the ratio between banded (juvenile) and segmented (adult) neutrophils can be indicative of infection
Lymphocytes	x10⁹/litre	**1.6–6.5**	Raised levels can be indicative of neoplasia of the lymphoid tissue, lowered levels follow viral attacks
Monocytes	x10⁹/litre	**0–.85**	Often raised as a result of viral infections
Eosinophils	x10⁹/litre	**0–.2**	High levels may be found following parasitic larval migration, and can be associated with allergic or hypersensitive conditions
Platelets	x10¹²/litre	**120–360**	Involved in clotting. High levels may be found in chronic suppurative disease, low levels following haemorrhage or viral infection
Fibrinogen	g/l	**1–4**	Level is increased during any inflammatory process
Coagulation time	mins	**10.6–14.6**	Used to test the efficiency of blood clotting
Prothrombin time	secs	**10–13**	As above, but especially if horse is on anticoagulation therapy
Erythrocyte sedimentation rate (ESR)	mm/hr	**22–57**	Level is increased during any inflammatory process

Biochemistry

Test	Range		Use
Albumin	g/l	25–37	Low levels are found in liver disease and following intestinal damage due to worms
Globulin a$_2$	g/l	8–13	Elevated after tissue damage
b$_1$		8–15	Elevated during larval worm damage
b$_2$		8–15	Elevated during liver damage
g		7–14	Elevated after bacterial infection, part of the antibody response
Total serum protein	g/l	60–80	A guide to general body condition
Triglycerides	mmol/l	0.12–0.35	High levels found in abnormal fat metabolism
Aspartate aminotransferase (AST)	iu/l	<300	Acute muscle damage causes high levels which peak 24–36 hours after insult. Levels persist in the serum for two to three weeks
Creatine phosphokinase (CK)	iu/l	<175	Acute muscle damage causes grossly elevated levels which peak two to three hours after insult. Levels return to normal after three days
Lactate dehydrogenase	iu/l	<585	High levels following damage to the liver, brain and muscles
LD3	% LD	43	% increases following heart damage
LD4	% LD	13	% increases following intestinal damage
LD5	% LD	2	% increases following damage to brain, liver and muscles
Gamma glutamyltransferase (GGT)	iu/l	<40	High levels following acute and chronic liver damage
Serum alkaline phosphatase (SAP)	iu/l	<350	Very variable levels in the young horse due to bone metabolism. Tends to increase in cases of chronic liver damage
Intestinal alkaline phosphatase (IAP)	iu/l	<20	Levels increase in cases of intestinal damage
Sorbital dehydrogenase (SDH)	iu/l	<6	High transient levels found after acute liver disease
Bilirubin (total)	mmol/l	10–50	Raised levels follow fasting
(direct)	mmol/l	4.5–15	Levels can rise after liver damage
Cholesterol	mmol/l	1–3	High levels found in abnormal fat metabolism
Triglycerides	mmol/l	0.12–0.35	High levels found in abnormal fat metabolism
Creatinine	mmol/l	100–180	Levels are elevated in cases of renal disease
Cortisol	nmol/l	50–250	Levels are raised during periods of athletic stress and in horses suffering from Cushing's disease
Glutamate dehydrogenase (GLDH)	iu/l	4–14	Levels rise during acute liver cell damage
Glutathiomine peroxidase (GSH-Px)	U/ml	>80	Indication of vitamin E/selenium levels
Urea	mmol/l	3.5–8	Kidney damage produces elevated levels

Blood Mineral Levels

MINERAL	RANGE		USE
Calcium	mmol/l	2.5–3.5	Might be low in acute cases of deficiency such as lactation tetany and in bran-fed horses
Chloride	mmol/l	100–108	Imbalances occur during heat stress and dehydration
Copper	mmol/l	8–18	Deficiency is rare in the horse
Glucose	mmol/l	3–6	Blood levels of glucose are used in oral glucose absorption test, used as an aid in determining intestinal disease
Lead	mmol/l	<1.2	Raised levels following lead poisoning
Magnesium	mmol/l	0.6–0.9	Deficiencies have occurred in foals and in horses suffering from travel stress
Phosphate	mmol/l	0.8–3	Deficiencies have been recorded in horses kept on phosphate-deficient soils
Potassium	mmol/l	3–4.5	Heat stress and dehydration cause imbalances, as chloride
Sodium	mmol/l	135–145	As chloride
Selenium	mmol/l		Deficiencies can occur on certain soil structures and toxicity has been recorded following contamination of mineral supplements

MUSCLES OF THE HORSE

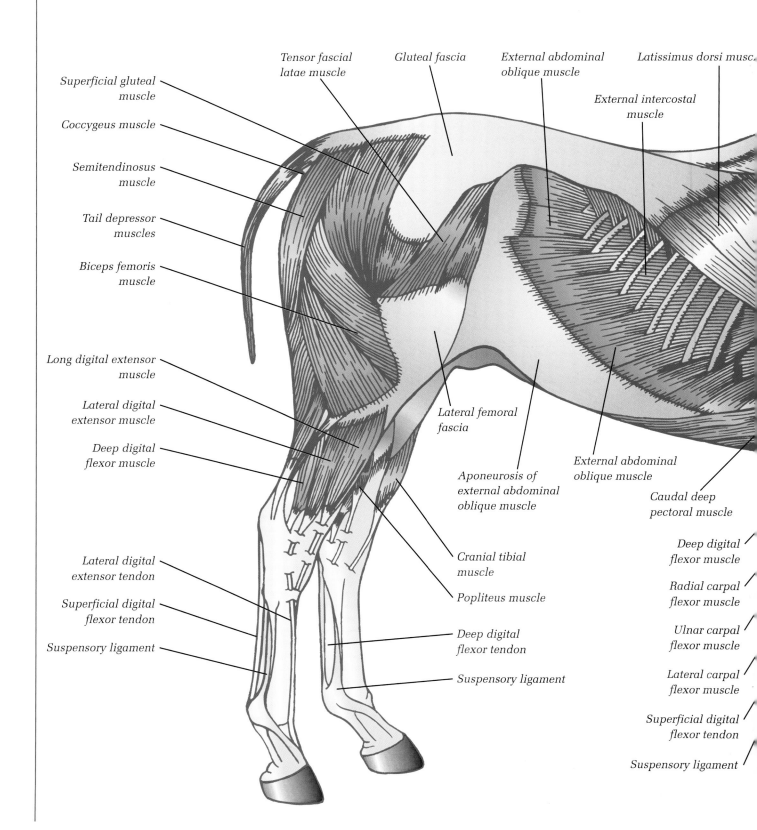

Tensor fascial latae muscle

Gluteal fascia

External abdominal oblique muscle

Latissimus dorsi musc.

External intercostal muscle

Superficial gluteal muscle

Coccygeus muscle

Semitendinosus muscle

Tail depressor muscles

Biceps femoris muscle

Long digital extensor muscle

Lateral digital extensor muscle

Deep digital flexor muscle

Lateral femoral fascia

External abdominal oblique muscle

Aponeurosis of external abdominal oblique muscle

Caudal deep pectoral muscle

Deep digital flexor muscle

Radial carpal flexor muscle

Cranial tibial muscle

Popliteus muscle

Ulnar carpal flexor muscle

Lateral digital extensor tendon

Superficial digital flexor tendon

Suspensory ligament

Deep digital flexor tendon

Suspensory ligament

Lateral carpal flexor muscle

Superficial digital flexor tendon

Suspensory ligament

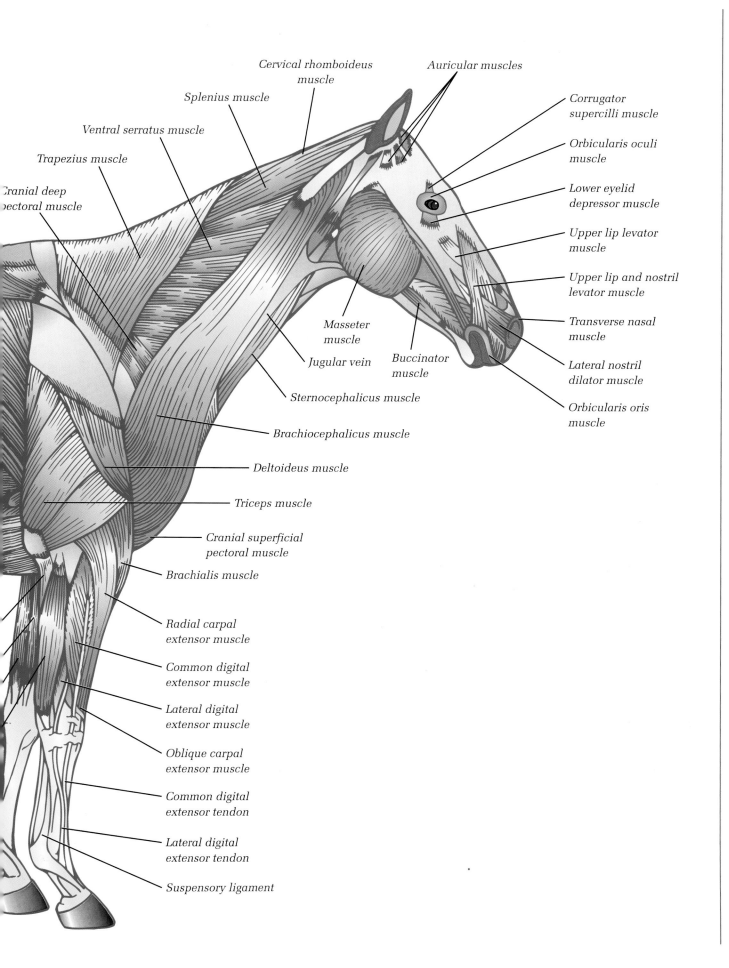

Cervical rhomboideus muscle

Splenius muscle

Ventral serratus muscle

Trapezius muscle

Cranial deep pectoral muscle

Auricular muscles

Corrugator supercilli muscle

Orbicularis oculi muscle

Lower eyelid depressor muscle

Upper lip levator muscle

Upper lip and nostril levator muscle

Transverse nasal muscle

Lateral nostril dilator muscle

Orbicularis oris muscle

Masseter muscle

Jugular vein

Buccinator muscle

Sternocephalicus muscle

Brachiocephalicus muscle

Deltoideus muscle

Triceps muscle

Cranial superficial pectoral muscle

Brachialis muscle

Radial carpal extensor muscle

Common digital extensor muscle

Lateral digital extensor muscle

Oblique carpal extensor muscle

Common digital extensor tendon

Lateral digital extensor tendon

Suspensory ligament

Nervous System

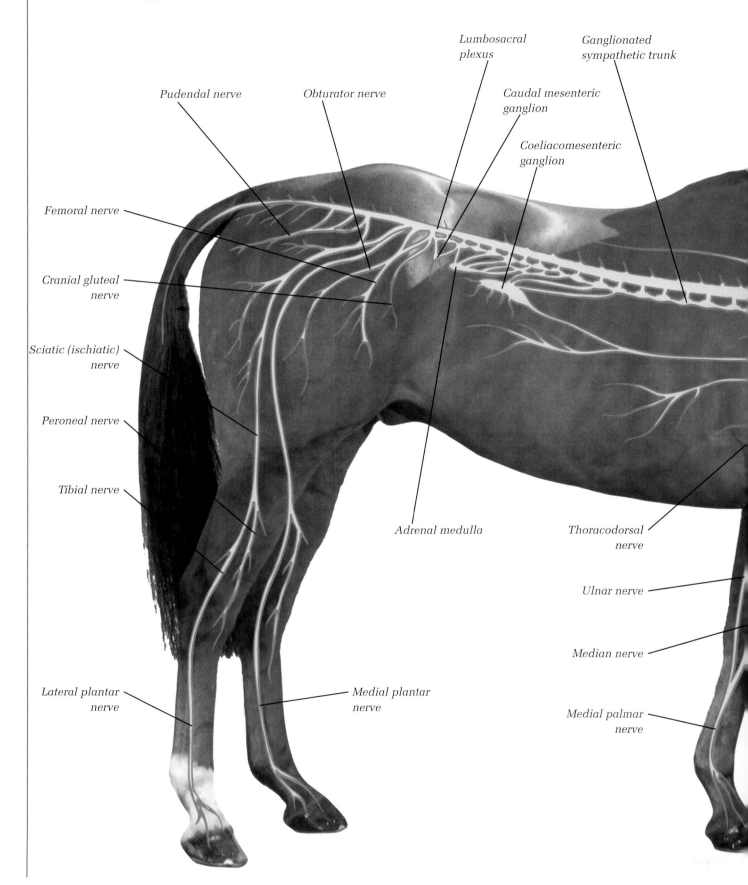

Pudendal nerve

Obturator nerve

Lumbosacral plexus

Ganglionated sympathetic trunk

Caudal mesenteric ganglion

Coeliacomesenteric ganglion

Femoral nerve

Cranial gluteal nerve

Sciatic (ischiatic) nerve

Peroneal nerve

Tibial nerve

Adrenal medulla

Thoracodorsal nerve

Ulnar nerve

Median nerve

Lateral plantar nerve

Medial plantar nerve

Medial palmar nerve

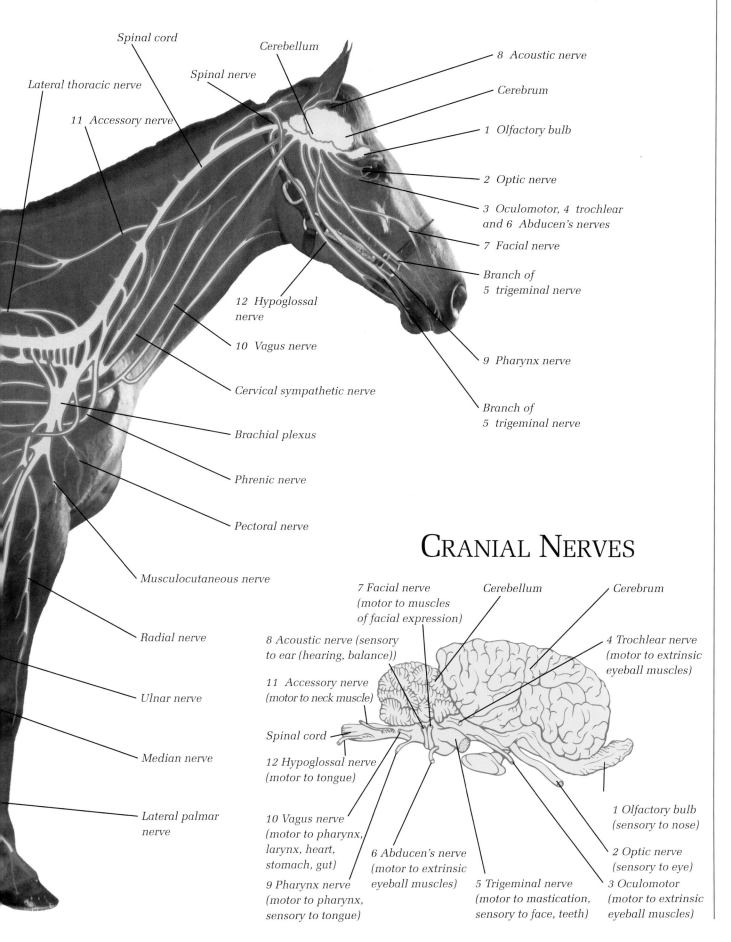

Spinal cord

Cerebellum

8 Acoustic nerve

Lateral thoracic nerve

Spinal nerve

Cerebrum

11 Accessory nerve

1 Olfactory bulb

2 Optic nerve

3 Oculomotor, 4 trochlear
and 6 Abducen's nerves

7 Facial nerve

Branch of
5 trigeminal nerve

12 Hypoglossal
nerve

10 Vagus nerve

9 Pharynx nerve

Cervical sympathetic nerve

Branch of
5 trigeminal nerve

Brachial plexus

Phrenic nerve

Pectoral nerve

Musculocutaneous nerve

CRANIAL NERVES

7 Facial nerve
(motor to muscles
of facial expression)

Cerebellum

Cerebrum

Radial nerve

8 Acoustic nerve (sensory
to ear (hearing, balance))

4 Trochlear nerve
(motor to extrinsic
eyeball muscles)

11 Accessory nerve
(motor to neck muscle)

Ulnar nerve

Spinal cord

Median nerve

12 Hypoglossal nerve
(motor to tongue)

1 Olfactory bulb
(sensory to nose)

2 Optic nerve
(sensory to eye)

Lateral palmar
nerve

10 Vagus nerve
(motor to pharynx,
larynx, heart,
stomach, gut)

6 Abducen's nerve
(motor to extrinsic
eyeball muscles)

3 Oculomotor
(motor to extrinsic
eyeball muscles)

9 Pharynx nerve
(motor to pharynx,
sensory to tongue)

5 Trigeminal nerve
(motor to mastication,
sensory to face, teeth)

CIRCULATORY SYSTEM

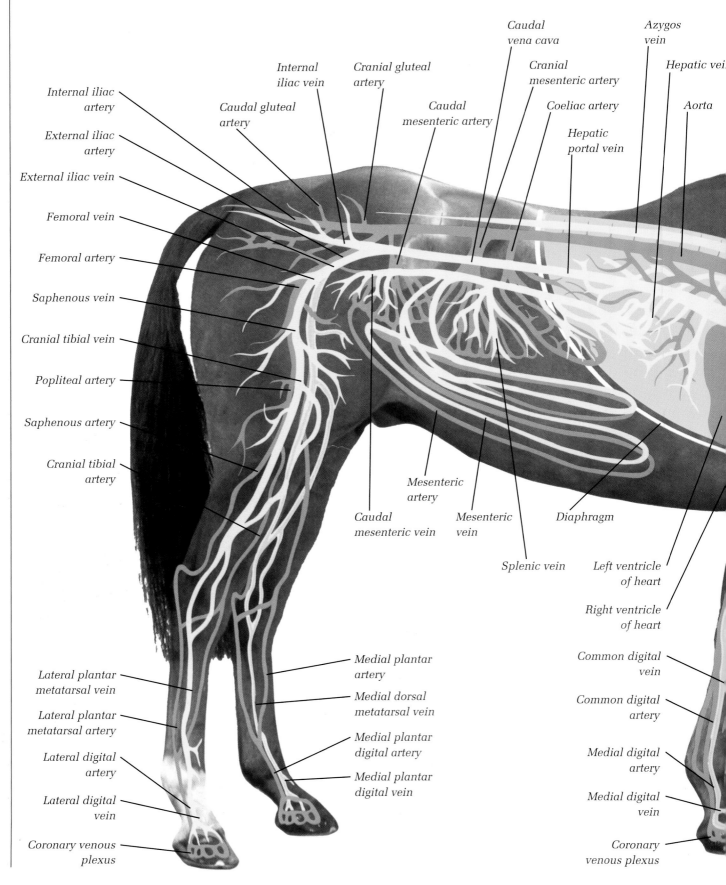

Internal iliac artery

External iliac artery

External iliac vein

Femoral vein

Femoral artery

Saphenous vein

Cranial tibial vein

Popliteal artery

Saphenous artery

Cranial tibial artery

Caudal gluteal artery

Internal iliac vein

Cranial gluteal artery

Caudal mesenteric artery

Caudal vena cava

Cranial mesenteric artery

Coeliac artery

Hepatic portal vein

Azygos vein

Hepatic vein

Aorta

Mesenteric artery

Caudal mesenteric vein

Mesenteric vein

Diaphragm

Splenic vein

Left ventricle of heart

Right ventricle of heart

Lateral plantar metatarsal vein

Lateral plantar metatarsal artery

Lateral digital artery

Lateral digital vein

Coronary venous plexus

Medial plantar artery

Medial dorsal metatarsal vein

Medial plantar digital artery

Medial plantar digital vein

Common digital vein

Common digital artery

Medial digital artery

Medial digital vein

Coronary venous plexus

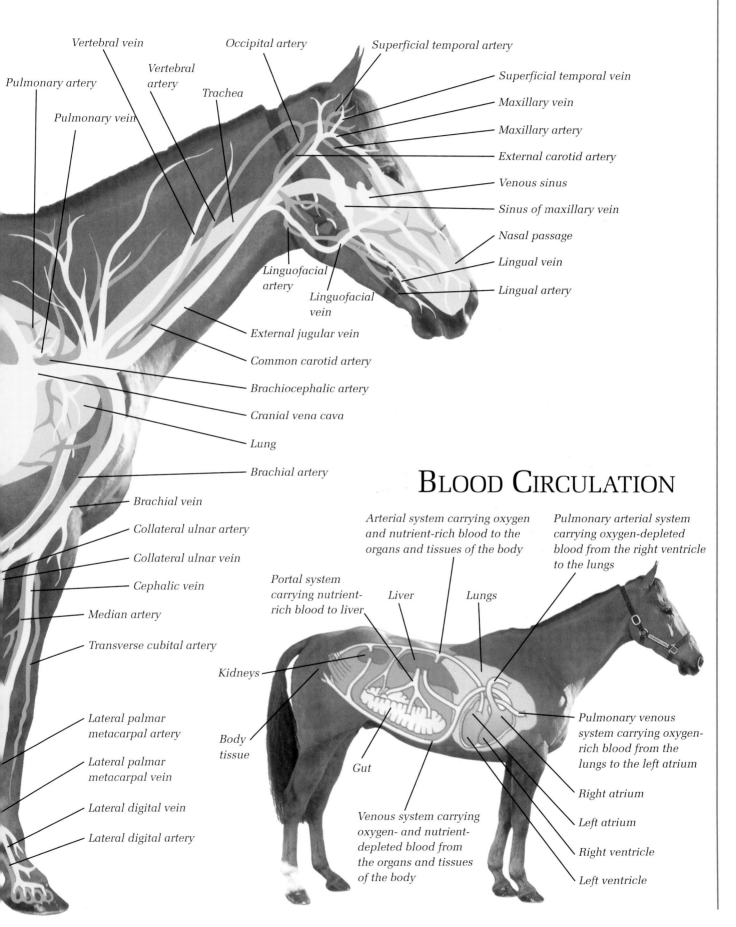

Vertebral vein

Pulmonary artery

Vertebral artery

Pulmonary vein

Trachea

Occipital artery

Superficial temporal artery

Superficial temporal vein

Maxillary vein

Maxillary artery

External carotid artery

Venous sinus

Sinus of maxillary vein

Nasal passage

Lingual vein

Lingual artery

Linguofacial artery

Linguofacial vein

External jugular vein

Common carotid artery

Brachiocephalic artery

Cranial vena cava

Lung

Brachial artery

Brachial vein

Collateral ulnar artery

Collateral ulnar vein

Cephalic vein

Median artery

Transverse cubital artery

Lateral palmar metacarpal artery

Lateral palmar metacarpal vein

Lateral digital vein

Lateral digital artery

BLOOD CIRCULATION

Arterial system carrying oxygen and nutrient-rich blood to the organs and tissues of the body

Pulmonary arterial system carrying oxygen-depleted blood from the right ventricle to the lungs

Portal system carrying nutrient-rich blood to liver

Liver

Lungs

Kidneys

Body tissue

Gut

Venous system carrying oxygen- and nutrient-depleted blood from the organs and tissues of the body

Pulmonary venous system carrying oxygen-rich blood from the lungs to the left atrium

Right atrium

Left atrium

Right ventricle

Left ventricle

33

DIGESTIVE SYSTEM

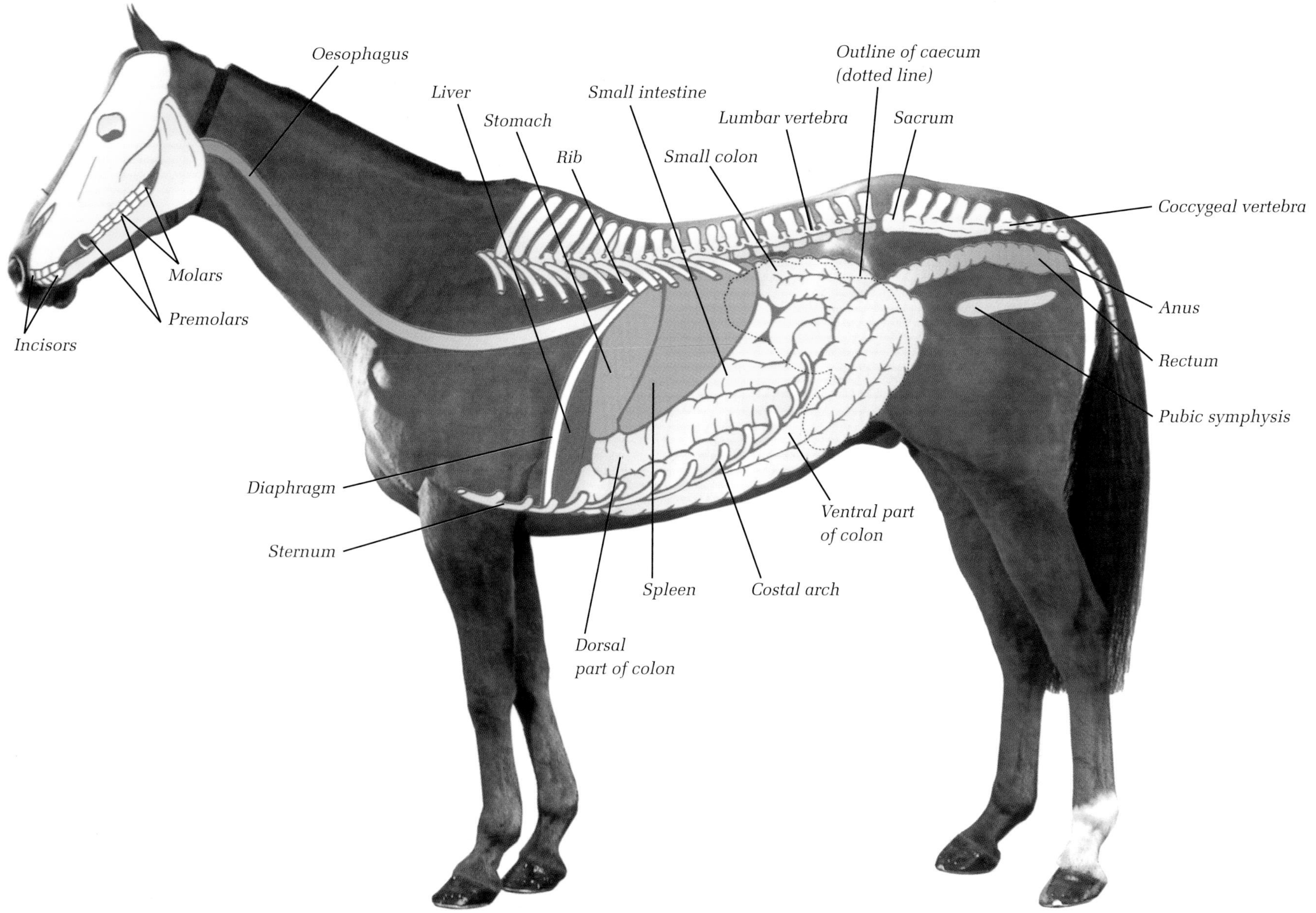

- Coccygeal vertebra
- Anus
- Rectum
- Pubic symphysis
- Outline of caecum (dotted line)
- Sacrum
- Lumbar vertebra
- Small colon
- Small intestine
- Rib
- Stomach
- Liver
- Oesophagus
- Molars
- Premolars
- Incisors
- Diaphragm
- Sternum
- Dorsal part of colon
- Spleen
- Costal arch
- Ventral part of colon

Urinogenital Systems

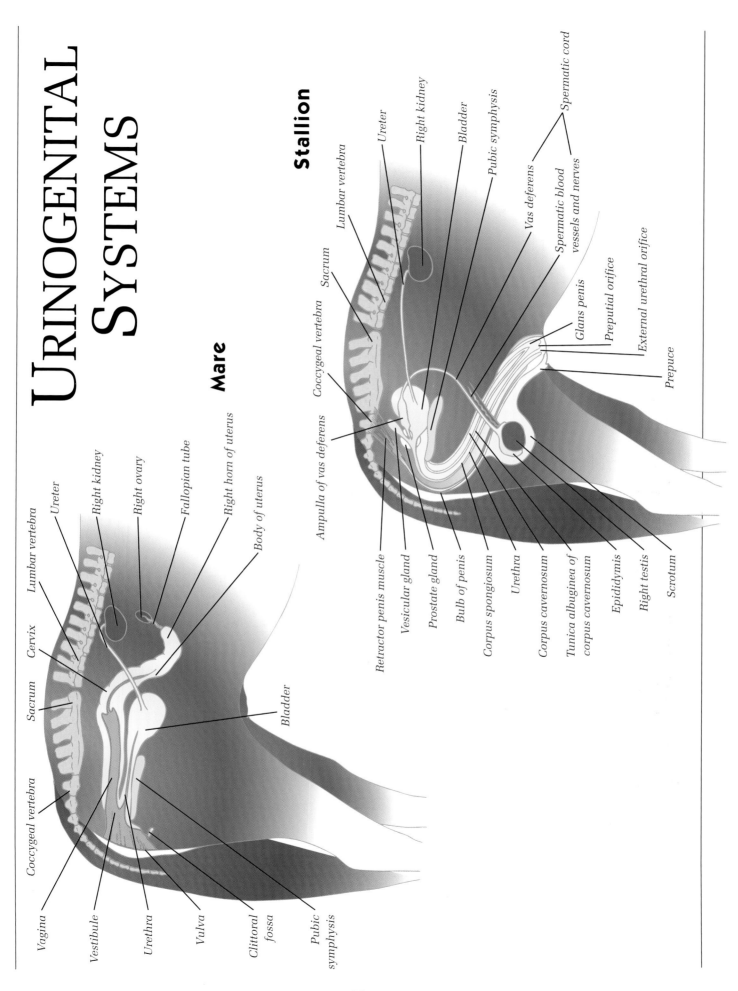

Mare

- Vagina
- Vestibule
- Urethra
- Vulva
- Clittoral fossa
- Pubic symphysis
- Bladder
- Coccygeal vertebra
- Sacrum
- Cervix
- Lumbar vertebra
- Ureter
- Right kidney
- Right ovary
- Fallopian tube
- Right horn of uterus
- Body of uterus

Stallion

- Ureter
- Lumbar vertebra
- Sacrum
- Coccygeal vertebra
- Ampulla of vas deferens
- Right kidney
- Bladder
- Pubic symphysis
- Vas deferens
- Spermatic blood vessels and nerves
- Spermatic cord
- Glans penis
- Preputial orifice
- External urethral orifice
- Prepuce
- Retractor penis muscle
- Vesicular gland
- Prostate gland
- Bulb of penis
- Corpus spongiosum
- Urethra
- Corpus cavernosum
- Tunica albuginea of corpus cavernosum
- Epididymis
- Right testis
- Scrotum

PREVENTATIVE TREATMENT

ROUTINE VACCINATION

TETANUS

Tetanus is one of the most distressing of all equine diseases. It is painful and immensely stressful for the horse and usually results in death unless treated aggressively with antitoxin at an early stage. The bacterial spores are endemic in the soil and can enter the body through the smallest of wounds, so that unprotected horses are at serious risk of contracting the disease. The incidence of tetanus is all the more unpleasant, given that complete immunisation is very easily achieved by vaccination.

Many people are confused by the various methods of dealing with tetanus. Put simply, your veterinary surgeon can treat a horse suffering from tetanus with antitoxin, or he can prevent tetanus from developing, post-injury, by using antitoxin, and also prevent tetanus permanently by using a vaccine, generally called tetanus toxoid.

Antitoxin is produced from specially treated horses with high levels of tetanus antiserum in their blood, and is used mainly as an essential part of the treatment of tetanus (see page 200). It may also be used by your veterinary surgeon at the time of an injury to neutralise immediately any toxin that may be formed. Unfortunately this effect does not last more

All horses should be vaccinated against tetanus. Vaccination against influenza is particularly important for horses coming into contact with each other at competitive events and shows

than about three weeks, so antitoxin is useless to prevent the disease in the long term.

Vaccination using tetanus toxoid is a completely different procedure from the above; it takes longer to become effective, but the immunity is then long-lasting. All foals should be vaccinated by the time they are four months of age, and older horses, if not already protected, should begin a course of vaccinations immediately upon acquisition. Tetanus toxoid is used for the vaccinations: it is a deactivated form of toxin which stimulates the development of the horse's immune system to destroy tetanus bacteria when they become established in the body. The first dose alerts the immune system; the second dose, given approximately one month later, stimulates a full response, and immunity develops gradually over the next week to ten days. This immunity is then long-lasting. A first booster is given after one year, then every two or three years according to current research recommendations. A booster given to the pregnant mare about one month prior to foaling maximises the immunity provided via the colostrum. The foal is then protected for about four months, when permanent vaccination can proceed. Foals born from mothers that are not vaccinated can be started much earlier, as soon as their immune system reaches maturity at two to three weeks of age.

If an unvaccinated horse is injured, vaccination alone at that time will not protect it from tetanus. Antitoxin and an initial dose of vaccine should be given, followed by a second dose of vaccine four weeks later.

INFLUENZA

The highly infectious nature of the influenza virus, the rapidity with which it spreads, the seriousness of the illness, and the protracted period for which it prevents affected horses from racing or competing, all combined to bring about the requirement for all racehorses and most competition horses to be compulsorily vaccinated against the disease. Owner-resistance to the vaccination programme due to cost and some reports of undesirable side effects have proved to have little or no impact on the overall success of the programme, and all owners, regardless of whether they take part in competitive events and shows, should be encouraged to have their horses vaccinated. This is particularly true since recent research has improved the period of immunity given, and the safety of the currently available vaccines. However, some authorities are sufficiently concerned about the continuing frequent epidemics that they are considering reducing the period between boosters from annually to every six months.

Racecourses nowadays are frequently used as venues for non-Thoroughbred equestrian events and all horses entering racecourse premises are required to be vaccinated in accordance with Jockey Club rules. Organisations running other competitive horse events are increasingly requiring participants to be vaccinated to a similar standard. The rules are as follows:

The Rules of Racing lay down that no horse for which a passport has been issued shall enter property owned, used or controlled by the Managing Executive of a racecourse unless the vaccination section in its passport is endorsed by a veterinary surgeon who is neither the owner nor the trainer of the horse, nor a person whose name is included in the Register of Stable Employees as being employed by the trainer of the horse at the time or by a recognised Turf Authority; and that it has also received two injections for primary vaccination given no less than 21 days apart and no more than 92 days apart. In addition, where sufficient time has elapsed subsequent to the primary vaccination the passport must be similarly endorsed to show that:

A. A horse foaled on or after 1 January 1980 has received a booster injection given no less than 150 days and no more than 215 days after the second injection of the primary vaccination and

B. A horse has received further/subsequent booster injections at intervals of not more than one year apart, commencing after the (first) booster injection required under A above or such lesser time as the Stewards of the Jockey Club may, in an emergency, decide, except that for horses foaled before 1 January 1980, the intervals between booster injections given before 16 March 1981 may have been not more than 14 months. None of the above injections has been given within the previous seven days including the day of entry into racecourse property.

C. A passport will not be regarded as being endorsed as required under the Rule if on or after 1 January 1988, any record of vaccination against Equine Influenza is altered in any way. An incorrect endorsement must be completely deleted and a new endorsement of the whole entry made, signed by the veterinary surgeon who was responsible for giving the vaccination.

HERPES VIRUS

Horses most at risk from equine herpes virus are youngstock and pregnant mares, especially where large numbers of horses, forming transient populations, are being managed. The various strains of the virus have proved particularly difficult to eradicate by vaccination as they are able to avoid destruction by the immune system. However, several vaccines are available which give a degree of protection from the effects of respiratory disease caused by EHV-1 and EHV-4 strains of the virus.

Studies have shown that the abortion follows a viraemia (an increase in the circulating levels of virus in the blood). The use of Duvaxyn EHV 1,4TM is known to reduce the level and duration of EHV viraemia and therefore might prevent EHV-induced abortion.

Research towards the development of improved vaccines is continuing. Meanwhile vaccination is probably an economic and realistic proposition only for those horses known to be at greatest risk.

VIRAL ARTERITIS

This is a contagious disease of major importance to the breeding industry, since infected stallions act as carriers and pass the virus on to mares via the semen, causing abortion. Serious outbreaks occurred in the UK and United States during the 1993 breeding season. The widespread use of artificial insemination increased the risk, especially using imported semen, until the production of safe and effective vaccines to immunise against the disease. Appropriate stud management to protect pregnant mares, testing of stallions to establish whether they are carriers and immunisation of non-carriers, mares who are not pregnant and young foals,

Common vaccines available in the UK are Duvaxyn IE Plus™ and Duvaxyn IET Plus™ manufactured by Solvay Duphar; Equip F™ and Equip FT™, manufactured by Schering-Plough Animal Health; and Prevac Plus™ and Prevac T Plus™, manufactured by Hoechst.
Manufacturers' recommendations for specific vaccines may vary, but the above is the minimum requirement.

VACCINES AVAILABLE FOR TREATMENT OF HERPES VIRUS:

Duvaxyn EHV 1,4TM (Manufacturer: Solvay Duphar)
Use: Prevention of respiratory disease caused by EHV-1 and EHV-4; prevention of abortion caused by EHV-1 virus
Vaccination: Foals from five months or earlier if immune-deprived.
Dosage: Primary doses separated by interval of four to six weeks, and boosters should be given every six months.
Contraindications: Slight local reactions might be noticed at the site of injection, but these should disappear in a few days.

Pneumobort KTM, (Dist: Willows Francis)
Use: Prevention of abortion due to EHV-1.
Vaccination: Pregnant mares at risk need to be vaccinated during the fifth, seventh and ninth months of pregnancy.
Unvaccinated pregnant mares should be vaccinated immediately and then every two months until foaled.
Maiden or barren stock running with vaccinated pregnant mares should be treated in the same way as the mares.
Stallions and youngstock can be vaccinated twice with a gap of two months, and subsequently six-monthly.

especially those intended as future stallions, has gone a long way to control the spread of the disease over the past decade.

Many countries do not allow the importation of seropositive horses, so if there is any likelihood that the horse will travel abroad, blood tests should be taken before vaccination to determine if the horse has previously been in contact with the disease. However, it can be argued that except for breeding stock, general vaccination of horses against EVA is not necessary.

ROUTINE CARE

WORMING

Parasitic worms are a major cause of unthriftiness in all types of horses and ponies. It is impossible to eradicate them from the body system completely and permanently, so regular dosing with an appropriate anthelmintic is necessary. Even a low-level infestation can affect the horse's health and performance, whereas a high-level infestation can result in serious illness, and sometimes even death.

There are a number of different worming preparations on the market, in different forms such as paste, powder, or granules. The easiest method of being sure to administer the full dose is to use a proprietary syringe, containing the dose in a paste. Dosage is determined by reference to the animal's bodyweight, remembering that most people underestimate a horse's weight when it comes to worming. In general horses should be dosed more frequently in summer and autumn, when parasite activity increases.

Youngstock and pregnant mares may be at risk of infection by equine herpes virus, particularly when forming temporary herds at stud during the breeding season

---

VACCINES AVAILABLE FOR TREATMENT OF VIRAL ARTERITIS:

Arvac™ (a modified live virus vaccine)
Artervac™ (an inactivated virus vaccine).

Dosage: At least two vaccinations – a primary course, followed by a booster a year later – appear to give long-standing protection (see Appendix A).

RESISTANCE TO WORMERS:

It is impossible to eliminate worms from the horse's system. This, coupled with increasing resistance to the fenbendazole (Panacur™) and pyrantel (Strongid-P™) groups of anthelmintics, and emerging evidence that future resistance is likely to develop to the newer macrocyclic lactones group (ivermectin, avarmectin and moxydectin), poses a serious future threat to the health of many horses.

It is vital that owners ensure that their worming regime takes into account all the appropriate measures and does not rely simply on regular dosing according to manufacturers' recommendations. The most useful and important of these is probably good pasture management, ideally with at least weekly collection of droppings (more frequently in smaller or heavily populated paddocks). Almost as useful is rotational grazing with sheep or cattle, which are susceptible to different parasites and help to clear the ground by breaking the life cycle. Thirdly, harrowing the ground in hot sunny weather will expose the eggs which will be killed by the sun; this may help in temperate climates.

Too frequent anti-worming treatment, for example every two months as traditionally recommended, even when rotating the three main drug groups, is likely to encourage resistance eventually, especially if the other methods of control mentioned above are ignored. One recent study (Little, Flowers, Hammerberg and Gardner, 2003) reported resistance to both fenbendazole and pyrantel on a breeding farm in North Carolina. This study sought to overcome the problem by reducing the number of treatments but specifically targeting more severely infested animals, identified by means of faecal worm egg counts. The cost of the egg counts was offset by savings on anthelmintic preparations. The researchers were able to reduce the number of doses used on the mare group by an astonishing 77.6 per cent. The programme was less successful on the foal group but a reduction was still achieved. The researchers considered that better results would have been obtained had the farm also practised pasture management controls. However, they concluded that the parasite population in the herd would remain resistant to fenbendazole, while the use of pyrantel may be possible in the future in conjunction with ivermectin.

The worry in this situation is that there is now only one effective group of wormers, the macrocyclic lactones, and should resistance develop to these, the last barrier against parasitic disease will have fallen. A further complication is that the use of moxydectin, which is particularly effective against larval stages, including encysted cyathastome (small redworm) larvae, but which also remains longer in the horse's body, may result in increased resistance from any parasites surviving

Larvae of the bot fly

Left: *Large redworm (*Strongylus vulgaris*) and small redworm (*Cyathostomes*) in the faeces*

Right: *Tapeworm*

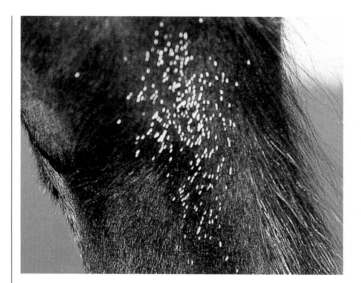

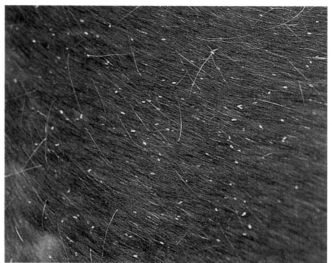

moxydectin treatment, which would also have the side effect of increasing resistance to ivermectin. Extrapolated to the world population at large, there are very real fears for the future and research is continuing into how resistance develops and better means of detecting it.

In conclusion therefore, at present the most effective measures to take against parasitic worms are:

Left: *The bot fly lays its sticky eggs on the horse's coat, to be swallowed when the horse licks them*

Right: *Evidence of lice seen on the horse's coat*

1. **Practise good pasture management** with frequent removal of droppings and rotational grazing if possible, and avoid overstocking. This removes a high proportion of both eggs and larval forms, those resistant to treatment as well as those susceptible to it.

2. **Aim to target any worming programme to actual conditions**, based on faecal worm egg counts or any improved tests that may become available in the near future. If this is impossible, opt for a strategic programme, using all three drug groups, three or four times a year, with specifically targeted extra treatments if necessary, particularly for youngstock. Avoid the traditional blanket programme of treating every two months without taking into account specific factors of pasture management, stocking intensity, climate and the actual worm burden indicated by egg counts.

Giving a proprietary paste wormer by syringe

Lice: Another common parasite, lice appear in the winter, when the horse's coat is long, causing itching and the loss of patches of hair. Serious infestations cause loss of condition and anaemia. There are two types, one affecting the mane and tail, the other living in the coat. The eggs or the creatures themselves are visible in good light. Treatment requires a suitable insecticidal wash, or dousing with louse powder, while the anthelmintic ivermectin also kills lice.

FOOT CARE

The horse's foot is truly a miracle of evolution, a rigid outer structure encasing and protecting delicate, sensitive inner tissues, the whole combining to transfer not only the considerable bodyweight of the horse to the ground, but also the additional energy created by movement. When the horse is galloping or jumping, these exertional forces test the strength and resilience of the hoof capsule, the internal structures and, indeed, the whole limb to the limit. The weight-bearing area of the feet is very small in relation to the weight of horse and rider, and it should be easy to understand why perfect balance through the whole combination, including the feet, is essential to minimise the risk of strain.

In the wild, horses' feet evolved to grow as required to counteract the effects of wear on the hoof wall. Through domestication, primarily because selective breeding has paid insufficient attention to hoof conformation and horn quality, and because horses are reared in different environments, their feet vary in strength and resilience. Some breeds such as native ponies retain very good feet; others, such as the Thoroughbred, often have very poor quality feet. These basic differences are greatly exacerbated by the need to nail steel shoes on the feet for work, and by the standard of farriery employed.

The visible outer structures of the foot comprise the hoof capsule, the sole and the frog, all of which are formed from the same horny material, developed as an extension of the epidermis (skin). Three types of tissue make up the hoof capsule: the hair-like cylinders of tubular horn are bound together by inter-tubular horn, while inside the tubules is found intra-tubular horn. The tubules of the sole are more widely spaced, with more inter-tubular horn which is capable of flaking away as new horn grows, while the frog obtains its resilient texture from a fat-secreting gland. As they grow, a process called keratinisation hardens the tubules, but they bend or are compressed according to the varying pressures received by the hoof capsule as it performs its functions of weight bearing and energy transference.

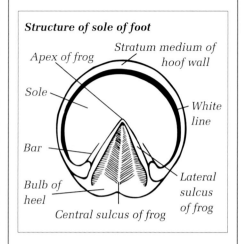

Structure of sole of foot

Apex of frog
Stratum medium of hoof wall
Sole
White line
Bar
Bulb of heel
Lateral sulcus of frog
Central sulcus of frog

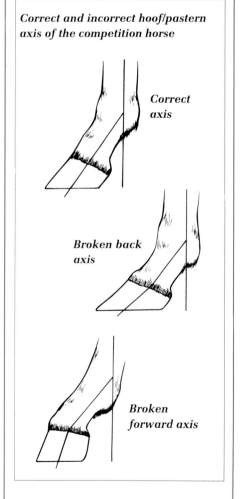

Correct and incorrect hoof/pastern axis of the competition horse

Correct axis

Broken back axis

Broken forward axis

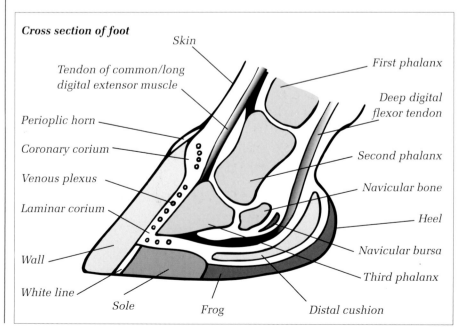

Cross section of foot

Skin
Tendon of common/long digital extensor muscle
First phalanx
Deep digital flexor tendon
Perioplic horn
Coronary corium
Venous plexus
Second phalanx
Laminar corium
Navicular bone
Heel
Wall
Navicular bursa
White line
Third phalanx
Sole
Frog
Distal cushion

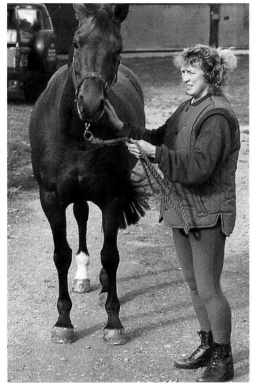

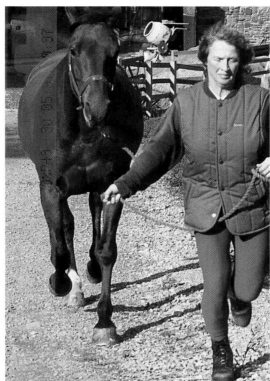

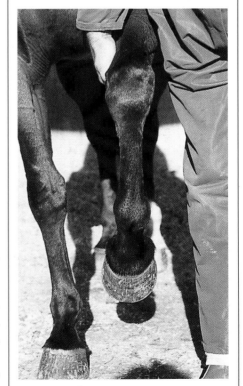

Assessment of foot balance should be carried out: (far left) with the horse standing square; (left) with the horse in movement; and (below) with the limb raised and supported with the lower leg falling free

The foot has evolved a design which enables it to expand and relax to facilitate this process: that is, the combination of concave sole and deeply cleft frog with the flexible tubular horn of the hoof wall. The horse's conformation, with straight forelegs and rounder front feet, and more angular hind legs and oval hind feet, reflects the fact that the greater proportion of weight (60 per cent) is carried by the forelimbs, while the propulsive power is effected by the hind limbs and quarters. Each foot, however, should be evenly balanced, the angles made by the toe and the heel with the ground should be the same, and the axis of the front of the hoof wall with the pastern should be continuous, maintaining the same angle with the ground. If the hoof/pastern axis is broken forward, more pressure is being exerted through the toe, predisposing to concussive injury; if it is broken back, as more commonly happens, more pressure is borne through the posterior part of the foot, resulting in compressed, collapsed heels, with excessive expansion and resultant strain, or even tearing of the internal structures, plus an increased risk of bruised soles.

That mythical creature, the perfectly conformed and balanced horse, would bear equal weight and transfer equal energy through each forelimb and through each hind limb, with that weight and energy evenly displaced through each foot. Good farriery, in conjunction with good training and good riding, seeks to achieve this ideal state of affairs. In practice, most horses have conformational or acquired defects or imbalances, for which a skilled farrier can compensate by means of trimming, rebalancing and adequately supportive shoeing.

The foot should be balanced in relation to the whole limb, not just to the symmetry of the hoof capsule itself. Therefore the horse should be assessed firstly standing square, secondly in movement, and thirdly with the leg raised and supported and the foot falling free, the shoe being fitted in a position central to the long axis of the leg.

The farrier will also take into account the type or breed of horse and its associated foot size and shape, also its hoof quality, plus the type of work it is expected to do. The choice of shoe size and section will depend upon these variables, as well as on conformational factors or acquired defects.

The sole and frog of the foot, like the hoof wall, grow continuously, so when the foot is prepared for shoeing, loose flakes of sole are removed and the frog is trimmed; this is particularly important with flat-footed horses which tend to grow large frogs, exacerbating the tendency for over-expansion at the heels. The hoof wall is trimmed with cutters and the foot is then rasped to complete the balancing process and the preparation for nailing on the shoe. The foot must be trimmed to achieve even balance, having regard to all these factors, in order to transfer energy from movement and bodyweight to the ground, without causing abnormal pressure in any part of the foot or leg. Shoes must be fitted appropriately to maintain this overall balance.

A further important point is that as the hoof grows, with repeated expansion, the hoof wall may overlap the outer edge of the shoe at the heels and if shoes are not refitted frequently enough, this is a common cause of corns. The farrier should be aware of this situation and new shoes should be fitted sufficiently wide to counteract the tendency and prevent it occurring before the next farriery session is due.

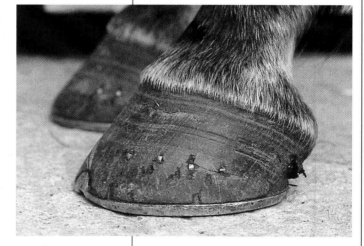

The shoe is usually lightly burnt on, to test the fit; excessive burning should be avoided as it draws moisture from the horn. Enough nails are used to secure the shoe to the foot, depending upon foot size and the workload; nails are not placed in the posterior quarters, to allow for heel expansion. Ideally the exit holes should be at least one third of the way up the hoof wall, and level all round, though this may not be possible if there is a defect in the horn. The exit holes should not be too low, as there is an increased risk of tearing off the hoof wall, should the horse lose a shoe. The toe is usually 'safed off' (slightly rounded) to assist easy break-over. Where extra support for low heels is needed, the heel of the shoe is extended beyond the back of the foot; even for well conformed feet, the heel of the shoe should extend slightly beyond the heel of the foot and should always be upright; the old practice of 'pencilling' the shoe heels, still unfortunately too commonly found, coupled with insufficient trimming of the toe, encourages collapsed heels and a broken-back hoof/pastern axis.

Nail exit holes should ideally be level with one another and appear approximately one third of the way up the hoof. The heel of the shoe should extend slightly behind the heel to offer support

The treatment of foot problems such as corns, sheared heels, seedy toe and cracks, or more serious ones such as separation of the laminae due to laminitis, fractured pedal bone or navicular disease, can all be greatly assisted by skilled supportive or corrective farriery, the farrier working in collaboration with the veterinary surgeon. Sometimes corrective trimming may be all that is required; in other cases the construction of special shoes, or drastic action such as surgical resection of the hoof wall is necessary.

The most useful and commonly used remedial shoe is the bar shoe, which may consist of a straightforward connecting bar joining the heels of the shoe, or which may provide additional rearward support as in an egg-bar shoe, or frog support, as in a heart-bar shoe. The forging and fitting of such shoes requires precise application of the farrier's art, combined with the veterinary input of accurate diagnosis, usually assisted by X-rays. The function of all bar shoes is to provide extra support where required, whilst equalising the pressure of weight bearing and energy transfer throughout the foot. For example, in treating sheared heels (separation of the bulbs of the heel due to uneven pressure – often the result of poor farriery), the bar shoe prevents the independent movement of the heels, allowing them gradually to recover to normal. Similarly with a fractured pedal bone, the bar shoe clamps the foot, helping to immobilise the structures so that healing can take place. Dorsal wall hoof resection is a dramatic operation which enables the dead and necrotic tissues resulting from the separation of sensitive and insensitive laminae (the tissues which join the outer casing to the inner structures of the foot) to be exposed and removed. It involves removing a section of hoof wall sufficient to expose fully the damaged area, which can then drain and be cleaned, then repeatedly hardened and debrided until only healthy, clean tissue remains. Constant, intensive nursing is required to maintain a hygienic environment and prevent infection of the open section. Provided the corium (the area which nourishes the coronary band and enables it to grow new horn) has not been damaged, the horse is able gradually to grow a complete new hoof. Similar techniques can be used to cope with foot infections (see page 102) and white line disease (see page 204).

Skilled farriery can perform two objectives: correction of problems in the immature, growing youngster; or compensation for problems which have developed in the older horse. All farriery, good or bad, affects the development and growth of the feet concerned in terms of balance and support for the limb above, hoof capsule development and heel expansion, the angles of the hoof/pastern axis, and so on. This in turn affects the athletic performance of the horse. However, there is now also an extensive movement that contends that horses should not be shod at all, and another that promotes a radically different form of shoeing: see Appendix C, p250.

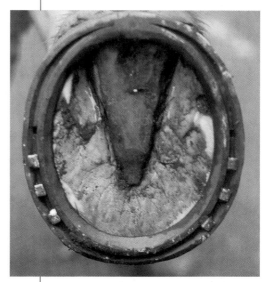

An egg-bar shoe

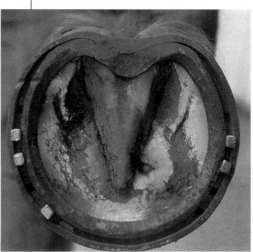

A partial heart-bar shoe

Resection of the dorsal wall of the foot, to treat a horse with separation of the sensitive and insensitive laminae

TEETH

The horse's teeth continue to grow throughout its life. This growth is necessary to replace the biting and grinding surfaces that are being worn down through constant use in masticating the feed, but the wear is usually uneven due to the circular action of chewing and the difference of width of the upper and lower jaws, the upper jaw being slightly wider than the lower jaw. In many horses sharp edges form on the outside of the upper jaw and inside of the lower jaw, and these can cause painful cuts or ulcers by rubbing against the cheek, resulting in discomfort, resistance to the bit and difficulty in eating.

Left: The horse's mouth is best held open by an expanding device called a 'gag', so that the veterinary surgeon can check the teeth for sharp edges, hooks, or other defects and gain access to the molars with special dental rasps. Some horses dislike the gag at first, but usually accept it if handled calmly and patiently

Below: The tables of the teeth are smoothed by rasping which is painless

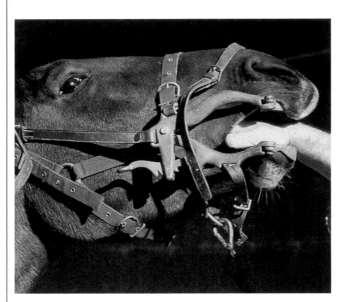

An annual check of the mature horse's teeth, or twice yearly for growing stock whose permanent teeth are still erupting, shows whether rasping to restore a level surface is necessary. Dental checks will also show tooth damage or the presence of wolf teeth, which need to be removed by a simple operation if the horse is to be able to carry a bit comfortably.

Aged horses may require more frequent attention, as gross changes in the apposition of the upper and lower tables might prevent them from chewing their food properly and gaining the best nourishment.

Those horses that are slightly pig- or parrot-mouthed do not wear the first or last teeth of the upper or lower tables properly, and these teeth develop a spike or grow in length to such an extent that chewing becomes very difficult. These teeth have to be cut and rasped to an even length if the horse is to regain normal mastication. Likewise horses suffering from peridontitis (see page 178) might lose a tooth, and the one opposite will then grow into the vacant space; again, this will eventually interfere with chewing and will need trimming.

In recent years both horse owners and the veterinary profession have become aware of the need for more careful attention to equine dentistry to keep the horse comfortable and healthy, both in terms of general well-being and efficiency of the digestive system, and with regard to improved performance by keeping the horse's mouth pain-free and able to carry a bit responsively.

As the law stands, anyone can rasp a horse's teeth in Britain,

Parrot mouth

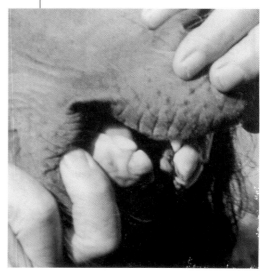

though not perform many of the other tasks of dental care that may be required. In 2001 the British Equine Veterinary Association in conjunction with the British Veterinary Dental Association launched a training course and examination for dental technicians to counteract the spread of unqualified laymen purporting to be equine dentists. Horse owners in Britain can now check that their dental technician is BEVA/BVDA accredited and suitably insured. When surgical intervention is needed, however, the dental technician must work in conjunction with a veterinary surgeon. New legislation under the auspices of DEFRA (Department for Environment, Food and Rural Affairs) is being prepared for 2004, that will provide a DEFRA approved training course. DEFRA has also listed the procedures that non-veterinarians can currently undertake, as laid down by the Veterinary Surgeons Act 1966. They include: examination of teeth, routine rasping (excluding power rasping), removal of sharp enamel points, small dental overgrowths such as hooks and spurs, bit seat shaping (a method developed in America to allow the bit to sit more comfortably against the teeth), removal of loose deciduous caps and removal of supragingival calculus.

Roaming a wide area and sharing grazing with sheep or cattle helps to break the parasite life cycle

PROGRESS OF EQUINE DENTISTRY

The new order will permit properly trained technicians to carry out more advanced procedures including some extractions, removal of dental hooks, and treatments using powered tools. However, any surgical procedures involving incisions and more complicated problems will still have to be done by a veterinary surgeon although the dental technician may work as part of the team supervised by the vet. It should also be remembered that any necessary anaesthetics or sedatives can only be administered by a vet.

America has been the major player in the progress of equine dentistry with the American School of Equine Dentistry and The Academy of Equine Dentistry in Idaho. The Worldwide Association of Equine Dentistry, first inaugurated in Nebraska, offers officially recognised qualifications which have now also been accepted by the Royal College of Veterinary Surgeons and DEFRA. Other schools can be found in Australia.

STABLE MANAGEMENT

The usual habitat of a stable and/or a field or fields is an artificial environment for the horse, intended by nature to roam freely over large areas of land. Thus even a large airy stable and a field of two or three acres is unnaturally restricted, and these imposed limitations can have an adverse effect on the horse's health, for several reasons.

In the Pasture

Moving over the same ground repeatedly, where it and others have already passed droppings, increases the extent to which the horse will pick up parasites. To minimise this, good field management requires that droppings are picked up and removed whenever possible, ideally at least twice a week, and the more heavily the land is grazed, the more important it is to do this. Harrowing helps in summer because it spreads out the droppings and allows the sun to kill the worm eggs; grazing with other species, such as sheep, also helps to interrupt the parasite life cycle.

If they are not carefully managed, modern horse pastures often become sour, with the herbage mix and cover depleted and an increased burden of plants of poor nutritional value and weeds, some of which – such as ragwort – are poisonous. To avoid these dangers, the pasture should be divided and the sections alternately rested; the weeds must be topped, sprayed or removed by hand (especially ragwort, which must be dug out by hand to be sure the whole plant is removed), and the land should be harrowed, reseeded, rolled and fertilised to an appropriate annual schedule. A top dressing of nitrogen-based fertiliser will provide early grass growth, although grazing must be controlled because a sudden flush of grass is the main cause of acute laminitis. Horse pastures also tend to become too acidic, and a slow-release organic dressing such as calcified seaweed applied every three years will help keep the land in good heart.

In the Stable

The biggest enemy of the horse in the stable is dust. The mould spores inevitably present in hay and straw fill the air, and if the stable is also poorly ventilated they build up and increase the risk to the delicate structures of the horse's respiratory system. Stables need to be well ventilated but without being draughty, and to this end a high-level exit is needed for polluted, used air. Dust-free bedding such as wood-shavings, shredded paper or the waste products from hemp and grape is preferable to straw, and has the added advantage that the horse cannot eat it.

If a horse must spend much of its time stabled, remember that its digestive system is designed to work on a continuous basis, so provide a steady supply of good quality forage. Concentrate feeds should be divided into several small feeds a day, rather than given as one or two large ones.

Finally the horse needs exercise to keep all its body systems working efficiently, and an hour a day out of the box on a hack is really not enough. All horses should be turned out for at least several hours daily to relax and stretch their legs, and to help keep the circulatory system working.

TRAVEL MANAGEMENT

Travelling to shows and competitions is a normal part of daily life for the average horse or pony, so it is easy to forget how potentially stressful it can be. Research shows that in horse transporters of all types, the air circulates upwards at the front, carrying ammonia fumes from urine, dust, spores and micro-organisms with it, past the horse's head, regardless of the position and design of ventilators. It is therefore vital that on a long journey, the vehicle should be kept as clean as possible, with faeces and wet, soiled bedding removed at regular intervals. Sawdust or shavings absorb urine and make it easier to clean out droppings, whereas straw is less absorbent and adds to the risk of dust and spores.

Soaked hay or haylage can be fed in transit, again to minimise the dust and mould spores in the air.

POLLUTED WATER

Water supplies should be constant, clean and unpolluted. This trough has been built into the boundary wall. Polluted water supplies can sometimes be the cause of illness or poisoning, so be sure that all field water, whether piped or from natural springs, comes from a pure source.

A COMFORTABLE RIDE

Refusing to load is often initiated by a bad travelling experience, so it is essential to give your horse as comfortable a ride as possible by driving with consideration, especially when cornering and braking. Also, make the horse as comfortable as possible. For example, some horses have difficulty in balancing in a trailer with a partition down to floor level because they find the width of the standing area insufficient to brace themselves against movement; however, removing the partition will often solve this problem for these horses. A breast bar is essential for horses travelling facing forwards, for support when the vehicle brakes.

Research has shown that horses sometimes prefer to travel facing backwards; however, this is not possible in most modern trailers due to the design for weight distribution. Lorries often provide sideways or herringbone-pattern travelling positions, which seem acceptable, and a horsebox normally provides better stability than a trailer, which is liable to sway. It is also thought that tying horses so that the head is held higher than normal during a journey may increase the risk of respiratory infection, so lower-level ties are to be preferred.

The length of the journey is another important factor. Water should be offered at least every four hours, and ideally horses should be unloaded and allowed to stretch their legs after this amount of time, before resuming a long journey. Horses tend to lose weight in transit, mainly due to fluid loss which also includes electrolytes, so it is important that a horse drinks enough following a journey to rehydrate its body adequately; this can be a problem if it has been transported to a new area and takes a dislike to the strange water supply. Various methods can be tried to encourage it to drink, such as flavouring the water with apple juice, cider vinegar, molasses or similar sweet additives that it is known to like, and obviously it is sensible to accustom the horse to these tastes at home first.

Horses facing very long journeys of more than twenty-four hours are sometimes given antibiotics before transit as an extra precaution against respiratory infections. Modern thinking now suggests that it is more important to monitor the horses *after* travelling, and *then* treat those that show a slight temperature rise or any other signs of respiratory disease. One of the most important and difficult things to achieve on a long journey, due to the change of routine and confinement in the transportation vehicle, is to keep the horse's digestive system functioning properly. Some horses eat well during transit, others go off their feed due to stress or anxiety. Giving a suitable probiotic preparation in the feed for three days before travel and continuing it through the journey and for three days afterwards, will help maintain the correct balance of flora in the horse's gut, encourage it to eat properly and reduce the risk of colic and other digestive upsets. Hard feed usually needs to be reduced or eliminated altogether during a long journey as the horse is not being exercised as much as usual, but clean forage should be provided and haylage in nets with small holes will keep the horse occupied for several hours, while also providing the ideal 'trickle feed' means of keeping the gut working.

Horses should always be walked for at least 30 minutes to one hour before being stabled at the end of a long trip. If the journey lasts several days, hand walking morning and evening, before departure and after arrival, should be considered essential.

As a general principle however, the best way to minimise travel stress, the risk of respiratory infection and the likelihood of impaired performance is to provide a clean environment, to offer food and water at regular intervals, to limit the time between stops and/or unloading, to allow the horse's head freedom to move up and down, and to give the horse as comfortable a ride as possible by thoughtful driving.

ELECTROLYTE REPLACEMENT

Electrolyte replacement is important if the horse will be competing the next day, and these can be given either diluted in water, or, if you are not sure the horse is drinking, in the feed or by syringe. Electrolytes are essential mineral salts which are needed for many vital body functions, and they cannot be stored in the body. In normal circumstances sufficient are obtained from the feed, but when these are depleted through sweating and the horse is subjected to the stress of competition before it can replace them naturally, supplementation is required. However, overdosing a dehydrated horse with electrolytes can cause a dangerous imbalance, so they should be administered with circumspection and not as a matter of routine.

All horses should be turned out daily and given the freedom to run and to relax

YOU
AND YOUR VET

THE CLIENT/VET RELATIONSHIP

Several factors make the question of when or whether to call out the veterinary surgeon a highly emotive and difficult one for many horse owners. On the one hand, the horse or pony is unlike the commercial animal in that it is often regarded as a friend and companion, so there is considerable emotional involvement on the part of the owner in its well-being, and much distress if it is thought to be suffering pain. On the other hand, veterinary fees represent one of the larger costs of horse keeping and there is often considerable pressure on the less wealthy owner to minimise expense whenever possible. This aspect is further complicated by the fact that many situations requiring veterinary treatment may be tackled in different ways at greater or less expense. Treatment may be conservative but take longer, or it may be more aggressive but with quicker results. More visits, more expensive drugs or surgical remedies can all add greatly to the cost.

In some cases, more expensive treatments are more easily justified than in others – for example, if the horse is used for commercial purposes to earn income such as in a

The horse or pony is unlike the commercial animal in that it is often regarded as a friend or pet; because of the emotional involvement there is therefore much distress if it is seen to be in pain or suffering and so the vet is called; alternatively, it may be a highly valuable asset as a top show, competition or racehorse; on this sort of business footing the owner may feel little emotional involvement, but will need the animal to be maintained in good health

riding school, or is a valuable competition or show horse, or a racehorse with the potential to affect the professional success or earnings of its owner or rider. Moreover the relative costs of different types of treatment are not always very easy to evaluate. For example, the latest wound dressings are expensive, but they promote quicker healing and so may ultimately mean fewer veterinary visits.

INSURANCE

Further considerations are whether or not the horse is insured, and if it is, the terms of the policy. Horse insurance policies are normally subject to an 'excess' on veterinary fees, ie the policy holder is responsible for the charges for each incident up to a certain figure. The insurance company imposes this excess in order to avoid having to pay out for many small claims, so when choosing a policy it is important to balance the excess against the annual premium you can afford and the extent of cover offered. It is vital that you read the small print and understand all the implications of any horse insurance policy, particularly with regard to matters such as when and how the insurance company must be notified of any incidents which may give rise to a claim. In practice, the best policy is to notify the company as soon as any incident occurs which requires treatment for which you may need to claim.

It is also important to know the limit of the amount which you may claim because policies differ in this, both as regards the number of incidents and the total limit over the term of the policy. If finance is an important consideration when dealing with your vet, it is far better to discuss your position and the terms of your insurance policy (if any) with him, so that he can tailor treatment and costs as far as possible to suit your situation. However, anyone considering purchasing a horse or pony should be aware of the likelihood of needing occasional emergency veterinary visits, perhaps followed up by longer-term treatment, and should budget accordingly. The purchase price is the least expensive part of horse ownership!

LOSS OF HORSE

The final aspect which may make the relationship between horse owner and veterinary surgeon a difficult one is that even the most expensive or most protracted course of treatment is not always successful. Sometimes a disease is incurable; sometimes an injury does not mend and the loss

of the horse either by natural death or humane destruction is the end result, still leaving the veterinary bill to be paid. In a few cases a horse may die unexpectedly, perhaps when treatment appeared to be going well, or on the operating table. It is important that the owner realises that these sad situations do occur, and through no fault of the veterinary surgeon; in such circumstances, insurance money may be some compensation, although obviously it will in no way mitigate the grief of losing a friend.

On rare occasions a veterinary surgeon may be held liable, if he is proved to have been negligent in his attention and treatment. However, the veterinary surgeon is by vocation a conscientious individual, and action by a horse owner on such grounds is usually unfounded. If you find yourself in a situation where you are unhappy with the progress your horse is making, or with the treatment the vet prescribes, you are entitled to ask for a second opinion and most vets will be perfectly happy to arrange this for you. Sometimes, if the problem is outside their own area of expertise, they will even suggest it themselves, or refer the horse to a specialist clinic.

TAKING THE MEDICINE

The best approach for the owner is to make a friend of the veterinary surgeon. Do not be afraid to ask questions, or to talk to him about your horse and its problems. Veterinary surgeons are aware that not all owners are experienced in horse management, and they will not think you stupid if you ask obvious-sounding questions or are unsure of yourself in matters such as giving medicines or injections which they may prescribe. If you do experience difficulty in administering prescribed treatment, it is much better to tell your vet and ask for help, than to struggle and fail to give the treatment, whether this is dosing, injecting or re-dressing a wound. A vet can only help you and, more importantly, your horse if he is made fully aware of the situation.

RECORD KEEPING AND NORMAL PARAMETERS

It is also advisable to keep your own stable management records so you can report the full details of the situation accurately to the vet, should you have to call him out. How is the horse behaving differently from normal? Has it been off colour in the preceding days? For how long? In what ways? Have the droppings or urine been normal? Has the horse been dull or depressed? Has its appetite been depressed or abnormal in other ways? What about its attitude to work? Has it had a higher than normal temperature, pulse rate or respiration rate? Has it been drinking more, or less than usual? All these observations can help the vet in making a diagnosis of illness.

The normal parameters of the healthy horse are given on page 24. Heart rate and temperature may

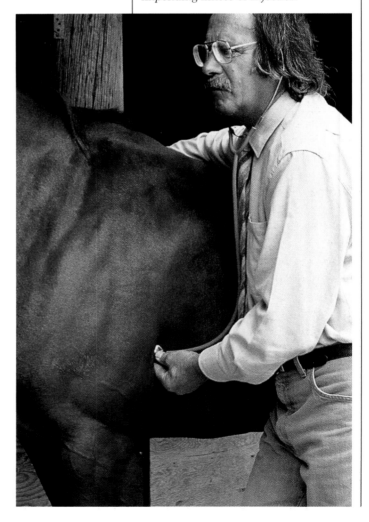

Obtain a stethoscope and keep a record of your horse's heart rate; any change from normal may indicate an impending illness or infection

vary slightly for individuals and it is useful to know your own horse's normal rates, which can be done by checking regularly and keeping a record. A stethoscope and thermometer are inexpensive items which should form part of your basic stable equipment. The heart rate is taken by listening with the stethoscope placed just behind the left elbow, and can be heard as a steady 'lub-dup' double-beat sound; each double beat is one heartbeat. Occasionally there may be abnormalities in the heartbeat: for example, some horses have very efficient hearts which actually miss occasional beats when the horse is at rest; this is nothing to worry about, however, and the heart will generally beat regularly once the horse begins to move and work. Other irregularities may be more serious (see page 160).

Any rise in rectal temperature from normal may also indicate a problem. The temperature should always be taken at the same time of day

To take the horse's temperature, first make sure the thermometer is well below 37.8° C (100° F) and grease it with Vaseline. Stand to one side of the horse to avoid being kicked, lift the tail and insert the thermometer into the rectum, rotating it gently and making sure that it lies against the wall of the rectum. Keep hold of the thermometer, wait one minute, and then take the reading. If you are unsure, ask your vet to show you how to take the heart rate (pulse) and temperature when he is making a routine visit.

HANDLING THE HORSE

All vets are trained to treat all animals but of course some specialise, and most horse owners prefer to have a vet who deals with horses on a daily basis, who is familiar with handling them and up to date on the latest equine research and treatments, to deal with their horse or pony. An equine vet should be confident, calm, kind and firm in his approach to your horse; an experienced practitioner will allow it a few moments to smell and get to know him or her, before attempting any diagnosis or treatment. A vet who takes the trouble to win the horse's confidence seldom has much trouble in handling and treating it.

It is the client's responsibility to have a well-mannered horse which has been taught to behave respectfully in the stable, to stand, to pick up its feet when asked, and not to bite or kick in normal circumstances. The environment around a sick or injured horse should be made as safe as possible for the benefit of both the horse and its handlers. This means the largest available stable with bedding appropriate for the situation; for example, a thick, deep bed of straw ideal for a foaling box would be unsuitable for a horse with a leg injury requiring splints. There should be no dangerous projections from the walls, and buckets, demountable holders, feed bowls and so on should be removed while the horse is being treated, and not left where they might cause an accident.

When handling the horse, the basic principles of safety should be applied. The horse is a large, strong animal which may react violently when frightened or in pain, even if it does not normally do so, and the handler should be aware of this, and of the risk that he or she accepts. The minimum number of people should be present in the box, and this will normally be only the vet and one handler. The lower door should be fastened. The handler should remain on the same side of the horse as the vet unless otherwise directed, and should wear gloves and an approved safety helmet. The headcollar or any other tack should be correctly fitted, and a leadrope or chain with a safe clip should be used; this should *never* be wrapped round the hand, but held close to the horse's chin. With strong horses it may be helpful to pass the leadrope over the noseband and through the side ring of the headcollar. A Chifney bit is often employed for horses inclined to rear, particularly stallions. Some equipment used by the veterinary surgeon may be potentially dangerous to the horse handler: for example, the metal gag inserted into the horse's mouth so the vet can rasp the teeth is heavy and could cause a nasty blow if the horse suddenly swung its head aside; also, protective clothing should be worn if X-rays are being taken.

The handler should avoid distracting the vet when injections are being given – a drug that is quite beneficial or safe for the horse may not be so if it is accidentally injected into the vet!

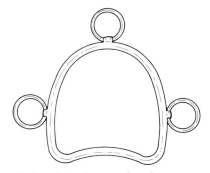

A Chifney bit, often used on horses inclined to rear

The handler should wear a safety helmet and gloves, and when the vet is treating it should stand in a safe position, usually on the same side of the horse as the vet

Some procedures, such as fertility investigations, require the veterinary surgeon to position himself where he is at least risk of being kicked. Large studs usually have stocks in which the mare can be restrained, the vet operating from outside. The individual owner will almost certainly have to compromise, however, and if a mare is known to be difficult, a barrier of straw bales is advisable.

Finally, the vet needs to have confidence in the ability of the handler, and if you are not sure that you can cope with your horse in a difficult situation, call in someone who is experienced to help. Sometimes the vet may bring a nurse or veterinary assistant with him, or it may be possible to have the horse transported to the clinic rather than being treated at home. In some cases it may be appropriate to sedate or tranquillise the horse for treatment. Whatever the case, if there is a difficulty, explain it to the vet when making your initial call, because a solution can nearly always be found.

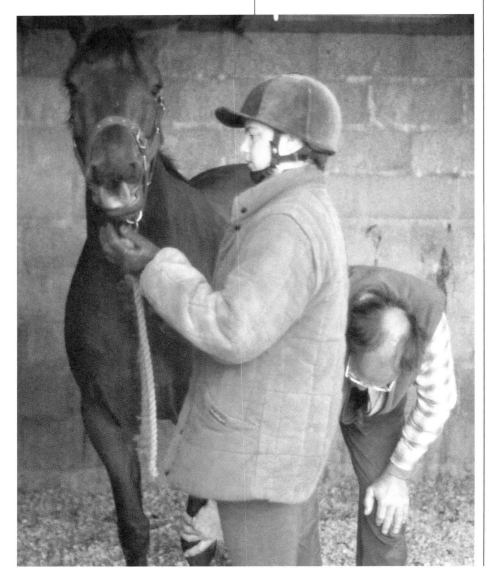

THE DECISION TO CALL THE VET

Sometimes this decision is easy to make, with obvious signs that immediate veterinary attention is necessary. At others, symptoms may be less obvious, but immediate attention may nevertheless be equally necessary to prevent a potentially serious illness from developing further and thus causing unnecessary pain, suffering and expense.

EASILY RECOGNISED CONDITIONS

Serious External Injury

For example as in a road accident or serious fall, with the horse suffering major wounds, profuse bleeding, perhaps unable to stand or to bear weight on one leg.

A TO Z CHECKLIST

back injuries, fractures, pelvic injuries, puncture wounds. See also the chapter on First Aid

This pony is grossly fat, and its obese condition and the way it stands on its heels is typical of a horse suffering from laminitis

Severe Lameness

Horse unable to bear weight on one leg. External signs of swelling or wounds may or may not be present. Or severe lameness in both front or all four feet, horse reluctant to pick up one foot or to move at all; 'laminitic stance' ie leaning back on the heels to relieve weight on front of feet.

A TO Z CHECKLIST

back injuries, fractures, laminitis, pedal bone fracture, pelvic injuries, tendon strain

Severe Abdominal Pain

Horse getting up and down, rolling violently, patchy sweating, pawing at ground and swinging the head round and biting or kicking at the flanks. Increased pulse and respiration rates, congested mucous membranes.

A TO Z CHECKLIST

colic

Severe Muscular Pain/Azoturia

Onset of condition rapid, with horse suddenly unable to move. Muscles of the hindquarters become swollen and hard. Horse sweats profusely, with increased pulse and respiration rates. Any urine passed may be discoloured red or even dark brown. Condition usually occurs early in exercise period. Milder cases have less severe symptoms and can be confused with muscle damage due to traumatic injury such as strain or tear.

A TO Z CHECKLIST

azoturia

Difficulty in Breathing

This may be accompanied by other symptoms: if the horse is **choking** because of impacted food material in the oesophagus, saliva builds up and is coughed up through the nose and mouth. This is accompanied by loud choking noises and severe distress.

In cases of **severe small airway disease**, breathing is laboured and wheezy, and may be accompanied by a cough and nasal discharge; the characteristic 'heave' line is present. Bacterial infections such as **strangles** (*Streptococcus equi*) cause difficulty in swallowing, swollen lymph glands, a high temperature and a nasal discharge. The swollen glands may constrict the airway so much as to make breathing very difficult, and in these cases an emergency tracheotomy might be necessary. **Lead poisoning** and **botulism** cause paralysis of the respiratory muscles and breathing difficulties.

This list is not exhaustive, and any case of respiratory difficulty should receive immediate attention.

A TO Z CHECKLIST

botulism, choke, chronic obstructive pulmonary disease (now called 'recurrent airway obstruction'), equine viral arteritis, poisoning, strangles

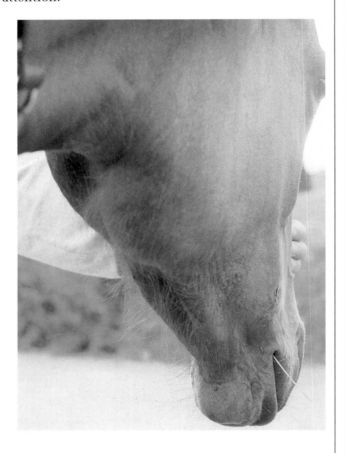

Swelling of the glands due to a strangles infection

Collapse

Various reasons, and a variety of accompanying symptoms: **heart conditions** which may or may not have been previously diagnosed may give rise to sudden collapse and sometimes sudden death. **Epilepsy** in the older horse can cause sudden collapse. **Damage to vital organs** due to accidental injury, which may not be visible externally, may lead to collapse shortly afterwards. **Worm damage** may lead to a ruptured aorta and haemorrhage. In summer, a common cause of collapse often associated with violent behaviour is **urticaria**, due to rolling in a patch of stinging nettles. Horses are very susceptible to **electric shock**, which may also cause collapse.

A TO Z CHECKLIST

aneurism, epilepsy, heart, and disease of, parasites, urticaria

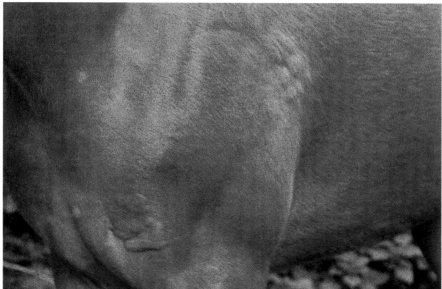

Urticaria can cause a severe reaction

Difficulty in Foaling

If a mare has not produced a foal within thirty minutes of the onset of the second stage of labour, sadly the prospect of a live foal is compromised and your vet should be called at once. At any time during foaling, if the process seems anything but straightforward, the safest course is to call the vet. He would rather arrive to find a live foal than be too late to help.

LESS OBVIOUS CONDITIONS

Diarrhoea

Diarrhoea may have many causes, but it is always potentially serious. Occasionally a change of diet or excitement may result in soft, cowpat-like droppings which soon return to normal, but severe diarrhoea which persists for more than a few hours, perhaps containing blood, requires urgent investigation. Accompanying symptoms vary according to the cause.

Lameness

Weight-bearing on one foot is difficult, but possible. Alternatively, the horse shifts from foot to foot, the walk shows short or shuffling strides, worse on hard surface.

Additional symptoms may include increased digital pulse, local heat, pain response to local pressure on the foot, heat, swelling and pain in the limb. Some conditions are more urgent than others (*eg* laminitis), but immediate veterinary attention is required for an accurate diagnosis to be made.

Tetanus

This horrific disease merits separate mention because the early symptoms are subtle, and early diagnosis is vital if there is to be any chance of successful treatment. Symptoms include the protrusion of the third eyelid across the corner of the eyes, especially if the horse is excited; ears pricked and dock slightly raised due to the onset of paralysis; and the face has an anxious expression, with the lips drawn back from the corners of the mouth (*see* page 79).

A TO Z CHECKLIST

dystocia, foaling

A TO Z CHECKLIST

colitis-X, diarrhoea, parasites, poisoning, salmonellosis

A TO Z CHECKLIST

laminitis sub-acute, navicular disease, pedal-ostitis, pricked foot, puncture wounds, pus in the foot, sesamoiditis, tendon strain

---

A TO Z CHECKLIST

tetanus

CONDITIONS NEEDING ATTENTION AS SOON AS POSSIBLE

Chronic Diarrhoea

If diarrhoea persists for more than a few days, chronic dehydration becomes a serious danger in addition to the underlying cause, and fluid therapy is necessary.

A TO Z CHECKLIST

see Diarrhoea p57

Eye Injuries and Diseases

The eye is a very sensitive structure: injuries need to be repaired as soon as possible, and antibiotic treatment administered to minimise the risk of infection, which may cause further, sometimes irremediable damage.

A TO Z CHECKLIST

cataract, conjunctivitis, corneal ulcer, entropion, recurrent uveitis. See also Anatomical Index: Conditions of the Eye p82

Inappetance

When not working or sleeping, the horse is usually eating, so a loss of appetite is a sign that something is seriously wrong. It is a symptom, not a disease in itself, and there may be many causes including stress or overwork, dislike of certain food ingredients, dental problems, difficulty in swallowing due to infection or injury, digestive problems, depression, fever or a number of other illnesses. The cause needs to be investigated and rectified.

A TO Z CHECKLIST

botulism, dental caps, parasites, peridontitis, poisoning, strangles, tetanus. See also Anatomical Index: Viral Infections p74; Bacterial and Other Infections p76; Diseases of the Teeth p82, and Parasitic Diseases p92

NON-LIFE-THREATENING INJURIES

The sooner any injury is treated, the more quickly healing and recovery can begin; neglect may considerably extend the recovery period and the expense of treatment. Examples include wounds large enough to require stitching, lacerations and penetrating wounds, less obvious tendon, ligament and muscle strain, facial injuries, back and pelvic injuries. In the case of orthopaedic injuries, diagnosis may not always be straightforward, but it needs to be accurate so that the correct treatment, coupled with rest or controlled exercise, can be prescribed.

A TO Z CHECKLIST

back injuries, pelvic injuries, puncture wounds, tendon strain. See also the following chapter, First Aid

Painful Swellings

These may have many causes, from bites or bee stings, to traumatic injury, or the growth of tumours which may be malignant or benign. Swellings may be hard or soft, bony or oedematous, or they may involve the development of granulation tissue, for example around a foreign body which has entered through a wound. Abscesses or cysts may develop. Hard, painful muscular swelling indicates congestion of the blood vessels due to tissue damage. Where the cause is not immediately obvious it must be investigated so that appropriate treatment can be given.

A TO Z CHECKLIST

abscess, azoturia, bog/bone spavin, boils, capped elbow/hock, curb, girth galls, haematoma, melanoma, puncture wounds, saddle sores, sarcoids, splints, strangles, tumours

Retained Placenta

If a mare has not fully passed the afterbirth within twelve hours after foaling, your vet should be called.

A TO Z CHECKLIST

placenta, retained

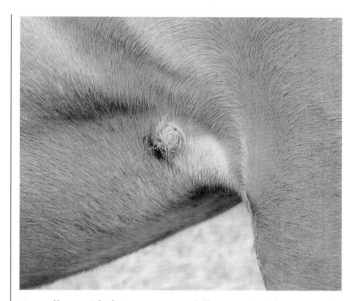

A small sarcoid; this was successfully treated with cryosurgery

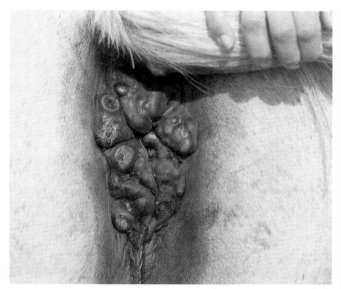

Malignant melanoma of the type which typically affects grey horses

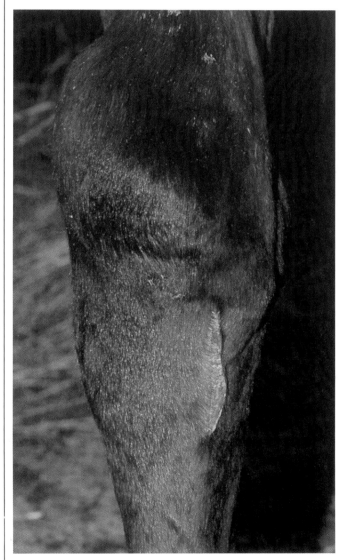

A capped hock

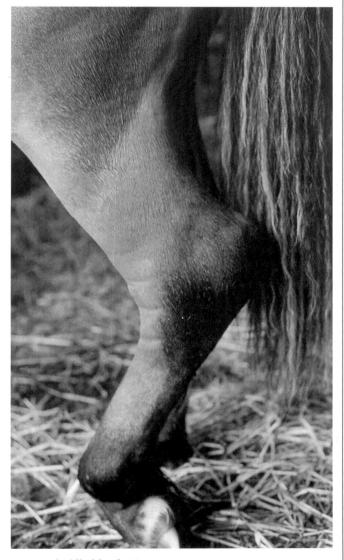

A severely filled hock joint

LESS URGENT CONDITIONS

Weight-Bearing Lameness Gait Abnormalities

Some minor lamenesses may resolve with rest alone, others may require a course of remedial treatment. For example, chronic **corns** may cause minor or intermittent lameness which is scarcely noticed, particularly if the problem affects both front feet; a **bruised sole** will cause minor lameness for a day or two – although bruised soles and heels are often recurrent and the result of poorly conformed feet which are inadequately shod. Prevention of all these problems is often possible with correct foot trimming and balancing by an experienced farrier. A shortened stride may go unnoticed, but it could be a warning precursor of **navicular disease** or longer-term damage due to **concussion** or jarring, which may ultimately lead to bony changes and conditions such as **ringbone** or **sidebone. Sore shins** due to overworking a young horse will also cause a shortened stride or uneven gait, and rest is needed. Minor muscle and ligament **strains** may also only be evident when the horse trots and shows that he is unlevel. Finally, minor physical injuries such as **over-reach** or **speedy-cutting** may cause lameness.

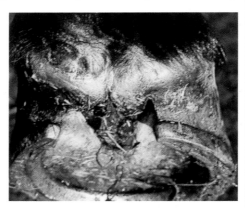

A typical over-reach. Keeping the wound clean and preventing infection is the most difficult aspect of this injury

A TO Z CHECKLIST

arthritis, corns, curb, navicular disease, over-reach, pedal-ostitis, ringbone, sandcrack, sheared heels, seedy toe, sidebone, sore shins, spavin, splints

Skin Conditions/Dermatitis

There are many conditions affecting the skin which, while not life-threatening, may be disfiguring, unpleasant or infectious and prevent the horse from working, or cause it discomfort. Individual diagnosis and treatment is needed.

A TO Z CHECKLIST

equine filariasis, lice, mange, mud fever, nodular skin disease, onchoceriasis, photosensitivity, rain scald, ringworm, sweet itch, warbles, warts

Non-Painful Swellings

(*See also* Painful Swellings.) Swellings which do not cause pain, even when subjected to pressure, may also have many causes. Some, such as fully formed splints, may never give any trouble and may simply be a disfigurement of no consequence to any horse but a show animal. Others, such as some sarcoids, may require surgical removal if situated where tack will cause rubbing, discomfort or further damage.

Where the cause of any swelling is unknown, a veterinary assessment is advisable, particularly if changes are noted.

A TO Z CHECKLIST

capped hock/elbow, hernias, melanoma, nodular skin disease, sarcoids, splints, thoroughpin

Poor Appetite

Poor appetite over a longer period may be due to a dietary deficiency which has the effect of suppressing the appetite, or to the horse being generally run down due to some underlying problem such as parasite infestation. Dental problems causing pain in the mouth may discourage the horse from eating, while elderly horses and ponies may have difficulty in biting or chewing their food due to wear on their teeth, in which case a special diet may be necessary. Horses which are bullied by others at feeding time may also give up trying to eat their share and, consequently, lose weight. Loss of condition due to poor appetite should always be investigated.

A TO Z CHECKLIST

dental caps, lampas, parasites, peridontitis, (also any deficiency diseases). See also Anatomical Index: Viral Infections p74; Bacterial and Other Infections p76; Parasitic Diseases p92; and the chapter on Preventative Treatment. See also Inappetance p58

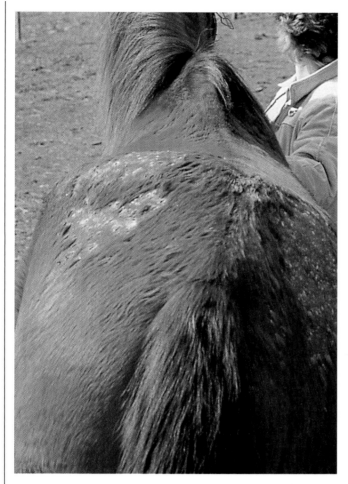

Rain scald is not life-threatening, but is unpleasant for the horse and usually combined with loss of condition due to insufficient protection from winter weather

A typical ringworm lesion

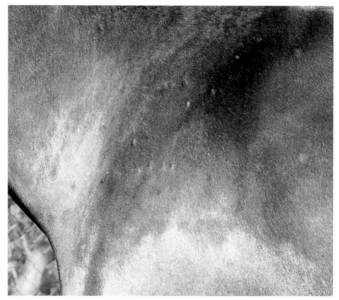

Nodular skin disease

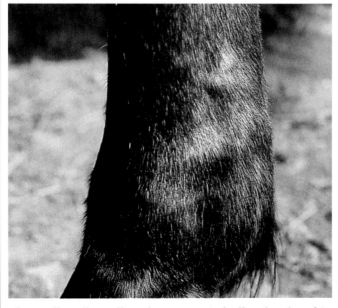

The small, puffy swellings known as windgalls, often found in hard-working horses. They may disappear when the horse is rested and may safely be ignored

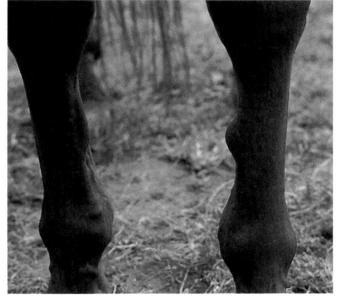

A large splint; when this is fully formed it is unlikely to cause any further trouble

61

FIRST-AID TREATMENT

Prompt first aid can minimise the trauma caused by injury, preventing further damage and helping maintain the situation until skilled veterinary assistance arrives. In minor cases, the right first aid may be all that is required, although all but the most trivial of wounds are best followed up with a course of antibiotics to prevent infection.

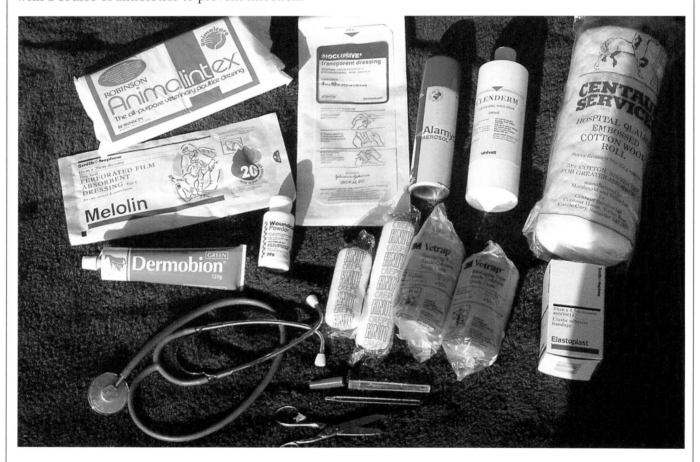

Essential contents of the equine first-aid kit

FIRST-AID KIT

Horses are among the most accident-prone of animals, and every tackroom should be equipped with a basic first-aid kit containing:
- Supply of conforming bandages, which mould to the shape of the limb, either 4 or 5in (7.5 or 10cm)
- Self-adhesive bandages to keep dressings in place, eg Vetrap™
- Proprietary hock and knee bandages, shaped to the joint
- Supply of sterile, non-stick gauze dressings, eg Melolin™
- Poultice dressing for use wet or dry, eg Animalintex™
- Scissors
- Thermometer

◆ Stethoscope
◆ Sticky-backed tape (not safety pins), for anchoring bandages
◆ Antibiotic spray or wound-dressing powder
◆ Antiseptic ointment
◆ Antiseptic cleansing liquid, for dilution to clean wounds
◆ Cotton wool
◆ A clean bucket, not used for feeding or other purposes

HOMOEOPATHIC TREATMENTS

Many owners nowadays also like to keep available some of the more useful alternative and homoeopathic treatments, such as arnica for bruising, aloe vera for healing or Bach's Rescue Remedy for shock. More detail of these increasingly popular methods is beyond the scope of this book, but there is no shortage of literature and advice available from suppliers. It should be pointed out, however, that the greatest danger of using so-called alternative treatments is the lack of any official regulation and the paucity of scientifically proven research, mainly due to the difficulty of proving or disproving the efficacy of such treatments. However, their growing use and the general desire for more holistic and natural methods of treatment and care will surely eventually stimulate more useful research into at least the most popular treatments. Some veterinary surgeons do practise alternative and holistic methods, notably, for example, acupuncture. Meanwhile, horse owners should beware of using any treatments without veterinary advice, and when doing so, should ensure they are as fully informed as possible about the likely outcome.

EMERGENCY TREATMENT

When a horse has an accident, first impressions can easily give rise to panic. Wounds may bleed copiously and a horse holding up a leg and refusing to move is very worrying. However, although tragic injuries inevitably occur, most accidents turn out to be less serious than they at first appear; blood spreads a long way and a great deal can be lost before the horse's life is endangered. With regard to fractures, some nowadays can be repaired; in the case of those that cannot, a few moments of calm assessment will not make the final outcome any worse.

ACCIDENTS

The first essential is to deal with any dangers to the horse and to other people in the vicinity. For example, if the accident occurs on a road and the horse cannot be moved, traffic must be warned to slow down or stop. If the horse can be moved, do so quietly and carefully to a safe place. In circumstances where the horse has been hit by a vehicle or has had any accident involving impact, it is wise to call for a veterinary examination, even if there is no outward sign of injury, in case of internal damage.

SHOCK

Shock is not just a nervous reaction, but a serious condition which may be fatal if appropriate treatment is not given quickly enough. The clinical signs include the horse appearing mentally depressed or dazed, showing an anxious expression, a rapid pulse and/or weakened pulse

FIRST-AID NOTES

ACCIDENTS
◆ Warn traffic if necessary
◆ Quietly move horse to safe place if possible
◆ Impact accidents: **call vet** even if no outward damage – there may be internal injury

SHOCK
◆ Symptoms: horse looks anxious; rapid, weakened pulse; pale mucous membranes
◆ **Call vet immediately**

BLEEDING
◆ If copious or prolonged, control with pressure bandage over pad of gamgee and/or gauze
◆ If one pad not sufficient, apply further pad and bandage over top; **call vet**
◆ For wound containing a foreign body: use a ring bandage, particularly where joint involved
◆ For dirty wounds, cold hosing

BRUISING
◆ Treat with cold water or ice packs applied over a bandage
◆ *Haematomas* (blood clots): small ones resolve themselves; large ones can be drained by the vet

SIMPLE PUNCTURE WOUNDS
◆ *In foot*: remove cause (eg nail); keep open to drain; apply poultice; call vet to vaccinate against tetanus

INCISED WOUNDS
◆ *Small cuts*: clean with an antiseptic solution
◆ *Larger cuts*: superficial cuts can be cleaned; pull edges together; dress; cover with pressure bandage
◆ *Cuts which penetrate skin thickness*: need stitching: **call vet**

LACERATED WOUNDS
◆ *Small*: grazes and scratches can be cleaned and anointed with antiseptic. If extensive, antibiotics needed: **call vet**
◆ *Large*: **call vet**; control bleeding; clean carefully with water (cold hosing) or antiseptic solution. **Do not apply ointments or creams**

FRACTURES
◆ Keep horse still
◆ Immobilise damaged limb with temporary splint such as inflatable vacuum splint or Robert Jones splint (see p67)
◆ **Call vet**

TENDON INJURIES
◆ **Call vet**
◆ Cold compresses: replace them as soon as they cease to be colder than the leg

and pale mucous membranes. The symptoms appear in response to interruptions to the normal circulation and a decrease in volume of the blood which may result from many different causes, from internal haemorrhage to endotoxaemia, dehydration or actual blood loss. If your horse appears to be suffering from shock, whether due to accidental injury or to illness, call your veterinary surgeon immediately.

BLEEDING

Bleeding must be controlled before a wound can be treated. Blood leaking into a wound from broken blood vessels and clotting is the first stage of healing and in most cases bleeding stops or slows to a trickle quite rapidly following injury. If bleeding is more copious or prolonged, a pressure bandage should be applied, over a pad of gamgee or gauze. The size of the pad and strength of pressure required depend upon the seriousness of the wound and the extent of the bleeding. If the first application is insufficient, a further pad and bandage can be applied over the top, whilst waiting for veterinary help. If arterial damage is involved, with bright red blood being lost in spurts, the vet should be called immediately.

Where there is a risk that a foreign body has penetrated the wound, a ring bandage around the centre of the wound should be used instead of a pad, to avoid any risk of exacerbating the damage. This is especially important where joints are involved.

For dirty wounds such as broken knees, cold hosing for up to half an hour is a more effective way of reducing bleeding and cleaning the damaged tissues.

WOUNDS

Four types of wound may be defined: bruises, or contused wounds; puncture wounds, involving deeper penetration, usually with a small surface area; incised wounds, such as a cut; and lacerated wounds, involving torn tissues.

Bruising

Most bruises heal quickly and the skin is unbroken. In some cases, where bleeding occurs under the skin, a haematoma (blood blister) may develop. Eventually the increasing pressure stops the bleeding and the blood clots, and will ultimately be re-absorbed by the body; or if the haematoma is large and unsightly, it can be drained by your veterinary surgeon.

Bruising is best treated with cold water or ice packs. Cold constricts the blood vessels, thus reducing the flow of blood into the injured area, therefore minimising inflammation and swelling. Ice and deep-frozen materials must never be applied directly to the skin, but over a bandage or in a specially designed pack, to avoid cold burns. Various types of proprietary ice pack are available that can remain cold for several hours, however research indicates that ice therapy to reduce inflammation and pain is most effective when used for 15–20 minutes, then removed and repeated hourly or with reasonable frequency in the early stages after injury.

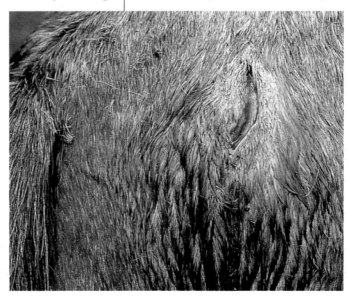

A cut caused by malicious wounding

Puncture Wounds

These occur most frequently in the feet, when a nail or some other foreign object enters the sole, causing a deep but often barely visible wound. Probably the first the owner will know of the injury is when the horse becomes severely lame due to infection. Occasionally the cause of the damage is found still protruding from the wound. Punctures through the centre of the foot are more dangerous than those at the edges, since there is a risk of the pedal bone being involved, resulting in long-term, chronic, or possibly permanent lameness. More common are simple punctures, which can be treated initially by opening up the tract and poulticing to draw out any dirt and debris. It is important that puncture wounds are kept open and allowed to drain and heal from the inside, and also that the horse is vaccinated against tetanus, which notoriously enters through this type of wound. A proprietary poultice such as Animalintex™ is easy to use, and it should be changed twice a day for about three days until the poultice is clean when removed, signifying that all dirt or infectious material has been drawn out.

Lacerated wounds, caused by a bite (below left) *and when healed* (below right)

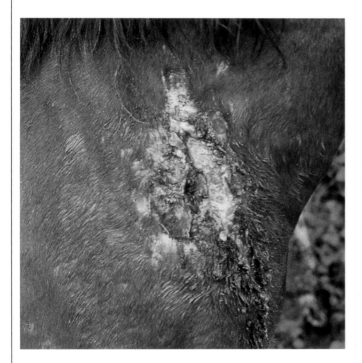

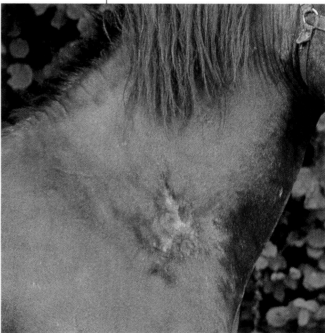

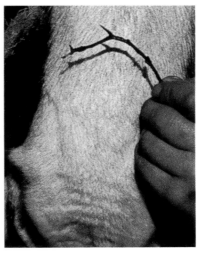

*Pus oozing from an infected wound at the back of the mouth (*far left*), caused by this twig of blackthorn (*left*)*

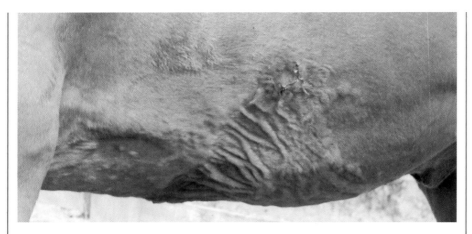

A burn

A gunshot wound

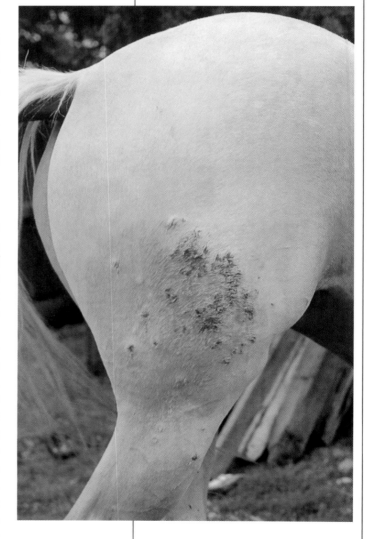

Incised Wounds

Small cuts under 1in (25mm) long will usually heal quite quickly, with no further treatment other than cleaning with an antiseptic solution to remove any dirt and debris, and to disinfect the wound. Dressings are not usually necessary.

Longer cuts which penetrate through the thickness of the skin require stitching to achieve healing by 'first intention', that is, where the edges of the wound are close and can easily knit together.

Lacerated Wounds

These require a similar approach. Small lacerations such as grazes and scratches can simply be cleaned, anointed with antiseptic and left to heal naturally. If the scratches are extensive – for example, if a horse has been caught in wire, an unfortunately common occurrence – a course of antibiotics is recommended to prevent infection.

Once the bleeding is under control, larger lacerations such as badly broken knees and deeper tissue damage require careful cleaning to remove dirt and foreign bodies. It is most important that wounds are cleaned as thoroughly as possible, to minimise the multiplication of bacteria which delay healing, but whether or not this can be done before the vet arrives depends upon the seriousness of the wound and the extent of the bleeding. Owners are sometimes afraid that swabbing the wound will hurt the horse, but most horses accept the process with little or no trouble. Plain water for hosing wounds, especially dirty wounds such as broken knees, or antiseptic solution for bathing, is all that is required at this stage. Ointments and creams should not be applied as they are difficult to remove should the vet decide to stitch the wound when he arrives.

With deeper wounds, the vet's first objective is to stop any further bleeding by clamping torn blood vessels. The area is then 'debrided' – thoroughly cleaned and any dead or damaged tissue removed. Deeper

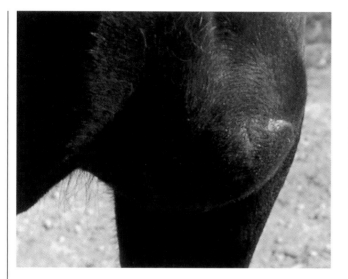

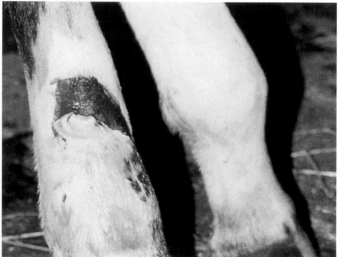

A large haematoma (above left) and (above right) a superficial leg wound. The edges were pulled together, dressed and covered with a pressure bandage, resulting in straightforward healing

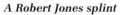

(a)

(b)

(c)

A Robert Jones splint

a) Apply at least four layers of gamgee tissue. After every two layers use a cohesive bandage to compress the gamgee as tightly as possible. For additional support a length of plastic drainpipe, cut in half lengthways, can be positioned between the padding and the bandages

b) Finish with a final layer of cohesive bandage

c) The finished bandage which should extend from the elbow to the hoof. There should be very little bend, to support the leg and keep it straight

A proprietary external splint

layers of tissue are sutured first, finishing with the skin. Some wounds, for example where areas of skin have been lost, cannot be repaired by stitching and will take much longer to heal.

FRACTURES

Today a fracture no longer automatically means the end of a horse's life, because many simple fractures, especially of the lower limb, can be satisfactorily repaired. Fractures of the upper limb, back and pelvis, however, have a poor prognosis and euthanasia is usually advised.

First aid for suspected fractures requires the horse to be kept as still as possible until professional help arrives. The next step is to immobilise the damaged limb by means of a temporary splint, such as an inflatable vacuum splint, or failing that, a Robert Jones splint which is devised by wrapping a layer of cotton wool thickly around the leg, then bandaging tightly, wrapping on another layer of cotton wool and again compressing by bandaging until several rolls have been used. Additional support can be obtained by placing a length of plastic drainpipe, cut in half lengthways, between the padding and bandages. (*See* diagram page 67.)

Cold-water boots can be used over a strain and are now frequently used as a preventative measure, to take the heat out of the legs following strenuous competition

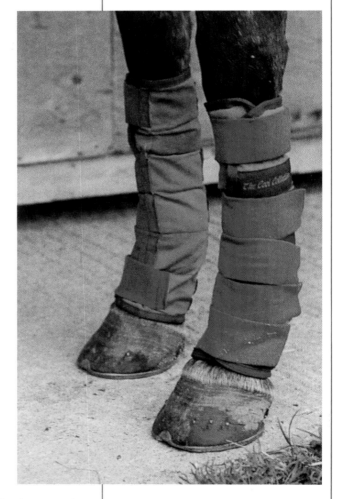

With this in place, the horse can then be transported to an X-ray unit where an accurate diagnosis of the extent of the damage can be made. Fractures involving a clean break heal more easily than 'comminuted' fractures, where the bone is shattered into several shards and realignment is difficult. Fractures involving joints are also less likely to heal well, as the new bone forming may interfere with the mobility of the joint and there is an increased risk of arthritis later on.

The major difficulty in coping with fractures is the combination of the length of time required for healing, and the disinclination of the horse, as a species, to remain immobile. The situation has been improved by the development of external splints, designed to transfer the horse's weight to the ground while keeping the injured leg supported. This also relieves the uninjured limbs of part of the stress of bearing extra weight.

In some cases, plating and screwing is possible: this process has the benefit of accurately aligning and immobilising the bones, but the disadvantages inherent in invasive surgery and the risk of infection.

Finally chip fractures, which are relatively common, can be dealt with successfully by surgically removing the offending chip of bone.

TENDON INJURIES

The most common form of tendon injury is a rupture due to excessive stress during exercise. Damage may be minor, affecting just a few fibres, or more extensive. It is easy to miss the small amount of heat and swelling indicative of minor strains, but in more serious cases, the whole length of tendon from behind the knee to the back of the fetlock may be hot, swollen and painful.

In all cases, the immediate first-aid treatment is the application of cold compresses, replacing them as soon as they cease to be colder than the leg.

This helps to minimise swelling, inflammation and pain. Veterinary treatment will then include anti-inflammatory drugs; in severe cases glucosaminoglycans (GAGS) may be prescribed, as they have been shown to help limit damage to tendon tissue caused by inflammation, and may help stimulate repair.

Complete rest is essential during the acute stage, until heat and swelling have disappeared and the horse is walking sound. The extent of the damage and the progress of healing can be monitored by ultrasound scanning.

The next stage involves carefully controlled progressive exercise over several weeks or months, depending upon the extent of the original damage. Research indicates that anything but a very minor strain is likely to require 12–18 months progressive rehabilitation, before the horse is ready to return to full work and resume its normal training programme. Reducing the rehabilitation period increases the risk of recurrence.

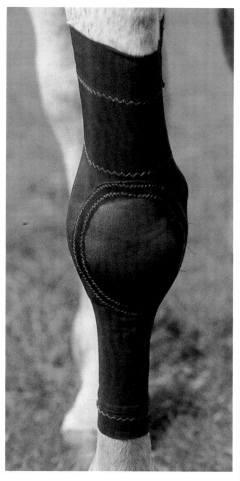

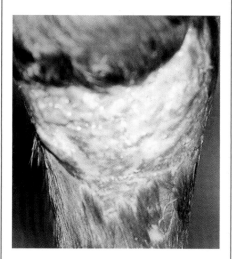

(left) *A proprietary conforming knee bandage, which helps keep dressings in place*

Granulation tissue, or proud flesh, has developed on this healing knee wound

The fully healed knee shows surprisingly little scarring

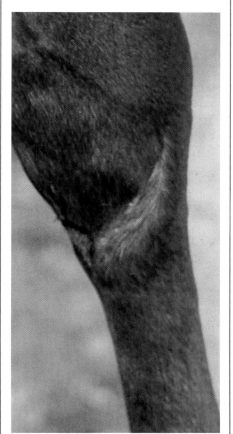

THE HEALING PROCESS

The body's first reaction to damage is to inundate the wound area with blood, which then clots; this is followed by inflammation and the migration of white blood cells to the area. These fight infection by digesting any foreign material and also the clotted blood, allowing new skin to form under the scab. Where the edges of broken skin are close together and able to reunite quickly, healing is said to take place 'by first intention'. However, where there is a gap, either because an area of skin was lost or a cut was not stitched immediately after the injury, granulation tissue must form to fill the gap before new skin can grow inwards from the edges. This is known as healing 'by second intention'. When this granulation tissue becomes too prolific, protruding from the wound and delaying healing, it is called proud flesh. It can be removed chemically or surgically, and where large areas are involved, pinch grafts of skin can be made; these are usually taken from the horse's neck.

The healing process of deeper tissues is similar, with cells called 'fibroblasts' multiplying and migrating into the damaged area until they meet those from the other side. The blood supply increases and granulation tissue forms, sometimes pushing through the surface of the wound as proud flesh. Next, as the fibroblasts lay down a strong fibrous tissue called collagen, the blood vessels and the white blood cells which fight infection decrease. Gradually the collagen contracts, decreasing the size of the wound, and is partly replaced with more elastic fibres, while nerves grow into the scar tissue to complete the process.

MEDICATION

BY MOUTH

Few medicines today have to be administered by mouth, except for those mixed with the feed, and also paste wormers, which are usually purchased in a proprietary syringe fitted with a screw nut which regulates the dose. Most owners are familiar with giving these and the procedure is simple. First screw down the nut to the mark on the plunger which gives the appropriate dose, then remove the cap on the nozzle. Make sure the horse's mouth is empty and not full of hay or grass. The easiest way to control the horse is to place your left hand (if you are right-handed) under its chin, around and over its nose, then slide the nozzle of the syringe into the mouth at the corner of the lips and depress the plunger. Most pastes are sticky and adhere to the tongue. However, it is as well to hold up the horse's chin until it has swallowed, to avoid the expensive paste being spat out on the floor.

Giving medication by mouth

Prescribed medicines which are to be mixed with the feed sometimes cause difficulty in that the horse dislikes the taste and refuses to eat the feed, thus avoiding taking the medicine. Various methods of disguising the taste can be tried, such as adding molasses or cider vinegar, which some horses enjoy. As a last resort, if the horse simply will not take the medicine in its food, the powder can be mixed with molasses or apple sauce and given by syringe; an old worming syringe, washed out and kept for the purpose, is ideal. The important thing is to be sure that the horse does take the medicine, one way or another.

INJECTIONS

Sometimes, to help minimise the cost of visits, the vet may leave injections, such as a course of antibiotics, to be given by the horse keeper. Giving intra-muscular injections is not difficult, but if you are not sure how to proceed, ask the vet to show you before he leaves.

First, shake the bottle and clean the plastic seal with an antiseptic swab. Next, in order to extract the injectable fluid, it is necessary to inject an equivalent amount of air into the bottle; after this you can draw off the appropriate amount of the drug. Detach the needle from the syringe and hold it between thumb and forefinger. Choose a well muscled area of the hindquarters, and standing close but to one side to avoid the risk of being kicked, briskly thump the outer heel of your hand several times against the muscle before tapping the needle straight through the skin. The 'thumping' desensitises the skin and hopefully distracts the horse from anticipating the needle, and provided you have chosen a well muscled spot, the horse is unlikely to feel the needle, nor move as it goes in. You can then re-attach the syringe and, provided no blood flows back into the syringe which would indicate that you had tapped a vein, slowly depress the plunger until the syringe is empty. In the unlikely event that blood does flow back, withdraw the needle and start again.

HOW TO GIVE INTRA-MUSCULAR INJECTIONS

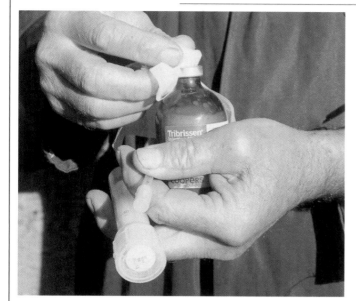

Shake bottle and clean seal with antiseptic swab

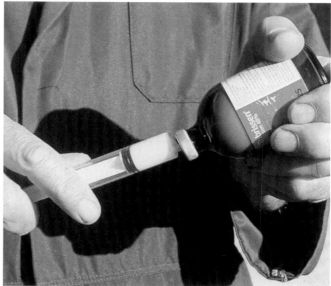

Inject equivalent amount of air into bottle to extract injectable fluid

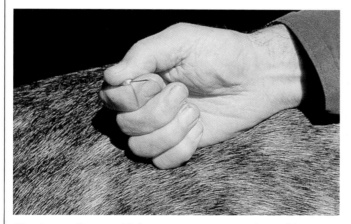

Give two or three rapid thumps on quarters to desensitise area

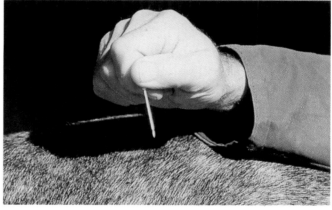

Quickly thump the needle in

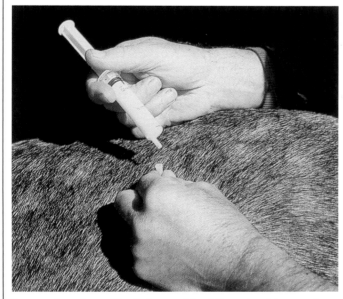

Re-attach syringe. Check that no blood flows back into syringe

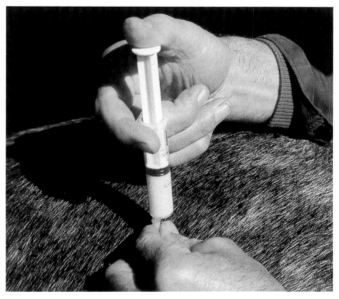

Slowly depress plunger until syringe is empty

71

Intramuscular injections can also be given into the chest – for example, anti-tetanus and influenza vaccinations are often given here. However, antibiotic injections involve quite a large amount of fluid, and the larger the muscle mass injected, the more easily the liquid is absorbed, and the more quickly the resultant bruising heals. For this reason it is not advisable to inject into the neck muscles, because they are smaller and cover many more sensitive and delicate organs which may be damaged by the penetration of a needle, or by infection.

Intravenous injections will usually be administered by your veterinary surgeon, and they should only be given by those who have learned the procedure under supervision.

ENEMAS

Virtually the only time when an enema is likely to be required is in treating the relatively common condition of retained meconium (*see* page 168) in foals, usually larger colts. The enema needs to be administered by an experienced person and comprises a mix of liquid paraffin and warm water, or soft soap solution.

Part II

ANATOMICAL INDEX OF DISEASES

INFECTIONS AFFECTING THE GENERAL SYSTEM

Viral Infections

Disease / Geographical Spread	Symptoms	Cause	Treatment
Adenovirus (p131) General.	High temperature, diarrhoea, nasal discharge.	Common pathogen of the young horse, causing moderately severe disease of the upper respiratory tract in the normal foal.	Warmth, good nursing, antibiotics, mucolytics; electrolyte fluids may be necessary.
African horse sickness (p132) Areas of Africa and the Middle East.	Three types: **Acute pulmonary** Fever, high temperature, sweating, severe respiratory signs, death within hours; survivors suffer prolonged respiratory distress. **Sub-acute cardiac** Fluid collects between heart and pericardium, lungs fill with fluid, endocarditis, swelling of head, neck and brisket, fever. **Chronic fever type** (Uncommon in the horse.) Less severe, raised temperature, loss of appetite, cough, breathlessness.	Viral disease spread by bite of Culicoides midges and perhaps mosquitos.	Non-specific, good nursing helps; prevention by vaccination and management.
Borna disease (p137) *See also* equine viral encephalomyelitis (p153) Germany.	Lethargy, inco-ordination, apparent blindness.	Virus probably transmitted by mosquito.	None specific.
Endotoxaemia (p149) General.	Sensitivity to endotoxic shock; marked depression, high pulse, dehydration, congested mucous membranes, colic symptoms, diarrhoea. Secondary laminitis may occur. Terminal shock, coma and death often follow.	Damage to integrity of intestinal mucosal barrier, allowing gram negative bacteria such as *E. coli* to enter general circulation, triggering acute inflammation.	Immediate intravenous fluid therapy and non-steroidal anti-inflammatory drugs. Surgery to remove portions of damaged gut. Recently developed specific hyperimmune serum effective if given in early stages.
Equine herpes virus (p150) (illus p75) General.	High temperature and slight, clear nasal discharge, which becomes thick and grey-yellow; performance badly affected; EHV-1 causes abortion and neurological complications.	A virus family classified into eight subtypes affecting horses and donkeys. Subtypes EHV-1 (associated with respiratory, reproductive and neurologic disease) and EHV-4 (associated with respiratory disease) are the major pathogens in the horse; (EHV-3: *see* coital exanthema).	Rest, good quality food, clean air; mucolytic drugs help and antibiotics for secondary infections. Prevention by vaccination possible; control by isolation of infected animals.
Equine infectious anaemia (p150) Endemic in the Americas, Middle and Far East, Russia and South Africa, present in parts of Europe.	High fever, moderate anaemia, oedema of the ventral body wall, increasing lethargy and in some cases death.	Virus spread by blood-sucking insects or contaminated surgical equipment or needles.	None specific.
Equine influenza (p151) World-wide.	High temperature, clear nasal discharge, cough.	Type A influenza virus (many subtypes) causes this major equine respiratory disease; young, unvaccinated horses in crowded, poorly ventilated conditions especially at risk.	Complete rest, good ventilation, mucolytic drugs and antibiotics to control secondary infection; prevention by vaccination.

INFECTIONS AFFECTING THE GENERAL SYSTEM

Disease / Geographical Spread	Symptoms	Cause	Treatment
Equine morbillivirus (p151) Australia.	Acute depression, very high temperature; severe respiratory symptoms, discharge at nose and mouth, oedema, ataxia and death.	A strain of the morbillivirus thought to be carried by fruit bats.	None; severe risk to humans, so slaughter essential.
Equine viral arteritis (p152) World-wide.	Many sub-clinical cases; more serious cases have fever, depression, inappetance, oedema of limbs, abdomen and around eyes, conjunctivitis, nasal discharge; pregnant mares may abort.	Virus spread by direct contact, either sneezing and coughing or venereally.	None specific; most recover quickly; prevention by vaccine possible.
Rabies (p188) General, but common in South and Central America. Great Britain, Australia, New Zealand and some islands free from rabies at present.	High temperature, dullness, progressive paralysis, death in 4–5 days.	A viral disease, relatively rare in the horse, transmitted through saliva by the bite of an infected animal (eg dog, fox).	None; notifiable disease in most countries; vaccination available.
Rhinovirus (p189) General.	Short-lived temperature rise, runny nose, cough.	Virus similar to human cold, frequently attacking young horses brought together for first time.	Nursing; antibiotics if secondary infection develops.

▲ EQUINE HERPES VIRUS

The type of nasal discharge that you often see with herpes EHV-1, or 4, infection

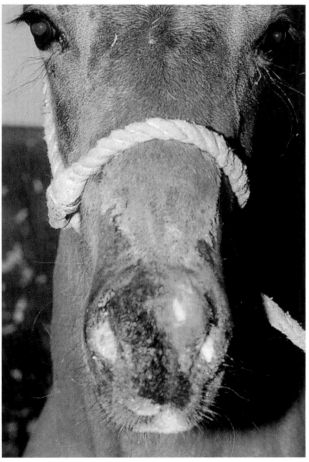

RHINOVIRUS ▶

The typical snotty nose associated with a rhinovirus infection in a weanling

INFECTIONS AFFECTING THE GENERAL SYSTEM

Disease / Geographical Spread	Symptoms	Cause	Treatment
Rotovirus (p190) (illus p77) Common in Central Kentucky, Ireland and Great Britain and in intensive horse-breeding areas.	Affects foals from 2 days to 6 months; diminished suckling response, foul-smelling diarrhoea, dullness, depression, young foals dehydrated.	Virus transmitted via ingestion with feed or licking contaminated surfaces.	Prevent dehydration, electrolyte fluids if necessary; absorbent drugs and lactobacillus-rich foods.
Vesicular stomatitis (p203) The Americas.	High fever and vesicles on tongue, lips and buccal mucosa; coronary band sometimes affected.	Viral disease, possibly carried by insects.	Most cases self-cure with appropriate nursing.

Bacterial and Other Infections

Disease / Geographical Spread	Symptoms	Cause	Treatment
Anthrax (p134) General; notifiable disease in the United Kingdom.	High temperature, depression, respiratory distress; in **acute cases**, sudden death, **sub-acute**, severe colic, enlarged spleen, bloody discharges from nose and mouth, death by 8 days.	Acute, rapidly fatal infectious disease, acquired by ingestion of spore-contaminated food, caused by *Bacillus anthracis*.	Large doses of penicillin; vaccines available in USA, but severe side-effects occur.
Botulism (p137) (illus p77) General.	General weakness, difficulty in eating and swallowing, shuffling gait, leading to collapse and death from respiratory paralysis.	Eating spoiled forage (often big bale silage) containing toxins produced by *Clostridium botulinum*.	Supportive therapy; only mild cases survive.
Brucellosis (p137) General.	Recurrent fever and stiffness, fistulous withers (p154) and poll evil (p185).	Infection with the bacterial organism *Brucella abortus*, mainly associated with disease in cattle, but now largely eradicated from world cattle population; related conditions in horse therefore rare.	Antibiotics unrewarding; vaccination treatment possible, but considerable reaction before resolution occurs.
Equine ehrlichiosis (p150) Northern California; also reported in other states, Sweden and UK.	High fever lasting several days, inappetence, disinclination to move, oedema of the limbs.	A seasonal disease during autumn and winter caused by the microscopic organism called *Ehrlichia equi*, possibly spread by ticks.	Course of antibiotic oxytetracycline.
Glanders (p157) Eradicated from Great Britain, but still occurring in the East and Middle East.	Acute pneumonia with a dry cough, a high temperature and a nasal discharge. Condition usually chronic in horse, with infection of nasal passages and weight loss.	The bacterium *Pseudomonas mallei*, causes acute disease usually in donkeys and chronic disease in the horse. One of few equine diseases which can cause a serious, often fatal disease in man.	Not advised due to risk to humans.
Intestinal clostridiosis (p162) World-wide.	General depression, acute diarrhoea, intensely congested mucous membranes.	The bacteria *Clostridium perfringens* and *Clostridium difficile* are generally associated with the disease. Considered that stress can trigger the condition.	Immediate fluid therapy, sour milk given by mouth, non-steroidal anti-inflammatory drugs.
Leptospirosis (p165) World-wide.	Most common clinical manifestation is recurrent uveitis, or periodic ophthalmia (see p189). Also thought to cause abortion, liver disease and kidney infections.	Bacteria *Leptospira pomona* and *L. icterohemorrhagiae* excreted via urine of infected animals and spread by contamination with infected food or water.	Antibiotics.
Lyme disease (p167) Widespread in northern hemisphere.	Numerous, including fever, arthritis, lameness and reluctance to move, poor appetite and lethargy.	Bacterium *Borrelia burgdorferi*, spread by ticks to both animals and humans.	Antibiotics.

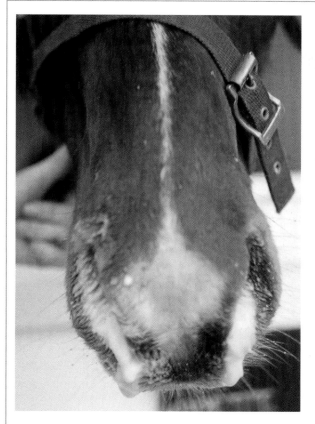

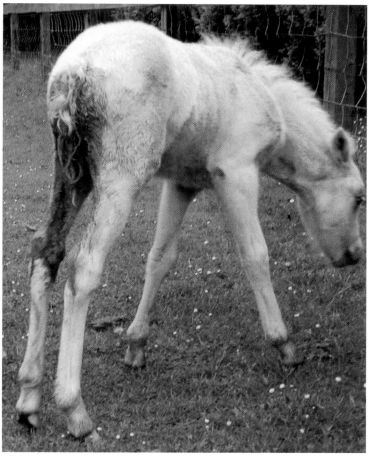

BOTULISM

(above) Paralysis of the muscles associated with swallowing cause this nasal discharge of mucus and food material

(below) Affected horses get gradually weaker, eventually becoming recumbent

▲ ROTOVIRUS

The type of diarrhoea associated with rotovirus infection in a foal

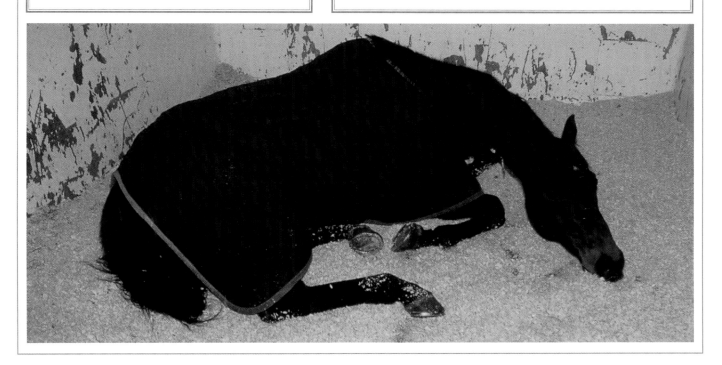

INFECTIONS AFFECTING THE GENERAL SYSTEM

Disease / Geographical Spread	Symptoms	Cause	Treatment
Malignant oedema (p168) General.	Rapid swelling of area surrounding wound, hot, painful with gas in subcutaneous tissues; frothy discharge; horse dull and depressed, death.	A micro-organism, usually *Clostridium septicum*, via cuts, wounds, surgery or contaminated needles.	Rarely successful; intravenous penicillin and treatment for shock.
Piroplasmosis (p179) (babesiosis, equine bilary fever, equine piroplasmosis, horse tick fever) Tropical and sub-tropical areas, eg South America, Caribbean, southern Europe, Africa, Asia, Middle East.	Fever, depression, weakness, yellow mucous membranes, sometimes oedema of affected areas and bloody urine.	Tick-borne blood parasites *Babesia equi* and *Babesia caballi*. Some horses have passive immunity and become carriers.	Anti-protozoan drugs; most recover.
Potomac horse fever (p185) Eastern states of America.	Two syndromes: **equine ehrlichial colitis** Fever, depression, colitis, diarrhoea, secondary laminitis; **equine ehrlichial abortion** Mares appear to recover, but then abort due to infection and death of foetus.	Infection by the organism *Ehrlichia risticii*.	Intravenous oxytetracycline.
Strangles (p197) (illus pp56 & below) World-wide.	Depression, high temperature, cough, thick discharge at the nostrils, difficulty in swallowing due to swollen lymph glands which finally burst, discharging pus.	The bacterium *Streptococcus equi*, spread by contagion.	Isolation, good nursing, heat applied to swelling abscesses to encourage maturation, steam inhalation, soft food; vaccines available in USA.
Tetanus (p199) (illus p79) General.	Closing of third eyelid, ears pricked, dock raised, progressive paralysis, leading to death.	The bacterium *Clostridium tetani*, which persists in spore form in the soil and enters via wounds, particularly punctures. The bacteria become active in anaerobic conditions, producing a toxin which progresses to the brain.	Large dose of tetanus anti-toxin, ideally into spinal canal to neutralise toxin, coupled with antibiotic and tranquillisers; horse kept in darkened box; expert nursing required. Up to 60 per cent recover if treated early. Easily prevented by vaccination.

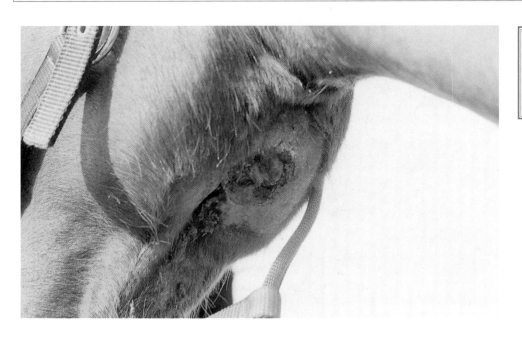

◀ STRANGLES

A typical strangles abscess developing between the angles of the jaw

INFECTIONS AFFECTING THE GENERAL SYSTEM

PROGRESSIVE SIGNS OF TETANUS

1 (above left) Increasing paralysis causes the ears to be fixed in a pricked position
2 (above right) Raising the head causes the third eyelid to close across the eye, a characteristic early symptom
3 (below) The trestle-like stance and the clearly visible third eyelid typical of tetanus

INFECTIONS AFFECTING THE GENERAL SYSTEM

Poisons

plants, chemicals, snake venom: *See* poisoning (p180)

Disease / Geographical Spread	Symptoms	Cause	Treatment
Kimberley disease (p163) Western and northern states of Australia.	Drowsiness, mood changes, inco-ordination, loss of appetite, weight loss, eventual coma and death.	The poisonous plant, *Crotalaria retusa.*	None.
Poisoning (p180) General.	Varied according to cause.	Poisonous plants, chemicals, insects or snake bites.	According to cause.
Rye grass staggers (p191) Australia, New Zealand, America, recently in UK.	Horse becomes increasingly unsteady, some become paralysed.	Grass infected with parasitic fungus, which produces a toxin.	None.

POISONING

(above left) Ragwort

(above right) Yew trees. Horses should never be grazed on land that has access to yew trees

(right) Horses grazing on poor grass with ample bracken, the scenario that can lead to bracken poisoning

DISEASES AFFECTING THE HEAD

General

Disease / Geographical Spread	Symptoms	Cause	Treatment
Head shaking (p159) General.	Violent jerks and shaking of head, often worse in summer.	Intense irritation, possibly allergic reaction, or associated with strong sunlight.	Surgery to desensitise nostrils may be successful; most recently, anti-allergic human drug apparently successful.

Conditions of the Brain

Disease / Geographical Spread	Symptoms	Cause	Treatment
Brain trauma (p137) General.	Varying degree of inco-ordination, circling gait, unsteadiness, dull vacant eyes and slack lips. Bleeding from the nose common following trauma to sinus areas; bleeding from ears signifies more serious damage eg fractured skull.	Accidents involving a blow to the head, especially the poll.	Rest and quiet, corticosteroids and diuretics to reduce bruising and swelling; antibiotics against infection.
Cerebella hypoplasia (p139) *See also* **Diseases Affecting the Foal** (p124) General.	Found in Arab foals, loss of balance and collapse.	Degeneration of cells in cerebellar region of brain.	No cure.
Eastern encephalomyelitis (p147) Eastern states of America.	*See* equine viral encephalomyelitis.	*See* equine viral encephalomyelitis.	*See* equine viral encephalomyelitis.
Equine protozoal myeloencephalitis (EPM) (p152) North and South America.	Paralysis of lips or ears, drooping eyelids, difficulty in chewing or swallowing, muscle wastage, sometimes unsteadiness or paralysis.	Protozoal organism called *Sarcocystis neurona*.	Corticosteroids, DMSO in acute phase; then potentiated sulphonamides and anti-malarial drugs.
Equine viral encephalomyelitis (p153) Middle and Far East, North and South America, Africa, Europe.	Fever, then nervous signs, irrational behaviour and inco-ordination. Mortality up to 80 per cent.	Virus carried by birds, spread via mosquitos.	No specific treatment; vaccines available.
Japanese encephalomyelitis (p163) Far East.	*See* equine viral encephalomyelitis.	*See* equine viral encephalomyelitis.	*See* equine viral encephalomyelitis.
Venezuelan encephalomyelitis (p203) South America and Southern States of America.	*See* equine viral encephalomyelitis.	*See* equine viral encephalomyelitis.	*See* equine viral encephalomyelitis.
Western encephalomyelitis (p204) Western States of America.	*See* equine viral encephalomyelitis.	*See* equine viral encephalomyelitis.	*See* equine viral encephalomyelitis.
West Nile Fever (p204) Africa, Middle East, North America, Europe, Russia.	Increasing weakness and inco-ordination, muscle tremors, loss of appetite, head pressing, aimless wandering and apparent loss of vision. Severe cases develop hyper-excitability, eventual coma, and death in 30–40% of cases.	Virus carried by birds, spread by mosquitos.	No specific treatment other than supportive treatment. Vaccines are available.

DISEASES AFFECTING THE HEAD

Disease / Geographical Spread	Symptoms	Cause	Treatment
Epilepsy (p149) (illus p83) General.	Initially a glazed, vacant look and trembling of ears and tail; horse may rear then fall, with legs outstretched and quivering, followed by gradual relaxation and variable period of unconsciousness.	Unknown.	Anti-convulsant drugs to control seizures.
Equine toxoplasmosis (p152) General.	Similar to EPM.	Food contaminated with cat faeces infected with the organism *Toxaplasma gondii*.	No satisfactory treatment.

Diseases of the Teeth and Jaw

Disease / Geographical Spread	Symptoms	Cause	Treatment
Dental cap (p146) General.	Slow eating, excessive salivation, quidding of food.	Temporary molar that has become impacted on top of underlying permanent molar.	Removal of cap.
Lampas (p164) General.	Swelling of tissue immediately behind upper front teeth.	Symptom of young horses changing their teeth, especially when in poor condition.	None necessary.
Parrot mouth (p177) (illus p46) *See also* Diseases affecting the Foal (p122) General.	Upper jaw protrudes over lower.	Congenital.	None.
Peridontitis (p178) (illus p83) General.	Loss of condition, bad breath, slow eating and presence of poorly digested grain in droppings.	Infection of the structures around the teeth found mainly in aged horses due to poor apposition or abnormal mastication.	Regular dental care.
Pig mouth (p179) *See also* Diseases affecting the Foal (p122) General.	Lower jaw protrudes beyond upper jaw.	Congenital.	None for minimal abnormality; possible euthanasia for more severe cases, as foal unable to suckle.
Wolf teeth (p205) General.	No clinical symptoms, but cause of refusal to accept bit.	Vestigial premolars immediately in front of upper cheek teeth.	Removal of wolf tooth/teeth.

Conditions of the Eye

Disease / Geographical Spread	Symptoms	Cause	Treatment
Cataract (p139) (illus p83) General.	Opacity of the lens, either small discrete area in body of lens or affecting whole lens.	Congenital in foals; in adults sequel to periodic ophthalmia or to trauma.	Removal of affected lens; most successful in foals.
Conjunctivitis (p142) (illus p83) General.	Reddening of eye, clear discharge, becoming mucopurulent, eyelids swollen and closed, especially in strong light.	Infection of conjunctiva, often occurring in dusty, dry, hot conditions.	Antibiotic eye ointment.
Corneal ulcer (p143) (illus p83) General.	Pain, eyelid closed, tears, surface of cornea cloudy.	Trauma or infection.	Remove horse from strong light, antibiotics locally or by injection, surgery may help healing.
Entropion (p149) (illus p84) *See also* Diseases affecting the Foal (p121) General.	Affects new-born foals; eye closed and watery, eyelid rolled inwards, rubbing on cornea.	Congenital.	Temporary stitching to turn eyelid outwards.

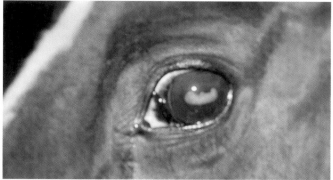

▼ EPILEPSY

Usual appearance of a horse after an epileptic attack

▲ CATARACT

This cataract has probably been present since birth

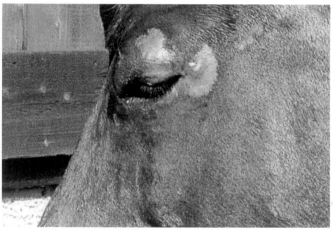

▼ CRIB-BITING

A good example of a crib-biting horse; note the worn front teeth

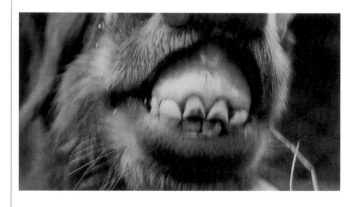

▲ CONJUNCTIVITIS

Acute conjunctivitis; note the self-mutilation that has occurred around the eye

▼ PERIDONTITIS

A case of peridontitis in an old horse; note the lesion in the top of the central incisor and also the red stippling of the gum showing a gingivitis

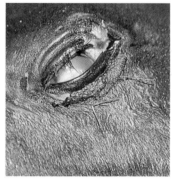 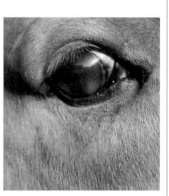

▲ CORNEAL ULCER

(above left) Acute severe corneal ulcer caused by entropion; note stitches to evert lower eyelid; (above right) A partially healed corneal ulcer in the lower right corner of the cornea

DISEASES AFFECTING THE HEAD

Disease / Geographical Spread	Symptoms	Cause	Treatment
Keratitis (p163) General.	Swelling and greying of cornea due to corneal oedema; photophobia and blepharospasm (closed eyelids); eyes water, conjunctiva red and inflamed; corneal ulcers usually present.	Trauma and infection.	Antibiotics.
Recurrent uveitis (p189) General.	Acute pain, pupil constricts and eyelids are tightly shut, often with tears; conjunctiva and iris inflamed; posterior portion of eye filled with grey inflammatory exudate; blindness follows repeated attacks.	Inflammation of ciliary body and iris, possibly due to exaggerated immune response to various organisms.	Immediate veterinary treatment essential; NSAIDs, antibiotics if bacteria indicated, corticosteroids and atropine.

Conditions of the Ears

Aural plaque (p135) General.	Crusty plaques on inside surface of ear; when removed, thickened pink skin is exposed.	Infection by the virus that also causes warts, aggravated by fly bites.	No cure, though lesions may be reduced by removing plaques and treating with anti-inflammatory ointment; ear protectors in summer aid prevention.
Ear mites *See* parasites (p175) General.	Acute irritation, rubbing and scratching.	Mites of the Psoroptes family.	Application of antiparasitic ear preparation.
Otitis externa (p173) General.	Rubbing affected ear, head shaking and tilting to one side; ear is painful and possible purulent discharge.	Foreign body eg grass seed in ear canal, or bacterial or fungal infection.	Removal of foreign body; cleansing of ear canal and application of antibiotic/anti-fungal/anti-inflammatory ear drops.

ENTROPION▶

Note turned-in lower lid

▼ RECURRENT UVEITIS

Typical clinical appearance showing acute conjunctivitis and obvious signs of inflammation in the anterior chamber

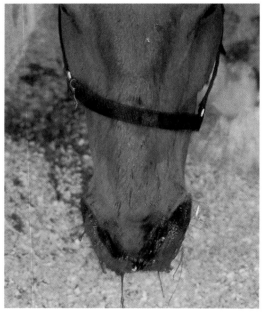

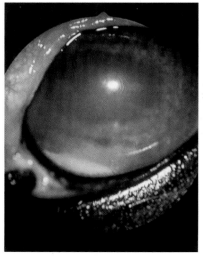

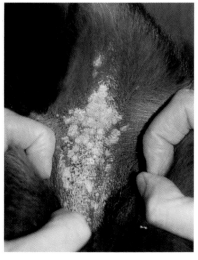

▲ BLEEDER

A quite serious bleeder

◀ AURAL PLAQUE

The typical appearance of aural plaque

DISEASES AFFECTING THE HEAD

Conditions of the Upper Respiratory Tract

Disease / Geographical Spread	Symptoms	Cause	Treatment
Bleeder (p136) General.	Bleeding from nostrils.	Pulmonary haemorrhage, infections, tumours.	Depends upon cause: covered in relevant section. *See* exercise-induced pulmonary haemorrhage; guttural pouch disease.
Ethmoid haematoma (p153) General.	Initially slight haemorrhage from one nostril, then noisy breathing, foetid breath.	Unknown, but thought to start from submucosal haemorrhage.	Surgery.
Guttural pouch disease (p158) General.	Intermittent purulent nasal discharge from one or both nostrils, difficulty in swallowing, hard, painful swelling usually evident at angle of jaw. Life-threatening haemorrhage from eroded carotid arteries may occur.	Bacterial infection usually secondary to respiratory infection; cause of mycosis unknown, but associated with poor stable environment and bacterium *Aspergillosis*.	**Early** cases of bacterial infection: antibiotic irrigation; **chronic** cases: surgical exposure of pouch and daily flushing; **mycosis** cases: little can be done.
Guttural pouch tympany (p158) General.	Large, hollow-sounding swelling on one or both sides behind angle of the jaw; more common in young female horses.	Unknown, probably abnormal development of folds at entrance to guttural pouches.	Surgery.
Laryngeal hemiplegia (p165) General.	Roaring or whistling noise as horse breathes in.	Dysfunction of left recurrent laryngeal nerve.	Surgery – Hobday or tieback operation.
Nasal polyps (p169) General.	Noise when breathing, later foetid breath and discharge, sometimes bleeding.	Soft growths in nasal chamber.	Surgery, but poor prognosis.
Sinusitis (p194) General.	Thick nasal discharge, sometimes also from the eye, area below eye might be swollen.	Follows respiratory infection, or may be caused by dental disease.	Antibiotic and mucolytic drugs; surgery may be required; removal of infected teeth if they are the cause.
Soft palate dislocation (p194) General.	Gurgling, choking sound, and horse stops running abruptly.	Believed to be connected with size of epiglottis and action of throat muscles.	Tongue-strap or straight bit might help. Surgery possible.

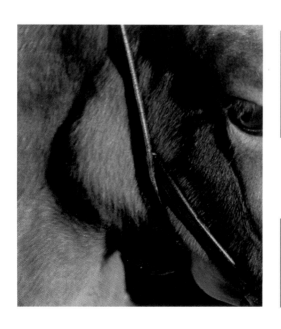

◀ **GUTTURAL POUCH TYMPANY**

A young horse with a typical tympanic guttural pouch

NASAL POLYP ▶

A large nasal polyp protruding from the right nostril

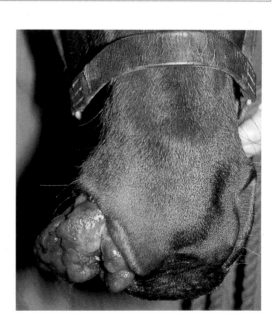

DISEASES AFFECTING THE CHEST

Conditions of the Respiratory System: Allergic Diseases

Disease / Geographical Spread	Symptoms	Cause	Treatment
Chronic obstructive pulmonary disease (COPD) Now known as Recurrent airway obstruction (RAO) (p140) (illus p87) General.	Chronic cough, breathlessness, wheezing, appearance of 'heave' line, reduced performance.	Inhalation of mould spores from forage, causing allergic response.	Remove from contact with cause; feed dust-free forage and use dust-free bedding. Drugs may be used to improve air passage, disperse mucus or desensitise cells which produce allergic reaction.
Exercise-induced pulmonary haemorrhage (p153) (illus p87) General.	Blood from one or both nostrils after strenuous exercise may be apparent; majority have no obvious symptoms, but endoscopic examination shows presence of blood in bronchial tree.	High blood pressure in upper rear tips of lung ruptures capillaries, causing haemorrhage.	Generally unrewarding, clean environment essential.
Inflammatory airway disease (p162) General.	Affects stabled horses. Cough, nasal discharge, mucus accumulation shown on endoscopic examination; possible exercise intolerance, loss of performance especially in young racehorses.	Uncertain but exposure to stable dust contributory factor; bacterial infection may contribute in young horses.	Antibiotics, bronchodilators and mucolytic drugs are conventional treatments; change of environment away from continuous stabling effects rapid improvement.

Bacterial Infections

Bronchitis (p137) General.	Breathlessness, together with a hollow chronic cough. Reduction in exertional capacity, increase in lung sounds.	Secondary to viral or other infection.	Antibiotics, plus mucolytic and expectorant drugs, plus clean air régime.
Pleurisy (p179) General.	Fever, lethargy, loss of appetite, rapid shallow respiration, short cough, and reluctance to move and lie down. Rasping sound from within chest.	Normally associated with pneumonia.	Early antibiotics and NSAID treatment essential.
Pneumonia (p180) General.	Rapid respiration, inappetance, high temperature. In foals: sometimes caused by organism found in soil and occurs in hot, dry, dusty conditions; symptoms accompanied by gradual loss of condition and chronic cough.	Any infective agent, viral or bacterial.	Prompt antibiotic treatment, plus broncholytic agent and bronchodilators.

Parasitic Diseases

Dictyocaulus arnfieldi, lungworm (see parasites: roundworm) (p175) General.	Chronic cough present at rest and exercise. No nasal discharge, and little effect on appetite or condition.	Usual host the donkey; horses grazing alongside or where donkeys have grazed may be affected.	Effective worming dose.
Parascaris equorum (see parasites: roundworm) (p175) See also Conditions of the Foal). General.	In foals: dirty nose and cough followed some weeks later by loss of appetite, dullness and lethargy. Impaction or rupture of the intestines can sometimes occur.	Large whiteworm up to 20cm (8in) long which lives in foals' intestines.	Regular dosing with appropriate anthelmintics.

Conditions of the Circulatory System: Diseases affecting the Blood Vessels

Anaemia (p132) General.	Reduced performance, followed by depressed appetite, dull hair, possible heart murmur; finally, pale mucous membranes and profound weakness.	Shortage of haemoglobin in the blood due to acute or chronic haemorrhage, stress or folic acid deficiency.	Diagnose and treat primary cause.
Haematoma (p158) (illus pp67 & 87) General.	Large swelling that forms rapidly under the skin or in a muscle.	Often from a kick or running into a fence.	Cold compresses to begin with; when initial injury healed, excise and remove contents.

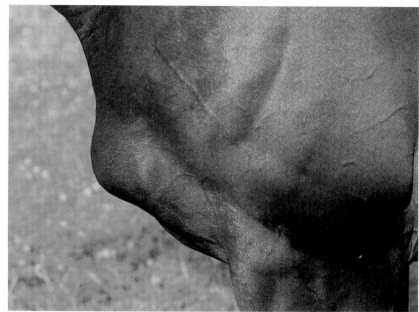

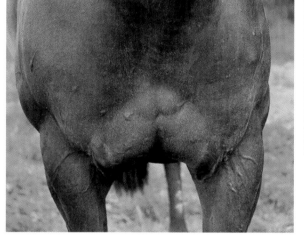

EXERCISE-INDUCED PULMONARY HAEMORRHAGE

(above left) The typical trickle of blood from a horse with exercise-induced pulmonary haemorrhage (EIPH)

(below) Looking down the trachea of the same horse. Note the streams of blood rising up the trachea

HAEMATOMA

(above right) Haematoma due to a kick on the breast

(left) One month later, after being treated by draining and an injection of long-acting steroids

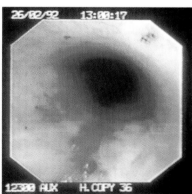
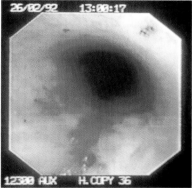

COPD (RAO) ▶

A case of COPD (RAO) showing a heave line along the abdomen

DISEASES AFFECTING THE CHEST

Diseases affecting the Heart

Disease / Geographical Spread	Symptoms	Cause	Treatment
Aneurism (p133) (illus 89) General.	Rarely observable; aneurism might burst causing fatal haemorrhage.	Migrating larvae of the redworm, *Strongylus vulgaris* (*see* p176; illus p40), weaken artery wall allowing development of aneurism.	Too late once aneurism has burst; aneurism can be prevented by removal of larvae before damage occurs.
Heart disease: *abnormal rhythm* (p159) a) missed beats b) atrial fibrillation General.	a) **missed beats**: one or more missed beats in normal pattern. b) **atrial fibrillation**: Sometimes breathlessness, jugular pulse and ventral oedema (illus below); more commonly a decreased exercise tolerance is the only symptom.	a) **missed beats**: lack of signal from pacemaker. b) **atrial fibrillation**: stream of impulses sent by pacemaker to the atria which respond by fibrillating; the condition may follow a viral attack; often a complication of myocarditis.	a) **missed beats**: none needed. b) **atrial fibrillation**: the drug quinidine sulphate will sometimes arrest the arrhythmia.
Cardiac murmurs (p160) General.	Variable, sometimes a murmur only, sometimes decrease in performance with cough and oedema. Congestive heart failure develops and damage to heart valves increases.	Disease or congenital defect prevents effective closure of valves.	No curative treatment but diuretics and ACE inhibitors can help manage the condition.
Myocarditis (p160) General.	Loss of performance, sometimes arrhythmia; may cause sudden death from heart failure.	Viruses, especially equine influenza.	Prolonged rest.

Conditions of the Lymphatic System

Filled legs (p153) (illus pp59 & 89) General.	Lower legs fill with fluid.	Poor circulation, usually in stabled horses overnight.	Adequate turnout and exercise, larger stable; diuretic drugs may be required if there is a physical reason for poor circulation.
Lymphangitis (p167) (illus p89) General.	Infection spreading up lymphatic vessels of leg; hot, painful swelling; acute lameness, high temperature.	Consequence of infected cut or mud fever.	Antibiotics, phenylbutazone and diuretics.

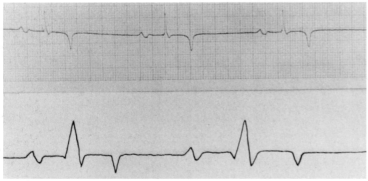

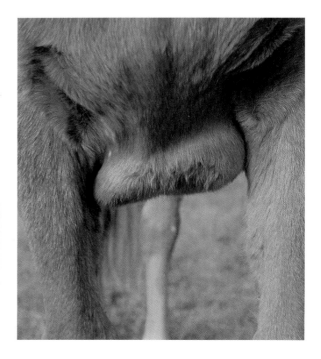

HEART PROBLEM

(above) A normal electrocardiogram trace, measuring the electrical impulses passing through the heart. The trace allows irregularities in the heart to be examined more closely

(right) Ventral oedema as a result of a heart condition

DISEASES AFFECTING THE CHEST

ANEURISM▶

Extensive haemorrhage in the chest following a ruptured aneurism in the pulmonary artery

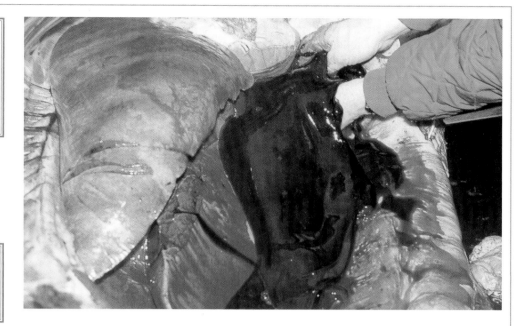

▼LYMPHANGITIS

A case of lymphangitis of the hind limb

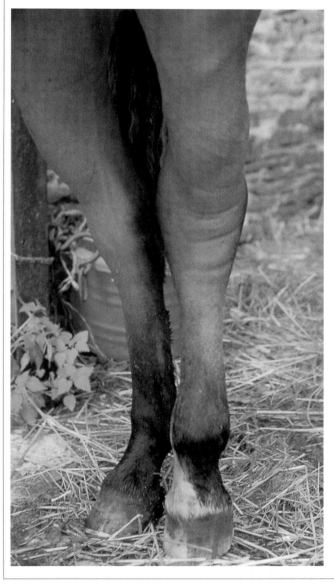

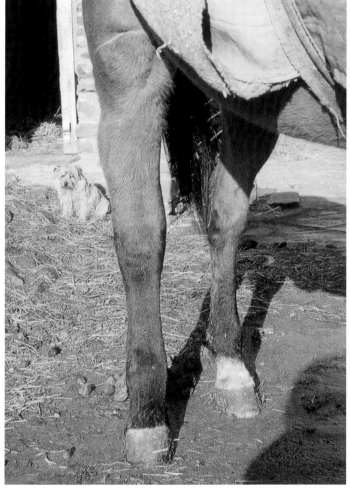

▲FILLED LEG

The filling will disappear when the horse is exercised

DISEASES AFFECTING THE ABDOMEN

Conditions of the Intestinal Tract: Acute Diseases

Disease / Geographical Spread	Symptoms	Cause	Treatment
Choke (p139) General.	Saliva-stained food material runs from nose and mouth. Head and neck arched and horse retches loudly. Very distressed and panicky.	Impacted food material in the oesophagus.	Anti-spasmodic drugs and sedatives; most blockages clear in a few hours; surgery occasionally needed.
Colic (p141) General.	Abdominal pain.	Three main types: **tympanitic**: build-up of gas due to fermentation in gut; **spasmodic**: usually caused by migration of worm larvae; **obstructive**: impaction of food or mechanical obstruction.	**Tympanitic**: anti-spasmodic and analgesic drugs; **spasmodic**: anti-spasmodic drugs and sedatives; **obstructive**: may require urgent surgery; **impactive**: liquid paraffin and saline by stomach tube, surgery sometimes required.
Colitis-X (p142) General.	Sudden onset, horse acutely depressed with discoloured mucous membranes; pulse and temperature high, then dropping. If it survives more than a few hours, profuse watery diarrhoea develops.	Unknown, but associated with stress.	Unrewarding; fluids and corticosteroids, but disease usually fatal.
Diarrhoea (p146) (illus p91) General.	Loose, watery faeces.	Not a disease itself, but a symptom of many diseases in which faeces become soft and cow-like, even completely fluid. Can occur naturally when a horse moves on to lush grass.	Diagnose and treat primary cause.
Poisoning (p180) General.	See Poisoning p80.	See Poisoning p80.	See Poisoning p80.

See Poisoning p80.

▼ CHOKE

A choking horse, probably due to some impacted sugar beet. Note the anxious expression, and the large amounts of saliva coming from the nose and mouth

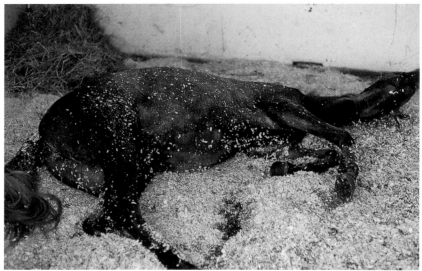

▲ COLIC

A horse with colic will try to roll, will look round at its flanks, may paw the ground and have patchy sweating

DISEASES AFFECTING THE ABDOMEN

Disease / Geographical Spread	Symptoms	Cause	Treatment
Peritonitis (p178) General.	Severe abdominal discomfort, reluctance to lie down, depression, loss of appetite and rapid weight loss.	Penetrating wound to abdominal wall, rupture of uterus or intestine, penetrating ulcer of stomach wall.	Usually fatal; aggressive antibiotic therapy may cure that caused by abdominal wound.
Salmonellosis (p191) General.	Acute diarrhoea, colic, fever, increased heart and respiratory rates. Progressive weakness and depression, followed by dehydration, circulatory collapse and death.	Infection by *Salmonella* bacteria, often associated with stress.	Fluid therapy, anti-inflammatory drugs, good nursing and hygiene.
Chronic Diseases			
Constipation (p142) General.	Lack of droppings, straining.	Rare in adult horse and secondary to other diseases; occurs in foal due to retained meconium.	Diagnose and treat primary condition. Foals: *see* retained meconium (p122).
Coprophagy (p143) General.	Eating droppings.	Natural in foals (*see* Conditions of the Infant Foal p121); rare in adult horse, may be due to deficiencies or lack of fibre in diet.	Foals, none; adults, provide fibre in diet.
Malabsorption syndrome (p167) General.	Chronic diarrhoea associated with gradual weight loss; appetite normal.	Inflammation of small intestine.	No successful treatment.
Neoplasia: *See* diarrhoea (p146) General.	Chronic diarrhoea and weight loss.	Tumour of stomach and intestines, usually in older horses.	Surgical removal.

▼ DIARRHOEA

The evidence of acute diarrhoea – loose faeces and stained bedding

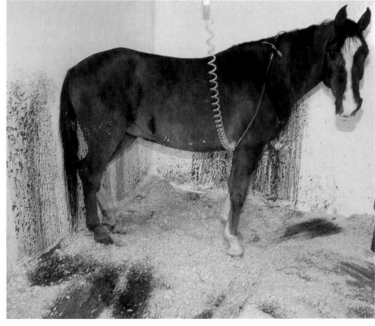

▲ SALMONELLOSIS

The profuse acute diarrhoea that is associated with salmonellosis in the horse. Note the drip line administering fluids

Chronic Diseases continued

Disease / Geographical Spread	Symptoms	Cause	Treatment
Ulcers (p201) General.	Strained, uncomfortable appearance, worse after feeding; irritability and depression. Perforation can occur, followed by collapse and death. Can also affect foals	Not known, but stress is major factor, especially in stabled, high performance horses. Serious diarrhoea or long-term treatment with NSAIDs can also be a cause.	Antacids and human gastric ulcer drugs; remove underlying cause and restore natural lifestyle. Condition improves when natural lifestyle and turnout restored.

Parasitic Diseases

Disease / Geographical Spread	Symptoms	Cause	Treatment
Bots *See* parasites (p174) (illus p40 & 93) General.	May cause unthriftiness in late winter/early spring.	Bot flies lay yellow/orange eggs on lower legs and abdomen and larvae pass via mouth to stomach.	Remove eggs by grooming with bot knife; dose with effective wormer.
Strongyles *See* parasites: roundworms (p175) (illus p93) General.	**Large strongyles** (three types): larvae can cause spasmodic colic, weight loss, depression and fever. Adult worms in large numbers cause chronic anaemia and diarrhoea. **Small strongyles:** large number of larvae cause colic, weight loss and lethargy in late autumn.	Major intestinal parasites of the horse.	Clean pasture management is vital. Targeted or strategic dosing with the three main groups of anthelmintics: benzimidazole group, tetrahydropyrimidines and macrocyclic lactones to minimize development of resistance (see p176)
Oxyuris equi, pinworms: *See* parasites: roundworms (p175) General.	Intense irritation around perineum, hair loss around head of tail, skin damage.	A threadworm up to 7cm (2.7in) long which lays eggs around the anal region.	All modern anthelmintics effective.
Tapeworms: *See* parasites (p177) (illus p93) General.	Acute colic; when chronic, unthriftiness, diarrhoea and weight loss, with sporadic colic.	The tapeworm *Anoplocephela perfoliata* infests junction of large and small intestines.	Twice-yearly preventative treatment with an effective wormer.

Conditions of the Liver

Disease / Geographical Spread	Symptoms	Cause	Treatment
Hepatitis (p160) General.	**Acute**: inappetance and dull abdominal pain, high pulse and respiration, jaundice and nervous signs. **Chronic**: nervous signs, severe weight loss and constant diarrhoea.	**Acute**: virus infection or poisoning. **Chronic**: ragwort poisoning most common; occasionally liver fluke.	**Acute**: supportive, with antibiotics. **Chronic**: supportive, with antibiotics.
Hyperlipaemia (p161) (illus p94) General.	Slow and lethargic, loss of appetite, severe weight loss; may show nervous signs eg circling and head pressing.	Rare but serious disorder of fat metabolism occurring in overweight ponies and donkeys due to stress.	Urgent replacement of energy deficit and dispersal of fat in the blood.
Liver fluke: *See* parasites (p175) General.	As for any chronic liver disease; rare in horses.	Grazing wet pasture infested with liver fluke.	Most of the drugs used for cattle. Triclabendazole useful though not licensed for horses.
Ragwort (illus p80) poisoning (p182) All temperate zones.	As for chronic liver failure.	Toxins in ragwort slowly poison the liver.	Supportive, but often fatal.

Conditions of the Urinary Tract

Disease / Geographical Spread	Symptoms	Cause	Treatment
Cystitis (p145) General.	Frequent, painful urination; urine thick, cloudy and may contain blood.	Usually secondary to urinary calculi, or vaginal infection; also injury to urethra and bladder after foaling.	Remove primary cause, then anti-bacterial drugs.
Infection of the sheath (p196) (illus p94) General.	Swelling, oedema, foul-smelling discharge, inflammation of prepuce and penis; urination may be difficult.	Common with increasing age; damage to lining of prepuce or penis.	Wash and clean prepuce and penis with warm, soapy water, and apply antibiotic ointment.
Nephritis (p171) General.	Initially high temperature; pain and swelling of affected kidneys; possibly blood and pus in urine.	Infection from bladder; common complication of foal septicaemia.	Antibiotics.

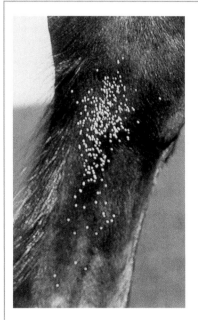

BOTS

(left) Bot eggs on the lower leg of a horse
(below left) Bots in the stomach seen through a fibrotic endoscope

(below right) An odd circular lesion that is probably caused by the larvae of the rare bot fly G. haemorrhoidalis *entering the lip*

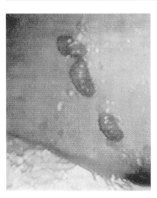

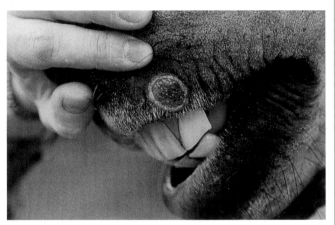

◄ PARASCARIS

A clump of the large whiteworm
Parascaris equorum

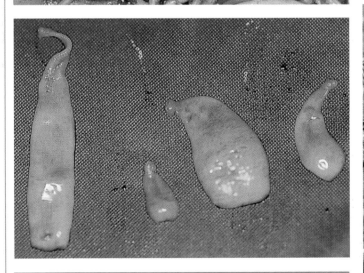

▼ STRONGYLES

If you look carefully you can see large numbers of the small redworm called Cyathostomes

▲ TAPEWORMS

A group of Anoplocephela perfoliata, *the horse tapeworm*

DISEASES AFFECTING THE ABDOMEN

Conditions of the Reproductive Tract: Physical Conditions affecting the Male

Disease / Geographical Spread	Symptoms	Cause	Treatment
Cryptorchidism (p144) General.	Physically the horse appears to be a gelding but shows stallion behaviour.	One or both testicles of the stallion have not descended into the scrotum.	Surgical removal of undescended testicle(s).
Infections			
Coital exanthema (p140) (illus p95) General.	Numerous small fluid-filled vesicles on the external genitalia; inflammation and vaginal discharge in mares.	Herpes virus subtype EHV-3.	Local antibiotic/antiseptic treatment.
Dourine (p146) Mainly tropical; sometimes found in Europe and America.	Penile or vulval discharge; genital swelling; blisters and ulceration of penis and vulva; fever, inappetance, loss of condition and difficulty in urinating.	Venereally transmitted blood parasite *Trypanosoma equiperdum*.	Drugs available, but strict control of breeding régimes more effective.
Orchitis (p173) General.	Painful swelling of one or both testicles; raised temperature and loss of appetite.	Infection or trauma.	Antibiotics.
Venereal disease (p202) General.	Unnoticed until infection passed from stallion to mare.	Bacterial infection.	Daily washing of penis and sheath and application of antibiotic cream. Mare: *see* endometritis.

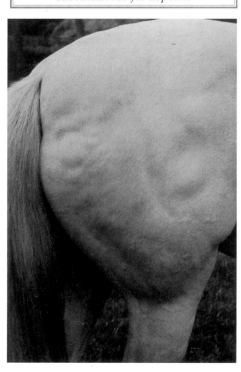

▼ HYPERLIPAEMIA

A case of hyperlipaemia; note the subcutaneous fat deposits

▲ SHEATH INFECTION

Infection of the sheath causes oedema and swelling

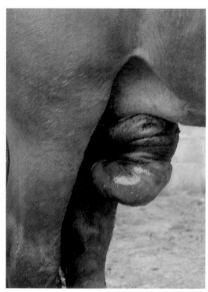

▼ INJURIES TO THE PENIS

A case of strangulated penis in a stallion

DISEASES AFFECTING THE ABDOMEN

Injuries

Disease / Geographical Spread	Symptoms	Cause	Treatment
Injuries to penis (p196) (illus p94) General.	Bruising, rupture of blood vessels, swelling; penis enlarged and hanging down.	Kicking, fighting, jumping fences to mares.	Support to prevent further damage; ice packs and cold hosing; antibiotics.
Paralysis of penis (p197) General.	Paralysis.	Side-effect after use of promazine group of tranquillisers.	Prompt support and manual compression; otherwise amputation.

Infectious Conditions affecting the Female

Disease / Geographical Spread	Symptoms	Cause	Treatment
Coital exanthema (p140)	*See above* Conditions affecting the Male: Infections.	*See above* Conditions affecting the Male: Infections.	*See above* Conditions affecting the Male: Infections.
Contagious equine metritis (p142) General.	Profuse, grey, mucopurulent vaginal discharge occurring 24–48 hours after service; reduces over next 10 days but inflammation of the cervix remains.	Organism *Taylorella equigenitalis*.	Antibiotics; also preventative code of practice.
Dourine (p146) General.	*See above* Conditions affecting the Male: Infections.	*See above* Conditions affecting the Male: Infections.	*See above* Conditions affecting the Male: Infections.
Endometritis (p147) General.	**Acute**: vulval discharge. **Chronic**: (a) **vulval aspiration:** 'windsucking' which may be obvious or subtle. (b) **loss of local immunity:** early return to oestrus after service; discharge.	**Acute**: infection of lining of uterus, following damage, or venereal bacterial infection transmitted from stallion. **Chronic**: (a) **vulval aspiration:** contamination and infection of vagina. (b) **loss of local immunity:** unknown; age and wear and tear implicated.	**Acute**: uterine irrigation with antibiotic. **Chronic**: (a) **vulval aspiration:** surgery to prevent windsucking. (b) **loss of local immunity:** depends on severity; uterine irrigation with antibiotics, minimal contamination techniques for service, lavage of uterus post service all effective.

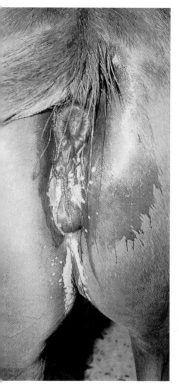

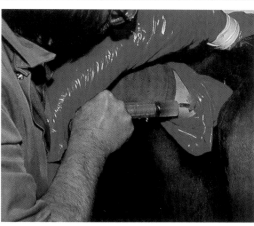

◀ COITAL EXANTHEMA

A classic case of coital exanthema

▼ ENDOMETRITIS: 1

Uterine irrigation on a mare with chronic endometritis

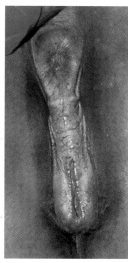

▲ ENDOMETRITIS: 2

(above left) Caslick's operation recently performed
(above right) The same Caslick's six months later

DISEASES AFFECTING THE ABDOMEN

Non-Infectious Conditions affecting the Female

Disease / Geographical Spread	Symptoms	Cause	Treatment
Anoestrus (p133) General.	None apparent; on examination, ovaries show no cyclic activity – normal condition in winter, but can extend into spring.	Normal condition of mare in winter, but can be caused by excessive poor condition and adverse environmental factors.	Exposure to increased period of light and rising energy intake encourages onset of cyclic activity.
Dioestrus (p146) General.	None.	Period of breeding cycle between each oestrus or heat period.	*See* prolonged dioestrus.
Lactation anoestrus (p163) General.	No oestrus activity.	The hormone prolactin, responsible for stimulating milk let-down, suppresses ovarian activity.	Partially affected mares respond to hormone treatment.
Oestrous cycle (p171) General.	Normal reproductive cycle; mare in oestrus crouches in docile attitude, with tail raised and 'winking' of vulva (illus p97); frequent passing of small amounts of urine.	Hormonal activity.	Hormonal drugs and environment control can be used to manipulate the cycle.
Oestrous cycle, transitional period (p172) General.	*See* anoestrus, *and* oestrus cycle.	*See* anoestrus, *and* oestrus cycle.	*See* anoestrus, *and* oestrus cycle.
Prolonged dioestrus (p187) General.	Absence of heat.	Persistence of corpus luteum and high levels of progesterone.	Prostaglandin injection breaks down corpus luteum and normal heat develops.

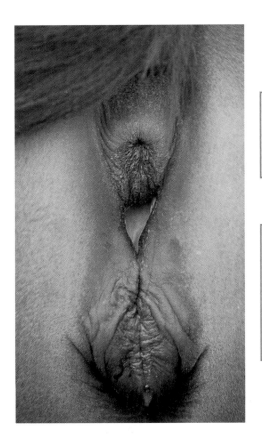

◀ RECTO-VAGINAL FISTULA

Perineal damage following foaling; the vulval seal is no longer present

ABORTION ▶

This mare has a retained placenta which shows a badly twisted cord. It probably caused the death of the foal and subsequent abortion

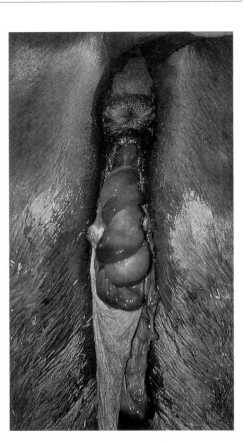

DISEASES AFFECTING THE ABDOMEN

Physical Conditions affecting the Female

Disease / Geographical Spread	Symptoms	Cause	Treatment
Prolapse of vagina, uterus (p187) General.	**Vagina**: pink, grapefruit-sized swelling protruding from vulva. **Uterus**: larger, more flaccid prolapse, always associated with foaling.	**Vagina**: mismatched or brutal covering. **Uterus**: oversized foal, or associated with aged mare, or long second stage of parturition.	Immediate replacement of prolapsed organs.
Recto-vaginal fistula (p189) (illus p96) General.	Faeces passed through both anus and vagina.	Tear occurs as complication of foaling.	Surgical repair.
Uterine cysts (p202) General.	Cysts protrude into lumen of uterus in mares over 10 years.	Probably part of natural ageing.	None unless contributing to infertility, when removed by laser or direct puncture with biopsy instrument.
Vulval aspiration (p203) *See also* endometritis (p147) General.	Audible sound of 'windsucking' as air is drawn into vagina; infection noticeable on examination by vet.	Faulty conformation of vagina, or damage during foaling.	Surgery to prevent windsucking.

Problems of Pregnancy

Abortion (p130) (illus p96) General.	Similar to those of natural parturition.	**Non-infective** eg twinning, twisted umbilical cord (illus p96); congenital abnormalities; or **infective** eg bacterial, fungal or viral.	Rarely necessary except to check for residual infection.
Pregnancy diagnosis (p185) General.	Lack of heat.	Pregnancy.	*See Table 5.* **Methods of diagnosis:** assessment of oestrus behaviour; manual diagnosis by rectal palpation; ultrasonic examination; hormonal tests.

DISEASES AFFECTING THE ABDOMEN

Disease / Geographical Spread	Symptoms	Cause	Treatment
Pregnancy, normal (p186) General.	Normal pregnancy.	Fertilisation of the ovum to birth of new foal without problems or complications.	None.
Twinning (p200) General.	None, unless mare aborts.	Two embryos develop; tends to be hereditary. Twins seldom carried full term; survivors tend to be weak.	If diagnosed early, the embryos can be aborted and the mare covered again.

PREGNANCY

(left) A typical pregnant mare

(above)'Waxing' just before foaling; note the droplets of milk coming from the teat

◀ TWINNING

Unfortunately this mare had twins; one is only just alive and the other is dead, although clear of its placenta

PREGNANCY AT VARIOUS STAGES

Examples of ultrasound pictures taken at various stages of pregnancy

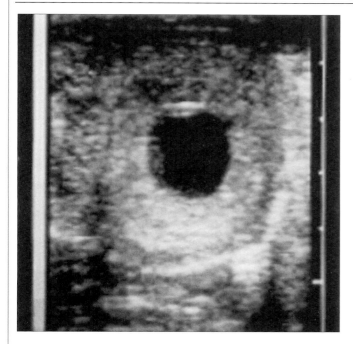

▲ *14-day conceptus, showing light grey uterine wall and the circular conceptus filled with fluid*

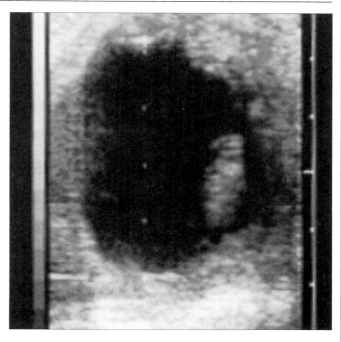

▲ *32-day conceptus; at this stage the grey 'blob' of the developing foetus can just be seen on the right*

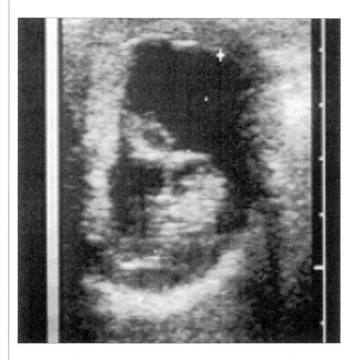

▲ *35-day conceptus; both conceptus and foetus are now growing rapidly*

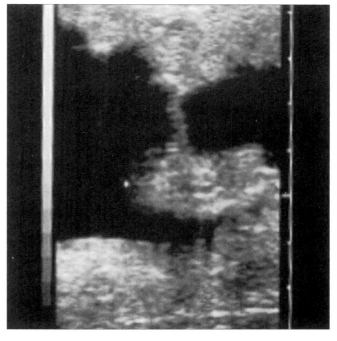

▲ *45-day conceptus; the umbilical cord is clearly visible at this stage*

PROBLEMS OF FOALING

Disease / Geographical Spread	Symptoms	Cause	Treatment
Dystocia (p146) General.	Delay in second stage of labour.	Abnormality in birth process where the foal cannot be delivered by its mother's efforts; usually malpresentation, ie where the foal is coming the wrong way.	Urgent assistance to enable delivery of foal essential.
Foaling, normal (p154) General.	*Stage 1*: similar to colic with discomfort, pacing, sweating; *stage 2*: propulsive stage, contractions develop in intensity, foetal membranes appear and rupture, delivery takes maximum 40 minutes from this stage; *stage 3*: expulsion of afterbirth (placenta).	Normal parturition.	None unless second stage delayed, when vet should be called immediately.
Lactation tetany (p163) General.	Stiffness, eyes glazed, gait unsteady with tetanic spasms, eventual recumbency.	Metabolic disorder of lactating mares involving fall in blood calcium, often associated with stress.	Intravenous calcium injection.
Mastitis (p168) General.	Glands become hot, hard and swollen; raised temperature, depression, stiffness; loss of appetite; milk clotted and discoloured.	Bacterial infection of mammary gland(s), often around weaning or just before foaling.	Anti-bacterial treatment, plus intra-mammary antibiotic.
Placenta (afterbirth), retained (p179) General.	Rope of placenta hanging from vulva more than 12 hours following parturition.	Unknown.	Manual removal, or injection of saline and oxytocin (a hormone), which causes contractions and expulsion of placenta.

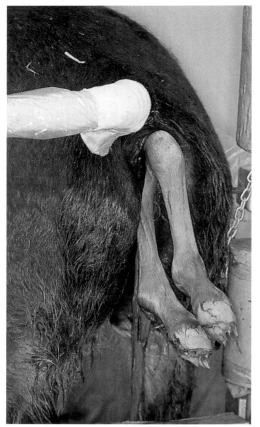

◀ DYSTOCIA

Both fore limbs but no head; a case of dystocia requiring urgent help

RETAINED PLACENTA▶

A mare with retained placenta

◀ MASTITIS

The hot swollen udder typical of mastitis

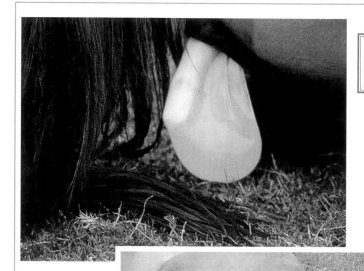

◄ *The early part of stage 2*

▼ *Some two to three minutes later*

◄ *Five minutes later the fore limbs, one in front of the other, and nose, are presented*

▼ *A different view of the same stage*

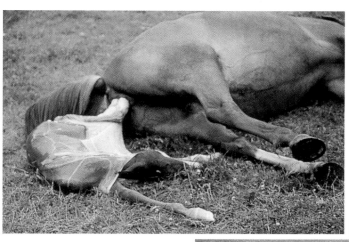

▲ *Two to three minutes later the foal is presented; notice the hind limbs still in the vulva*

The mare and foal beginning to recover ▶

DISEASES AFFECTING MOVEMENT

Conditions of the Foot

Disease / Geographical Spread	Symptoms	Cause	Treatment
Bruised sole (p138) General.	Varying degrees of weight-bearing lameness, discoloration when sole trimmed.	Trauma from hitting stone or similar object.	Rest; cold tubbing.
Buttress foot (p138) (illus p103) General.	Initially, sudden lameness, foot held with toe just touching ground; often painful swelling of front of coronary band.	New bone formation and soft tissue swelling at point of insertion of tendon into front of pedal bone, sometimes small fractures due to strain or trauma.	Complete rest; surgical removal or pinning of fracture.
Corns (p143) General.	Varying degree of lameness, or pottery action if both feet affected.	Bruising at heels usually caused by ill-fitting shoes.	Removal of shoe, trimming of affected area; replacement of shoe, sometimes seated out, to correctly balanced foot; if infected, treat as for solar abscess.
Cracked heels (p143) General.	Soreness, inflammation and swelling; sticky exudate forms scabs which crack.	Wet, muddy conditions provide opportunity for bacterial infection (*Dermatophilus congolensis*).	Prevention by keeping legs clean and dry; removal of scabs by bathing, then antibiotic applied to the cleaned and dried area.
Greasy heels (p158) General.	Affects area under fetlock. *See* cracked heels.	*See* cracked heels.	*See* cracked heels.
Laminitis (p163) (illus p103) General.	**Acute disease**: severe pain in the feet, sweating and distress, standing with hind legs underneath the body and front legs extended. **Sub-acute**: horse lifts one foot after the other.	Overloading of the digestive tract with carbohydrate leads to endotoxin production, increased blood pressure and 'short circuit' of blood supply to the feet, resulting in degeneration and separation of laminae.	Liquid paraffin to prevent absorption of endotoxins; phenylbutazone for inflammation and pain; immediate administration of acepromazine to dilate blood vessels of foot; topical nitro-glycerine patches applied to digital arteries behind fetlocks also help; supportive nursing, stable litter to support sole and prevent rotation of pedal bone essential. Fitting of heart-bar shoe in most cases. Surgical hoof resection (illus p45) in severe acute cases.
Navicular disease (p169) General.	Lameness when in one foot, often pointed forwards at rest; when in both may be pottery rather than lame; tendency to trip; in long-established cases heels appear contracted, and the foot boxy.	*Three theories:* **1.** physical trauma; **2.** changes in and loss of blood supply to navicular bone; **3.** degenerative change to navicular bone.	Correct foot balancing, with egg-bar shoe (illus p45) with rolled toes. Also drugs: warfarin under supervision as anti-clotting agent; isoxsuprine as vasodilator; new research shows success with Tiludronate to normalise bone metabolism. Surgery: sectioning of collateral navicular suspensory ligaments can be successful; neurectomy used but may have serious complications.
Pedal bone fracture (p178) General.	Sudden, severe lameness; X-rays show fracture.	Severe localised trauma.	Rest and immobilisation of foot with bar shoe (illus p45) and side clips; alternatively surgery to fit bone screw. Recovery to soundness unlikely if joint is affected.
Pedal-ostitis (p178) General.	Low-grade shifting lameness, pottery action; X-rays show thinning of anterior edge and roughening of bottom margin of pedal bone.	Severe bruising and repeated low-grade trauma.	Seldom successful; NSAIDs may help; protective pads and frog bar on shoes also helpful.
Pricked foot (p187) (illus p103) General.	Pain while nail driven in; possible bleeding; subsequent lameness.	Incorrect angle of entry of nail.	Remove nail, dress with antiseptic; tetanus antitoxin if horse not vaccinated; may need antibiotics.
Pus in the foot (p188) (ilus p103) General.	Acute lameness, foot becomes hot and pulse felt at mid-pastern; sometimes swelling higher up leg, and later pus appears at coronary band.	Infection following a penetrating wound, bruised foot or corn.	Sole cleaned and tract of infection opened and drained; hot tubbing and poulticing; antibiotics following draining.

DISEASES AFFECTING MOVEMENT

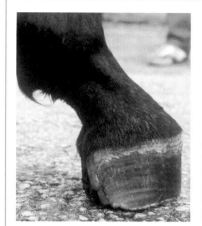

◀BUTTRESS FOOT

Typical malformation of the hoof

PUS IN FOOT▶

Pus in the foot; note the drainage channel that has been created opposite the thumb

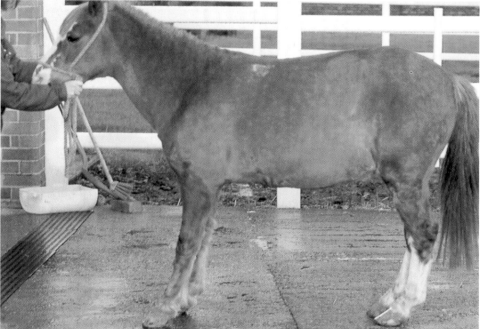

LAMINITIS

(left) The typical stance of a laminitic pony
(above) Protrusion of the pedal bone through the sole of the foot, a complication of laminitis

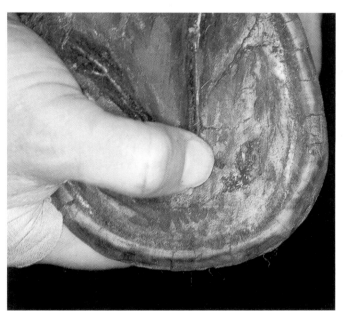

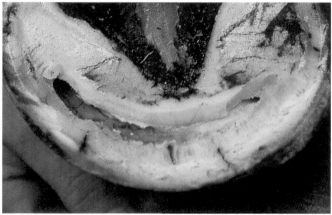

PRICKED FOOT

(left) Pus indicating where infection has set up; (above) the affected area removed

DISEASES AFFECTING MOVEMENT

Disease / Geographical Spread	Symptoms	Cause	Treatment
Quittor (p188) General.	Pain, swelling and heat at heel; sinuses discharging pus at coronary band.	Trauma to lateral cartilage, followed by infection and death of sections of cartilage.	Unrewarding, but antibiotics used; also surgery to remove dead tissue.
Ringbone (p189) General.	Chronic condition showing low-grade lameness, usually with hard swelling above coronary band. X-rays show new bone formation. Pastern trauma causes more acute condition.	Trauma to pastern bones or strain of ligaments joining the bones; conformational faults predispose to ringbone.	Rest and anti-inflammatory drugs usually resolve problem unless joint is affected.
Sandcracks (p191) (illus p105) General.	Pain and lameness.	Cracks starting from coronary band caused by damage to hoof-forming epidermis of coronary band; cracks starting from ground surface usually initiated by uneven pressure in unbalanced foot.	Short, partial-depth cracks resolved by correct shoeing. Full-depth infected cracks opened out to expose infected area; treated with antibiotics, then new, growing hoof filled with hoof compound and stabilised.
Seedy toe (p192) (illus p105) General.	Gap filled with soft, crumbly tissue or impacted mud develops at toe; chronic lameness usual.	Damage due to chronic laminitis; trauma to sole.	Removal of hoof wall to expose cavity and remove diseased horn; application of eucalyptus oil and formalin or iodoform.

QUITTOR

(above) A long-standing case of quittor

(right) The same case six months later, showing how it deforms the foot

▲ RINGBONE

The type of lump often associated with ringbone

DISEASES AFFECTING MOVEMENT

Disease / Geographical Spread	Symptoms	Cause	Treatment
Sheared heels (p193) General.	Heels are uneven, the wall of the lower, generally the medial heel is more upright, best seen when viewed from behind; chronic lameness usual.	Uneven trimming of foot, excessive use of large road studs fitted to one side only.	Remedial trimming, fitting a bar shoe to provide good heel support.
Sidebone (p194) General.	Lameness sometimes present with associated pain, heat and swelling. X-rays show degree of ossification.	Increase of concussive forces acting on back of pedal bone, eg delayed shoeing.	Rest and NSAIDs; grooving foot may help if lame.
Thrush (p200) General.	Black, tarry discharge in sulci of frog; separation of frog; area becomes soft and foul-smelling.	Wet, dirty conditions encourage thrush, especially soiled stables.	Paring to remove all diseased tissue; treat with antibiotics, formalin or iodoform twice daily until healed.
White line disease (p204) General.	Under-running of the hoof wall, starting at the ground surface and extending up the foot between the white line and surface of the hoof. Cavity full of a crumbly, foul-smelling material.	Opportunist infection of the hoof with various strains of fungi. More common in conditions of high humidity and moisture. Thought to occur secondary to other hoof problems that lead to separation of the laminae.	Correction of hoof balance defects with appropriate trimming; removal of all infected hoof material, and treatment with tincture of methiolate or iodine. Support with egg-bar shoes if required.

SANDCRACKS▶

A typical sandcrack, of the neglected foot variety

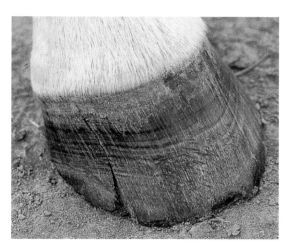

SEEDY TOE▶

A case of seedy toe; the hoof has been removed to expose the infected tract

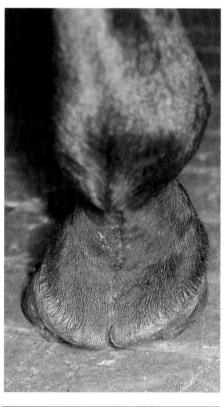

▲ SHEARED HEEL

A good example of sheared heels, showing the uneven growth of each side of the hoof

DISEASES AFFECTING MOVEMENT

Conditions of the Limbs

Disease / Geographical Spread	Symptoms	Cause	Treatment
Ankylosis (p133) (See also p121). General.	One or more joints fused in flexed position.	Injury, disease; elective surgery (eg for bone spavin); congenital flexural deformity in new-born foal.	None; if foal born alive, euthanasia should be considered.
Arthritis (p134) (illus p107) General.	**Acute**: pain, swelling and heat in affected joint, loss of appetite and high temperature; **Chronic**: increasing stiffness and swelling in one or more joints, accompanied by lameness which often wears off with exercise.	**Acute**: sequel to wound or infection of joint; **Chronic**: repeated trauma and strain, with loss of cartilage from bearing surfaces of joint and growth of new bone.	**Acute**: antibiotics essential; maybe lavage of joint; immobilise. **Chronic**: changes irreversible, prevention important; initial rest then gradual return to work, with drug therapy. Hyaluronic acid, glycosaminoglycan polysulphate and pentosan polysulphate help maintain cartilage. NSAIDs (phenylbutazone) to control pain.
Brushing (p138) General.	Injury caused by foot of one limb striking inside of opposite limb.	Bad conformation, fatigue.	Good foot balance and shoeing may help.
Capped hock or elbow (p138) (illus pp59 & 107) General.	Soft swelling on point of hock or elbow.	Kicking back at a wall or trailer ramp or similar trauma causes damage to bursa.	Early drainage of fluid, application of pressure bandage and local injection of long-acting corticosteroid; surgery often unrewarding.
Carpitis (p139) (illus p107) General.	Lameness, with swelling over the front of the knee.	Repeated trauma to joint, poor conformation, resulting in new bone growth.	**Acute**: rest, with injections of corticosteroid into joint might help; **Chronic**: NSAIDs to alleviate inflammation and pain.
Curb (p144) (illus p107) General.	Enlargement of the plantar ligament at the back of hock. Early lameness.	Poor conformation or excessive strain.	Rest, reduction of inflammation. **Chronic stage**: no treatment required.
Degenerative joint disease (p145) General.	Pain in affected joint, with lameness, sometimes swelling and warmth.	Changes in structure of cartilage; occurs naturally in old age or following strain, or overfeeding young horses.	Rest followed by controlled exercise; drug therapy may help.
Epiphysitis (p149) General.	Enlarged, painful joints, with knuckling and shifting lameness.	Overfeeding youngstock, combined with sudden activity interspersed with idleness.	Reduce level of nutrition; ensure well balanced ration with correct ratios of vitamins and minerals is fed.
Fractures (p156) (illus p108) General.	Acute pain, swelling, abnormal angulation, non-weight-bearing; fractures of small bones may require X-ray for diagnosis; fractures of head and trunk may go unnoticed initially.	Excessive force applied to bone.	Horse kept immobile until vet arrives; lower leg fractures immobilised by Robert Jones splint (illus p67) or similar; surgical repair may be possible at specialist centre.
Over-reach (p174) (illus p60) General.	Injury to heel area of forefoot, struck by toe of hind foot.	Faulty conformation, fatigue, bad trimming or shoeing.	As for minor injury; prevent by correct trimming and shoeing.
Ringbone (p189)	See Conditions of the Foot (p104).	See Conditions of the Foot (p104).	See Conditions of the Foot (p104).
Sesamoiditis (p193) General.	Acute lameness with pain over one or both sesamoids.	Abnormal stresses cause ligaments to tear from sesamoid bone; bone to split.	Immobilisation of injury, long rest; fractures sometimes surgically screwed.
Sore shins (p194) General.	Swelling, initially warm and painful, to front of cannons; lameness if unilateral, otherwise shortened stride.	Excessive force applied to immature bones in strong work causes periosteum to tear from cannon.	Good farriery, better work surface and training régime; rest, anti-inflammatory drugs.
Spavin (p195): (bog spavin and bone spavin) (illus p108) General.	**Bog spavin**: Soft swellings on inside and outside of hock joint, rarely causing lameness. **Bone spavin**: Indefinite hind-limb lameness, reduced flexion, shortened stride.	**Bog spavin**: Probably poor conformation and strain. **Bone spavin**: Constant strain to hock.	**Bog spavin**: Immobilisation, cold hosing and rest. **Bone spavin**: Surgical fusion of joint, or work horse while controlling pain with NSAIDs, to speed up fusion; once bones are fused, lameness disappears.

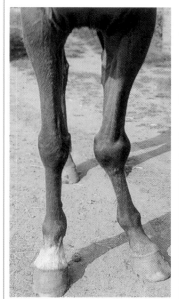
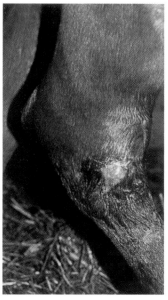

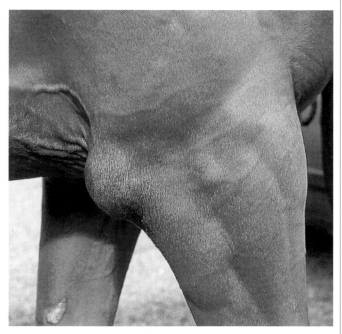

▲ ARTHRITIS

(above left) Chronic arthritis following an old injury to the left knee

(above right) Infected arthritis due to a penetrating wound to the hock

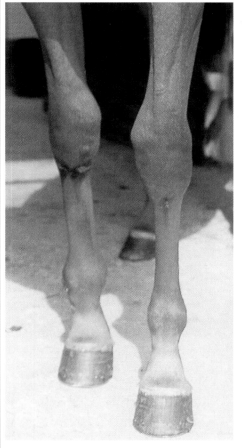

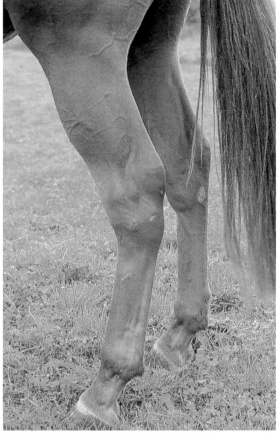

CARPITIS

(far left) Note the enlarged, asymmetric carpi

CURB

(left) A good example of a curb in the left hind leg; note the swelling just below the point of hock

DISEASES AFFECTING MOVEMENT

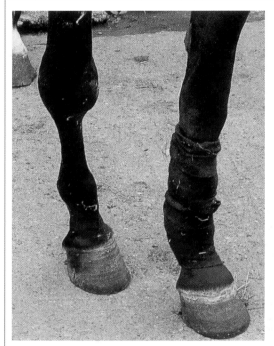

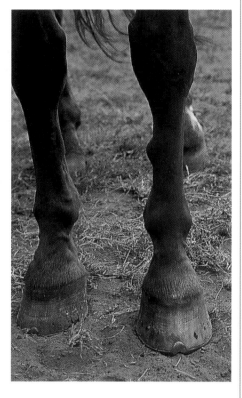

▼ SPLINT

A bad splint in the left fore leg

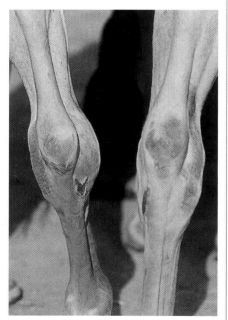

▲ FRACTURES

(above left) An old fracture of the carpal joint showing medial deviation (above right) An X-ray of a well defined chip fracture of the intermediate carpal bone

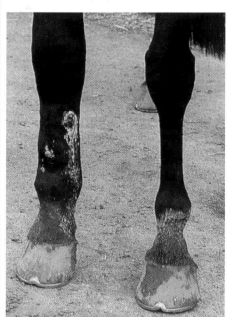

▼ BOG SPAVIN

A soft, fluctuating swelling typical of a bog spavin

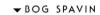

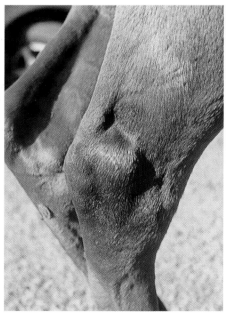

▲ PUNCTURES

A penetrating wound, and the type of infection and swelling it can cause

▲ BONE SPAVIN

The swelling associated with spavin affecting the left hock

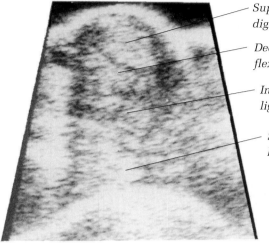

Superficial
digital flexor tendon

Deep digital
flexor tendon

Inferior check
ligament

Suspensory
ligament

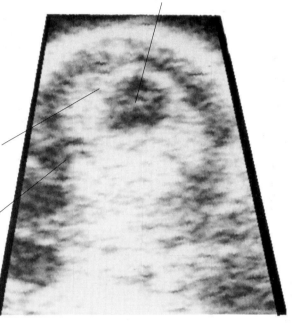

The hypoechoic appearance
of a large core lesion of the
superficial digital tendon

Swollen
superficial
digital tendon

Fluid
accumulation
in the tendon
sheath

▼ TENDON STRAIN

(below) A case of tendon strain in the flexor tendon of the forelimb

(right) A tendon strain which has been fired at some time in the past

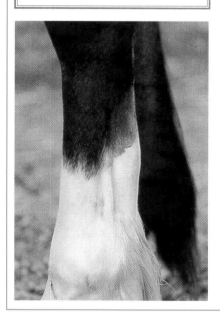

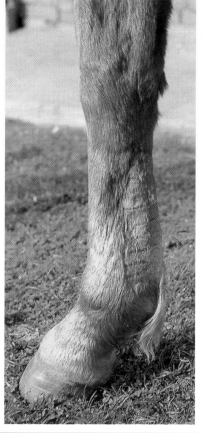

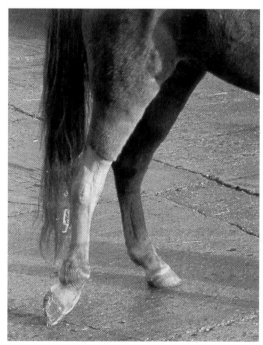

▲ UPWARD FIXATION OF THE PATELLA

The locked hind leg typical of upward fixation of the patella

DISEASES AFFECTING MOVEMENT

Disease / Geographical Spread	Symptoms	Cause	Treatment
Splints (p195) (illus pp61 & 108) General.	Hard, bony swelling usually on inside of front cannon, initially warm and painful.	Concussion to immature bone bruises ligament which binds splint bone to cannon; trauma; or sudden change to hard work in older horses.	Conservative; anti-inflammatory lotions might help reduce size.
Tendon strain (p199) (illus p109) General.	Varying degrees of lameness, heat, swelling and pain.	Strain exceeding natural ability of tendon to stretch and rebound.	Immediate cold compresses essential, anti-inflammatories to ease pain; immobilisation of leg in cast, box rest until sound, followed by controlled exercise. The drug Adequan has proved helpful.
Thoroughpin (p200) General.	Soft swelling above and behind hock joint.	Probably poor conformation.	None needed. Intra-lesional injection of cortisone may reduce large thoroughpin.
Upward fixation of the patella (p201) (illus p109) General.	Hind leg 'locked' in place; release accompanied by loud crack.	Abnormality of stay mechanism of hind legs, preventing release of patella from medial condyle of femur when horse changes from rest to movement.	Many cases resolve with time and improved condition. Alternatively injection of an irritant to cause thickening of the ligament, or two methods of surgery. All treatments are successful, but can lead to future chronic lameness problems.
Windgall (p204) (illus p61) General.	Soft swelling above and behind fetlock, often in hard-worked horses.	Wear and tear, or slight fetlock strain.	None required as blemishes not significant except for being unsightly. Intra-lesional injection of cortisone may help reduce a large windgall.

Conditions of the Musculature
Additional entries on page 126

Azoturia (p135) General. Chronic: eg recurrent equine rhabdomyolysis (RER); see also equine polysaccharide storage myopathy (p126).	**Sporadic:** Affects older, competing horses when work level increased. **Chronic:** Affects younger horses, with recurrent attacks when exercised. Both showing anxiety, sweating, stilted movement, unwillingness to move, dark or discoloured urine; hot, swollen, painful muscles.	Unknown, but recent research suggests that factors involving calcium build-up in the muscle cells are responsible, especially in cases of RER.	Anti-inflammatory drugs; local heat; intravenous electrolytes to flush kidneys of muscle breakdown products. Severe cases: box rest until pain and stiffness relieved, then gentle exercise and paddock rest. Mild cases: gentle exercise. Controlled diet and controlled progressive programme to return to work.
Shivering (p194) General.	Hind leg is flexed in exaggerated way and shivers, horse may fall.	Unknown.	None; euthanasia should be considered for severe cases.
Stringhalt (p197) General; also in Australia, NZ and USA	As horse moves, hind leg drawn sharply upwards and forwards, then sharply down; degree varies.	Unknown, except as in Australia, New Zealand and USA, due to consumption of dandelion weed.	Muscle relaxant, Mephanesin; alternatively surgical treatment; in cases of Australian stringhalt, remove from cause.

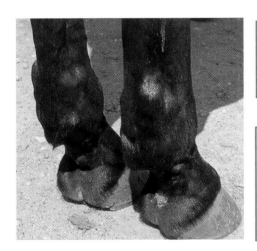

◀ WINDGALL

Windgalls on hind fetlocks

BACK INJURIES ▶

An old injury to the back showing dissymmetry of the pelvis

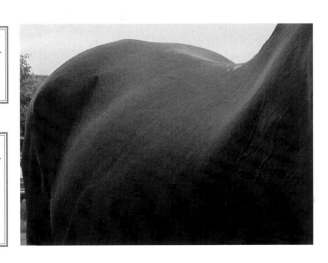

DISEASES AFFECTING MOVEMENT

Conditions of the Skeleton

Disease / Geographical Spread	Symptoms	Cause	Treatment
Back injuries (p136) (illus p110) General.	**Acute injury**: pain at the site of injury with varying degree of immobility, especially in hindquarters; **chronic injury**: increasing unwillingness to carry out accustomed movements, and objection when rider mounts.	Injuries due to fall(s), badly fitting saddle, arthritis of sacro-iliac joint, spondylitis ('kissing spines').	Some cases respond to surgery; otherwise anti-inflammatory treatment and rest.
Fistulous withers (p154) General.	Withers swollen, hot and painful; swellings eventually burst to leave large suppurating mass. Condition where infected tracts develop in and around the withers.	Possibly infection with *Brucella abortus*; also trauma to wither area.	Antibiotics, or surgery sometimes necessary.
Pelvic injuries (p178) General.	**Fractures**: varying lameness, sometimes obviously visible. **Pelvic strain**: disinclination to move forwards freely, sometimes stiffness, jumping performance impaired.	**Fractures**: severe trauma. **Pelvic strain**: strain of sacro-iliac ligaments.	**Fractures**: usually rest; surgery sometimes appropriate. **Pelvic strain**: rest and anti-inflammatory treatment, local heat.
Poll evil (p185) General.	Swelling, heat and pain in poll area; infected tracts exude pus.	Trauma followed by infection.	Antibiotics, poulticing and NSAIDs in early stages. Long-standing cases require surgery to drain sinuses.
Spondylitis (p196) General.	Inflammation and new bone formation of thoracic and lumbar vertebrae, evidenced as back pain, irritability and abnormal sensitivity during saddling; refusal to jump; decreased athleticism; unco-ordinated hind-leg action.	Repeated trauma.	Rest provides immediate relief, but problem returns when horse ridden. Surgical treatment effective for 'kissing spines'.

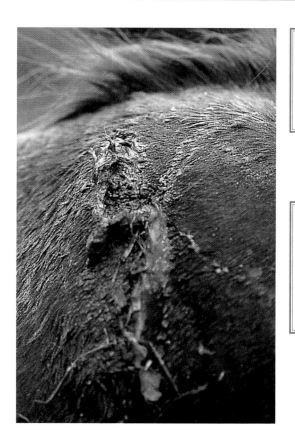

◄ FISTULOUS WITHERS

A case of fistulous withers. Note the discharging tracts

PELVIC INJURIES ►

Note the severe asymmetry of the hindquarters following this fracture of the pelvis

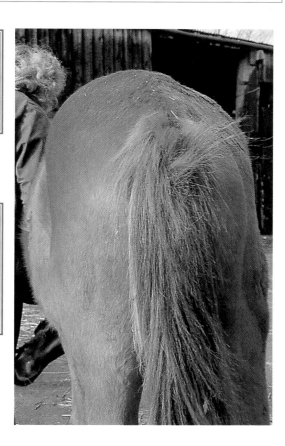

DISEASES AFFECTING THE SKIN

Allergic Diseases

Disease / Geographical Spread	Symptoms	Cause	Treatment
Nettle rash (p171) General.	Large areas of raised hair, hot and painful, nervous signs, ataxia, violent behaviour.	Hypersensitive reaction to nettle stings.	Usually resolves in few hours; painkillers and anti-inflammatory drugs.
Photosensitivity (p179) General.	Skin reddened, thickened and inflamed, dies and sloughs off, heals leaving scar.	Photosensitive agents build up in skin and increase sensitivity to sunlight.	Removal to darkened box, cortisone and antihistamine injections, local antiseptics.
Sweet itch (p198) (illus p113) General.	Localised dermatitis of mane, poll and root of tail; skin thickened and oedematous; intense itching causing constant rubbing; loss of hair, skin becomes ridged and scaly.	Reaction to saliva of midges of Culicoides group.	Prevention by stabling horse at critical times of day, combined with weekly spray with synthetic pyrethrum.
Urticaria (p202) (illus p113) General.	Sudden appearance of skin weals.	Systemic reaction usually due to sudden change in diet eg new spring grass.	Antihistamines.

Conditions of the Skin

Disease / Geographical Spread	Symptoms	Cause	Treatment
Abscess (p131) (illus p113) General.	Swelling under skin, develops from hot and hard to softer and less painful until skin ruptures and releases pus.	Sequel to penetrating wound, or infection, eg strangles.	Prevention by scrupulous cleaning of wounds; if abscess forming, poultice to encourage maturation.
Boil (p136) General.	Small painful papules which enlarge, exuding serum.	Infection of hair follicle which spreads, often following clipping.	Hot water bathing to encourage abcess to burst, then antibiotic or antiseptic treatment.

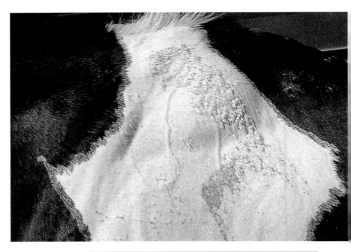

▲ NETTLE RASH

A case of nettle rash; note the raised hair over the shoulder

▲ PHOTOSENSITIVITY

A case of photosensitivity in a skewbald horse due to eating St John's Wort; you can clearly see the hardening and wrinkling of the white areas of the skin

(left) St John's Wort, the weed that can cause photosensitisation in horses

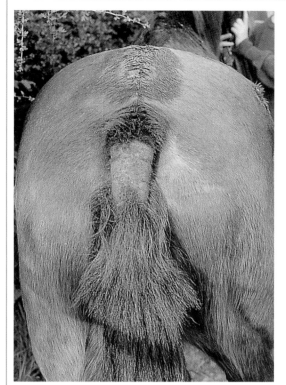

SWEET ITCH

(left and below) Sweet itch, showing typical lesions at the tail root and along the crest of the neck

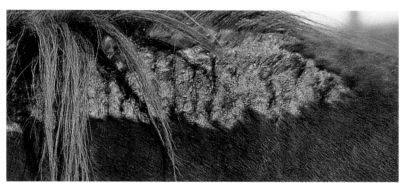

CYST ▶

A dermoid cyst in the eye of a yearling

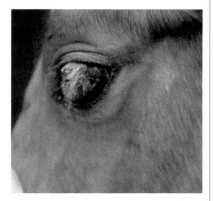

ABSCESS

(right) An abscess just about to burst
(below) A large abscess buried in the left thigh of a foal

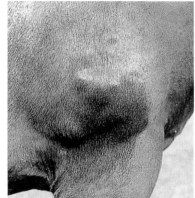

▼ URTICARIA

The cutaneous swellings typical of an allergy

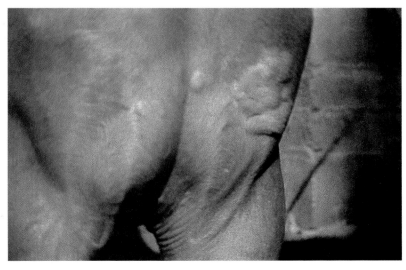

DISEASES AFFECTING THE SKIN

Disease / Geographical Spread	Symptoms	Cause	Treatment
Cyst (p145) General.	Swellings in the skin, commonly at the base of ear or in false nostril.	Congenital abnormality.	Surgical removal.
Girth gall(s) (p156) General.	Raised skin, hair loss or raw wound(s) in girth area.	Dirty or unsuitable girths, tight girthing, sensitive skin, prolonged use.	Antiseptic or anti-inflammatory and antibiotic ointment, and rest until healed. Take preventative measures.
Melanoma (p168) (illus p59) General.	Small, firm black lumps in the substance of the skin, often around the anus, eyes or in the glands of the neck.	Tumours of the melanin-producing cells of the skin, occurring first in middle age; common in greys.	Surgery possible, but risk of spread; anticarcinogenic drugs may help.
Nodular skin disease (p171) (illus p61) General.	Sudden appearance of painless nodules on neck or back varying in size from a grain of rice to a pea.	Thought to be allergic reaction to insect bites or parasitic larvae after worming.	Usually resolves in time; surgical removal if necessary.
Saddle sores (p191) General.	Hair loss at point of friction, developing into open sore, usually at sides of withers or on loins.	Ill-fitting saddle, dirty or wrinkled numnahs or poor riding technique, causing uneven weight distribution.	Rest, treat sore(s) with healing ointment.
Sarcoids (p192) (illus pp59 & 115) General.	Non-spreading skin tumours. Six types: see descriptions on p192.	Thought to be due to a virus, possibly due to previous non-productive infection.	Surgery, cryo-surgery, radiation techniques, cytotoxic ointments may be successful depending on type and location of sarcoid.
Seborrhoea (p192) (illus p115) General.	Hair greasy and clogged with scurf.	Secondary to other skin complaints, eg lice or mange.	Eliminate primary cause; use sulphur and coal-tar shampoo.
Sunburn (p198) (illus p115) General.	Reddening of skin on white or hairless areas of nose.	Sensitive skin, burned by sunlight.	Removal of horse from direct sunlight, use of sun-blocking creams.
Tumours (p200) (illus p115) General.	*See melanoma, sarcoids (above).*	*See melanoma, sarcoids (above).*	*See melanoma, sarcoids (above).*
Warts (p203) (illus p115) General.	Small groups of lumps in skin of young horses, commonly around eyes, muzzle and under tail.	Equine papilloma virus.	None necessary, as warts are self-curing over several months.

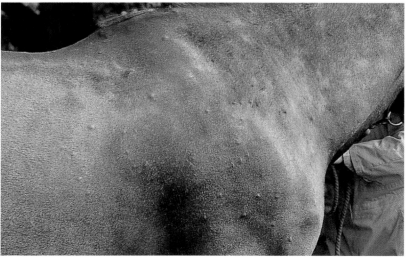

▼ NODULAR SKIN DISEASE

The small hard nodules characteristic of nodular skin disease

▲ MELANOMA

Severe case of melanoma in a grey mare

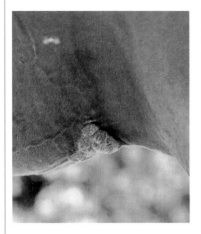

▲ SARCOIDS

Sarcoid under the jaw line of a horse

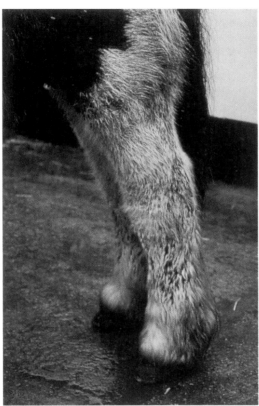

SEBORRHOEA ▶

Greasy skin

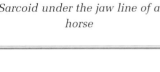

SUNBURN

A bad case of sunburn on the nose; sun-block factor 20 is needed here

TUMOURS

(left) Typical appearance of a carcinoma of the penis
(below) Lymphosarcoma in a Welsh cob mare

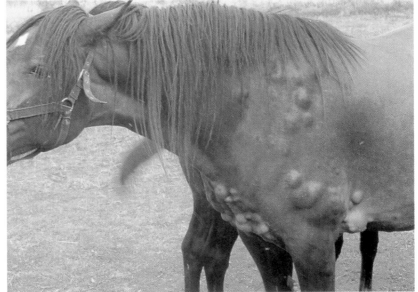

◀ WARTS

Juvenile papillomata in a three-year-old

DISEASES AFFECTING THE SKIN

Infections of the Skin

Disease / Geographical Spread	Symptoms	Cause	Treatment
Folliculitis (p156) General.	Small, painful papules in skin, which burst leaving hairless patches on healing.	Bacterial infection, secondary to poor skin hygiene.	Antibacterial washes, possibly antibiotics.
Furunculosis (p156) General.	Area of skin becomes nodular with large, crusted ulcers.	Usually sequel to untreated folliculitis.	Local and systemic antibiotics; removal of underlying cause.
Mud fever (p168) (illus p117) General.	Crusty lesions affecting legs up to knees and hocks, legs swollen and very painful, horse lame and sometimes quite ill.	Infection by *Dermatophilus congolensis*, in wet, muddy conditions.	Bathing to remove scabs, then legs kept dry and clean, antibiotics may be required.
Rain scald (p189) (illus p61 & 117) General.	Scabby lesions along back and neck, skin inflamed, discomfort, loss of condition.	Primarily bacterial infection with *Dermatophilus congolensis*, after rain washes out protective oils and softens skin.	**Early cases**: skin kept dry, gentle grooming; **more advanced cases**: medicated shampoo to remove crusts, application of antibiotic ointment. Protect from weather.
Ringworm (p190) (illus p117) General.	Round, crusty scab appears which multiplies and develops to cover large area.	Two groups of fungae, trichophyton and microsporon.	Course of the antibiotic Griseofulvin, or topical washes with Natamycin.

Parasitic Diseases

Disease / Geographical Spread	Symptoms	Cause	Treatment
Equine filariasis (p150) Southern Europe and Asia.	Malaise, fever, subcutaneous swellings, conjunctivitis.	Larvae of filariad worm *Seruria equina*; disease spread from horse to horse by mosquitos.	The anthelmintic Ivermectin.
Habronemiasis (p158) (illus p117) General.	Sores on lower limbs, corners of the eyes and prepuce and penis of males.	Larvae of stomach worm, Habronema, when deposited on wounds or mucous membranes.	Ivermectin to kill larvae; large lesions require surgery or cryosurgery.
Leishmaniosis (p165) South America, Southern Europe.	Ulcerating or crusty, hairless lesions in skin of face.	Protozoan parasite of Leishmania family, living for a stage in the body of sand flies and occasionally skin of horses.	No specific treatment, appears to resolve spontaneously in 4–5 months.
Lice *See* parasites **(p174) (illus p117)** General.	Irritation, dull coat, hair loss, mane and tail become matted, loss of condition and anaemia.	Small, active parasites which breed in long winter coats and feed from skin debris; two types, biting and sucking.	Coat clipped if possible; insecticidal wash, or louse powder; ivermectin wormers also kill lice.

▼ FURUNCULOSIS

Acute furunculosis caused by a Staphylococcus equi *infection*

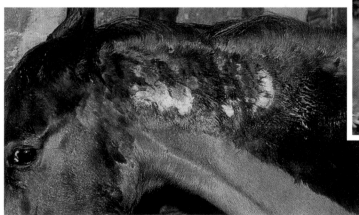

▲ FURUNCULOSIS

The same horse twelve months later, showing the odd hair growth where the lesions had occurred

DISEASES AFFECTING THE SKIN

▼ MUD FEVER

The crusty lesions typical of mud fever

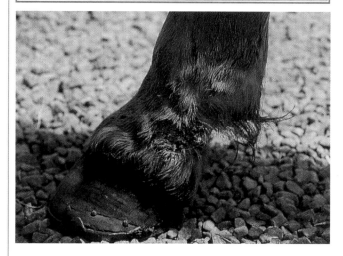

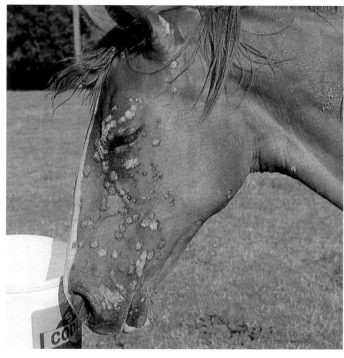

▲ RAIN SCALD

Skin lesions seen in cases of rain scald

▲ RINGWORM

The round crusty scabs associated with ringworm can rapidly cover a large area

LICE

(right) Typical dermatitis caused by a severe lice infestation

(below) The usual type of bald patches caused by lice

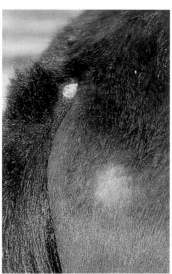

▲ HABRONEMIASIS

Habronemiasis granuloma

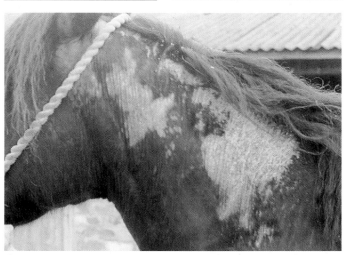

DISEASES AFFECTING THE SKIN

Disease / Geographical Spread	Symptoms	Cause	Treatment
Mange *See* parasites (p175) General.	*Three types:* **chorioptic**: affected horses stamp the ground. **Psoroptes equi**: moist, bloody patches at base of mane and tail, head shaking. **Sarcoptes scabei**: hairless patches exuding serum, around head, neck and shoulders (notifiable disease).	Infestation by mites causes intense itching.	Weekly washes with acaracide; ivermectins.
Mites *See* parasites (p175) General.	Itching rash on lower legs, usually in late summer.	Larval bites.	Washes with insecticide, anti-inflammatory ointments.
Onchoceriasis (p173) World-wide.	Patches of scaly dermatitis along mid-line, face, withers and chest, which may become de-pigmented; eye lesions.	Microfilariae of worm *Onchocerca cervicalis* migrating to skin.	The anthelmintic ivermectin.
Ticks *See* parasites (p177) General.	Heavy burdens cause anaemia and loss of condition; sometimes infected abscesses.	Tick bites.	Wipe-on or spray acaracides; reduced grazing on rough ground.
Warble *See* parasites (p177) General.	Hard lump on back, caused by reaction to dying warble-fly larva.	Presence of warble-fly larva, which cannot complete its development in the horse.	Removal of undeveloped larva manually, by poulticing, or surgically.

▼ MANGE

Mange-like lesions occurring on the head due to a chorioptic mange infection

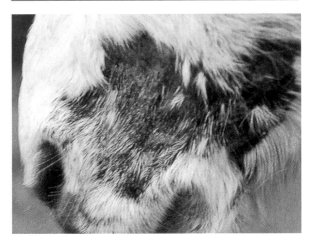

▲ ONCHOCERIASIS

Alopecia and depigmentation due to dying microfilariae

DISEASES AFFECTING THE METABOLISM

Disease / Geographical Spread	Symptoms	Cause	Treatment
Anhydrosis (p133) Humid environments, eg Gulf States, Hong Kong, Southern States of America.	Increasing inability to sweat, hair loss on face and flanks, panting, poor appetite, loss of condition.	Unknown; probable over-stimulation of sweat glands by high levels of adrenalin present in working horses in tropical conditions.	Non-specific; electrolyte therapy may help, also working in cooler hours, and air conditioning.
Azoturia (p135) *See* Conditions of the Musculature (p110) General.	*See* Conditions of the Musculature.	*See* Conditions of the Musculature.	*See* Conditions of the Musculature.
Dehydration (p145) General, especially in hot conditions.	Dull, depressed attitude, sunken eyes and dry, tight skin.	Complication of other disease, or loss of fluid through sweating during strenuous exercise.	Prompt administration of large quantities of water and electrolytes, by mouth or intravenously.
Grass sickness (p157) United Kingdom, Northern Europe, Southern America, Australia.	**Acute cases:** death in 2–3 days following severe colic, regurgitation of stomach contents and trembling muscles. **Chronic cases:** dull abdominal discomfort, severe loss of condition; horse stands with dipped back and feet together.	Interruption of autonomic nervous control of gut. Evidence suggests could be toxico-infection caused by overgrowth of *Clostridium botulinum* type C in the small intestine, triggered by nutritional and environmental changes.	Usually fatal, but high quality nursing aids survival of some chronic cases. As a result of interest in *Clostridium botulinum* type C as causal agent, work has started on production of a vaccine.
Heat stroke (p160) Anywhere in hot, humid conditions.	Rapid respiration, high pulse and temperature, red mucous membranes and unwillingness to move; heartbeat becomes chaotic and muscles twitch; collapse and death unless immediately treated.	Inability to dissipate bodyheat quickly enough, usually due to strenuous work in adverse conditions.	Cooling with large quantities of water, plus intravenous fluid and electrolytes.
Myoglobinuria (p169) General, first major outbreak in Scotland.	More than one in group of horses usually affected; seen lying down, frequently unable to rise from lateral to sternal recumbency; if standing, lethargic and disinclined to move; appetite often normal; blood tests show severe muscle damage; urine coffee-coloured.	Unknown.	Large quantities of intravenous fluids with anti-inflammatory drugs and vitamin preparations, calcium and steroids; however, disease is often fatal.

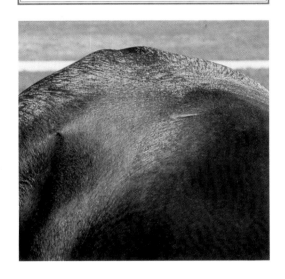

▼ DEHYDRATION

Salt deposits on the hindquarters of a dehydrated endurance horse

▲ GRASS SICKNESS

The emaciated condition that rapidly develops in chronic grass sickness

DISEASES AFFECTING THE FOAL

▼ ANGULAR LIMB DEFORMITY

A bilateral valgus deviation of the distal limbs – a common deformity of the foal

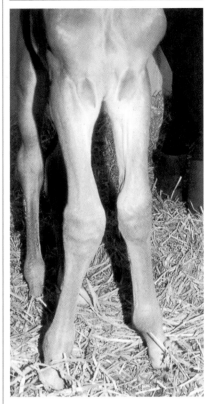

ANGULAR LIMB DEFORMITY

(left) A slight flexural deformity of both fore fetlocks in a large new-born foal

(below) A more severe case of congenital flexural deformity

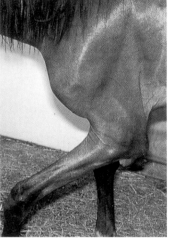

◄ ANGULAR LIMB DEFORMITY

A case of acquired flexural deformity in a well-grown four-month-old foal

▼ ANKYLOSIS OF JOINTS

Condition seen in a new-born Shetland

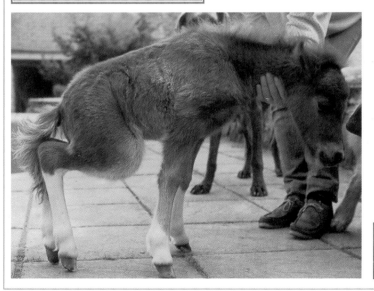

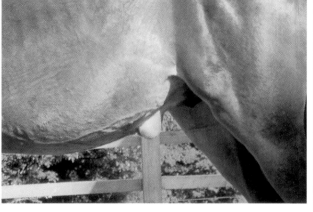

▲ HERNIAS

Umbilical hernia in a two-year-old

DISEASES AFFECTING THE FOAL

Conditions of the Infant Foal

Disease / Geographical Spread	Symptoms	Cause	Treatment
Ankylosis of joints (p133) (illus p120) *See also* Conditions of the Limbs (p106) General.	One or more joints fused in flexed position.	Congenital.	None; if foal born alive, euthanasia should be considered.
Atresia ani (p135) General.	Foal strains to pass first motion, colicky symptoms soon occur.	Foal born with anus and some or all of rectum missing.	Immediate surgery to construct anal opening.
Contracted tendons (p142) (illus p123) General.	Knuckling over of forefoot in young foals, with toe worn and bruised. Knuckling of fetlock joint in older foals and yearlings with pastern upright and fetlock moving forwards.	Disparity of growth between flexor tendons and bones of limb.	Emergency treatment necessary; decrease nutritional intake, plus corrective shoeing or surgery depending on condition.
Coprophagy (p143) General.	Eating dung.	Normal for young foals, probably to enhance intestinal flora and vitamin intake.	None.
Diarrhoea (p146) (illus p91) *See* Conditions of the Intestinal Tract (p90)	*See* Conditions of the Intestinal Tract.	*See* Conditions of the Intestinal Tract.	*See* Conditions of the Intestinal Tract.
Entropion (p149) (illus p84) General.	Eye closed and watery, eyelid rolled inwards, rubbing on cornea.	Congenital.	Temporary stitching to turn eyelid outwards.
Haemolytic disease (p158) General.	Frequent yawning, sleepiness, rapid breathing and heartbeat; whites of eyes and mucous membranes become yellow, urine may be bloodstained, progressive weakness.	Foal's red blood cells different to those of mare; antibodies absorbed via colostrum attack foal's red blood cells.	Transfusions of washed blood cells from mare.
Hernias (p161) General.	**Umbilical**: Swelling at umbilicus. **Inguinal**: Swelling in inguinal region.	**Umbilical**: Defect in abdominal wall. **Inguinal**: Abdominal contents herniate through inguinal ring.	**Umbilical**: Most regress, no treatment unless strangulated when surgical repair required. **Inguinal**: Surgical repair.
Hypothyroidism (p162) General.	Enlarged thyroid gland; foal lethargic and weak initially, then rapid recovery.	Deficiency of iodine in mare's ration during pregnancy, or more commonly, an excess of iodine in the diet, thought to suppress the ability of the thyroid gland to secrete thyroid hormone.	Rarely needed once the foal is standing and suckling.

Limb Deformity in Foals

Disease / Geographical Spread	Symptoms	Cause	Treatment
Angular limb deformity (p166) (illus p120) General.	Deviation of distal portion of fore or hind limb from normal line.	**New-born foals**: incomplete ossification of limb bones, slack joint capsules and ligaments; **older foals**: abnormal bone development.	In **new-borns** often self-correcting; if not, limb is splinted; in **older foals** surgical intervention is necessary.
Hyperextension (p167) (illus p122) General.	Fetlock joints fully extended.	Unknown.	Protection of pastern joints; refractory cases require heel extension fitted using plastic glue-on shoe.
Hyperflexion (p166) (illus p123) *See* Contracted Tendons General.	Contraction of tendons, fetlock joint and sometimes knee affected.	Unknown.	Often self-righting, otherwise splinting; extreme cases may never be athletically sound.

DISEASES AFFECTING THE FOAL

Disease / Geographical Spread	Symptoms	Cause	Treatment
Meconium, retained (p168) (illus p123) General.	Discomfort, tail twitching, foal increasingly lying down, often in awkward position; straining.	Difficulty in passing the large balls of meconium.	Liquid paraffin by mouth or as enema, surgery as last resort.
Navel ill (p169) General.	Navel cord hot and swollen, high temperature, loss of appetite, depression, discharging abscess forms in navel cord and joint ill may follow.	Infection of navel cord.	Navel treated with antiseptic after birth; once infected, repeated hot water bathing to encourage abscess to burst, plus antibiotics.
Neonatal maladjustment disease (p170) (illus p123) General	Vary from slight vagueness and staring attitude to complete seizure; loss of ability to suckle, fits or twitching of limbs.	Brain damage due to trauma during birth.	Stabilisation of foal, anti-convulsant drugs, light anaesthesia, constant supervision, feed by stomach tube or intravenous fluid therapy.
Orphan foal (p173) General.	None specific, foal may be weak or sickly.	Death of dam during or after birth, or rejection of foal.	Rear on foster mother (preferred), or by bottle-bucket-feeding.
Parrot mouth (p177) (illus p46) General.	Upper jaw protrudes beyond the lower jaw.	Congenital.	None if displacement minimal; regular dental care required for adults.
Patent urachus (p177) General.	Urination difficult, and urine seeps from stump of naval cord with infection of soiled area.	Failure of urachus to close on birth.	Cleaning and cautery of umbilicus; surgery may be required; course of antibiotics.
Pig mouth (p179) General.	Lower jaw protrudes beyond upper jaw.	Congenital.	None for minimal abnormality; possible euthanasia for more severe cases, as foal unable to suckle.
Pneumonia, foal (p180) Hot, dry climates eg Australia, California; rare in UK.	Loss of condition, chronic cough, variable appetite, sometimes nasal discharge, raised temperature and respiratory rate.	Inhalation of dust containing infective organism.	Long course of antibiotics.
Premature foal (p187) General.	Low bodyweight, weakness, difficulty in suckling and keeping warm, silky hair and skin, mucous membranes and tongue often brick red.	Failure of mare to sustain pregnancy to full term.	Warmth and adequate supply of colostrum essential, feeds small and frequent, preventative antibiotic cover.

HYPEREXTENSION▶

Hyperextension of the fetlock, a common condition in the new-born foal

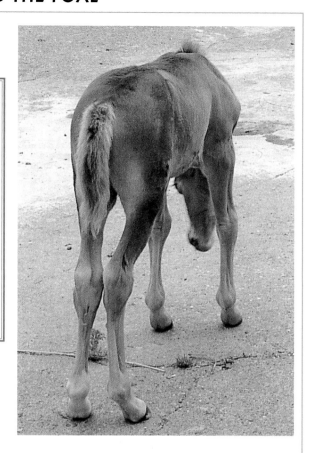

◄ HYPERFLEXION

A case of contracted tendons in a four-month-old foal

NEONATAL MALADJUSTMENT DISEASE ►

A typical attitude and posture of a foal with neonatal maladjustment disease

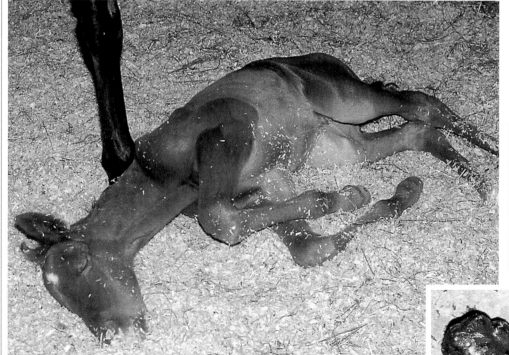

MECONIUM

A foal with retained meconium, exhibiting the usual low-grade colic

The typical appearance of a pellet of meconium

DISEASES AFFECTING THE FOAL

Disease / Geographical Spread	Symptoms	Cause	Treatment
Ruptured bladder (p190) General.	Similar to retained meconium, ie straining, rolling, lying in abnormal positions, abdomen distended.	Excessive pressure on foal's abdomen during birth.	Urgent surgical repair necessary.
Septicaemia (sleepy foal disease) (p193) General.	Loss of appetite, fever, depression, then coma and death.	Infection via placenta which rapidly spreads through bloodstream; development depends upon foal's level of immunity derived from colostrum.	Immediate commencement of course of antibiotics, intravenous fluid probably required, good nursing essential.
Septic arthritis, joint ill (p193) General.	Lameness, affected joints become hot and swollen, raised temperature, foal stops suckling and appears ill; irreparable joint damage quickly occurs.	Frequent sequel to navel ill or septicaemia, bacteria spreading to joints.	Long course of antibiotics starting immediately on diagnosis.
Wry nose (p205) General.	Foal is born with a twisted nose; varying degrees of malformation occur.	Malposition of foetus in the uterus, causing pressure on the developing head.	None if malformation is slight; surgery may be possible in a few cases; humane destruction in severe cases.
Conditions of the Suckling Foal			
Cerebella hypoplasia (p139) General.	Affects Arab and part-Arab foals; gradual loss of balance, high-stepping gait and head nodding; frequency of attacks increases until foal is recumbent.	Degeneration of cells in cerebellar region of brain.	No cure.
Combined immunodeficiency disease (p142) General.	Foal normal at birth, but within few weeks begins to suffer from a variety of respiratory diseases, intractable to treatment.	Genetic condition of Arab foals; due to recessive gene which causes failure of developing immune system.	Unrewarding; disease usually fatal.

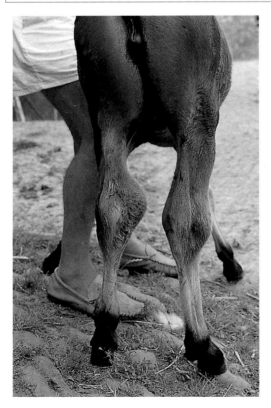

◀ SEPTIC ARTHRITIS, JOINT ILL

Joint ill in a two- to three-week-old foal

WRY NOSE ▶

A severe case of wry nose

DISEASES AFFECTING THE FOAL

Disease / Geographical Spread	Symptoms	Cause	Treatment
Parascaris equorum See parasites: roundworms (p175) *Also see* Conditions of the Respiratory System (p86) General.	Dullness, lethargy, loss of appetite; may have dirty nose and cough.	Large white worm present in the small intestine during first 9 months of foal's life.	Worm dam two weeks before foaling to reduce risk; worm foal every 6 weeks with effective anthelmintic.
Strongyloides westeri See parasites: roundworms (p177) General.	Transient scour; heavy infestations cause chronic diarrhoea and weight loss.	Small threadworm common in intestine of foals.	Dose with effective anthelmintic.
Tysser's disease (p201) General.	High temperature, depression, rapidly followed by collapse and death.	The organism *Bacillus piliformis* causes acute hepatitis.	No cure.
Ulcers (p201) General.	More marked after feeding; disinterested in suckling; grinding of teeth and chewing on straw; signs of stomach pain.	Unknown but associated with stress.	Antacids and human gastric ulcer drugs; removal of underlying cause.

Conditions of the Yearling

Wobbler disease (Cervical vertebral stenotic myelopathy [CVSM]) (p204) General.	Gradual loss of control of hind quarters and ability to stand.	Affects 1–2-year-old male Thoroughbreds; caused by narrowing of spinal canal which constricts spinal cord.	Medical: NSAIDs to reduce odema; control of diet in attempt to slow growth. Surgical techniques have been developed but risk severe complications.

DISEASES OF OLD AGE

Cushing's syndrome (p144) General.	Increased drinking and amount of urine; prone to laminitis and reduced exercise tolerance; coat becomes long, curly and shaggy; weight loss; decreased resistance to infection.	Affects aged horses and ponies; result of increased secretion of hormones due to a tumour in the pituitary gland.	Drugs: Pergolide™, cyproheptadine hypochloride and bromocriptine have been used with some success. A new drug called trilostane appears effective but more research needed.
Neoplasia (intestinal tumours) *See* Conditions of the Intestinal Tract (p91) General.	Chronic diarrhoea and weight loss.	Tumour of stomach and intestines, usually in older horses.	Surgical removal.

CUSHING'S SYNDROME▶

Note the shaggy, curly coat

Disease / Geographical Spread	Symptoms	Cause	Treatment
Clostridial myonecrosis (p140) General.	Acute soft swelling on site of intramuscular or extra vascular intravenous injection, usually chest, neck or gluteal muscles. High temperature, pain at affected site.	Infection of injection site with the bacteria *Clostridial perfringens* or *Clostridial septicum*, usually following injection with an irritant substance.	Emergency needing immediate treatment for survival. Removal of all dead tissue in affected area, with intense antibiotic and supportive treatment.
Equine polysaccharide storage myopathy (p152) General.	Affects heavier-muscled horses. Attacks can be regular or sporadic and are induced by exercise. Tucked-up appearance, abnormal sweating with twitching, tenseness and pain in large muscle groups. In severe cases muscle weakness leads to recumbency. Chronic cases show hind muscle wastage. Abnormal hind-limb gait also occurs.	Uncertain but apparently due to a genetically transferred abnormality of glycogen production in the muscle.	Dietary control, replacing carbohydrates with roughage and fats. Turnout, allowing constant natural exercise; slow build-up of work programme; stabling is contra-indicated.
Glycogen branching enzyme deficiency (p157) General.	Affects the Quarter Horse. Foals are born weak and lethargic. Weakness increases, resulting in death within about a month.	Inherited deficiency of glycogen branching enzyme (GBE) essential for glycogen production, leading to accumulation of abnormal glycogen molecules in skeletal and heart muscle.	None.
Hyperkalaemic periodic paralysis (p161) General, more common in America.	Periodic episodes of muscle stiffness and trembling spreading to more muscle groups as attack proceeds. Contraction of small muscles of face and sometimes prolapse of third eyelid. Often increased flaccidity of muscles leads to swaying, stumbling and recumbency. Full recovery occurs until next attack.	Genetic abnormality limited to descendants of the Quarter Horse stallion, Impressive.	Dietary control. IV isotonic saline or 5% dextrose solutions are used to decrease high serum potassium levels.

GLOSSARY OF TERMS

abscess Localised accumulation of pus surrounded by a fibrous capsule

acute The rapid onset of disease

aerobic Involving or requiring oxygen

anaerobic Living or occurring without oxygen

aneurism Ballooning of an artery or vein, or the wall of the heart

anthelmintics Drug effective against parasites

antibiotic A drug which kills bacteria or stops them multiplying

anti-protozoan A drug which kills protozoa or stops them multiplying

arrhythmia Irregular rhythm

asymptomatic Not showing or causing symptoms or signs

ataxia Inco-ordination

atrial fibrillation Rapid or inco-ordinated ventricular contraction of heart muscle

blepharospasm Spasm of eyelids

bronchodilator A drug which dilates the lung passages

broncholytic Substance that liquifies mucus in the bronchioles

buccal mucosa Lining of the oral cavity

carcinoma A cancerous growth

carotid Artery supplying the heart with blood

carpi Bones of the carpus (knee)

cerebellar Of the cerebellum

chronic Long-standing stage of disease or injury

ciliary (body) A body in the eye that stabilises the lens

clinical (manifestation of disease) Observable symptoms

congenital An abnormality that develops in the foetus *in utero*

COPD (RAO) Chronic obstructive pulmonary disease (now known as 'recurrent airway obstruction')

corpus luteum A gland that develops in the ovary in response to hormonal changes during the heat cycle

corticosteroid Generic term for cortizone family of drugs

dermoid (cyst) Within the skin

diuretics Drugs which cause the kidneys to excrete more water

DMSO (Dimethylsulphoxide) Used as an agent to transport substances through the skin; has pain-killing effects

EIPH Exercise-induced pulmonary haemorrhage

elective surgery Surgery done through choice

electrolyte Essential ions contained in plasma

endocarditis Infection of internal surface of heart, generally involving the valves

endoscopy Internal examination using an endoscope

endotoxic (shock) Acute illness caused by the spread of toxins through the bloodstream

endotoxin A chemical contained in the coat of gram-negative bacteria, commonly *E coli*

EPM Equine protozoal myoencephalitis

ethmoid (haematoma) Vascular growth occurring in the posterior nasal cavity

expectorant (drugs) Drugs that encourage the expulsion of phlegm

fibrillation *See* atrial fibrillation

filariad (worm) A nematode spread by mosquitoes affecting various parts of the body

fistula A long, narrow opening connecting the lumen of an organ or a cavity with the skin surface

gram negative/positive bacteria A method of separating bacteria into two main groups depending upon which colour they stain with Gram's stain: pink = negative; purple = positive

haematoma Blood-filled swelling, due to trauma

haemoglobin A protein that is contained in red blood cells and has the ability to absorb oxygen

haemorrhage A discharge of blood from the blood vessels due to rupture

Hobday/tieback operation Two surgical procedures to improve the movement of air through the larynx

impaction Obstruction of the gut by impacted food material or a foreign body

lactobacillus (-rich) Beneficial bacteria needed in the gut for good digestion

lavage Washing

lesion Wound

lumen (of uterus) The space (within the uterus, or other body part)

medial condyle (of femur) Inner protuberance

mucolytic Substance that liquifies mucus

mucopurulent Containing mucus and pus

myocarditis Inflammation of the heart muscles

myocosis Fungal disease

neurectomy Operation to sever nerves

NSAIDs Non-steroidal anti-inflammatory drugs

oedema Fluid-filled swelling

papillomata Warts

patella Knee-cap (in horse = stifle)

pathogen Organism causing disease

perineum The area of skin surrounding the external genitalia and rectum

phenylbutazone A non-steroidal anti-inflammatory drug (NSAID)

photophobia A dislike of sunlight

polyps Pedunculated growths emerging from mucous membrane

potentiated (sulphonamide) A mixture of two anti-bacterial drugs, the combined effect of which is greater than the sum of their individual effects

purulent Full of or exuding pus

rupture Broken or burst tissues due to internal pressure

secondary (eg laminitis, infection) Complication predisposed by an initial or primary illness/condition

sectioning (of collateral navicular suspensory ligaments) Separation or severing

sedative Calming and relaxing drug

sub-acute Less severe than acute form of early stage of disease

sub-clinical Not visually apparent

subcutaneous Under the skin

submucosal Under the mucous membranes

sulphonamides Synthetic anti-bacterial drugs

sulci (of frog) The indentations to either side of the frog

synthetic pyrethrum Insecticidal drug

tieback/Hobday operation *see Hobday/tieback operation*

vasodilators Drugs which dilate blood vessels

Part III

A–Z OF DISEASES

ABORTION (illus p96)

The failure of a pregnancy before the foetus is capable of independent survival, between 0–300 days of gestation. Beyond 300 days, early parturition is defined as premature birth. The factors that lead up to an abortion, and the process of abortion, vary according to the stage at which it occurs:

Between 0–15 days
Failure of the fertilised egg to develop may be due to lethal gene mutations or because the maternal environment is unsuitable to sustain foetal growth.

16–35 days
The conceptus is resorbed; however, the other signs of early pregnancy such as a closed cervix, a tonic uterus and a persistent corpus luteum can remain for up to three months. Normal cyclic behaviour will not return until lysis (breaking down) of the persistent corpus luteum occurs either naturally or as a result of prostaglandin treatment. Known as pseudopregnancy type 1.

36–140 days
The maintenance of pregnancy comes increasingly under the control of the hormone equine chorionic gonadotrophin (eCG) which is secreted by the endometrial cups. These clearly defined groups of specialised cells which develop at the base of the pregnant horn of the uterus continue to be active even if pregnancy failure occurs, and they secrete enough eCG hormone into the circulation to prevent the mare from returning to normal oestrus activity. Very little can be done to avoid this and it can be 90 to 150 days after the embryonic loss before the mare returns to oestrus. Known as pseudopregnancy type 2.

140 days to term
This stage of gestation begins when the role of eCG hormone ends and when the maintenance of the pregnancy is taken over by hormones secreted from the placenta and foetus; it ends with birth. Death of the foetus causes a rapid drop in circulating oestrogens and progesterone; these hormonal changes relax the cervix and stimulate contractions of the uterine muscle which in turn cause rapid expulsion of the foetus. This process is what is traditionally called an abortion.

The mare returns rapidly to normal cyclic activity if the abortion occurs during the summer months; in the winter she might go straight into winter anoestrus (see p133).

The signs of imminent abortion may be identical to those of normal parturition, such as development of the mammary glands, waxing and milk formation. They are more common when abortion is due to twinning or a developing infection, when the first and second stages of labour occur but are shorter than in a normal birth and are generally uncomplicated. If an infection of the placenta is the cause of the abortion then its expulsion can be prolonged, and treatment necessary to ensure complete removal. In some cases the warning signs of abortion are absent, and expulsion of the foetus is rapid and uncomplicated.

There are non-infective and infective causal agents of abortion.

Non-infective reasons
■ *The presence of twins:* A common occurrence, but as the mare's placenta is designed to support only one foetus, all too often one of a pair finds that the division of resources is unequal and its share of the essential nutrients is not sufficient to support growth. At some time, normally during early pregnancy, the smaller twin gives up the unequal struggle and dies. This generally upsets the regulatory hormones enough to cause the expulsion of both twins. Less frequently the live twin is carried to full term and is born alive, but often so underweight that the prospect of survival is severely compromised.

Early diagnosis of twinning is obviously very important, as 65 per cent of twins are aborted at or before the eighth month, and the survival rate in those that continue to full term is calculated to be only about 50 per cent. Also, any attempt to remove one conceptus by manipulation must be made before the endometrial cups start to produce the hormone eCG at about 40 days; after this stage an aborted mare will not breed again for several months. Sometimes the smaller twin is resorbed, leaving only one embryo to complete its development. However, if twins are diagnosed, the most practical course is probably to abort both and start again.

■ *Twisted umbilical cord:* The umbilical cord, especially when too long, may twist upon itself or around the trunk or a limb of the foetus. This may so impede the circulation of blood from placenta to foetus as to endanger the health of the foetus, even causing its death and abortion.

■ *Congenital abnormalities:* When unduly serious, these will cause the death of the developing foetus.

■ *Mare reproductive loss syndrome:* MRLS is the term used to describe an abortion storm that occurred in Kentucky during the spring of 2001 and since. It is now reasonably certain that it is caused by ingestion of the eastern tent caterpillar which lives on wild black cherry trees. When weather conditions are favourable, large numbers of caterpillars develop and although the specific causal agent has not been identified, abortions are always associated with these rises in caterpillar numbers.

Infective reasons
■ *Bacterial:* Bacterial infection of the uterus and placenta can occur via the vagina or from the mare's bloodstream. The bacterial types most often implicated are b-haemolytic streptococci and coliforms. Local infection spreads from the vagina through the cervix and causes a varying degree of placentitis (infection of the placenta); this is common in later pregnancy when the weight of the uterus and loss of body condition of the mare may cause vulval distortion and breakdown of the vaginal seal. The resulting pneumovagina with associated bacterial infection and vaginitis can lead to infection spreading through the cervix to the placenta: this placentitis may affect the health of the foetus and eventually cause abortion.

Symptoms = 🔲   Cause/diagnosis = 🔲   Treatment = 🔲

Septicaemic infections of the foetus (those that spread from infection in the mare's bloodstream) can enter the foetus via the mare's blood supply, the placenta and the foetal blood supply. The resultant septicaemia can cause foetal death and subsequent abortion.

■ *Fungal:* A mycotic abortion is generally first seen as a small, unhealthy foetus lying on the floor, often surrounded by a thickened, diseased placenta. Mycotic infections can occur following the ingestion of mouldy hay, or more commonly due to contamination of the uterus at the time of the previous birth. The fungus normally infects the placenta causing large, thickened areas of inflammation. Abortion generally occurs later in pregnancy.

■ *Viral:* Viral abortion can be caused by two different families of virus: **Equine herpes type 1 (EHV1, rhinopneumonitis)** is the most common, being endemic in Britain and the United States. It causes an upper respiratory tract infection, more common in young horses that are in contact with the virus for the first time. It causes a short-lived immunity and spreads rapidly through a susceptible population; in the pregnant mare it can cause sufficient damage to the uterus to compromise the viability of the foetus. In these cases no virus or viral damage can be demonstrated in the aborted foetus. EHV1 can also cross the placental barrier and enter the body of the foetus where it damages the internal organs, especially the lungs, liver and kidneys. Death of the foal follows rapidly and abortion occurs. Infection of the nearly full-term foal results in a stillbirth or the delivery of a weak, sickly foal that does not survive long. The virus can also remain dormant in the mare for long periods, causing no symptoms until activated by some form of stress. Again, in the pregnant mare this resurgence can cause damage to the foetus and subsequent abortion; also serious neurological complications to the mare (see p150).

Control of the disease is difficult. Pregnant mares should be kept away from young animals and preferably in small groups. Any aborting mares should be isolated at once, and the products of the abortion should be burnt. Visiting mares should not be allowed on to infected premises, nor should any mares be allowed to leave. Two vaccines against EHV1 are available in this country, and both are licensed for use against abortion (see p150). There is some doubt about its efficiency, but from a practical point of view, frequent and regular use in the pregnant mare reduces the incidence of abortion storms.

Equine viral arteritis (see p152): this virus had not caused disease in Great Britain for many years, but in 1992 it was introduced by an imported Polish stallion, a symptomless carrier. It spreads by aerosol infection and also by venereal routes. The resulting outbreak caused illness and abortions amongst the susceptible mare population. A voluntary freeze on all horse movement and vigorous control measures on infected and in-contact studs eradicated the disease, and no other outbreaks have occurred.

Diagnosis

Every attempt should be made to diagnose the cause of any abortion. A full examination of the placenta and the foetus should be carried out, and samples sent to a specialist laboratory. It is often more satisfactory to send the complete foetus. Bacteriological swabs and perhaps a biopsy of the endometrium should be taken to check uterine pathology as a possible cause. The recent finding that EHV1 can cause abortion by damaging the uterus rather than by infecting the foetus leads to the scenario where a foetus with no viral pathology present could still have been aborted as a result of EHV1 infection. Only a uterine biopsy could lead to the correct diagnosis if this were the case.

Rarely necessary. Following abortion the mare rapidly returns to normal, and the only procedure which might be prudent is to ascertain whether any residual infection is present. If so, the infection must be treated before any attempt is made to get the mare back in foal.

ABSCESS (illus p113)

The reaction produced by the body in attempting to overcome a local infection.

Initially a swelling developing under the skin, in the early stages diffuse, hot and painful but which then becomes harder. As it matures, the swelling becomes more discrete, and the centre becomes softer and cooler and less painful. The skin over the centre becomes thinner and eventually ruptures, releasing quantities of pus; this can take 2–7 days. In the early stages the horse is off colour, often with a high temperature, and off his food; as the maturation process proceeds the horse reverts to normal.

In most cases the result of a penetrating wound allowing a foreign material into the body, either a splinter of wood, or dirt, grass seeds or metal such as a nail penetrating the foot. Some systemic infections such as strangles (see p197) cause abscessation of the lymph glands.

■ In the early stages, to prevent an abscess from developing, it is essential to clean the wound thoroughly with an effective antiseptic preparation, paying special attention to the depth of the wound; hibitane- or iodine-based scrubs are best.
■ Antibiotic treatment, at an early stage, might nip the developing abscess in the bud and resolve the situation.
■ Anti-tetanus treatment will be needed if the horse has not been vaccinated.
■ If an abscess is forming, antibiotic treatment is contra-indicated, and the only treatment necessary is the application of hot poultices or drawing agents such as magnesium sulphate paste. This will encourage the abscess to come to a head and perhaps to burst; if not, your veterinary surgeon might have to lance it. Either way the cavity should be kept open by regular irrigation whilst healing takes place from the base outwards.

ADENOVIRUS

A common pathogen of the young horse, generally credited with causing the cold that most foals seem to catch soon after weaning.

A moderately severe disease of the upper respiratory tract may occur in the normal foal. The first signs of a problem are a high temperature, often associated with diarrhoea, and a nasal discharge which rapidly becomes muco-purulent. A blood sample will reveal a drop in the total number of white blood cells.

Adenovirus is the cause of a fatal pneumonia in immunodeficient Arabian foals (see p142).

 ■ Warmth and good nursing are all that is usually needed.
■ Antibiotic cover to treat the inevitable secondary infection might be necessary.
■ The use of mucolytic drugs such as Sputulosin (Boehringer Ingleheim) might help.
■ Electrolyte fluids, either intravenous or by mouth, might be necessary where the diarrhoea is persistent.

AFRICAN HORSE SICKNESS

Synonym: horse sickness fever

A seasonal (summer) viral disease endemic in areas of Africa and occurring in the Middle East. It causes damage to the circulatory and respiratory systems and is spread via the bite of species of Culicoides (biting midges) and perhaps mosquitoes. Outbreaks occurred from 1987 to 1990 on the Iberian peninsula, although a vigorous control programme has, for the moment, eradicated it from these areas. Characterised by a persistent fever which, in the chronic type, can last for up to a month. The incubation period is usually between 5 and 7 days. Amongst the Equidae, horses are the most susceptible, followed by mules, donkeys and lastly zebra, which are resistant and show little sign of the disease.

Appears as one of three distinct clinical syndromes; also, the pulmonary type and the cardiac type might combine to form a fourth mixed type.

Acute pulmonary type

High fever with a temperature in excess of 40.5°C, accompanied by profuse sweating and associated with severe respiratory signs; these include uncontrollable coughing, laboured breathing, and a yellow frothy nasal discharge. The membranes of the eyes, nose and mouth rapidly become very congested, and collapse and death can occur in a few hours. Those few horses that survive suffer severe respiratory distress for many weeks.

Subacute cardiac type

This form attacks the heart: fluid collects between the heart and the pericardium (the tough fibrous sac surrounding the heart), the lungs also fill with fluid and an endocarditis develops. Externally the head swells, followed by the neck, brisket and chest. The mucous membranes become cyanotic (blue in colour) due to the heart damage, and petechiae (blood specks) develop in the mouth, especially under the tongue. Intermittent fevers occur, with temperatures up to 41.5°C.

Chronic fever type

Less severe, in fact clinical signs often go unrecognised. A rise in body temperature, up to 41.5°C, is apparent in the first few days of infection, also a loss of appetite. A slight cough and breathlessness, also conjunctivitis may be present. The fever abates in a few days and the horse returns to normal. This form is uncommon in the highly susceptible horse, but may be seen in donkeys and mules.

 Diagnosis

Appreciation of the various clinical and epidemiological signs should lead to an initial diagnosis which can be confirmed by positive complement fixation and serum neutralisation tests on samples of blood.

■ Nothing specific, but good nursing will help ensure recovery in the less severe cases.
■ The spread of the disease can be controlled by the use of vaccine; by removing horses from the areas where the insect vectors (disease carriers) are active, ie by housing horses; and by preventing infected horses from being bitten by the midges.

AFTERBIRTH, RETAINED

see **Placenta**

ANAEMIA

A shortage of haemoglobin in the blood, due to either a reduction in the number of circulating red blood cells or a reduction in the haemoglobin concentration in

those cells. It is never a primary disease, but occurs secondary to an underlying condition.

 Poor performance is probably the most significant indicator because it is directly related to the lack of haemoglobin which is an essential part of the oxygen-carrying function of the blood, oxygen being vital to the energy pump within the cell. The result is a weak, lethargic horse, and as the anaemia worsens the appetite is depressed and the hair becomes dull and lifeless. The heart sounds might develop a murmur, and as the condition becomes severe the mucous membranes appear pale. Anaemia of this severity leads to profound weakness, together with increasing inco-ordination and finally collapse and death.

Acute haemorrhage

Copious blood loss as a consequence of injury or after a major operation will lead to acute anaemia. If the horse survives the immediate effects of the haemorrhage the bone marrow is stimulated to produce more red blood cells and in approximately three weeks they are back to normal numbers.

Chronic haemorrhage

Commonly found in the horse with a heavy worm burden. The redworm which affects the horse is a bloodsucker (*Strongylus vulgaris*), and in large numbers can rapidly produce a severe anaemia: the constant drain of blood and the attempts to replace the red blood cells can lead to a situation in which the body reserves of iron and the bone marrow's ability to produce blood cells are both exhausted. These deficiencies can take a long time to correct.

Lice and ticks also suck blood, and when present in large numbers can cause this type of anaemia.

Dietary deficiencies

Rarely a cause, because the levels of those chemicals necessary for the production of haemoglobin – iron, copper and cobalt, vitamins and trace elements – are present in adequate amounts in the normal feed of a horse. However, strenuous training can sometimes cause a temporary anaemia because high levels of work demand a fast turnover of blood and tissue, and this can use up the available stores of iron and vitamin B12. Stress in its own right can cause erythropoesis (depressed red blood cell production) and increased red blood cell destruction together with an increased fragility, all leading to anaemia and loss of form.

One vitamin, folic acid, plays an essential part in the production of both red and white blood cells. Folic acid is found in abundance in fresh grass, alfalfa or haylage but is destroyed as grass is made into hay, especially badly made hay. Thus stabled horses fed on a diet of hard food and hay can become deficient in folic acid and, as a result, develop anaemia.

The primary cause of the anaemia must be established and corrected, and then the anaemia, a secondary condition, will disappear.
■ Obviously acute haemorrhage must be quickly controlled (see p64) and the loss of body fluid made good. Then a high-protein diet and an iron-rich supplement will help the bone marrow to replace the missing red blood cells. Injections of vitamin B12 will also help.
Chronic anaemia due to parasitic disease will respond to the same treatment once the initial cause has been removed.
■ Treatment of anaemia due to a deficiency is simple once the deficiency is known: for example, the anaemia of the winter-fed horse on a diet of hay and grain can be cured by the addition of folic acid to the diet, or it can be prevented by feeding alfalfa or silage, both rich sources of this vitamin.
■ Exercise-induced anaemia can also be cured very easily if the high level of stress is reduced: just give the horse a few months' complete rest. However, it is much more difficult to reverse the anaemia and still keep the workload high. In this circumstance a complete check of the diet is essential, any imbalances should be corrected, and the major components changed if necessary; though remember that any change of diet should always be gradual. It might help to alter the mental stimuli: introduce some fun into the daily training, or even branch out into a completely different discipline for a few hours a week.

ANEURISM (illus p89)

A swelling in an artery caused by a weakening of the arterial wall. This allows the positive pressure of the blood passing through the artery to balloon the lumen of the vessel.

Rarely anything that can be observed in the live horse, but it is possible that the aneurism might burst, causing a fatal haemorrhage. This is more likely to occur during a period of maximal effort and is often why horses on the racetrack or cross-country course will suddenly collapse and die.

The migrating larvae of the redworm *Strongylus vulgaris* (see p176) spend part of their life cycle in the walls of the mesenteric arteries; their presence weakens the wall and allows the development of an aneurism. This is by far the most common cause of an aneurism. However, the development and use of ivermectins, which are very effective at removing redworm in both its adult and larval stages, has markedly reduced the incidence of aneurism formation from this cause.

Until an aneurism has burst there are no clinical signs, and so no indication that treatment is needed – and once it has burst it is too late. Preventing the formation of the aneurism by removing the larvae before they have the chance to damage the arterial wall is a much better course of action.

ANHYDROSIS

Synonym: dry coat

An inability to sweat. Occurs in horses that are kept in an environment that is permanently hot and humid, eg racehorses performing in the Gulf States, Hong Kong and the southern states of America.

An increasing inability to sweat as the ambient temperature and humidity increase. However, most horses retain the ability to sweat under the mane, along the brisket and perineum. Hair loss occurs on the face and flanks. Panting is a common feature, as the horse attempts to regulate body temperature, which can rise to 42°C (107°F) after moderate exercise. Performance at competition level becomes impossible. Appetite is poor and it becomes increasingly difficult to maintain body condition.

Unknown, in spite of considerable investigation. Probably the continual high levels of adrenalin in the blood present in horses working in the tropics overload the ability of the sweat glands to function.

 ■ There is no uniformly successful treatment.
■ Oral and also intravenous electrolyte therapy help in some cases.
■ Air-conditioned stables, attention paid to cooling out at all times, and working out in the cool of the early morning will all reduce the effects of the condition.
■ Most horses improve as the cold season approaches, but intractable cases have to be moved to a colder climate before the ability to sweat returns.

ANKYLOSIS OF JOINTS (illus p120)

The complete inability of a joint to flex or extend. This can occur at any age.

Injury or disease, or as a result of elective surgery ie as a treatment for spavin (see p195). More often found in the new-born foal suffering from congenital flexural deformities (see p166).

None, once a joint has ankylosed.

ANOESTRUS

A condition where the ovaries show no cyclic activity whatsoever. A normal state for mares in the depths of winter, but can extend into spring and early summer especially if the mare is in poor condition. In spring the state of anoestrus changes, through a transitional period, into the cyclic activity of summer and autumn; it then returns as winter approaches. Lactating mares can be an exception (see p163). During anoestrus the ovaries are small and hard with a few small follicles present.

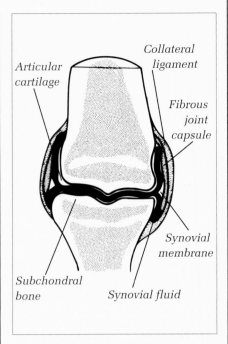 The normal state for a mare during the winter months. A long cold spring and poor condition in the mare can extend anoestrus into the spring and early summer.

■ Exposing mares to an extended daily period of light, and increasing the energy intake of food from December onwards, will encourage an early return to cyclic activity.

■ At least 16 hours of good quality light each day are necessary.

■ Drugs are relatively ineffective.

ANTHRAX

An acute, rapidly fatal infectious disease caused by *bacillus anthracis*. A notifiable disease (ie the appropriate government department must be informed) in the UK and most other countries.

Most common are the per-acute and acute forms typified by sudden death. In the living horse a high body temperature 42°C (107°F), depression and respiratory distress are the usual clinical signs.

Sub-acute and chronic forms of the disease appear less often; manifested initially as a severe colic. An enlarged spleen can be palpated by rectum, the throat often swells, and bloody discharges appear from nose and mouth. If untreated, death intervenes by 8 days.

The ingestion of spore-contaminated food.

■ The drug of choice is penicillin administered in large doses intramuscularly every 8 hours.

■ Vaccines against anthrax are available in the United States, but severe side-effects have been recorded.

ARTHRITIS (illus p107)

Synonyms: degenerative joint disease, DJD, osteo-arthrosis, secondary joint disease

An inflamed joint, resulting from infection, such as seen following a wound to a joint or as a sequel to septicaemia in the foal; or that is associated with the more common syndrome, degenerative joint disease.

Acute arthritis
Pain, swelling and increasing warmth of the affected joint, often associated with loss of appetite and a rise in body temperature. If untreated, abscesses might form in the damaged or infected joint and irreversible damage to the joint surfaces occur.

Chronic arthritis
Increasing stiffness and swelling associated with one or more joints. Lameness which often wears off with exercise.

Acute arthritis generally follows an insult to the joint, either trauma such as a penetrating wound and subsequent infection, or localisation of a general infection in one or more joints (see below).

The causes of *chronic arthritis*, or *degenerative joint disease*, are not so clear cut. Repeated trauma to the synovial membrane and the cartilaginous surfaces of the joint is certainly one of the more important reasons. Sports which call for a high degree of twisting and turning, ill-conceived training schedules that put unacceptable strain upon immature joints, and a body conformation that stresses one or more joints, all have a part to play in the development of this disease. Inside the joint the problem seems to be twofold: there is a gradual loss of cartilage from the bearing surfaces of the joint, sometimes right down to the underlying bone; and a concurrent growth of new bone, probably in an attempt to realign the weight-bearing surfaces.

The treatment of *acute arthritis* should be considered an emergency.

■ Antibiotics are essential in cases of infective arthritis, and should be considered as a precaution in all cases of hot, painful joints.

■ In serious cases where the joint is grossly infected, joint lavage might be necessary.

■ The joint should be immobilised whenever possible.

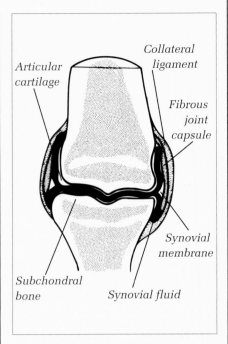

Articular cartilage

Collateral ligament

Fibrous joint capsule

Synovial membrane

Subchondral bone

Synovial fluid

Chronic arthritis or degenerative joint disease cannot be cured, as once the degenerative changes have occurred they cannot be reversed; therefore every effort should be made to prevent the condition in the first place.

■ Young horses should not be overfed and should be allowed to develop naturally.

■ Training methods should always be commensurate with the horse's age and experience.

■ Joint trauma should be investigated thoroughly and the correct treatment instigated immediately.

For those horses unfortunate enough to develop the condition there are treatment régimes that will help:

■ An initial period of rest seems to be beneficial, but in my experience regular in-hand exercise and a gradual build-up to previous levels of fitness allows the normal repair processes to catch up with the damage, and seems to keep more horses functionally sound.

■ Treatment with intra-articular steroids is certainly beneficial in the early stages, but there is mounting evidence that their long-term use is contra-indicated.

■ Non-steroidal anti-inflammatory drugs, of which phenylbutazone (bute) is the most common, are widely used to control the pain associated with the long-standing case. This use of bute causes an emotional response in some people, but there is no doubt that many thousands of elderly

Symptoms = ⦿   Cause/diagnosis = ✕   Treatment = ⊞

horses and ponies would be denied the quality of life that they are entitled to expect in their declining years, were it not for the odd sachet of bute.

■ For the long-term treatment of chronic osteo-arthritis, pentosan polysulphate, hyaluronic acid and glycosaminoglycan polysulphate – a group of slow-acting drugs – are useful. The latter is not licenced for use in the UK but is used in other parts of the world in preventing osteoarthritis in that most demanding sport, endurance racing. They can be given intra-articularly or by intramuscular injection and seem to work by providing the building blocks to build and maintain healthy cartilage.

ATRESIA ANI

A condition found in the new-born foal. The foal is born with the anus and some or all of the rectum missing.

The foal strains continually trying to pass the first motion. Colicky symptoms appear quickly.

Examination of the perineum region shows no anal opening, although if the rectum is present the impacted faeces cause a swelling where the anus should be located.

Immediate surgery is necessary to construct an anal opening.

AURAL PLAQUE (illus p84)

Synonym: aural papilloma

Affects the skin inside the ear; seen in any breed and age of horse.

White plaques of crusty material develop in collections on the inside surface of the ear. When this material is removed, thickened pink skin is exposed. The lesions do not appear to irritate the horse in that they are not accompanied by head shaking and ear twitching, but the lesions are painful and the horse will resent any interference to the affected ear.

Previously thought to be a reaction to the constant bites of the small black flies

that are found in the ear during the summer months. Although reaction to these fly bites certainly aggravates the condition, the primary cause is now thought to be an infection by the virus that causes warts in horses. Once the plaques have developed, they remain indefinitely.

■ None, once the plaques have formed, although removing the plaque material and treating the area with an anti-inflammatory ointment does reduce the size of the lesion.

■ Ear protectors worn throughout the summer are of some use in preventing flies from irritating the lesions.

AZOTURIA (EXERTIONAL RHABDOMYOLYSIS)

Synonyms: Monday morning disease, 'setfast'; tying up

Traditionally this disease affected draught horses that were rested on Sunday but still received full rations and were then expected to do a full day's work on Monday. The condition is now seen more often in competition horses, especially those on a high plane of nutrition and an irregular workload. Mares seem to be more prone to the condition and some horses develop recurrent attacks. It affects horses while they are working, and is often more prevalent when they are also subjected to environmental stress.

It is now considered that there are two forms of ER: sporadic and chronic.

■ *Sporadic ER:* seen in horses that have always worked well but suddenly show signs of tying up. It occurs commonly when the level of training suddenly increases forcing the muscles to work harder than they are used to. It can also occur during exhaustive exercise such as an endurance race. In these cases it is probably due to a collection of insults. High body temperature, loss of electrolytes and depletion of energy stores all have a role to play in an attack of this nature. Most horses suffering this type of ER recover completely and rarely have another attack.

■ *Chronic ER:* is seen in the younger horse and is typified by recurrent attacks that occur whenever the horse exercises. One type of chronic ER is Equine polysaccaride storage myopathy (see p152). Another is known as Recurrent Exertional Rhabdomyolysis (RER) which occurs in

many breeds of horse and seems to be due to an abnormality in which muscle cells regulate calcium during contraction. Excitement and stress also seem to play a part in the development of the condition in that it often occurs in fillies at their first maiden race, in inexperienced endurance horses being held to a slower pace than they want, or during a horse's first show.

Initially an unwillingness to continue working. The horse becomes anxious, sweats copiously and moves in a stilted fashion. If only mildly affected, its gait might just be a little short behind; more seriously and it can come to a complete halt. The urine can vary from red-brown to black in colour, this depending upon the amount of damage done to the muscles and the concentration of breakdown products (mainly myoglobin) circulating in the blood and excreted in the urine. The affected muscles, generally those of the hindquarters, rapidly become hot, very hard, swollen and very painful. The muscle-specific enzymes creatine kinase (CK) and aspartate aminotransferase (AST) are elevated following an attack: 3 to 6 hours after the insult CK can reach a peak of 500,000 iu/l, falling back to a normal level in 3 to 4 days, whilst 24 to 48 hours after the insult AST reaches a lower peak of up to 20,000 iu/l, falling to normal 10 to 14 days later. These enzyme levels provide a useful diagnostic aid as long as due attention is paid to the time the sample is taken relative to the attack. CK levels especially rise and fall very quickly. However, CK and AST levels tend to remain higher in horses that suffer from RER.

An enigma. Traditionally explained as being due to the build-up of blood lactate following the rapid breakdown of the glycogen store accumulated during the period of rest; it was suggested that the level of lactic acidosis was sufficient to damage the muscle fibres. Although many cases are associated with horses on a high plane of nutrition, and those subjected to changes in feeding and workload, recent research can find no evidence that lactic acidosis is the cause. Certainly in cases of RER it is likely that unknown factors affecting the levels of calcium within the muscle cell are responsible for a build-up of calcium within the cell which in turn causes damage and death of the cell.

Strict attention to the diet and workload are essential in order to prevent further attacks. Changing the ratio of nutrients to include a higher fibre content might also help.
■ Immediate treatment: reduce the pain and swelling with non-steroidal anti-inflammatory drugs; provide local heat over the affected muscles; in milder cases, gentle exercise. Severe cases should be box-rested until the pain and stiffness disappear, then gentle exercise and paddock rest are indicated.
■ Intravenous electrolytes are essential in all but the mildest cases so that the breakdown products of this condition are adequately flushed through the kidneys.

BACK INJURIES (illus p110)

The spinal column, and hence the back of a horse, is an immensely strong and rigid structure, therefore injuries and disease affecting it and causing a 'bad back' (as suffered in human terms) are consequently rare in the horse. However, injury and disease to the structures that make up the back can occur, causing considerable pain and loss of athletic ability.

Acute injury
Pain at the site of injury – this identified by careful examination – and a varying degree of immobility. Often only the forequarters can move, the hindquarters remaining rooted to the ground.

Chronic injury
Initially an increasing unwillingness/inability to carry out movements that previously caused no problems. Thus back injuries/disease should be suspected in those horses which suddenly refuse to jump or start knocking the top rail; which 'hollow out' over a jump; which cannot 'flatten' when asked for that 100 per cent

racing effort; and which start complaining when their rider tries to mount.

Most commonly injury. A badly fitting saddle causes bruising and acute spasm of the thoracic and lumber muscles. A crashing fall whilst jumping causes pelvic injuries, while even rolling in the field onto a badly placed rock can damage the back sufficiently to interfere with normal function. In the older horse, arthritis of the sacro-iliac joint can cause considerable pain, quite enough to prevent normal activity.

Other horses (fortunately few in number) develop a condition where the dorsal processes of the lumbar vertebrae grow too close together ('kissing spines') and start rubbing against each other. This can cause considerable pain.

Surgery: some pelvic fractures might respond to plating or pinning the fractured portions together, but generally the internal forces that act within the pelvis render surgery inappropriate. The kissing spine syndrome, however, can be relieved by surgically increasing the space between spines.
■ Anti-inflammatory drugs and rest are generally effective for other back injuries.
■ The attentions of 'back people' who claim to be able to 'replace the misplaced disk' or 'align the cervical vertebrae': considerable argument exists about their effectiveness. Whilst it is difficult to understand how a puny human, even with the help of the horse's weight, can manipulate such a rigid structure, success, according to some owners, does sometimes follow such procedures.

BLEEDER (illus p84 & 87)

A horse that bleeds from one or both nostrils, most often during or after exercise.

Appearance of blood at one or both nostrils, commonly associated with a period of extreme effort. The amount of blood is variable, normally minimal but in cases of guttural pouch haemorrhage due to erosion of the carotid artery it is usually profuse, even life-threatening.

Bleeding from ethmoid tumours is associated with foetid breath.

■ Exercise-induced pulmonary haemorrhage (see p153); this is the most common.
■ Infections of the guttural pouch; these can cause life-threatening haemorrhage (see p158).
■ A non-neoplastic growth found at the back of the nose called an ethmoid haematoma (see p153).

Depends upon the exact cause of the haemorrhage and is covered in each relevant section.

BOIL

A localised infection of the skin.

Occurs either as a single entity as a result of an infection developing in a break in the skin; or more commonly, as a generalised infection throughout the skin. A boil starts as a small, painful papule which enlarges over the next few days exuding serum and developing a covering scab. Significant oedema can accompany the development, especially if the boils are few in number. The lesions can be extremely painful while active.

Typically starts off as an infection developing in the hair follicle, and this spreads into the surrounding skin, causing the above symptoms. The bacteria *Staphylococci* are usually to blame.

Boils are commonly seen after the horse has been clipped, especially if the rug used is dirty. In fact unhygienic conditions and boils are usual companions.

■ Bathe the individual boil with hot water to encourage it to mature and burst. Antibiotic or antiseptic ointment should then be applied.
■ If the boils are numerous, a systemic antibiotic should be used.
■ Antiseptic skin washes such as Hexocil or iodophor shampoos used daily are effective for the generalised type.

BONE, BOG SPAVIN

see **Spavin**

Symptoms = 👁 Cause/diagnosis = 🦴 Treatment = 💊

BORNA DISEASE

A virus disease of horses and sheep that has been known in central Europe from the Middle Ages. The disease attacks the brain of infected horses causing a polioencephalomyelitis. It was thought to be sporadic in nature and confined to Germany and Switzerland, but recent work has found that antibodies to the disease exist in horses from other countries in Europe, the USA and Israel, although active disease is so far unknown in these countries.

Borna disease has an incubation period of 2–3 months. An affected horse becomes lethargic, unco-ordinated and appears blind; behaviour changes occur – it might head-press or seek out dark areas in the stable. Eventually progressive paralysis and increasing weakness lead to recumbency and death. Mortality rates vary between 60 and 100 per cent and survivors usually demonstrate permanent nervous defects.

A viral disease affecting the brain and thought to be transmitted by direct contact via nasal secretions and saliva or from contaminated food between many species. The disease is thought to produce symptoms by causing an inflammatory reaction in the brain rather than by direct viral action.

None specific.

BOTULISM (illus p77)

Synonyms: Clostridial disease, forage poisoning

An uncommon disease associated with the eating of spoiled forage containing the toxins produced by *Clostridium botulinum*. Since big bale silage has become a major source of roughage for horses the incidence of the disease has increased.

Clinical signs start appearing four or five days after the toxins have been eaten. A general weakness develops, but specifically, the muscles controlling mastication fail and the affected horse shows difficulty in eating and swallowing; eventually swallowing becomes impossible.

Food material, saliva and mucus appear down the nostrils. The horse moves with a shuffling, stumbling gait and often stands with the head lowered to the ground. Collapse occurs five to eight days later, often associated with slow paddling movements of the limbs. Death occurs from respiratory paralysis.

Ingestion of the toxins produced by bacteria *Clostridium botulinum* (type C). Bales of silage which have been made from soil-contaminated grass, especially with a high pH, allow the organism introduced with the soil to multiply and produce toxins; this is now the most common cause of the disease.

Only mildly affected cases survive.
■ Supportive therapy is important; food and electrolytes should be given by stomach tube. Liquid paraffin and activated charcoal by mouth will help to remove any intestinal toxin.
■ Vaccination against the disease is possible.
■ If treatment is instigated early enough, hyperimmune serum obtained from human medical sources can help.

BRAIN TRAUMA

Horses are animals of flight and unfortunately uncontrolled flight often leads to traumatic accidents. When these involve the head the possibility of brain trauma or concussion is high.

Vary, depending upon the degree of trauma. A horse with a slightly bruised brain might appear normal except for an obvious headache, whilst the more seriously injured will show a varying degree of inco-ordination, circling gait and unsteadiness, together with dull vacant eyes and slack lips. Blood appearing from the nose is quite common following trauma to the sinus areas, but blood from the ears signifies serious damage, probably a fractured skull. Extreme damage to the brain causes coma and often death.

Many potential causes; the more common include running into gate posts, rearing and hitting low beams, road traffic accidents and sporting mishaps. The

young horse that rears and falls over backwards whilst being haltered or led is also at risk. A heavy blow to the poll is probably the most dangerous of all accidents.

■ Rest and quiet in a darkened box will discourage the aimless wandering that so often occurs with brain injuries.
■ Corticosteroids and diuretics will reduce the bruising and swelling in the brain.
■ Antibiotics will reduce the risk of infection.

BRONCHITIS

An infection or inflammation of the bronchial tubes in the lung.

Breathlessness, together with a hollow, chronic cough. A reduction in exertional capacity develops, and an increase in lung sounds is present.

Rarely a primary condition but occurs secondary to a viral infection or together with other pulmonary disease. Various bacterial species – *streptococci, staphlococci, pseudomonas* and *E. coli* – can be found in samples taken from the trachea and undoubtedly contribute to the pathogenicity of the disease.

■ A long course of antibiotic, generally a penicillin/streptomycin mixture or potentiated sulphonamide.
■ A clean-air regime.
■ Mucolytic drugs (drugs that liquefy tacky mucus in the bronchia tree) and expectorants are helpful.

BRUCELLOSIS

Caused by infection with the bacterial organism *Brucella abortus*. This organism is mainly associated with disease in cattle, and since *Brucella* has to a large extent been eradicated from the cattle population throughout the world, the related conditions in the horse have become uncommon.

Fistulous withers and poll evil, a generalised illness characterised by recurrent bouts of fever and stiffness, has also been reported. The *Brucella* organism has a predilection for synovial areas causing inflammation, swelling and pain in these, commonly the supraspinous and atlantal bursae (the wither and poll). Swelling and eventual fistulation, together with secondary infection with a wide range of organisms, then cause the typical picture of fistulous withers and poll evil.

Infection with the bacterium *Brucella abortus*. *Brucella* has also been reported as having caused abortion in the mare.

■ Antibiotic therapy is unrewarding, probably due to the intracellular nature of the bacteria.
■ Vaccination with various *Brucella* vaccines has given good results, but treatment by vaccination is always accompanied by a considerable systemic and local reaction before resolution occurs.

BRUISING

The body's response to trauma. Normally relatively superficial involving the subcutaneous tissues and superficial muscles.

A hot, painful swelling appears at the trauma site. In areas of light-coloured skin, discolouration might be present. In cases involving the deeper muscles where the trauma was sufficient to rupture larger blood vessels, enough blood might escape to form a haematoma (see p158). Where the bruise involves an area over the bone, the lining covering the bone (the periosteum) might be involved and if untreated could lead to new bone formation.

■ Immediate application of cold; either cold water hosing or an ice pack to reduce inflammation, pain and swelling.
■ Non-steroidal anti-inflammatory drugs and antibiotic cover might be necessary in more serious cases.

BRUISED SOLE

Synonym: stone bruise
A common cause of lameness, especially in the more flat-footed Thoroughbred

type of horse. It occurs frequently during endurance competitions or in any other activity that involves the horse moving fast over rough, hard ground.

A moderate to severe lameness, usually in the front foot, that becomes more evident some hours after the event. Careful cleaning and examination of the sole will usually demonstrate a red or discoloured painful area. Gentle pressure with hoof-testing callipers will cause a pain response. The full extent of the bruising might not be evident visually for several days as it takes time for the blood to leak into the horn.

Rest the horse and protect the bruised foot: most bruises will then resolve over a week or ten days.

BRUSHING

Synonyms: cutting, speedy cut
The foot or shoe of one limb strikes the inside of the coronary band, pastern, fetlock or cannon of the opposite limb.

A bruise or cut appears on the inside of the leg, generally between the coronary band and the mid-cannon.

Bad conformation or fatigue, and more often both.

Brushing boots will prevent the injuries but do not correct the cause. Strict attention to good shoeing and foot balance sometimes cures the problem.

BUTTRESS FOOT (illus p103)

Synonym: pyramidal disease
A sudden lameness of moderate severity. The foot is held with the toe just touching the ground and moderate heat might be felt on the anterior aspect of the foot. A painful swelling on the front aspect of the coronary band is present in the early stages of the disease.

As the condition becomes more chronic the shape of the foot changes, becoming more upright, narrower and

boxy. At this stage X-rays of the foot will show the new bone forming on the front of the pedal bone.

Trauma, either as a result of a blow or due to excessive strain to the tendon which runs down the front of the lower leg; this causes new bone formation and soft tissue swelling at the point where the tendon inserts into the front of the pedal bone. The damage and reaction cause severe lameness, with swelling, heat and pain at the coronary band. Where excessive strain has occurred the proximal part of the pedal bone might fracture forming one or more chips.

■ Complete rest for up to three months. Severe cases might never become completely sound.
■ Small fractures should be removed through a window cut in the wall of the hoof, whilst an attempt can be made to pin larger fracture chips.

CAPPED ELBOW (illus p107)
CAPPED HOCK (illus p59)

A soft swelling that develops on the point of the hock or elbow. The fluctuating swelling can reach the size of a melon, but is normally non-painful.

Damage to a bursa, or cushion, that lies under the ligaments passing over the point of hock or elbow; typically when the horse kicks back at a wall or the closed ramp of a trailer. The resulting damage and inflammation cause a large, unsightly swelling on the point of hock.

■ The fluid should be drained from the swelling as soon as possible and an elastic pressure bandage applied in an attempt to prevent more fluid accumulating. Injection of a long-acting corticosteroid into the empty sac improves the chances of resolution. Good cosmetic results can be achieved with this method if treatment is started soon after the appearance of the capped hock or elbow. ■ Surgical removal is technically simple but the range of movement that occurs at the point of hock or elbow can lead to breakdown of the wound, making treatment unrewarding.

CARPITIS (illus p107)

Acute or chronic inflammation that can affect the carpus (knee) and its associated structures.

Initially a varying degree of lameness in conjunction with swelling over the front of the knee, involving one or more of the joints. With repeated trauma, new bone is laid down in these areas and the swellings become hard and less painful. However, if the new bone should interfere with the joint surfaces or with ligamentous attachments, chronic lameness can result.

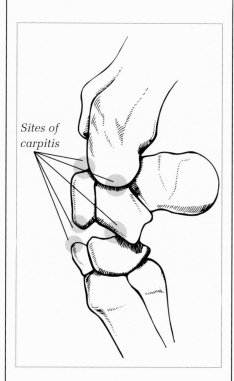

Sites of carpitis

Repeated trauma to the knee joint, coupled with poor conformation of the carpus. Over-extension of the ligamentous attachments binding the knee joint together, or bruising of the periosteum (the lining of the bone), causes new bone

to form. Repeated injury compounds the growth until the function of the joint is compromised.

■ In the acute phase, injections of corticosteroid into the joint and a long period of rest might resolve the condition. ■ Once new bone formation has occurred there is little that can be done except hope that the use of non-steroidal anti-inflammatory drugs might improve the patient's quality of life to an acceptable degree.

CATARACT (illus p83)

An opacity of the lens; this can appear as a small discrete area in the body of the lens, or as a stellate structure, or affect the whole lens.

 Most cataracts develop over a several years in the older horse, and are generally first noticed when the light strikes the eye at a particular angle. A grey haze or denser opacity covers the whole of the lens; close examination may reveal the smaller opacities that can be present. These irregularities are usually picked up by a veterinary surgeon when he examines the eye with an ophthalmoscope. Cataracts become denser and larger as time goes on, but horses seem to retain a degree of sight even when the opacity is marked.

Cataracts in foals under one year of age will probably be of congenital origin. One or both eyes may be affected, the amount varying from a pinpoint of opacity to a diffuse area causing complete blindness. Senile cataracts are rare in horses and if present are a sequel to periodic ophthalmia (see p189, recurrent uveitis) or due to damage following a fall or blow. Hunting or jumping accidents are a typical and frequent cause.

Removal of the affected lens will restore some vision; this is most successful in foals under six months.

CEREBELLA HYPOPLASIA

A disease found in Arab or part-bred Arab foals.

A gradual loss of balance, generally starting with the hind legs but rapidly leading to complete ataxia. The forelegs show an exaggerated, high-stepping gait and the head nods in a typical, almost shivering motion. The frequency of the attacks increases until the foal becomes permanently recumbent.

A degeneration of the cells in the cerebellar region of the brain.

Incurable.

CERVICAL VERTEBRAL STENOTIC MYELOPATHY

See **Wobbler disease,** p205

CHOKE (illus p90)

Food or foreign material becomes lodged in the oesophagus.

The horse is usually found in a very distressed state: saliva stained with food material runs from the nose and mouth as it retches noisily in an attempt to remove the blockage; the head and neck are arched as it attempts to swallow. It often becomes uncontrollable in its panic at the situation in which it finds itself.

Food material becomes impacted in the oesophagus. It usually occurs after rapid eating of food; dry sugar-beet cubes, windfall fruit and bread are commonly involved. Choke also occurs occasionally when exhausted, dehydrated horses – for example, endurance horses at the end of a 100-mile competition – are offered hay. Tumours or fibrosis following injury of the oesophagus can cause recurrent blockages.

■ Antispasmodic drugs to relieve the spasm of the oesophagus.
■ Sedatives to calm the horse.
Most blockages clear themselves in a few hours. A few persistent cases may need surgery to remove the blockage.

Symptoms = 👁   Cause = 🦴   Treatment = 💉

139

CHRONIC OBSTRUCTIVE PULMONARY DISEASE (COPD)
NOW KNOWN AS RECURRENT AIRWAY DISEASE (RAO) (illus p87)

Synonyms: allergic bronchitis, broken wind, heaves, small airway disease

An allergic condition affecting the lungs of older horses.

 A chronic deep, hollow cough which is constant; more severely affected horses will appear always out of breath and often wheeze badly. In cases of this severity, breathing out can be so difficult that the horse grunts with the effort of expelling the last bit of air, and a long line called the 'heave line' appears between the abdomen and chest wall; hence the old name for the condition, the 'heaves'. Even horses that are only slightly affected show some signs of breathlessness; exercise tolerance is always decreased, with a corresponding reduction in performance.

Horses with RAO (COPD) improve when they are turned out to grass, only to regress when they are re-stabled.

Traditional RAO is thought to be caused by the inhalation of mould spores found in stable dust. These moulds grow in poorly made hay and straw, and form spores which, when inhaled, irritate the lining of the respiratory tract and cause an allergic response in the lungs.

A similar condition occurring in horses grazing summer pasture has recently been recognised in the UK and the USA. The symptoms are much the same as RAO, and one survey (T.S. Mair, *Veterinary Record* 1996, 138, 89–91) found that more than half had a history of traditional RAO. **Summer obstructive pulmonary disease** is thought to be due to an allergic response to some pollens, possibly complicated by an increase in air pollution. The allergic response causes bronchospasm – a narrowing of the lumen of the small bronchioles – and increased mucus production, which tends to block these airways.

The moulds thought to cause RAO are *aspergillus fumigatus* and *micropolyspora faeni*, but the high levels of ammonia found in poorly ventilated boxes and concurrent infection with respiratory viruses also predispose to full-blown RAO. Thus horses in poorly ventilated, stuffy boxes are more likely to develop the syndrome, especially if they are recovering from a virus infection.

Preventative

■ Remove the horse from any contact with the mould spores.
■ Keep him out at all times.
■ Use a compound concentrate feed and ensiled grass or haylage, and soak hay for at least 24 hours before feeding. The latter method will only work in mild cases as it ignores the effect of spores contained in the bedding; it also removes many of the nutrients in the hay.
■ Shredded paper, peat or coarse shavings used as bedding material will lessen the concentration of spores, but it is important not to allow a deep litter bed to form as, under suitable conditions, moulds can develop in this material as quickly as they do in straw bedding.

All these precautions will come to naught if dust from feed or bedding in neighbouring stables can reach the affected horse. So in a stable-yard environment it is as well to insist that a RAO sufferer is stabled in the end box, or better still, is completely isolated from horses kept uner 'normal' conditions.

Drugs to control the disease

■ The most useful is clenbuterol hydrochloride, or Ventipulmin®: this relaxes the constricted bronchioles, thus making the airway wider and allowing a free passage of air into and out of the lungs, and also stimulates the clearance of mucus from the small airways.
■ The mucolytic drugs such as Sputolosin®: these decrease the viscosity of the mucus produced in the bronchioles, making it easier to expel and thereby clearing the airway.
■ Cromovet® is a drug given in a nebulised form. It acts as a blocking agent and will prevent the disease appearing, but only if treatment is carried out when the horse is normal. The drug acts on the cells involved in the reaction, desensitising them; thus the mould spores cannot cause any reaction and the lungs remain clear and functional. This drug has the added advantage of prolonged action, two days' treatment protecting the horse for up to 10 days.

■ Other drugs, namely corticosteroids, also used in a nebulised form or administered intramuscularly, combat the effects of RAO. Nebulisation has the advantage of delivering small but effective doses of potentially harmful drugs to the area where they are able to exert their full pharmacological effect. Correctly used and carefully monitored, corticosteroids are the most effective way of controlling this condition.

CLOSTRIDIAL MYONECROSIS

Synonyms: cellulitis, gas gangrene, clostridial myositis, malignant oedema

Clostridial myonecrosis is a very serious condition most commonly following the intramuscular injection of an irritant substance.

An acute soft tissue swelling, often with a gassy feel, develops where an intramuscular injection has occurred. The muscles of the chest, the neck and the gluteals are most often affected. The horse has a high temperature and shows acute pain around the affected site. Clostridial myonecrosis must be considered an emergency and treatment must commence immediately if the horse is to survive.

Clostridial myonecrosis is caused when an injection site becomes infected with *Cl. perfringens* and *Cl. septicum*. The condition develops more often when the injected substance is an irritant, or when it is injected into a non-vascular, poorly oxygenated area.

Immediate treatment is necessary. All dead tissue in the affected area should be removed and intense antibiotic and supportive treatment started. Pencillin G in high doses is probably the most effective antibiotic to use.

COITAL EXANTHEMA (illus p95)

Synonym: horse pox

An acute, sexually transmitted disease that affects the external genitalia of mare and stallion.

Symptoms = 👁   Cause/diagnosis = ✖   Treatment = 💊

Numerous, small, fluid-filled vesicles develop on the external genitalia, the prepuce and penis of the stallion and the vulval lips and perineum of the mare. The development of secondary infection leads to an acute inflammation of the affected area, and in mares, a vaginal discharge. The disease does not appear to cause infertility, although the accompanying soreness might prevent covering and therefore cause problems in a busy stud. Affected mares and stallions should not undertake any breeding activity until the lesions have healed; a period of three weeks is normally sufficient.

This is a member of the herpes virus family, subtype EHV-3 under the new classification.

Local applications of an antibiotic or antiseptic ointment; however, most cases heal with no complications within 10 to 14 days.

COLIC (illus p90)

Abdominal pain, caused by distension of the gut due to a build-up of gas or over-eating, or as a result of a blockage. Colic should always be treated as an emergency and is one of the conditions where professional help should be obtained immediately. Most cases are successfully treated medically, but the few serious cases that need surgery must be operated on within a few hours if a successful outcome is to be obtained.

There are three main types of colic: tympanitic, spasmodic and obstructive.

Tympanitic colic

Synonyms: bloat, gastric tympany, wind colic

Acute, continuous pain, caused by an overproduction of gas which distends the gut, with the attendant signs of sweating, a high pulse and a tense abdomen. The right flank is often full. The gut sounds are over-pronounced and are of a high-pitched tympanitic quality. The horse might make violent attempts to lie down and often has an anxious expression on its face. Frequent attempts to urinate occur and flatulence is common.

Food material starts to ferment in the stomach or the large gut. Common in horses being fed large quantities of fermentable food such as grain or coarse mix. Rich green grass grazed in the spring has much the same effect.

■ Analgesics to control the intense pain.
■ Anti-spasmolytic drugs.
■ Oral medication of antibiotics and vegetable oils will reduce the fermentation process. Fermentation in the stomach can be relieved with the use of a stomach tube, which will reduce the tension by allowing reflux of gas and fluid.

The treatment of uncomplicated cases of tympanitic colic is generally rewarding and most cases make an uneventful recovery.

Spasmodic colic

Probably the most common type of colic, generally mild in character and short in duration, an attack lasting only a few hours. Seen more often in younger horses.

Bouts of acute gut pain are interspersed with periods of normality; during the pain episodes the pulse rises to around 70 beats per minute and the horse looks round repeatedly at its flank. Sweating, restlessness and a tense abdomen are common symptoms. Gut sounds are always present and are slightly louder than normal. Frequent rolling occurs and, contrary to popular belief, does no harm as long as the horse does not damage itself against wall or door.

1 Migrating worm larvae: as these travel along their migratory route (see p175ff) they damage the small blood vessels supplying the gut. This interferes with the normal rhythmic contractions of the gut so that gas and intestinal contents build up and distend the gut wall and gut pain results.
2 In exhausted, dehydrated horses a lack of sodium and chlorine ions, common in the dehydrated horse, causes a similar interference with normal gut contractibility, and gas pressure causes a spasmodic pain.

Anti-spasmodic drugs and also sedatives.

Obstructive colic

Can be subdivided into two main types: obstructive, and the less severe impacted.

■ *Obstruction* of the stomach and mechanical obstruction of the small or the large intestine all cause acute pain. The horse rapidly becomes shocked due to the release of toxins into the system. The pulse rises to a high level and stays there in spite of treatment, the mucous membranes become a dirty red colour, and in the early stages the temperature might rise. The intensity of pain increases until the approach of death when the horse becomes cold and clammy and quiet.
■ *Impacted colic* is more insidious in nature. As the impaction builds up, the horse stops eating and passes increasingly dry and scanty faeces. A low-grade pain is present. The horse spends a lot of time lying down and frequently looks at its flank. Internal examination will reveal a mass of hard dry material at the pelvic flexure.

Obstructive colic is potentially the most serious type of colic. Obstruction can occur:
(i) in the stomach when it is due to over-eating, especially dry material such as nuts or worse still, unsoaked sugar beet;
(ii) in the small intestine as a mechanical obstruction caused by developing tumours, or by a twist or volvulus, and as a result of a strangulating hernia. Food material that impacts at the junction of the small and large intestine is a common cause;
(iii) in the large intestine, the most usual site. Mechanical obstructions, generally due to torsion of the gut, are rare, and impaction, usually at the pelvic flexure, is more common. The cause is a sudden change in diet, such as from grass to dry hay or straw. Feeding large quantities of poor quality roughage can also cause impaction.

■ *Obstructive colic:* an emergency, and in most cases surgery is indicated to relieve the condition. The decision to operate has to be made quickly, as irreversible changes soon occur in the obstructed tissues.

■ *Impacted colic:* responds to liquid paraffin and saline given by stomach tube; these soften the impacted mass and allow it to pass along the intestinal tract. Massage per rectum will help break up the mass. Treatment might be necessary for a few days before the impaction is cleared completely. Surgery may be required in refractory cases.

COLITIS-X

An acute, usually fatal disease of the adult horse considered to be associated with stress.

Of sudden onset, typified by an acutely depressed horse with discoloured mucous membranes. In the early stages the pulse and body temperature are high, but the temperature soon falls to subnormal levels as shock intervenes. Death often occurs at this stage, but if the horse survives for more than a few hours, a profuse watery diarrhoea develops. Mortality rate is close to 100 per cent.

The exact cause is unknown, but it has been associated with stress. Cases are sporadic and have followed extended surgery, or a long course of treatment with oral antibiotics, especially of the tetracycline group.

Unrewarding: prompt fluid therapy, and high doses of corticosteroid so as to combat the shock may help.

COMBINED IMMUNODEFICIENCY DISEASE (CID)

A genetic condition found in Arab foals.

The foal appears normal at birth but within a few weeks begins to suffer from a variety of respiratory diseases which prove intractable to treatment.

Thought to be due to a recessive gene which causes a failure in the developing immune system. Thus, once the protective effect of maternally transmitted antibodies

wanes, the foal is unable to combat any of the normal infections of infancy.

Generally unrewarding, and few foals live to adulthood.

CONJUNCTIVITIS (illus p83)

An infection of the conjunctiva, the lining of the eye.

The first signs are a reddening of the eye and the appearance of a discharge, clear at first but rapidly becoming mucopurulent. The eyelids become swollen and remain closed, especially in the presence of strong light.

Infection of the conjunctiva: a variety of organisms may be involved, either as a primary infection, or secondary to physical damage to the conjunctiva. Attacks often occur when horses are kept in a dusty, dry, hot environment.

An eye ointment containing an appropriate antibiotic applied to the affected eye twice or three times a day.

CONSTIPATION

Rare in the adult horse, and generally occurs only secondary to other conditions. In the foal, can be caused by retention of the meconium (see p168).

CONTAGIOUS EQUINE METRITIS (CEM)

A sexually transmitted, highly contagious disease which can be carried by symptomless mares or stallions.

Typically characterised by a profuse grey mucopurulent vaginal discharge occurring 24–48 hours after service. This diminishes over the following 10 days, but inflammation of the endometrium and cervix remains, and by interfering with the passage of spermatozoa and causing early luteolysis of the corpus luteum a high percentage of mares become repeat breeders. The disease is self-limiting, but a high percentage of

mares carry the organism in the clitoral sinus and fossa and become symptomless carriers. Stallions can carry the organism on all parts of the penis but show no clinical signs of infection.

First described in the 1977 breeding season by Crowhurst, Newmarket. The organism concerned was finally isolated and identified in 1978 when it was suggested that it be called *Haemophilus equigenitalis*. This name was later changed to *Taylorella equigenitalis*.

The disease spread rapidly to all the major horse-breeding centres of the world, and until effective control measures were developed, became a disease of major economic importance.

The organism is sensitive to most antibiotics and the condition responds well to local and systemic treatment. However, the ability of the CEM organism to remain hidden in the clitoral sinus and fossa of mares, and in the folds of the prepuce and the urethral fossa of stallions, makes complete eradication from the genital tract difficult.

Prevention

In view of the serious economic implications of this disease, a code of practice comprising a series of tests has been developed; this should be applied to all breeding mares and stallions. The type and scope of tests taken depends upon the risk status of the mare or stallion. Details of what constitutes a high risk or a low risk animal and the suggested code of practice are described in Appendix A (see p206). The routine checking of mares and stallions in this way has markedly reduced the incidence of the disease in the United Kingdom.

CONTRACTED TENDONS (illus p123)

A condition seen in the rapidly growing foal or yearling.

The forefoot or fetlock knuckles over. Knuckling of the foot is seen more often in the younger foal between 6 weeks and 6 months of age, the toe eventually becoming worn and bruised. The resulting lack of weight-bearing on the limb

---

Symptoms = 👁   Cause/diagnosis = ✴   Treatment = 🧴

accelerates the severity of the condition. In the older foal or yearling, knuckling of the fetlock joint is more common, where the ground surface of the foot remains normal but the pastern becomes more upright and the fetlock moves forwards.

A disparity of growth between the flexor tendons and the bones of the limb, the bones growing faster than the tendons which fail to accommodate that growth; principally the consequence of a sudden increase in the plane of nutrition, as witnessed by the high incidence of contracted tendons seen in young animals being prepared for show or sale.

Emergency: once the ligaments of the affected joint accommodate to the new position it becomes more difficult to reverse the changes.
■ Minimal changes can be corrected by cutting down the nutritional intake, thus retarding limb growth and allowing the imbalance to adjust towards normality.
■ For cases involving the coffin joint, trimming the foot into a low-heel, built-up toe profile and fitting extended toe pieces is necessary.
■ Severe changes to the joints will require surgery to alleviate the condition. The procedure is to section the check ligament. This can be likened to cutting a bowstring, thus allowing the bow – in this case the joint – to straighten into a normal position.

COPROPHAGY

Eating dung, a normal practice for the young, growing foal which at some time between 3 and 8 weeks will suddenly start eating its mother's dung. This practice only lasts for a short time and is thought to inoculate the foal's gut with necessary bacterial flora and to supply essential vitamins that the foal cannot manufacture at that stage of its life.

Adult horses will practise coprophagy if they are fed a low-fibre diet with no chance of making up the deficit from natural sources.

CORNEAL ULCER (illus p83)

Usually a response to trauma. Bearing in mind the prominent position of the equine eye, it is surprising that corneal ulcers are not more common.

Acute pain. The eyelids are generally closed and tears run down the cheek. The surface of the cornea becomes dull and cloudy especially in the area around the ulcer.

Ulcers become infected with bacteria very easily, and in the horse, some bacteria have the ability to liquefy the cornea, thus rapidly increasing the size and depth of the defect. In these cases full-depth ulceration or penetration and prolapse of the iris into the ulcer are common complications.

The conjunctiva becomes red and inflamed, extra blood vessels develop opposite the ulcer and grow through the cornea to the ulcer. Once the vessels reach the ulcer, healing proceeds quickly.

Trauma from foreign objects. However, bacterial or viral infections can cause primary ulceration. Fungal infection of an ulcer generally occurs secondary to antibiotic treatment of a bacterial infection.

■ Prompt removal of the horse from strong light is essential. Because the potential for loss of sight is so great, professional help should be obtained without delay.
■ Suitable antibiotic treatment, either locally 6 times a day, or as an injection into the conjunctiva once daily, should be started.
■ Severe ulceration might need surgery in the form of a conjunctival flap sutured into the defect, to aid healing. A period spent with the eyelids sutured together also helps healing.

CORNS

Bruising that can occur in the sole at the angle of either or both heels of the foot.

Chronic lameness associated with pain and bruising of the sole at the angle of the heel.

An ill-fitting shoe, most notably when the shoes have not been changed frequently enough. Since the hoof continues to grow while the shoe does not, the foot overlaps the outside of the shoe, allowing the shoe to apply pressure to the sole, especially in the angle of the heels. The excessive pressure causes haemorrhage in the sensitive corium and renders hoof growth poor. Trimming of the surface hoof material generally reveals the bruising which shows as a blood-stained area on the sole, between the bars and the hoof wall. The damage to the sensitive corium, coupled with poor hoof growth, often allows the entry of bacteria and the development of an abscess.

A varying degree of lameness is always present, although if both feet are affected a pottery action is generally more common.

■ Ill-fitting shoes must be removed at once and the corn trimmed out.
■ If infection is present, treat as for any solar abscess.

Prevention
To avoid corns, the shoes should be removed regularly, the foot trimmed back and the shoe re-applied in the correct position, ensuring that the foot is balanced and that the heels are adequately protected.

CRACKED HEELS

Synonyms: greasy heel, mud fever
Cracked heels are the result of a dermatitis or infection which is situated below the back of the fetlock and between the heels. When the infection extends up the leg to involve the fetlocks and the cannon, it is more usually called mud fever.

The area first shows soreness and becomes inflamed and swollen. The skin exudes a sticky serum which hardens rapidly into a crusty scab. As the condition progresses, the skin begins to crack open, hence the term cracked heels, and the pastern and fetlock become swollen and painful.

Permanently wet hair and skin, combined with frequent or constant exposure to muddy conditions, predispose to infection with the bacteria *Dermatophilus congolensis*. The state of being constantly wet softens the skin and removes essential protective oils, and the mud acts as an abrasive. Both factors allow the bacteria to enter and infect the skin.

A similar condition occurs in endurance horses, but is more likely to be an allergic reaction to the constant abrasive effect of miles of contact with dust and sand, and the use of large quantities of water for cooling.

 Preventative

■ Keep the lower legs dry and clean.
■ Once lesions have developed, bathe gently to remove all scabs; it is essential to do this, but can cause so much pain that a sedative might be needed.
■ Once the area has been thoroughly cleaned and dried, apply an antibiotic ointment.

CRIB-BITING, WINDSUCKING
(illus p83)

Problems of the domesticated horse unknown in populations of wild ponies.

 Crib-biting
The horse grasps a fixed object with his teeth, and pulls against it, arching his neck at the same time.

Windsucking
The horse swallows air as it cribs, often with an audible grunt. Recent research has shown that the air is not actually swallowed, but is moved in and out of the anterior oesophagus without reaching the stomach. The horse can windsuck without having to grasp onto anything.

Unknown, but certainly associated with the stress of stable routine, because recent work has shown a positive link between stabling and vices – although established cases crib and windsuck as much at pasture as when stabled. Perhaps developed as a substitute for grazing: the horse's natural inclination is to spend the day alternately grazing and resting, and because the sensation of an empty stomach is therefore completely unnatural to it, some may develop the vice as a method to avoid this sensation.

Generally unsuccessful.
■ Surgery can remove portions of the nerves and muscles of the neck so as to prevent flexing, but although this has some effect in the short term, most cases resume the vice when returned to the same environment.
■ Application of a throat strap performs the same function.
■ Prevent the horse grasping onto things, either by rounding all protruding objects in the stable, or by anointing them with a noxious substance. (These methods are perhaps of more use as therapy for the owner of the vice-afflicted horse than the horse itself, which generally shows considerable ingenuity in finding new objects to grasp.)

The best course of action is to prevent these vices from developing at all. If the horse must remain stabled, then increase the time it spends eating by making it more difficult for it to get at the hay, and consider using extruded concentrates which are bulkier than grain.

CRYPTORCHIDISM

Synonym: rig
A stallion where one or both testicles have not descended through the inguinal ring into the scrotum.

 Complete rig
Both testicles remain in the abdominal cavity. Physically the horse is like a gelding, but shows stallion-like behaviour. Hormone tests can be carried out to determine the presence of testicular tissue.

False rig
Stallion-like behaviour is shown by horses that have no demonstrable testicular tissue and are thought to have been castrated. The condition is associated with incorrect castration where not all the testicular tissue has been removed.

Both complete rigs and false rigs are infertile. Cryptorchid horses with one testicle in the scrotum and the other in the inguinal ring or under the skin are fertile but because of the hereditary factor should not be used at stud.

Complete or partial failure, due to developmental reasons, of one or both testicles to descend.

■ Surgical removal of the undescended testicle.
■ The 'riggy' behaviour of false rigs can sometimes be improved by shortening the stumps of the spermatic cords.

CURB (illus p107)

An enlargement of the plantar ligament which runs down the back of the hock joint. Particularly common in young horses and often resolved spontaneously.

The line from the point of the hock down the back of the hock to the cannon bone should be straight. Horses that have thrown a curb develop a firm swelling some 4in (10cm) below the point of hock, just above the junction of the hind cannon bone with the first bone of the hock joint. In the early stages of development the curb might be warm and the horse slightly lame.

The combination of poor hock conformation, and excessive strain and damage to the plantar ligament.

■ In the early stages is aimed at reducing inflammation, but once the chronic stage is reached, treatment is unnecessary.
■ A long rest period is essential, to allow complete healing of the damaged tendon.

CUSHING'S SYNDROME (illus p125)

Found in aged horses, with pony breeds more often affected, and is due to an adenoma (tumour) of the pituitary gland.

The first signs are an increased intake of water (polydipsia) – up to 12 gallons (55l) might be consumed every day – with a parallel increase in the amount of urine passed (polyuria) though this is often not noticed until the pony is housed. Affected ponies are especially prone to laminitis and develop a reduced exercise tolerance. The coat becomes long, curly and shaggy, the hair feels coarse and brittle and is not shed in the spring. Frequently the pony loses weight and changes shape, becoming sway-

---

Symptoms =   Cause/diagnosis =   Treatment =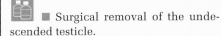

backed and pot-bellied, and as the disease progresses, seems to become more prone to infection: small cuts that should heal with no trouble do not, and ulcers develop in the mouth.

A tumour in the *pars intermedia*, a part of the pituitary gland; this causes an increased secretion of powerful hormones which control many functions in the body.

Pergolide™ returns many ponies to a more normal life; the usual regime is a high dose of 4–5mg daily to stabilise the pony, reducing to a lower dose. Because of the high cost, a low dose regime of 1–2mg a day has been used with some success. Other drugs that have been used with some success are Cyproheptadine hypochloride and Bromocriptine. A new treatment with a drug called trilostane seems to be effective but more work is needed to compare its efficiency with tradditonal treatments.
■ Strict attention must be paid to any developing infection because of the low resistance which affected ponies develop.
■ A high plane of nutrition is needed to prevent loss of weight.

CYSTS

Synonyms: dentigerous cysts, atheromas, sebaceous cysts

Cysts are not commonly found in horses. Epidermoid cysts are the most usual and are congenital malformations that appear in the skin of the horse. The cyst is lined with a normal epithelium and may be contained in the skin, or it may have an opening to the surface.

Swellings that appear in the thickness of the skin, commonly at the base of the ear when they are known as **dentigerous cysts** or in the false nostril where they are called **atheromas**. The lesions become nodular as they fill with keratinaceous debris. Dentigerous cysts commonly discharge a grey gelatinous material.
Foals can be born with a dermoid cyst present in the cornea (illus p113). These appear as a small area of skin often with normal hair in the middle of the cornea.

Congenital abnormalities of the epidermis.

Surgical removal is the treatment and is generally successful.

CYSTITIS

A condition characterised by an inflammation of the bladder; not common in the horse. Mares are affected more often than geldings or stallions.

Frequent urination, the quantity passed small, and the process obviously painful. The urine is thick, cloudy and may contain pus and clots of blood.

Generally secondary to urinary *calculi* (stones) or an infection of the vagina. May be a consequence of injury to the urethra and bladder following foaling.

■ Remove the primary cause.
■ Then antibacterial drugs to cure the cystitis.

DEGENERATIVE JOINT DISEASE (DJD)

Synonyms: osteo-arthritis, arthritis
Degenerative joint disease (*see* arthritis, p134) covers a whole range of joint disorders. The condition occurs naturally as a consequence of old age, and as a secondary condition, following trauma to a joint or due to the modern fashion of overfeeding young horses so as to obtain maximum growth.

Pain in the affected joint or joints, associated with lameness. Some degree of swelling and joint warmth might be present.

Thought to be changes in the composition and structure of cartilage, due to a biochemical change in the levels of

essential chemicals and enzymes present, or to the application of abnormal stresses on the supporting bone under the cartilage. Overworking young, rapidly growing horses, the abnormal loads applied to the joints due to badly designed race tracks and many more equine activities, all play a part in the development of degenerative joint disease.

No cure once established.
■ Rest in early stages, but controlled exercise should start within three to four weeks.
■ Intra-articular corticosteroids in early stages.
■ Hyaluronic acid and a chemical called glycosaminoglycan polysulphate have given promising results. The cost of these drugs is high, however.
■ Probably the most practical means of relief is phenylbutazone: it is cheap, in the adult horse its side-effects are minimal, and in mild cases it is effective.

DEHYDRATION (illus p119)

Loss of water from the body tissues, always associated with a corresponding loss of essential minerals such as sodium, chlorine, potassium and calcium that together with less significant chemicals are collectively called electrolytes.

Dull, depressed attitude with sunken eyes and dry, tight skin. Blood tests show a high blood protein level together with a concentration of the blood constituents.

Acute dehydration and electrolyte loss are a normal complication of many diseases: diarrhoea, colitis-X, anaphylactic shock, endotoxaemia and acute burns can all cause life-threatening dehydration.
More common is that which follows vigorous exercise such as endurance riding, long-distance racing, eventing and trail riding. The only way a horse can lose the heat generated by work is to sweat, and this results in the loss of large quantities of water and electrolytes which may not be adequately replaced by eating and drinking. The consequent dehydration and electrolyte depletion inhibit the horse's natural

ability to recover to normal, and a vicious circle develops which can cause a life-threatening situation demanding prompt treatment.

Chronic electrolyte imbalance and dehydration can also develop in horses that work hard in hot climates and do not have an available source of extra electrolytes.

 The immediate administration of large quantities of water and electrolytes by intravenous injection or by mouth will correct the fluid and electrolyte imbalance and should return the horse to a stable condition. Any underlying disease can then be treated.

DENTAL CAP

A temporary molar that has become impacted on top of the underlying permanent molar.

Eating becomes slow and painful with excessive salivation and quidding.

In the normal horse the erupting permanent molars push out the temporary teeth and replace them. A dental cap occurs when the temporary tooth is stuck on top of the erupting permanent tooth.

Removal of cap with dental forceps.

DIARRHOEA (illus p91)

Synonym: scouring

Diarrhoea is not a disease in its own right but is rather a symptom of many diseases in which the faeces become soft and cow-like or even completely fluid. It is a condition that can occur naturally when the horse moves into lush grass, but long-term diarrhoea is not common in the adult horse. The diseases that cause acute and chronic diarrhoea are listed below, but are described in full in their own sections.

Acute diarrhoea
colitis-X (see p142)
endotoxaemia (see p149)
intestinal clostridiosis (see p162)
poisoning (see p180)
rotovirus (see p190)
salmonellosis (see p191)

Chronic diarrhoea

PARASITIC (see p176)

Heavy infestation with intestinal worms is probably the most common cause of diarrhoea in the younger horse, occurring most frequently in the late winter or early spring. It can be acute or chronic, and is associated with sudden weight loss. Swelling in the lower limbs might also be present in more serious cases.

 Generally caused by bad pasture management or an inadequate worming programme.

An effective anthelmintic (a drug that is effective against worms) should be given at once.

NEOPLASIA

Tumours of the stomach and intestines can occur in the older horse, causing chronic diarrhoea with an associated weight loss. The tumour mass can sometimes be felt when performing a rectal examination.

Surgical removal.

MALABSORPTION SYNDROME (see p167)

Chronic diarrhoea associated with a gradual weight loss. The appetite remains normal.

 Characterised by a chronic inflammation of the small intestine: the wall becomes thickened and unable to absorb essential food material.

None successful.

DIOESTRUS

Synonym: inter-oestrus period

The period of the oestrus cycle that lies between each oestrus, generally lasting between 10 and 16 days depending upon seasonality and the individual. Sometimes the dioestrus period might be extended, a condition known as **prolonged dioestrus** (see p187). It is that part of the oestrus cycle which is controlled by the corpus luteum (CL). Injection of a prostaglandin causing lysis (destruction) of the CL will bring a mare back into oestrus.

DOURINE

A venereal disease of horses transmitted by a parasite and found mainly in the tropics, although cases have occurred in Europe and America.

In the initial stages, a discharge might be present from the penis or vulva. The genital organs become swollen and tender, the swelling often extending along the abdomen, and the surface of the penis and vulva become covered with blisters and ulcers.

General symptoms are a fever, inappetance and loss of condition, and difficulty in urinating. Later, weakness of the hind quarters develops. A peculiarity of the disease is the development of skin plaques, circular swellings under the skin, which appear and disappear over the flanks and shoulders.

The blood parasite *Trypanosoma equiperdum*, transmitted venereally by infected horses. Symptomless carriers do exist and cause a great problem in the control of the disease.

Drugs are available to treat dourine, but control of the disease depends upon identification of infected animals and strict control of their breeding régimes.

DYSTOCIA/DYSTOKIA (illus p100)

An abnormality in the birth process whereby the foal cannot be delivered by the mother's efforts alone. Surveys have demonstrated that only 4 per cent of Thoroughbred mares and fewer non-Thoroughbreds have trouble during foaling so the chances of problems occurring are remote. However, there are stages during birth which, if delayed, suggest that something is wrong and should be investigated. These are:
■ The second stage of parturition should

Symptoms = ◉   Cause/diagnosis = ✶   Treatment = ⬚

be a progressive process with no long periods of inactivity.

■ The fluid-filled amnion, like a white balloon, should be visible at the vulva soon after the start of the second stage, firstly seen only during strong contractions, then continuously.

■ The front feet, one often behind the other, and the right way up, should be followed by the tip of the nose which should be at the level of the knees.

■ Once the front feet, head and chest are present they should be followed by the hips; any delay could mean that the hips have become obstructed in the mare's pelvis.

If any changes from normal are noticed, then an examination should be made to find out what is delaying the birth process. The most usual reason is a malpresentation, where the foal is coming the wrong way: these vary from a slight deviation from normal which, if immediately recognised and corrected, allows the smooth continuation of the second stage and completion of the birth, to a more serious malpresentation that will require the immediate attention of your veterinary surgeon.

Types of malpresentation which can be corrected easily can be grouped as follows:

■ Where *one or both forelimbs are flexed at the elbow:* this is easily recognised, as the front foot or feet are at the same level as the nose. Gentle pulling on one or both feet whilst pushing the head back will usually correct this situation.

■ Where *the front feet are crossed:* again, the head needs to be pushed back whilst the front feet are uncrossed and pulled forwards.

■ *One or both front feet bent at the fetlock:* the feet are generally flexed under the cannon, but occasionally they can be flexed dorsally with the feet pointing up towards the roof of the vagina. In the latter case the foal has often failed to rotate completely. The resultant mix-up is best left to your veterinary surgeon to sort out, as it is very easy for the feet to penetrate the vaginal wall and cause a large recto-vaginal tear. In the former case, where the foal's foot is bent under the forearm, the malpresentation can be corrected by repelling the head so as to gain a little working room, and uncurling the flexed limb with the foot in the palm

of the hand. This ensures that the sharp toe does no damage as the limb is straightened.

■ Where the foal has been delivered normally up to the point where *the front legs, head and thorax are out* but in spite of considerable effort by the mare *no more progress is made.* In these cases the hips have either become jammed in the mare's pelvis, or – more rarely – the hind legs have flexed, and the hind feet together with the foal's trunk have become wedged in the pelvis. Diagnosis and correction of the second condition is very difficult and should be left to your veterinary surgeon, but the first condition might be solved with a little helping traction. This should be applied when the mare forces, in the direction of her hocks. The foal should be twisted at the same time: note that a major rotation of the front of a foal only rotates the hips a little, but this may be enough to release the hip lock.

Other, more serious malpresentations should be attended to by your veterinary surgeon. However, it helps to be able to recognise the serious so that no time is wasted in futile attempts to correct the malpresentation:

■ If nothing is visible, and nothing can be felt in the vagina after 10 to 20 minutes of the start of the second stage, then expect problems. The forelegs and/or the head might be deviated laterally, or the foal's trunk may have engaged the pelvic inlet (the *breech presentation*). Occasionally the legs and neck can be recognised but are in the wrong position, and feel rigid with no normal joint movement. This condition, described as *hyperflexion and ankylosis of the lower limb joints*, is serious and normally requires a caesarean section to resolve the situation.

■ Posterior presentation, when the hind legs come first, is rare in the mare. It can be recognised by the presence of a tail in the mare's pelvic inlet and the shape of the hocks. Be careful here as, in the heat of the moment, the hocks can easily be mistaken for the elbows. The feet are normally upside down in a posterior presentation. This is one situation where speedy, vigorous traction is required as the cord quickly becomes compressed between the foal's chest and the mare's pelvic girdle and the resultant lack of blood will compromise the foal's health.

EASTERN ENCEPHALOMYELITIS

A viral disease of the brain and spinal cord occurring in the eastern states of America (*see* equine viral encephalomyelitis, p153).

ENCEPHALOMYELITIS

(*See* equine viral encephalomyelitis, p153)

ENDOMETRITIS (illus p95)

An infection of the lining of the uterus, the endometrium; it can be acute or chronic in nature.

Acute endometritis

A persistent discharge from the vulva which can be liquid or tacky, but is always cloudy. Can cause a serious generalised illness. Mares show a high temperature, are off their food and can develop endotoxic shock and a severe laminitis.

Can follow uterine damage due to foaling accidents, and is a common sequel to the delayed or inexpert removal of a retained placenta. Also by infection with some strains of *Streptococcus, Staphylococcus, Klebsiella* and *Proteus.* These bacteria, like the organism causing CEM (contagious equine metritis, see p142), are venereal, that is, they can be transmitted from one mare to another by an infected stallion.

■ Daily uterine irrigation with large volumes of saline.
■ Systemic and inter-uterine treatment with a suitable antibiotic preparation.
■ The use of NSAIDs, which block the effect of bacterial toxins capable of causing endotoxic shock (see p149), is also to be recommended.

Chronic endometritis

Chronic endometritis, like the acute form, is an infection of the endometrium but which in this case is slow and insidious, with no external signs. It occurs when the mare, for one reason or another, cannot remove the normal bacterial contamination that occurs in the uterus. A diagnosis can be made in three ways:

1 From examining swabs taken from the uterus, where the presence of pathogenic bacteria or a higher-than-normal number of the cells which fight infection suggests that a chronic infection is present.
2 From a uterine biopsy, a more useful test which can give a certain amount of prognostic information: a small sample of uterine wall is taken with a special biopsy instrument, and by examining it microscopically an assessment can be made regarding the health of the endometrium and its ability to support implantation of the conceptus.
3 By ultrasound examination of the uterus.

Chronic endometritis is due, in the main, to two conditions:

Vulval aspiration (**syn.** windsucking, pneumovagina)

 Mares that 'windsuck' have a faulty shaped vulva. Thus, instead of the vulval lips sloping slightly forwards from the vertical with the greater length below the floor of the pelvis, some are too vertical with most of the length of lip above the floor (common in young Thoroughbred fillies), and others are almost horizontal with a sunken anus and open lips (the old multiparous mare syndrome): both of these anatomical abnormalities cause the aspiration of air into the vulva. This can be obvious, with a rude sucking noise occurring with every step; or subtle, only occurring when the mare is relaxed and moving from one leg to another. Air and faecal contaminants then enter the vagina. The air dries out and damages the lining of the vagina, and the inevitable contamination causes a chronic infection of the vagina and cervix which soon spreads to the uterus.

Chronic infection of the endometrium has no outward signs, but is a common cause of infertility.

Surgical techniques to prevent the aspiration of air into the vagina; once this is prevented, contamination of the uterus

ceases and the endometrium has a chance to return to normal.
■ Caslick's operation, where the upper portion of the vulval lips are abraded and sutured together; simple and effective.
■ Pouret's operation, carried out when the basic geometry of the vulva needs to be corrected. This is a more elaborate operation more suited to the old mare with a sunken anus and horizontal vulva; when successful it also reduces the bacterial contamination of the vagina and uterus.

Loss of local immunity

Some mares seem unable to cope with the normal bacterial challenge that occurs during service because of some decrease in the level of local immunity in the uterus.

Early return to oestrus following service. Sometimes a muco-purulent discharge occurs post-service.

Not known, but increasing age, and wear and tear of the endometrium play an important part in the syndrome.

Varies according to the severity of the condition:
■ In the simple case, uterine irrigations with a suitable antibiotic given during the anoestrus period will reduce infection and inflammation, and allow successful implantation once the breeding season has started.

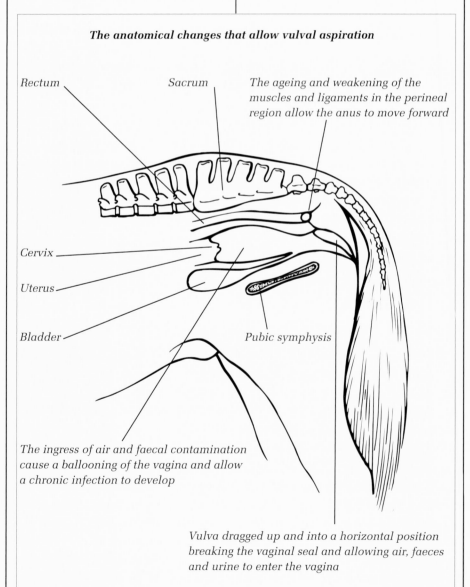

The anatomical changes that allow vulval aspiration

Rectum

Sacrum

The ageing and weakening of the muscles and ligaments in the perineal region allow the anus to move forward

Cervix

Uterus

Bladder

Pubic symphysis

The ingress of air and faecal contamination cause a ballooning of the vagina and allow a chronic infection to develop

Vulva dragged up and into a horizontal position breaking the vaginal seal and allowing air, faeces and urine to enter the vagina

Symptoms = ⬛   Cause/diagnosis = ⬛   Treatment = ⬛

■ Where the uterine resistance to infection is low, other attempts to reduce the normal contamination which occurs during service should be made, for example the use of artificial insemination in situations where it is allowed. Using AI, the semen can be treated before it is inseminated so that the majority of contaminants are removed. Unfortunately the negative attitude of some breed societies and the Thoroughbred industry to AI restricts the use of this method of control.
■ Another method to minimise contamination is to flood the uterus with an extender containing antibiotics *before* service (the minimal contamination technique). This dilutes the contaminants and minimises post-service infection.
■ Lavage of the uterus with antibacterial agents and saline for two to three days after service will reduce the normal post-service inflammatory response and increase the chance of normal implantation. Because the timing of these treatments is critical, this method can only be used in those mares which receive one service.
■ Uterine cautery, either chemical or physical, has also been tried, with encouraging results.

ENDOTOXAEMIA

The consequence of gram negative bacteria entering the system from the contents of the gut.

The horse seems particularly sensitive to endotoxic shock. Depression is marked and the pulse rate rises rapidly to in excess of 80 bpm. The horse becomes extremely dehydrated with packed cell volumes in excess of 75 per cent. The mucous membranes become congested and dirty-looking, and the horse might show colic symptoms and develop acute diarrhoea. Affected horses often stand at a water trough slurping water through their lips. Secondary laminitis commonly develops in those horses that survive the initial stages of the disease.

An extremely serious disease, and in spite of prompt, aggressive treatment many horses relapse into terminal shock, coma and death.

Associated with any condition that damages the integrity of the intestinal mucosal barrier and allows gram negative bacteria such as *E. coli* to enter the general circulation. Conditions such as colitis (inflammation of the colon), twisted, strangulated gut, concentrate overload and acute metritis all allow this to happen. The presence of endotoxins in the circulation triggers off an acute inflammation, far in excess of what would normally be expected. The severe clinical signs are caused by this out-of-control inflammatory response.

Must be immediate to be of benefit:
■ Large quantities of fluid, to be given intravenously.
■ Also non-steroidal anti-inflammatory drugs may be given.
■ Surgery to remove portions of damaged gut may be attempted.
■ Recently a specific hyperimmune serum has been developed, which although very expensive, has produced good results if given early enough in the course of the condition.

ENTROPION (illus p84)

A condition affecting one or both eyes of the new-born foal. The foal is born with eyelids in such a shape that they roll in and rub on the cornea, causing an intense irritation.

One or both eyes run continually. If neglected, the surface of the eye, the cornea, becomes grey, and an acute conjunctivitis (see p142) develops.

Close examination of the eyelids will show that the lid margin everts onto the surface of the eye allowing the eye lashes to rub against the cornea.

Temporary stitching of the eyelid so that it is turned out; this is normally sufficient to correct the condition.

EPILEPSY (illus p83)

Uncommon in the horse, but can occur more often in the older pony type.

The first signs that a seizure is about to take place are a glazed, vacant look and trembling of the ears and tail. The horse then often rears up and falls to its side, legs outstretched and quivering. The body gradually relaxes and the animal spends a variable time unconscious on the ground before getting up apparently normal. In mares that suffer from epilepsy the attacks occur more often when they are in oestrus, and appear to be triggered by abrupt stimuli.

Many intercranial conditions such as tumours, worm damage and infection can cause seizures, but the cause of epilepsy is unknown. Attacks of epilepsy can appear at a certain stage in a horse's life, and then seem to disappear spontaneously.

An anticonvulsant such as Valium™, Diazapam™ or Phenobarbitone will control the convulsions that occur during a seizure, but there is no long-term treatment that will prevent the seizures.

EPIPHYSITIS

Synonym: rickets

A condition of the ends of the long bones rather similar to rickets. The joints become enlarged and painful. Another common condition which is associated with osteochondrosis and overfeeding, and is frequently seen in Welsh Cob colts and fillies that are being prepared for show.

The knee joints are often affected and the first signs appear as a rapid knuckling of the joint, almost a quivering, together with a shifting lameness. The knees and fetlocks might appear swollen and painful. As the condition develops, an imbalance between the relative lengths of flexor tendons and cannon leads to an apparent contraction of the flexor tendons and a knuckling over of the fetlock joint (see p167).

Overfeeding fast-growing youngsters. Mineral and hormonal imbalances brought about by such overfeeding also have an influence in the development of epiphysitis.

■ Reduce the level of nutrition, making sure that a well balanced ration is substituted.

■ Make sure that the correct ratios of minerals and vitamins are fed.

EQUINE EHRLICHIOSIS

A seasonal disease occurring during autumn and winter, common in horses living in the foothills of Northern California. Cases have been reported in other American states and also in Sweden and the UK.

Initially a developing high fever lasting for several days. The affected horse does not eat, is disinclined to move and develops oedema of the limbs. The incubation period is between 10 and 14 weeks. Untreated horses are ill for 1 to 2 weeks before a gradual return to normality occurs. Young horses are less severely affected than adults.

A microscopic organism called *Ehrlichia equi*. The method of infection is unknown, but the seasonal pattern of occurrences suggests that ticks might play a role in its transmission and recent work in the UK supports this hypothesis.

The antibiotic oxytetracycline: within a day of starting treatment the fever abates and appetite returns. A week-long course at daily intervals is generally sufficient to return the horse to normality.

Once infected, horses are resistant to further infection for a period in excess of twenty months.

EQUINE FILARIASIS

A disease of horses found in Southern Europe and Asia caused by the larvae of the filariad worm *Seturia equina*.

General malaise and fever which is associated with subcutaneous swellings and conjunctivitis.

The disease is carried by the mosquito from one horse to another; the adult worms lay eggs in its tissues, and these are sucked up into the mosquito while it is feeding. They develop into larvae in the tissues of the mosquito and are re-introduced into a new host.

The anthelmintic drug ivermectin.

EQUINE HERPES VIRUS (illus p75)

Synonym: the virus, equine rhino-pneumonitis

The classification of the herpes virus family has recently been changed and it is now considered that there are 8 subtypes of the herpes virus, the first 5 found in horses and the last 3 in donkeys. The two subtypes known as EHV-1 and EHV-4 are the major pathogens in the horse, while EHV-3 is associated with the common venereal disease known as **coital exanthema** (see p140). EHV-1 is the subtype associated with respiratory, reproductive and neurological disease, whilst EHV-4 causes respiratory disease only.

Young horses are usually infected with EHV-1 or EHV-4 as yearlings. The incubation period is between 2 and 10 days, and the infected horse first develops a high temperature and a slight clear nasal discharge. The glands of the head and neck sometimes become enlarged.

The clear discharge becomes muco-purulent, thick, grey-yellow and smelly, as secondary infection takes place.

Performance can be badly affected, and horses can take up to three months to return to their previous fitness.

Pregnant mares that are infected with EHV-1 for the first time, or those that suffer a resurgence of the disease, can abort. Abortion can occur from a few weeks to several months after the initial infection, which might be asymptotic. Abortion might be a single episode, or if a group of mares is exposed to the virus, multiple abortions might occur. It is thought that abortion results from the death of the foetus: this follows multiplication of the virus in the mare, with subsequent infection of the foetus across the placental barrier. Some foals are born alive but rapidly deteriorate and die as a result of virus damage to the liver, kidneys and lungs.

Neurological complications can also follow EHV-1 infection. They can occur as an isolated incident with no evidence of prior infection, or as multiple cases when a group of horses is infected. The clinical signs occur rapidly and vary from slight hind-limb weakness, ataxia and gait abnormality, to complete paralysis.

Spread mainly by respiratory means; the copious nasal discharge is a potent source of viral particles. The equine herpes viruses EHV-1 and 4 can be considered the Houdinis of the virus world. They are very good at evading capture and destruction by the immune system of the horse, and are capable of lurking in the body ready to multiply and cause a resurgence of the disease at any time. Thus in spite of the many available vaccines, the disease is still capable of causing devastating economical damage.

No cure. The only way of controlling the disease is to stop it spreading by prompt isolation of all infected horses (see Appendix A, p206).
■ Once the infection is present, ensure complete rest, good food and clean air.
■ The use of drugs that liquify the mucus that clogs the airways does speed recovery, and in conjunction with antibiotics, is useful where secondary infection exists.

Prevention
■ A vaccine called Rhinomune™ has been available in the United Kingdom for some time, and this has been joined by another called Duvaxyn EHV1,4™. The immunity produced is short-lived, thus the vaccine must be given every three to six months. Although the efficiency of Duvaxyn EVH1,4™ in preventing herpes abortion has not been tested, it does prevent the virus multiplying in the body. As this multiplication of viral particles seems to be a major factor in causing abortion, there is a good case to suggest that the vaccine will also prevent abortion in susceptible mares, and it was licensed for this use in 1997.
■ Another vaccine that can be used to prevent abortion is Pneumabort K™; it should be given in the 5th, 7th and 9th month of pregnancy.

EQUINE INFECTIOUS ANAEMIA (EIA)

Synonyms: horse malaria, swamp fever

A viral disease present in many areas of the world: endemic in the Americas, the Middle and Far East, Russia and South Africa, and present in parts of Europe.

The Coggins test developed in 1970 is

Symptoms =   Cause/diagnosis =   Treatment =

most efficient, and has allowed a certain control over the spread of the disease; many countries demand a negative result before allowing any horse imports. The close relationship between this and the HIV virus has prompted a lot of research into EIA, but so far no effective vaccine or treatment has evolved.

Acute/subacute symptoms of high fever, moderate anaemia, oedema of the ventral body wall, increasing lethargy and in some cases death. More usually, however, horses recover from this phase and appear normal for a few weeks; then recurring episodes of fever and depression start to occur. These die down after a year or so and the horse becomes a symptomless carrier of the virus. Once infected, horses never get rid of the virus.

Some horses do not return to apparent normality and the recurring attacks of fever and resulting anaemia cause a chronic wasting disease, characterised by anaemia, oedema and weight loss. An enlarged spleen can be felt per rectum. Death is the usual sequel to this uncommon complication.

A virus which is transmitted from horse to horse by blood-sucking insects such as the horse- and deerfly. It can also be spread via contaminated, unsterilised surgical instruments or uncleaned, recycled needles and syringes.

None specific, and the variability of the virus makes the production of an efficient vaccine difficult.

EQUINE INFLUENZA

Synonym: the flu

A worldwide distribution: can be considered the major respiratory disease affecting horses. It exerts its main effect in young, unprotected horses that are crowded into poorly ventilated buildings.

A severe, acute respiratory disease with a short incubation period of 3 to 4 days. The virus gains entry through the nasal mucosa and attacks the lining of the respiratory tract causing damage and eventual death of large areas of mucosa.

The older horse develops a high temperature, a clear nasal discharge and a cough; in the absence of secondary infection these clear up in a week or so, although it takes at least three weeks before the damaged mucosa repairs itself. The muscle of the heart and the cells of the liver can also be damaged by the virus infection, especially if exercise is resumed too soon.

Young animals can become very ill and sometimes die, although death is more usually due to pneumonia caused by secondary bacterial infection.

Type A influenza virus: it has developed into many subtypes, some of which are immunologically distinct, while others are similar. Unlike the human strains of influenza, the equine varieties are reasonably stable and new strains do not occur very often.

In both old and young horses a carrier state is possible. This occurs when for some reason or other a poor immune response develops and the virus is not eliminated from the system. These horses are a grave risk to other healthy equine populations as they remain virus shedders in spite of appearing in normal health.

■ Complete rest, for at least six weeks, is vital in order that the damaged tissues can heal.

■ Good ventilation is essential, as there is evidence that horses suffering from influenza are especially susceptible to the effects of stable dust and readily become sensitised to its affects.

■ Mucolytic agents (drugs that liquidise tacky mucus) and antibiotics will help to control the secondary infections that so often occur.

Prevention

Vaccines against equine influenza have been in existence for decades and where it has been possible to vaccinate more than 70 per cent of a local population, they have been successful at preventing the development of an epidemic. However, the duration of immunity in these earlier vaccines was not good and it was necessary to boost the initial immunity by vaccinating high-risk horses every 3–4 months.

In the last few years an intense effort has gone into developing new vaccines

which are based on new adjuvants and using purified and reconstituted virus particles. These vaccines have extended the period of immunity to a more useful 10–15 months.

EQUINE MORBILLIVIRUS

Synonym: acute equine respiratory syndrome (AERS)

The virus responsible for AERS belongs to the morbillivirus group, members of which cause measles in humans, distemper in dogs and rinderpest in cattle. In September 1994 a strain of this virus was the cause of a new respiratory disease which appeared in horses kept on properties in Brisbane, Australia. The disease caused acute respiratory symptoms in a pregnant mare, and two weeks later in a total of twenty-one horses on the property, fourteen of which died or were put down. More seriously the trainer and a stable lad who looked after the first case were also affected with severe flu-like symptoms, and the trainer subsequently died from pneumonia and renal failure. Up until December 1995 one more case involving another horse has been recorded in the Brisbane area.

Most affected horses showed an acute depression and had a body temperature in excess of 41°C (106°F). Severe respiratory symptoms followed: the respiratory rate increased, breathing became laboured, and a frothy discharge appeared at nose and mouth. Dependent oedema occurred in the angle of the jaw and in the legs and sheath. Later, some horses showed ataxia (unsteadiness) and nervous symptoms. Death, generally *in extremis*, followed quickly from respiratory failure.

Source and cause is still uncertain. Recent work has suggested that the virus might be spread by fruit bats. The cause of death in most horses is a very severe interstitial pneumonia associated with gross alveolar (air sac) oedema and lung haemorrhage.

None, and in view of the seriousness of the risk to horse handlers, a swift and strict standstill order coupled with a slaughter policy is essential to control the spread of the disease.

EQUINE POLYSACCARIDE STORAGE MYOPATHY

A metabolic disease affecting the skeletal muscles of the heavier type of horse: Warmbloods, American Quarter and American Paint horses, draught horses and crosses of these breeds. EPSM appears to be more common in mares and is more serious in the heavier draught breeds.

 Exercise intolerance. Attacks occur some minutes after exercise has started and can occur after every attempt at exercise or sporadically. The horse appears tucked up, sweats abnormally and shows a reluctance to move. The flank muscles twitch and muscle groups, most often the gluteals, the biceps and semitendinosus become tense and painful. In severe cases the horse becomes recumbent, a profound muscle weakness resulting in an inability to rise. Chronic cases show a wasting appearance of the rump and thigh regions. Abnormal hind gait, such as a short, stiff hind-limb action or abnormal flexion of one or both hind limbs is also a common finding.

Blood tests show rises in the levels of the enzymes creatininekinase (CK), lactate dehydrogenase (LH) and aspartatetransaminase (AST). The more severe the attack the higher the level.

Thought to be due to a genetically transferred abnormality of glycogen production in the muscle. Large quantities of unsuitable polysaccharides accumulate in the muscles. When asked to work the affected muscles rapidly run out of fuel. Microscopic examination of biopsy material taken from suitable muscles show changes, which allow a positive diagnosis.

■ No effective treatment for this condition but alterations to the diet and a controlled exercise regime can return most cases of EPSM to a normal life.
■ All carbohydrates such as concentrates, grain, sugar beet and molasses should be replaced with good quality roughage and the necessary energy should be supplied from vegetable fats.
■ Exercise levels should be slowly built up to at least 30 minutes a day and the horse should be kept out as much as possible. Stable rest is contra-indicated.

EQUINE PROTOZOAL MYELOENCEPHALITIS (EPM)

A protozoan disease affecting the brain and spinal cord. It has only recently been recognised as a disease entity and is found in horses throughout North and South America. Cases have also developed in horses exported to other countries, and it has been recognised in animals in France and Great Britain which were imported from the USA. Seems to affect young horses, and broodmares close to foaling.

The cranial nerves are often affected, causing paralysis of the lips or ears, drooping of the eyelids and sometimes difficulty in swallowing and chewing. Muscle wasting often occurs, and if the brain stem is affected the horse can become unsteady on its feet or even completely paralysed.

Recently found to be the protozoal organism *Sarcocystis neurona*; the intermediate host believed to be the possum, and birds are also incriminated in the transmission of this disease.

■ In the acute phase corticosteroids and DMSO are considered to help.
■ Potentiated sulphonamides and antimalarial drugs carried out for a period of at least 30 days work well.

EQUINE TOXOPLASMOSIS

The organism *Toxaplasma gondii* is responsible, found in the intestine of cats. Capable of forming cysts in the tissues of many species.

The horse seems to be resistant to the organism, as many surveys have shown that a high percentage of horses have antibodies to toxaplasma but have never shown any signs of infection. On little evidence it seems that toxaplasma could cause symptoms like that of EPM.

Ingestion of food contaminated by infected cat faeces.

None satisfactory.

EQUINE VIRAL ARTERITIS (EVA)

Synonyms: infective equine cellulitis, pinkeye

An extremely contagious viral disease with a wide distribution throughout the world. Capable of remaining unnoticed in horse populations, only rarely causing a serious outbreak, as in Kentucky during 1984 and in the United Kingdom in 1993. Spreads either via the respiratory system or venereally with a high morbidity and a low mortality rate.

Many subclinical cases with little or no external signs occur. In more serious cases, a persistent high fever, 42°C (108°F), develops some 3 to 14 days after infection; this period is shorter in cases of venereal infection. Depression and inappetance are common. The limbs, ventral abdomen and the area around the eyes develop a varying degree of oedema. Conjunctivitis (red inflamed eyes) and a nasal discharge are often present.

Pregnant mares infected with the virus, whether or not they show clinical signs, can abort; in a naive population up to 60 per cent of mares can be affected. Abortion occurs at the end of the acute phase of the disease, and can affect mares at any stage of pregnancy.

Mature stallions might show a transient loss of fertility during the acute phase but this soon recovers. They do, however, become symptomless carriers of the disease, as the virus is capable of persisting in the testicles, and virus particles are shed in the semen for many years.

Spread from horse to horse by direct contact, either via the respiratory route by sneezing and coughing, or by carrier stallions by the venereal route. The increase in the use of AI, and the ease with which chilled semen is moved from stud to stud, is another potent source.

None specific. Apart from the rare case of acute pneumonia in young foals, infected horses recover quickly.

Prevention
■ A live, attenuated vaccine, Artevac™, is available. Following the initial vaccination course, a long-lasting immunity

---

Symptoms = 👁 Cause/diagnosis = 🦴 Treatment = 💊

develops. Re-vaccination a year later should confer adequate protection for at least three breeding seasons.

■ All at-risk breeding stallions should be vaccinated to prevent infection and the development of the carrier state, this would drastically reduce the risk of venereal spread of the disease.

EQUINE VIRAL ENCEPHALOMYELITIS

A group of six virus diseases of the brain, found in the Middle and Far East, North and South America and Europe: **Eastern** and **Western encephalomyelitis** found in the eastern and western states of America; **West Nile Virus** found in North America, Europe and Africa; **Venezuelan encephalomyelitis** found in South America; **Near East encephalomyelitis** found in Russia and the Middle East; and **Japanese encephalomyelitis** in the Far East. A very similar disease that affects horses, sheep, cattle and man, called **Borna disease** (see p137), is found in middle Europe.

Initially a generalised fever which often goes unnoticed, followed by a period of increasingly serious nervous signs: the horse becomes anxious and excitable, followed by irrational behaviour in which it circles, walks compulsively and crashes into fixed objects, until eventually it becomes unco-ordinated and sometimes recumbent. The mortality rate varies, but can reach 80 per cent. Laboratory tests are needed to differentiate between the various types.

A small virus whose main hosts are birds and which is spread via mosquito from bird to bird. Causes a mild illness in the avian host. When the mosquito population is high, some feed on and infect the occasional horse. The disease is thus sporadic in nature, but epidemics can occur when the level of infection in the primary host is high.

None specific, but intensive supportive care is needed to ensure recovery. Effective vaccines are available for all forms of equine encephalomyelitis.

ETHMOID HAEMATOMA

An encapsulated mass which originates deep in the ethmoid turbinate at the rear of the nasal chambers.

The appearance of slight, sporadic haemorrhage from one nostril. As the mass grows, noisy breathing might be noticed, together with a foetid breath. X-rays of the upper nostrils and endoscopic examinations will confirm the diagnosis.

Unknown, but the haematoma is thought to start from submucosal haemorrhage. It is not known why it grows so quickly.

Surgery, which is difficult as any interference causes gross haemorrhage. Cryo-surgery has been used with some success. Smaller masses can be removed endoscopically with a surgical laser, but larger haematomas require an approach via a bone flap to get access to the seat of the lesion with the horse under general anaesthesia.

EXERCISE-INDUCED PULMONARY HAEMORRHAGE (EIPH) (illus p87)

Synonyms: epistaxis, nose-bleeders

Always considered a condition, causing bleeding from the nose, present in a few performance horses after strenuous exercise. Following many endoscopic surveys carried out post-exercise, we now know that the percentage of horses with EIPH is much higher than was previously thought: many were found with blood present in the trachea that would then be swallowed and therefore never became visible at the nose.

Bleeding from one or both nostrils after maximum exercise occurs in some horses, but these are the tip of the iceberg as regards the number suffering from EIPH; endoscopic examination of the bronchial tree reveals the presence of blood in a much higher percentage of competition horses.

Following years of research it is now thought that EIPH is caused by the uneven pressure gradients and high capillary blood pressure that occurs in the upper rear tips of the lung during intense exercise. These two factors cause tensions in the capillaries in this area that are high enough to rupture them, causing haemorrhage into the lung.

Generally unrewarding.

■ The diuretic drug Lasix™ given before exercise does help in some incidences, probably because a side action of the drug causes bronchial dilation.

■ Attention to a clean-air environment is essential.

■ Any lower airway disease that might further complicate the issue should also be treated.

FILLED LEGS (illus pp59 & 89)

Seen in the larger horse that spends most of the day in the stable.

The legs from the knee and hock down become filled with fluid. This is at its worst in the early morning; it disappears as soon as the horse is exercised, only to reappear the next morning.

The relatively poor blood circulation to the lower part of the horse's legs. When the horse is resting the heart rate drops to a very low rate; thus the efficiency falls, and the heart does not pump the blood out of the lower limbs very well. Lymph is also moved from the extremities of the horse by a combination of pressure and the massaging effect of adjacent muscles. The absence of muscle and the length of leg in the horse mean that lymph finds it very difficult to move up the limb, and during rest it stagnates. The combination of poor circulation and stagnant lymph allows fluid to escape from the blood and lymph vessels into the subcutaneous tissues. The fluid builds up during the night so that by morning the legs are quite oedematous.

Horses that are on a high plane of nutrition seem to suffer more, and any bumps or bruising will accentuate the swelling.

 ■ Provide an adequate period of turnout, and ensure a decent amount of exercise: this will tune up the circulation and minimise the degree of filling that occurs overnight.

■ A large stable, attuned to the size of the horse, will allow some movement through the night and prevent stagnation of blood in the lower extremities.

■ Some horses with lower limbs that have a physically impaired circulation due to old injuries or mud fever (see p168) might need treatment with diuretic drugs to remove the swelling.

FISTULOUS WITHERS (illus p111)

Infected tracts develop in and around the withers.

The withers become swollen, hot and painful, generally more on one side than the other. After a varying time the swelling bursts and becomes a discharging tract; other tracts might also develop, until the whole withers becomes a large suppurating mass.

Historically the bacteria that cause abortion in cattle, *brucella abortus*, is thought to be responsible. Certainly the bacteria can be found in the discharges from the sinus tracts, but some doubt remains as to whether this is the primary cause. Trauma to the ligaments surrounding the withers is certainly one of the predisposing factors.

The sooner fistulous withers is treated, the more likely that a cure is effected.

■ A long course of a suitable antibiotic is necessary.

■ Surgery to expose the infected tracts might also be needed.

■ The vaccine S19, which is used to prevent cattle abortion, has effected cures – another reason to suppose that *Brucella abortus* might be involved in the cause of fistulous withers.

FOALING (NORMAL) (illus p101)

Contrary to popular belief the mare manages the whole process of foaling very well, so well in fact that we very rarely see it happening. The great difficulty in anticipating the start of the foaling process (parturition) is that the mare shows few signs that it is imminent. The length of time from conception to birth – known as the gestation period, and which is stated as being 11 months – is actually very variable, as a slow-growing, small foal takes longer to reach a weight that maximises its chances of survival than a normal, healthy foal. If the waiting becomes unbearable, ask your veterinary surgeon to examine the mare and check that everything is progressing normally. There are, however, a few clues that tell us that the birth of the foal is imminent:

■ The mammary glands become very tense as foaling approaches, and a honey-coloured secretion forms at the end of each teat, a phenomenon called 'waxing'.

■ In the last hours before parturition, changes occur in the chemical consistency of the colostrum (the first milk). The levels of calcium and of potassium salts increase, and that of sodium decreases just before foaling, and by measuring the concentration of these salts every day the time of birth can be estimated to within 24 hours.

Other physical changes that occur are less dependable:

■ The pelvic ligaments slacken, and the musculature around the anus and vagina relaxes.

■ The behaviour of the mare alters: first she might become antisocial, then anxious, seeking human company. The margin for error is unfortunately wide, and these signs can occur several times before foaling actually starts. One fact that has emerged from the large amounts of information collected about foaling, is that the majority of births occur during the hours of darkness or the first moments of dawn.

For those mares that must be made to foal for medical reasons, foaling can be induced by the administration of either prostaglandin or oxytocin, two hormones associated with birth, but the attendant risks may outweigh the advantages. The problem is the difficulty in judging the right time to induce the mare, because if it is done too early or too late, the health of the foal might be jeopardised.

Labour can be divided into three stages, although most people will see only the last stage, the passing of the afterbirth.

First stage

The first signs are very much like colic. The mare shifts her weight from foot to foot, she is generally uncomfortable, and may now and then break into a sweat as she paces anxiously round the box. She passes frequent small amounts of faeces and urine, and will look round at her flanks, very often holding her tail up. These signs are due to the beginning of uterine contractions and are brief; in many mares they may not occur at all.

Second stage

This is the propulsive stage, and the developing signs of discomfort are due to increasing uterine contractions and dilation of the cervix. However, in the early stages the mare is often relaxed enough to wander round the box, perhaps to eat some hay, before more contractions cause further discomfort. Older mares seem hardly bothered during these early stages, although young first-timers can get upset.

During these early stages the foetus changes position. In late pregnancy, the normal position of the foetus is on its back with legs folded to its belly, but as the first stage advances, the head and forelimbs flex and extend as if trying to butt the cervical opening, indeed this might be one of the factors that initiates cervical relaxation; then the fore-body twists into a dorsal position. As the intensity of the contractions builds up, the cervix starts to open and the uterine pressure forces the foetal membranes into the vagina; they can sometimes be seen protruding from the vulva rather like a thick white balloon. The foetus has by now turned so that the head and forelegs are the right way up and are engaged in the pelvic opening. The hindquarters are still upside down. When the membranes rupture, releasing 10 to 20l (2 to 4gals) of amniotic fluid, the second stage of labour can be said to have started.

Noting the onset of the second stage is important, as from now on labour is irreversible and should take only 30 minutes

The changing position of a foal during normal parturition

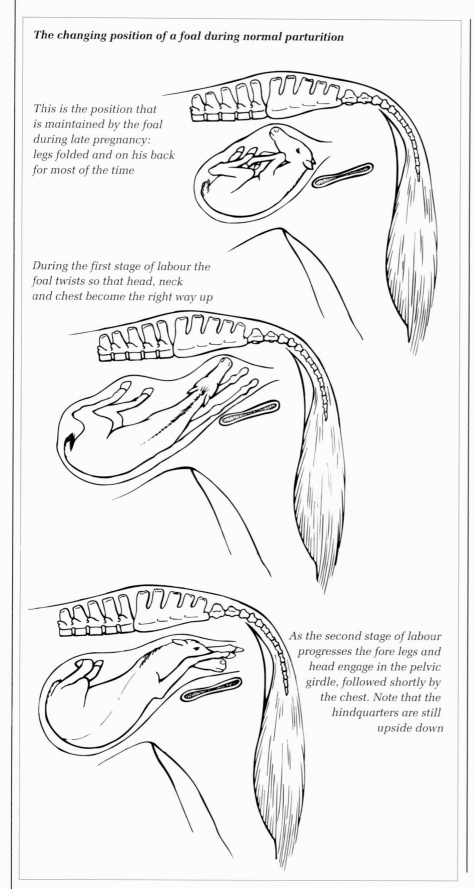

This is the position that is maintained by the foal during late pregnancy: legs folded and on his back for most of the time

During the first stage of labour the foal twists so that head, neck and chest become the right way up

As the second stage of labour progresses the fore legs and head engage in the pelvic girdle, followed shortly by the chest. Note that the hindquarters are still upside down

or less to complete. The mare lies down and starts to strain, attempting to push the foal further into the pelvic opening. At first she gets up and down several times, we think to help reposition the foetus. How the mare and foetus manage to time and co-ordinate this complicated series of movements is not understood, but the frequent getting up and down of the mare, the contractions of the uterus and the foal's own movements are all involved. One rather appealing habit that the mare shows during the second phase of birth is the tendency to lick areas where the amniotic fluid has spilt; this includes your own person if you are present. It is not known why this happens, but probably it is an attempt by the mare to minimise the olfactory evidence that she has just given birth, or perhaps it is a way of marking out the 'maternity ward'.

As the second phase proceeds, the mare spends more time lying down, frequently raising her head to look at her flanks. The contractions increase in power and severity and soon the front feet can be seen, enclosed in the shiny membrane of the amnion, one just in front of the other, followed shortly by the nose, head and chest of the foal. It is at this stage that the foal's movements should rupture the membrane. If this does not happen, the amnion should be broken to free the foal's head and allow breathing to start. The whole process is fast and violent, taking only 5 to 15 minutes. Even now, at this late stage, it is normal for the mare to get up several times and lie down again, generally on the other side.

The second phase is completed as, after a short rest, one last effort produces the foal's hips and hindquarters. At this point the mare should not be disturbed, because if she should get up, the umbilical cord could break and the last flow of blood from the placenta into the foal be lost; the loss of this quantity of blood could make the difference between survival and death of the new-born foal. Also, the hind legs often lie in the vaginal passage for a few minutes, and this is perhaps nature's way of plugging a potential gateway for infection to enter the uterus.

After this essential rest, which may seem forever to the watching attendants and can be up to 40 minutes, the mare rises to her feet to turn and inspect the new arrival and to start the cleaning process. This action imprints the image of his mother in the foal's mind and stimulates the reflexes necessary for him to cope with the outside world. During the resting period another vital change takes place: the umbilical cord becomes brittle. This allows either the foal's movements or the mother rising to break the cord at the correct place, about 4cm (1.5in) from the abdomen. This physical change occurs in order to minimise the chances of infection entering via the cord, or haemorrhage occurring from the stump. All that needs to be done at this point is to treat the end of the cord with an antibacterial powder or solution. At the same time the part of the placenta that is visible should be bundled up and tied into a parcel. Some mares, especially young ones, are liable to become alarmed at this thing that is flapping about behind them, and tying it up reduces this risk.

Normally the second stage is completed smoothly and quickly, but anything giving cause for concern should be treated as an emergency. Once the strong contractions have started, the foal should arrive in 10 to 20 minutes; if not, get in touch with your veterinary surgeon immediately. In all probability he will arrive just in time to congratulate you and the mare on a strong, healthy foal, but a wasted journey is much better than a dead foal or a damaged mother.

Third stage

The expulsion of the afterbirth (the placenta) takes place within an hour of foaling. During this third stage, the contractions of the uterus, necessary to expel the placenta, can cause some discomfort and the mare can show quite colicky signs. These are normal, and unless they are very severe they can be ignored. The placenta is passed inside out, rather like pulling off a sock, and once completed it should be spread out and examined to check that it has all been expelled, as any pieces left in the uterus could cause acute endometritis (an infection of the uterus).

FOLLICULITIS

Small painful papules develop in the skin, generally in an area rubbed or covered by ill-fitting or dirty tack. The pustules come to a head and burst, becoming crusted ulcers which heal, leaving small areas of alopecia.

Bacterial infection of hair follicles, generally by the species *Staphylococcus* but occasionally by *Streptococcus* and *Corynebacterium* species. The condition is generally secondary to poor skin hygiene or skin trauma to the saddle area, caused by a combination of heavy workload, sudden warm weather and poor grooming.

■ Local antibacterial washes.
■ Systemic antibiotic treatment might be needed.
■ Attention should be paid to the underlying cause.

FRACTURES (illus p108)

Until very recently the great majority of horses which suffered fractures were destroyed. Fortunately this is no longer the case, as with modern materials and methods a surprising number of horses can be treated successfully. However, the materials, the operating and anaesthetic costs, and the expense of aftercare are so high that insurance cover is essential.

Acute pain over the fracture site is usual together with swelling, and if the fracture involves the limbs the affected leg is generally held off the ground in a non-weight-bearing position. Sometimes the leg might be angulated in an abnormal manner. Conversely, fractures of the smaller bones in the leg can show little external signs, and X-ray or scintigraphy might be needed. Equally, fractures of bones of the trunk and head might go unnoticed for some time.

When an unacceptable force is applied to a bone. This might be due to a kick or a fall, or it might happen on the racetrack when the strain on a bone is more than it can stand.

■ The horse should be kept still until expert help arrives. If the fracture is one that can be treated, then the horse will be removed to a specialist centre where surgical repair can be carried out.

■ If the fracture involves the lower limb then this should be immobilised by applying a Robert Jones splint (see p67) or one of the newer removable casts before the horse is moved.

FURUNCULOSIS (illus p116)

Many infected hair follicles coalesce to form a large infected area.

An area of skin becomes nodular, with many drainage tracts present and large crusted ulcers. Furunculosis generally develops in the saddle area or under any badly fitting tack.

Generally as a sequel to untreated folliculitis (see above).

Local and systemic antibiotic treatment, together with attention to the underlying cause.

GIRTH GALLS

Early signs: raised area of skin or hair, tenderness when touched or groomed, pain when girthed up. Horse may try to bite or move away, signifying discomfort. **Later signs:** hair loss, raised weals, skin in girth area rubbed raw, or scabby, often in wrinkled pattern, weeping or open wounds.

Girths made of unsuitable material for the type of horse (eg string girths will often pinch thin-skinned horses); girths dirty or sweat-soaked, or worn, and the material rough or torn. The horse may have been girthed up too tightly. Young horses being girthed for the first few times may have sensitive skin and show a reaction. Finally a nylon girth together with a sweating horse and worn for a long period may have a scalding effect.

Symptoms = 👁   Cause/diagnosis = ✷   Treatment = 🗋

Mild cases
- Apply antiseptic cream.
- Avoid girthing the horse until symptoms subside.
- Eliminate cause.

More advanced cases
- Rest horse until wounds are healed.
- Apply anti-inflammatory, antibiotic ointment to aid healing and avoid infection.
- Eliminate cause.
- When the horse resumes work, tighten the girth gradually, avoid girthing too tightly and stretch each foreleg forwards after girthing to smooth wrinkled skin.
- Use fleece or neoprene girth sleeves, or padded girths lined with a natural material (eg cotton). Use a clean girth each time the horse is worked.

GLANDERS

An ancient disease of the horse, ass and donkey, and one of the few which can cause a serious, often fatal disease in man. Glanders has been recorded over the centuries from every country where the horse is kept; today, cases occur in the East and Middle East.

 ### Acute
Typified by an acute pneumonia with a dry cough, a high temperature and a nasal discharge. Death occurs rapidly.

Chronic
Small nodules develop in the lungs and associated lymph glands. The nasal passages become infected and soon a foul-smelling nasal discharge develops; the horse rapidly loses weight. Another chronic form common in the horse is the cutaneous type known as 'farcy'. Nodules develop in the skin, and these ulcerate quickly, discharging a grey-yellow pus.

The bacteria *Pseudomonas mallei*. The acute form is generally in the donkey which is particularly susceptible, and the chronic in the mule or horse.

Not advisable because a notifiable disease. Identified by the Mallein test, and any positive cases should be destroyed.

GLYCOGEN BRANCHING ENZYME DEFICIENCY

A recently recognized glycogen storage disease. It is found in Quarter Horses as well as humans and Norwegian cats.

 Affected foals are born weak and lethargic. Within a month or so of birth increasing weakness and stiffness eventually lead to recumbency and death.

GBE is caused by an inherited deficiency of the enzyme, which is an essential part of glycogen production. The lack of GBE leads to the accumulation of abnormal glycogen molecules in skeletal and heart muscle.

None.

EQUINE GRASS SICKNESS, EGS
(illus p119)

A disease of the autonomic nervous system (controlling the action of the intestinal tract); originally restricted to the north-eastern area of the United Kingdom, it has gradually spread to cover virtually the whole country. Similar diseases have been reported from northern Europe, southern America and Australia.

The disease can vary from the extremely acute, with death occurring in two or three days, to chronic, showing gradual wasting over a period of weeks or months. The more acute cases show signs of severe colic, the regurgitation of fluid stomach contents down the nose, and paralysis of the throat. The muscles tremble in an uncontrolled manner. Initially there may be diarrhoea, but later no dung is passed and on examination the faeces are found to be hard and black.

Less severe cases show dull abdominal discomfort and severe loss of condition. Appetite is poor to non-existent and stomach contents are returned down the nose, the dung is hard and dry. When observed at rest, the horse stands with a dipped back and the feet brought together under the body. In the more chronic cases, where gradual wasting follows recurrent regurgitation of stomach contents, small quantities of soft cow-like faeces may be passed. Severe rhinitis, with a mucopurulent discharge, is a common finding in these cases.

One problem that has delayed the understanding of EGS is that it can assume many forms with few common features. Also, diagnosis can only be confirmed by post-mortem and the clinical signs are easily confused with colic. There is no predisposition in terms of age, sex or breed, but the disease is confined to animals grazing at pasture and has a higher incidence in ponies – this may be because ponies spend more time grazing. Young mares heavy in foal and moved to a stud to be foaled down and covered are a particularly high risk group.

Grass sickness occurs more frequently in the period May to July, especially during dry weather or during a cold wet period following warm, sunny weather. Extensive research work has led to the realisation that grass sickness is caused by an interruption of the nervous control of the gut. What agent causes this, leaving its evidence in the disruption of the autonomic nervous system, is not yet known. It has been shown that the substance is capable of moving up the sympathetic nerves and damaging the ganglia controlling the gut; also a guess can be made of the molecular size of the substance.

More evidence suggests that EGS is a toxico-infection caused by an overgrowth of *Clostridium botulinum* type C in the small intestine, triggered by nutritional and other environment changes. Until the effect of all these factors has been fully worked out, prevention of EGS will be difficult.

All acute and nearly all sub-acute cases die or have to be put down. Some chronic cases survive. Workers at the Royal Dick, Edinburgh have worked out a scoring system, based on the signs shown by each case, which can give some idea of the prognosis. Whatever the cause, very high quality nursing is needed if there is to be any chance of recovery. As a result of the interest in *Clostridium botulinum* type C as a casual agent, and earlier research, work has started on the production of a vaccine.

GREASY HEELS

An acute dermatitis affecting the area under the fetlock, generally of the hind limbs. Similar to **cracked heels** (see p143).

GUTTURAL POUCH DISEASE

The guttural pouches, one to each side of the neck, are unique to the horse. They lie in the angle of the jaw and are a natural enlargement of the eustachian tube which joins the middle ear to the pharynx. The function of these pouches is obscure, but from a practical standpoint they are important because vital structures – namely two branches of the carotid artery and numerous nerves – pass along the wall of each pouch. Therefore any disease affecting the pouch might involve these, with far more serious implications. Two main syndromes affect the guttural pouch.

Guttural pouch infection
Bacterial and fungal infections can occur in the guttural pouch.

Commonly an intermittent purulent nasal discharge, from either one or both nostrils. The horse might find it difficult to swallow, and a hard painful swelling is usually evident at the angle of the jaw. Occasionally, but more commonly with cases of mycotic infection, haemorrhage from the eroded carotid arteries can occur: this is a life-threatening condition.

Bacterial infection of the guttural pouch is generally a secondary condition following a neglected respiratory infection. The cause of *guttural pouch mycosis* is unknown, but in my experience is associated with a poor, humid stable environment and mouldy hay. The causal organism is generally one of the *Aspergillus* species.

■ Little can be done for guttural pouch mycosis. Early cases of bacterial infection can be cured by antibiotic irrigation of the pouch. More chronic cases need surgical exposure of the pouch and daily flushing.

Guttural pouch tympany
(illus p85)

A large swelling on one or both sides behind the angle of the jaw. The swelling sounds hollow when tapped, and by interfering with the normal air flow through the pharynx can cause a loud respiratory noise. The condition is found in young horses and is more likely to occur in females.

The tympany is caused by air being forced through the guttural pouch openings into one or both pouches during expiration. The actual cause is unknown but is probably due to abnormal development of the folds at the entrance to the pouches.

The offending guttural pouch can be temporarily deflated by passing a catheter into it, but a permanent cure requires surgery.

HABRONEMIASIS (illus p117)

Synonym: summer sores

Sores develop on the lower limbs, at the corners of the eyes and on the prepuce and penis of male horses. In some apparently hypersensitive horses, the sores quickly develop into large granulomatous masses.

The larvae of the stomach worms of the horse, *Habronema*. Normally this worm has a straightforward life cycle, from house and stable fly in which the larvae develop, to the horse's stomach where the adult worms feed and lay eggs. Habronemiasis is caused when the larvae are deposited on to wounds or moist areas of mucous membrane, where they cause intense irritation and the development of lesions.

■ Ivermectin to kill the larvae; the sores will then heal rapidly.
■ Larger granulomatous lesions might require surgery or cryosurgery.

HAEMATOMA (illus p67 & 87)

The swelling that results when bleeding occurs under the skin or into a muscle.

A large swelling that forms rapidly under the skin or in a muscle. If it forms under the skin it is generally floppy, whilst a haematoma that forms in a muscle is firmer and very painful. Depending upon the site, a haematoma can be very large, containing many litres of blood.

When a blow or damage to a blood vessel causes bleeding without an external wound; typical scenarios might be a kicking match between horses, and running into a fence. The pressure of the escaping blood lifts the skin away from the underlying muscle or separates the muscle fibres, causing a large swelling. When the tension around the haematoma equals the pressure of the blood escaping, the bleeding stops and the haematoma stabilises.

■ Initially cold compresses and pressure applied to the haematoma to help stop the bleeding.
■ Then the haematoma should be left for a few days until the original injury to the blood vessel has had a chance to heal. Once this has happened the haematoma can be excised and all the contents removed.

HAEMOLYTIC DISEASE

A rare condition of the new-born foal involving the blood system, characterised by a rapidly developing anaemia; it occurs in the first days of a foal's life.

In the early stages the foal yawns frequently and becomes increasingly sleepy; it will also breathe rapidly and have a fast heartbeat due to the developing anaemia. Later, the whites of the eyes and mucous membranes become yellow due to jaundice. Blood-stained urine is frequently present. As the disease progresses the foal becomes weaker and has often collapsed or died by the third day post partum.

When the mare's red blood cells are different from those of the foal: these

Symptoms = 👁 Cause/diagnosis = 💥 Treatment = 💊

mares develop high levels of antibodies to foal red blood cells with which they come into contact during pregnancy. The antibodies are concentrated in the colostrum, so when the foal first sucks, the antibodies are absorbed into the blood system and destroy the red blood cells. If untreated, a rapid, fatal anaemia develops. Rare in first-time mothers but once a mare has had a haemolytic foal she will to do so at each succeeding pregnancy.

■ Remove the foal from the mare and transfuse it with blood cells from the mother; these must be washed to remove all traces of antibody. If this is done before the anaemia becomes severe, the foal stands a good chance of a full recovery.
■ The condition can be prevented in known mares by muzzling the foal for the first 48 hours of life and feeding stored colostrum that contains no antibody.

HEAD SHAKING

Attributed to many causes: middle ear disease, ear mites, allergic rhinitis and many more conditions have been blamed for the violent vertical jerks and frantic shaking of the head that characterise the condition. However, until recently no physical cause for head shaking could be found in at least 90 per cent of cases, and traditional treatment has been generally unrewarding.

Episodes of head shaking usually start in the spring and occur more often during warm, sultry weather. Strong sunlight seems to be a constant trigger. Many cases are normal in the stable and only start head shaking when ridden out; others head shake when turned out to pasture. Many of these horses try to get out of strong sunlight by pushing their heads into dark corners or seeking areas of deep shade. The symptoms often disappear during the winter months.

Most typical is a violent, vertical head shake together with sudden jerking movements, as if trying to dislodge a fly. Snorting and tossing the head also occur and the affected horse often wipes his nostrils on the ground or across his forelegs. A state of high agitation is always present.

The cause is certainly intense irritation to some area of the head. For some years it was thought that the irritation could be due to ear mites in the ear canal or to some sinus problem, or an allergic reaction to some substance present during the summer, grass or tree pollen perhaps. However, in most cases no cause could be found and treatment of any type had no effect.

A recent survey by workers at Davis, California has suggested that sensitivity to strong light *could* be a major cause. They found that many cases ceased head shaking at nightfall, and that applying a blindfold had the same effect; in some cases, fitting the horse with dark goggles also diminished the episodes of head shaking. They suggested a parallel to the condition known as 'photic sneeze' in man, a seasonal condition occurring in spring and summer, in which exposure to strong light causes acute rhinitis and involuntary sneezing.

■ A surgical approach has been tried with some degree of success, whereby the nerves to the nostril are sectioned so that all sensation to this area is lost; this improves the situation, but does mean that the horse can no longer sense anything with his nostrils. He often becomes severely disorientated at night.
■ Medical treatment with various anti-inflammatory agents has been tried, but with little success.
■ The drug Cyproheptadine, used for treating acute rhinitis and allergic conjunctivitis in man, seemed to work very well in the small survey carried out by the Davis researchers.

HEART (AND DISEASE OF)

The heart is a large, powerful muscular pump surrounded by a tough fibrous sac called the pericardium. It consists of four chambers: the left and right atria, and the left and right ventricles; like any pumping machine, it is equipped with valves which direct the flow of blood from one chamber to another, and then into the net of vessels that circulate the body. These vessels start out from the heart as high-pressure, elastic-sided tubes called arteries, and spread in a branching network through the tissues becoming narrower as they go, until finally they are microscopic tubules called capillaries.

It is through the thin walls of the capillaries that the blood takes up nutrients from the liver and gut, and oxygen from the lungs, and releases this store to the tissues that need them, at the same time absorbing the waste products of energy production. Once through the capillary network the blood is returned to the heart by a system of low-pressure, thin-walled vessels called veins.

In order to achieve these many tasks, a complicated circulatory system has evolved: inside the heart, blood in the right ventricle is pumped into the pulmonary arteries and through the lungs where oxygen is taken up and the waste products water vapour, heat and carbon dioxide excreted, and returned via the pulmonary veins to the left side. The richly oxygenated blood, now bright red in colour, passes from the left atrium into the left ventricle and is pumped at high pressure through the arteries, and then the narrower arterioles. Finally it passes through the capillary network where the oxygen is extracted by those tissues that need it.

Once through the capillary network the blood is returned to the heart via the veins. They empty into the right atrium and then the darker, deoxygenated blood passes from the atrium into the right ventricle where once more it is pumped through the lungs.

To feed the system, nutrients are taken up into the blood as it passes through the gut wall.

Another system of blood vessels, called the portal veins, short-circuit the main cycle taking blood, enriched with nutrients, from the gut to the liver. Here the nutrients are broken down to carbohydrates, fats and amino acids and rejoin the general circulation to be used by the tissues as they are required.

Abnormal rhythm

The rhythm of the heart is controlled by a group of specialised nodules in the heart called the 'pacemakers'. They initiate and then control the waves of stimulation which spread across the heart muscle, making sure that the atria and ventricles contract in the correct sequence and, equally importantly, at the correct intensity.

Missed beats

When a horse, and in particular a well trained, fit horse is at rest, the occasional beats are quite commonly missed.

One or more beats are missed in a regular pattern. Generally there are four to eight normal beats, followed by one to three missed beats.

The pacemaker has forgotten to send out its signal. However, as soon as the horse starts to exercise, the pacemaker concentrates on its task and the rhythm becomes normal. This is quite a common condition and does not seem to affect performance in any way.

 None needed.

Atrial fibrillation

A condition seen in the competition horse. It is not known whether heart abnormalities are just noticed more often because the stethoscope is used more often in the sporting horse, or because the condition is associated with the stresses of competition. It causes failure of the atria to contract correctly and therefore insufficient blood is pumped into the ventricles. This in turn causes a fast, erratic ventricular beat and a low output of blood.

Very often further pathological change is found in the valves or heart muscle.

Serious cases show characteristic signs of heart disease: they become breathless very easily, show a jugular pulse, and have a ventral oedema. More commonly, the only symptom shown is a decreased exercise tolerance, the horse appearing normal at all other times.

The pacemaker for various reasons sends out a constant stream of impulses to the atria which respond by fibrillating (making a great many partial contractions). The condition can appear and disappear spontaneously; it can follow a viral attack, and is often a complication of myocarditis.

The drug quinidine sulphate, given by mouth or by intravenous drip, will sometimes arrest the arrhythmia and return the heart to normal function.

Cardiac murmurs

In the present-day climate of increased professionalism, more and more horses' hearts are being examined with a stethoscope, either to check pulse rates or to assess post-exercise recovery rates, and as an aside many supposedly normal horses with high athletic potential are found to have a heart murmur. This only goes to show how difficult it is to decide if a murmur is significant when advising upon a horse's future athletic career.

Murmurs are caused by changes in the geometry of the heart valves. These vary depending upon which valve is affected and to what degree. Most valvular lesions are slight and do not seem to cause any discernible symptoms except for the murmur. However, some lesions might be progressive and cause a gradual decline in the amount of work the horse can do. In these cases a cough might develop, together with oedema (a fluid swelling) present in the dependent areas of the body. As the damage to the valves increases other facets of heart function deteriorate and congestive heart failure develops.

Due to disease or congenital defect, the valves do not close properly. When this happens the smooth flow of the blood is interrupted and turbulence occurs. This is heard as a roaring sound between the normal heart sounds, and by pinpointing its position relative to these, the faulty valve can be identified. The valves on the left side of the heart are more commonly affected.

Infection of the heart valves is rare in the horse, and the most common cause of valvular defects is considered to be the wear and tear of age or sudden irregular bursts of high blood pressure such as happens in an ill-conceived training programme.

None, but the condition can be helped with the use of potent diuretics. More recently ACE inhibitors, developed for use in humans, have been shown to have a positive effect. Careful management of severe cases of congestive heart failure can regain a useful degree of health and live a relatively normal life.

Myocarditis

An inflammation of the heart muscle.

Loss of athletic performance, frequently towards the end of a race. Changes might occur in the ability of the pacemaker to orchestrate the heartbeat, and then arrhythmia might occur. Sudden death from heart failure is a possibility.

 Several viruses have the ability to affect heart muscle, equine influenza virus probably being the most important of these (see p151).

A long period of rest.

HEAT STROKE

Synonym: heat exhaustion

Occurs in horses that are working hard in a hot, humid environment.

The first signs are rapid respiration, disinclination to move, red mucous membranes and a high body temperature. The pulse is generally high, and as the condition worsens, the heartbeat becomes chaotic and the lip, cheek and forearm muscles twitch. Without fast cooling treatment, the horse collapses and dies.

The horse is unable to lose body-heat, either due to the workload, or environmental conditions, or more often both. Horses competing in the endurance phase of a three-day event or in endurance races held in hot, humid countries are especially at risk.

■ Large quantities of cold water, iced if necessary, should be poured over the horse immediately, to cool the body down as soon as possible. Shade and fans to provide an artificial wind will help.
■ Electrolytes and fluid given intravenously are also needed.

HEPATITIS (LIVER DISEASE)

The liver is an organ with immense recuperative properties, and three-quarters of its working capacity can be lost before disease becomes apparent. Unfortunately this means that by the time symptoms of liver disease do appear, it is almost too late to instigate treatment. Hepatitis can be split into acute and chronic forms:

Acute disease

Loss of appetite with a dull abdominal pain, and high pulse and respiration rates. Jaundice appears quickly. Nervous

---

Symptoms =   Cause/diagnosis =   Treatment =

signs such as head pressing, aimless wandering and apparent blindness develop as the disease progresses.

An extremely severe and dangerous condition. It can be caused by virus infection or by the ingestion of many chemical and biological toxins.

Chronic disease

Nervous signs predominate. The horse seems unaware of its surroundings – head pressing, circling and suffering apparent blindness. Profound weight loss and diarrhoea.

Generally the weed ragwort (see p182). Toxins in the weed slowly poison the liver cells, causing cirrhosis of the liver. When growing in a field, ragwort is extremely unpalatable and is rarely eaten; but in hay it is tasteless and it is after eating contaminated hay that most cases occur.

Liver fluke has also been recorded as having caused chronic liver disease.

Mainly supportive for both the acute and the chronic disease.
■ Antibiotics to control primary or secondary bacterial infections will reduce the liver damage caused by the effect of toxins.
■ Intravenous glucose to maintain blood glucose levels and vitamins, especially the B group, to support the damaged liver can help.

HERNIA

The two common types of hernia found in the foal are developmental abnormalities generally present at birth but often only noticed when the foal is older. A hernia is caused by a defect in the abdominal wall, either in the umbilical or inguinal regions. The peritoneum (the lining of the abdominal cavity) invaginates into the gap and a varying amount of abdominal contents follow.

Umbilical (illus p120)

A round swelling varying in size which appears at the umbilicus in the first six weeks of life. It can be differentiated from other swellings such as a navel cord abscess because the soft abdominal contents can be returned to the abdominal cavity with the application of gentle pressure, and the edges of the ring can then be felt. Unless the abdominal contents become constricted at the ring and strangulate, umbilical hernias can be left untreated as most will regress during the first year of life. If the contents should strangulate, immediate surgery is necessary; if the reason for repair is cosmetic, however, then there is no hurry to instigate surgery.

A congenital defect present at birth. Abscess formation in the umbilical cord, especially when it involves the body wall, might weaken the wall and allow a hernia to develop.

■ Small hernias tend to disappear during the first year of life.
■ Larger hernias, especially when treated in the first few months of life, respond well to the careful application of two elastrator rings (the rubber rings used to castrate lambs). Because of the danger of trapping abdominal contents, this procedure should be carried out by your veterinary surgeon.
■ Larger hernias might need surgery to correct them.

Inguinal

Potentially a more serious condition. In this case the abdominal contents herniate through a weakened or enlarged inguinal ring and are seen as a swelling in the inguinal region. The hernia is often involved with the scrotum and in these cases appears as a grossly enlarged scrotal sac. Inguinal hernias can be unilateral or bilateral and do not regress, indeed they tend to get bigger with age and are more likely to strangulate. For this reason surgery should be performed as soon as practicable to repair the defect.

Result from an over-large inguinal ring. They are often associated with a difficult birth with its attendant increase in abdominal pressure.

 Surgery is required.

HYPERKALAEMIC PERIODIC PARALYSIS

A muscular disorder confined to horses descended from the American Quarter horse stallion, Impressive.

Periodic episodes of muscle stiffness and muscle trembling occur. These spread to more and more muscle groups as the attack proceeds. Prolapse of the third eyelid sometimes occurs and often the small muscles of the face contract causing what looks like an evil smile. During mild attacks the horse remains standing but more often increased flaccidity of the muscles leads to swaying, stumbling and eventual recumbency. As the attack subsides, and after a few attempts, the affected horse regains his feet and carries on as if nothing had happened.

Considered to be a genetically transmitted abnormality which causes changes in the way sodium and potassium ions are handled by the muscle cell. Sodium ions leak into the cell and potassium ions are forced out.

■ The condition can be controlled by strict attention to the diet, which should contain less than 1% potassium. Foods to be avoided are alfalfa, sugar beet molasses and bran. General-purpose mineral and vitamin products should be checked for their potassium content.
■ In acute attacks attention is paid to decreasing the high serum potassium levels. I/V isotonic saline or 5% dextrose solutions are used.

HYPERLIPAEMIA (illus p94)

A disorder of the fat metabolism that occurs in overweight ponies and donkeys. A rare and serious condition with a high mortality rate.

Affected animals become slow and lethargic, appetite is lost and extreme weight loss develops. Nervous signs such as circling and head pressing are seen as liver failure develops in a few days. A blood sample will show the high levels of fat in the plasma.

Occurs in excessively fat ponies or donkeys that are suddenly starved or subjected to some other form of stress such as transportation or inclement weather. It is more common in those animals that have a resistance to the effects of insulin. In order to feed itself, the pony mobilises its fat reserves; the level of fat in the blood increases and the liver fails as it tries to cope.

Early treatment is essential to replace the energy loss and reduce the levels of fat in the blood.

HYPOTHYROIDISM

Synonym: goitre

A deficiency of thyroid hormone: a rare condition in the adult horse, but it occurs in new-born foals when it is more often known as 'congenital goitre'. It has been blamed as a cause of abortion, and has been associated with bone and tendon developmental abnormalities and loss of hair. Due to the difficulty of being sure that a deficiency of thyroid hormone actually exists, care should be taken when making this diagnosis in an adult.

The thyroid gland in affected foals is always enlarged, and foals with congenital goitre are born lethargic and weak. They often find it difficult to rise and have to be suckled on the floor. Once over this initial period of weakness, recovery is rapid, and apart from the enlarged thyroid gland foals appear normal.

Can be due to a deficiency of iodine in the mare's ration during pregnancy, especially during the latter months. More commonly, however, the condition arises because of an *excess* of iodine. It is thought that the high concentrations of iodine suppress the ability of the thyroid gland to secrete thyroid hormone. This effect disappears quickly after birth which explains why thyroid hormone levels in the young foal are normal, and why, once over the initial weakness, foals appear normal apart from an enlarged thyroid gland.

Rarely needed once the foal is standing and suckling. However, attention should be paid to the mare's diet during pregnancy in order to prevent the condition from ever happening. The normal dietary requirements of iodine for a mare are 1 to 2mg a day. In a recent case report (*Durham Equine Veterinary Education* 5,239–241) congenital goitre was found in two foals whose mothers had had a daily dose of approximating 26mg iodine a day. This amount could easily be reached if the usual practice of 'if one tablespoon is recommended, two must be better' syndrome of feeding supplements is adopted.

NOTE: This is a good example of the care that must be taken when adding supplements to the normal daily ration of horses. All too often two or three different supplements are fed in the mistaken belief that they must do good, and completely forgetting the fact that many trace elements are toxic and that the daily recommended dose of each element should not be exceeded.

INFLAMMATORY AIRWAY DISEASE

A chronic inflammation affecting the lower airways of horses that spend most of their life in stables. In populations of young racehorses it can cause a considerable loss of performance but recent work carried out in large populations of mature horses kept in a stable environment showed that IAD had little effect on performance.

Affected horses may show exercise intolerance: they might have a cough and a nasal discharge and an endoscopic examination shows an excessive collection of mucus. Unlike RAO (was COPD – see p140) affected horses do not have an increased respiratory effort at rest and often appear clinically normal to the outward eye.

The actual cause of this syndrome is unknown, but constant exposure to stable dust is a major component. In the young racehorse infection with various bacteria could also have a bearing on the development of the condition.

Conventional treatment consists of antibiotics, bronchodilators and mucolytic drugs. A rapid improvement occurs when affected animals are removed from the high dust levels of a stable environment.

INTESTINAL CLOSTRIDIOSIS

First described in the 1970s by workers in Sweden and America. The disease is sporadic in nature and can affect all breeds and ages of horse. It is usually associated with stress, either following surgery or treatment with antibiotics.

First usually depression, followed very quickly by a peracute diarrhoea which is projectile, foul-smelling and liquid in nature. Mucous membranes rapidly become congested and dark red in colour. The affected animal often stands by water, mouthing it repeatedly but not appearing to drink. The usual outcome is increasing weakness, recumbency and death.

Generally accepted to be an enterotoxaemia caused by the rapid growth of the bacteria *Clostridium perfringens* and *C. difficile*. The reasons for this overgrowth are unknown, but many cases are associated with treatment with the antibiotic tetracycline or following stressful surgery.

Immediate treatment is essential.
■ Large quantities of fluids should be given intravenously.
■ Early work from Sweden suggests that sour milk, given by mouth, is effective.
■ There is some evidence that the antibacterial drug metronidazole given orally, or systemically and orally, is also effective.
■ If available, *C. perfringens* antitoxin will help.
■ The drug Flunixin meglumine, used to combat the effects of toxaemia, should also be given. However, in spite of aggressive treatment, many cases die from this serious disease.

Symptoms = 👁 Cause/diagnosis = 💥 Treatment = 📋

JAPANESE ENCEPHALOMYELITIS

A viral disease of the brain and spinal cord occurring in the Far East, see **equine viral encephalomyelitis** p153.

JOINT ILL

A disease of the young foal affecting the joints, often associated with a generalised septicaemia. For further information, see **septic arthritis**, p193.

KERATITIS

An inflammation of the cornea.

 Swelling and greying of the cornea as a result of corneal oedema. Photophobia (dislike of light) and blepharospasm (closed eyelids) occur early in the condition, also the eyes water and the conjunctiva becomes inflamed. Corneal ulcers are present in nearly all cases.

Trauma; as a result of excessive heat or cold; or more commonly, by infection with bacterial, viral or fungal agents.

■ Check carefully for the presence of a corneal ulcer.
■ Suitable antibiotic treatment, either locally six times a day, or as an injection into the conjunctiva once daily, should be started immediately symptoms are seen.

KIMBERLEY DISEASE

Synonym: walkabout disease

The result of poisoning; seen in the western and northern states of Australia.

Early signs are the effect on the central nervous system. Sleepiness, lack of co-ordination and mood changes are common, with loss of appetite and extreme loss of condition. Affected horses head press for hours, and where able, may walk aimlessly in a straight line for many miles. Eventually recumbency, coma and death occur.

The plant *Crotalaria retusa* is responsible for the poisoning; it is found growing on the flood plains of river valleys in these areas.

None.

LACTATION ANOESTRUS

An absence of oestrus behaviour in mares that are suckling a foal.

Affected mares show no oestrus activity. This situation can occur from the time the mare foals, but more often develops four to six weeks after foaling. Ultrasound examination of the ovaries reveals that they are small and inactive and show no follicular development, much as they would be in the midwinter anoestrus phase of the reproductive cycle (see p133).

When the foal suckles, a hormone called prolactin is released. Its main function is to stimulate milk let-down, but it also has the effect of suppressing ovarian activity.

■ Full-blown lactation anoestrus is almost impossible to treat and normal ovarian activity does not return until late in the season.
■ Many mares are only partially affected, however, and treatment with Regumate™ followed by an injection of prostaglandin will bring them into oestrus.

LACTATION TETANY

Synonym: milk fever

A metabolic disorder of the lactating mare, associated with a fall in blood calcium.

Typically the mare is found standing stiffly, often with grass sticking out of locked jaws. The eyes are glazed and the gait unsteady. Tetanic spasms soon develop, in fact the condition is often confused with tetanus, and eventually the mare becomes recumbent and in the absence of treatment, falls into a coma and dies.

A sudden fall in the level of calcium in the mare's blood. Lactation tetany is often associated with the stress of travel to shows or market, with unaccustomed housing, or with weaning. It almost always occurs in the lactating mare.

An intravenous injection of calcium given by your veterinary surgeon.

LAMINITIS (illus p103)

Synonym: founder

Inflammation of the sensitive laminae which lie between the hoof and the bone of the foot (pedal bone). Traditionally considered a disease of fat ponies grazing on lush spring and autumn pasture, but it can affect any horse, donkey or mule, and it can be caused by over-eating or by any condition that leads to toxaemia or septicaemia, such as retention of foetal membranes after foaling, or even by excessive trauma to the feet. It can be an acute or a chronic condition.

In the acute disease, severe pain in the feet is a constant symptom, and the horse is generally distressed, sweating and trembling. A bounding, fast pulse can be felt in the arteries underneath the fetlock. The front feet tend to be affected more severely than the back, and as a result the horse stands with the hind legs underneath the body and the front legs extended in an attempt to lessen weight-bearing and, therefore, pain in the front feet. In the less affected case the horse

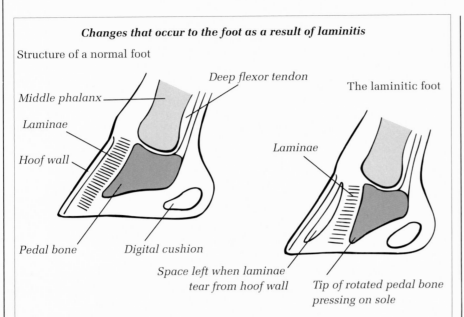

Changes that occur to the foot as a result of laminitis

Structure of a normal foot

Middle phalanx

Deep flexor tendon

Laminae

Hoof wall

Pedal bone

Digital cushion

Space left when laminae
tear from hoof wall

The laminitic foot

Laminae

Tip of rotated pedal bone
pressing on sole

stands alternately lifting one foot after the other. Later in the course of the condition the foot feels cold whilst the coronary band is hot.

Separation occurs at the bond between hoof and pedal bone and this, together with the pull of the deep flexor tendon, can cause rotation of the pedal bone. In turn, the point of the rotated pedal bone applies pressure on the sole, causing it to flatten from its normal concave position; in severe cases the bone penetrates the sole of the foot. If the separation between hoof and pedal bone is extensive then further complications develop, namely the unsupported bony column starts to sink within the foot, causing long-term changes that can be very difficult to control.

Typically a sudden overloading of the digestive tract with carbohydrate, either fresh young grass or cereals; this encourages a flush of lactic acid-producing bacteria. The high levels of lactic acid kill the normal bacteria in the large intestine and damage its mucosal lining; endotoxins from the dead bacteria and the lactic acid can then enter the vascular system. Any condition that causes the formation of endotoxins can therefore lead to laminitis. The presence of these poisons in the body results in an increase in blood pressure and the development of a peculiar short-circuiting of the blood to the foot, whereby the blood supply is shunted across the coronary band and never reaches the lower portions of the foot; this leads to a lack of oxygen and a lack of supply of essential amino acids to the laminae – the leaf-like fingers which interlock to hold the hoof onto the pedal bone beneath. The reduction in blood flow and the reaction of the sensitive laminae to this insult causes intense pain. The laminae degenerate, and blood and serum collect between the hoof and bone causing separation. As already mentioned, the resulting lack of support can cause rotation of the distal phalanx, or in more severe cases a sinking of the whole bony column within the external structures of the foot. In serious cases the reduced blood supply at the coronet kills the tissues at this point and the whole hoof may be sloughed off.

Irreversible changes occur in the laminae within the first twelve hours, so it is essential to start treatment immediately. This is aimed at preventing further damage and reducing the effect of the loss of blood supply to the laminae.

■ Administering large quantities of liquid paraffin helps to prevent further absorption of endotoxins.
■ Phenylbutazone will reduce the considerable pain, increase the blood supply to the foot and reduce inflammation. DMSO is also used with success.

■ The sedative acepromazine has a dilating effect on the vessels of the foot and should be administered immediately.
■ Topical nitro-glycerine patches applied to the digital arteries just under and behind the fetlocks will also dilate the vessels of the foot.
■ Nerve-blocking the feet with a long-acting local anaesthetic will increase the blood flow by exerting a vasodilator effect but should be used with caution.
■ In all cases, stabling with litter that supports the sole, to minimise lamella damage and to prevent rotation and sinking of the third phalynx, is essential. Sand or a mixture of peat and sand is the best, bark or wood chips will suffice.
■ In all but the mildest case a heart-bar shoe will support the pedal bone.
■ In severe acute cases, surgical removal of the front wall of the hoof might be necessary (illus p45).
■ A high proportion of acute cases do not respond and the condition becomes chronic. Treatment concentrates on controlling the pain with anti-inflammatory agents combined with regular corrective trimming and shoeing (every three to four weeks) so that the pedal bone assumes a more normal position.

LAMPAS

An apparent swelling of the tissue immediately behind the upper row of the front teeth, a condition that worries a great many horse owners. In fact this is quite normal in young horses that are changing their teeth, although it may be more marked in horses in poor condition.

An enlargement of the tissue immediately behind the top row of incisor (front) teeth. The swelling might be marked enough to protrude below the wearing surface of the teeth.

Unknown, but associated with poor condition, especially in the young horse.

Traditionally barbaric methods were used to remove the lampas; one method was to burn the tissue with hot irons. No treatment is necessary, however, since the condition will resolve itself as the horse gets older and improves in condition.

Symptoms = 👁   Cause/diagnosis = ✳   Treatment = 🗄

LARYNGEAL HEMIPLEGIA

Synonyms: roarer, whistler

The left vocal cord becomes paralysed. In the normal horse the muscles connected to the cartilages of the larynx contract when the horse breathes in, thus pulling the vocal cords up and out and increasing the size of the laryngeal opening; the heavier the breathing the wider the opening.

Changes that occur in the larynx of a roarer as exercise intensity increases

Normal larynx during rest

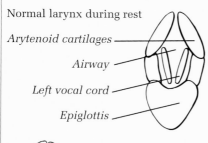

Arytenoid cartilages

Airway

Left vocal cord

Epiglottis

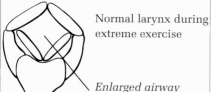

Normal larynx during extreme exercise

Enlarged airway

Larynx of a roarer during exercise

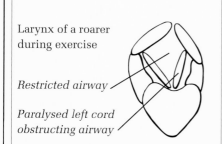

Restricted airway

Paralysed left cord obstructing airway

A roaring or whistling noise which occurs when the horse breathes in. The noise, normally absent at rest, increases in intensity with the speed of work. More common in large Thoroughbreds, hunters and warmbloods.

In affected horses the left vocal cord cannot be pulled back, and the entrance becomes asymmetric. This causes turbulence in the in-flowing air which vibrates the vocal cords and causes the whistling or roaring noise characteristic of the condition.

The reason for the paralysis is a progressive dysfunction of the left recurrent laryngeal nerve which controls the muscles responsible. Why this nerve becomes degenerate is not known. There might be an hereditary component, or physical chemical damage might play a part.

Surgical interference is the only way of treating this condition:
■ Traditionally the Hobday operation: the larynx is opened and a portion called the ventricle, which lies behind the vocal cord, is removed. The scar tissue which forms during healing is supposed to pull the vocal cords back and increase the size of the laryngeal opening.
■ A more modern method is the tieback operation: the larynx is opened and the cartilage supporting the paralysed vocal cord is tied back. The technical precision needed to perform this operation leads to variable results, but when performed successfully, the laryngeal opening is enlarged, allowing free passage of air. A Hobday operation is generally performed as well.

The success of the treatment is difficult to determine. Few horses stop making a noise, although the ability to perform does improve.

LEISHMANIOSIS

The condition is seen in South America, and recently cases have been seen in Southern Europe.

Nodular lesions develop in the skin of the face, inguinal and axillary regions. Some of these lesions ulcerate and others become crusty and hairless.

The actual cause of this condition is a protozoan parasite of the family Leishmania. Their life cycle consists of a stage in the body of sand flies and skin of dogs, man and occasionally horses.

There is no specific treatment and lesions appear to resolve spontaneously in 4 to 5 months. Control of sand flies will prevent the condition appearing in horses.

LEPTOSPIROSIS

A bacterial disease with a worldwide incidence affecting humans, companion animals and wildlife. The leptospires tend to be host specific: *L. hardjo* and *L. pomona* have cattle, sheep and pigs as their definitive hosts; *L. canicola* affects mainly dogs; *L. bratislava* has recently been associated with the horse. Some strains can cause severe disease in species other than their host.

The most common disease caused by *leptospira* infection is **recurrent uveitis** (periodic ophthalmia) (see p189). Liver disease and kidney infections, especially in the young foal, have also been attributed to it. It has long been recognised as one of the causes of abortion in cattle and pigs, and in the 1980s (probably due to improved diagnostic methods), leptospires were also found to be the cause of abortion and neonate disease in the horse.

Leptospira are excreted mainly via the urine of acutely infected animals. The horse is infected by eating contaminated food or water, or by standing in infected stagnant water.

The antibiotics streptomycin, potentiated penicillins and tetracycline.

LIMB DEFORMITY IN FOALS

Limb deformities originate in the young foal, either in the new-born as a result of congenital or developmental abnormalities, or in the rapidly growing older foal as a consequence of that growth. In the older foal most, if not all limb deformities are the result of this rapid growth, and of the mineral and vitamin imbalances caused by the persistent desire to overfeed young horses. The wish and belief that a fast-growing, obese foal is 'doing well' is erroneous, and the pressure – largely of economics – to get a young horse to adult weight as soon as possible is no friend to the horse or indeed to the owner.

Young bone grows by increasing its length and diameter at the growth plate and at the cartilaginous layers at the ends of the bone. In these two areas the immature cartilage grows, thus increasing the length and breadth of the bone. At the same time this new cartilage is changed into young bone. The process occurs smoothly across the whole width of the growth plates to ensure that the bone grows straight and is capable of bearing weight throughout its development.

Unfortunately a combination of events comprising overfeeding, too fast a growth rate, mineral imbalance and over-exercise conspire to create an overall imbalance in which the rate of ossification cannot keep up with the rate of new cartilage formation. As a result the deeper layers of the cartilage become degenerate and cannot support the weight of the foal. This condition is called 'oesteochondrosis' and is thought to be the root cause of most deformities of the limb bones of the actively growing foal.

Angular deformities (illus p120)

Angular deformities can occur either soon after birth when they are due to incomplete ossification of the limb bones and slack joint capsules and ligaments; or later in the foal's life when abnormal bone development is the cause.

 The distal portion of fore- or hind limbs deviates from the normal line. The deviation can be medial (varus, or turning in) or lateral (valgus, or turning out). In young foals a valgus (turning out) of the front legs is the most common type.

Angular deformities in most new-born foals generally right themselves as the foal becomes stronger and the joint capsule tighter. In a few cases the condition worsens, in particular in those foals that are born weak or premature, or those forced to exercise too much trying to follow the mare. In these it must be corrected before the continuing ossification makes the angularity permanent.

In the older foal, deformity is due to an unequal growth of the long bones. As the foal gets older the long bones increase in length: most of this increase occurs at the far end of the bone, in an active growing area called the growth plate, with a little occurring in the head of the bone.

However, occasionally the rate of growth across these regions differs, one side growing faster than the other, and as a consequence, the leg deviates from the normal. The reasons for this unequal development are complicated, but certainly the continual compressive trauma that occurs at the growth plate in foals that are born with a deviation, and the unequal forces acting on the joint as a result of developing oesteochondrosis, are factors in the development of displacement.

The condition is common in the fat, rapidly growing, overfed individual, which would substantiate the view that oesteochondrosis is more likely in animals in this condition – another reason to slow down the development of the foal to a more natural rate.

■ The leg of a new-born foal that is slow to straighten will generally respond well to splinting. It should be held straight by the splint, and care must be taken to ensure that it is well padded and not likely to cause pressure sores.
■ Successful treatment in the older foal relies upon altering the rate of growth of the deformed bone, either by persuading the shorter side to grow faster or to slow down the faster growing side. The latter has been the traditional method, and various techniques are used to achieve this. They all depend upon bridging the growth plate with a rigid structure, either staples or wire, so as to prevent any increase in size, thus allowing the shorter side to catch up and straighten the leg. Once this has been achieved the restraint is removed and the leg allowed to grow on normally.
■ More recent observation has found that damage to the covering of the bone (the periosteum) leads to a corresponding spurt in bone growth underneath the damaged area. This finding is used in a technique that involves transecting the periosteum over the growth plate on the shorter side and allowing the accelerated bone growth to level up the leg. An advantage of this method is that no staples or screws have to be removed once correction has been achieved and also, due to reasons unknown, once the leg is straight, the differential growth ceases.

Whatever the method of correction, it

is important that it is done at a period of maximum bone growth. In the case of deviations involving the fetlock this is during the first month of life, and for the knee and hock joints any time in the first four months.

Ankylosis of the joints

A condition that nearly always carries a serious prognosis.

 The foal is born with one, or more often multiple joints fused in a flexed position. These cannot be manipulated in any way, and the resultant shape of the foal often causes severe problems during birth.

Thought to be lack of space in the uterus, but it is possible that various plant toxins, mineral deficiencies or drug toxicity could be involved.

■ Very slight abnormalities will improve as the foal becomes stronger.
■ Foals with a badly affected joint or joints should be put down as there is no practical treatment.

Flexural deformities (illus p120)
Synonym: contracted tendons
The most common joint abnormalities found in the foal. They can be divided into two divisions: the deformities that occur in new-born foals, and those that develop in the older foal.

Congenital flexural deformities

 The fetlock joints of the front legs are most often affected and are flexed to a greater degree than normal. In most cases the degree of flexion is such that the foal walks on the points of its feet, but in the more severe case, weight might be born on the front of the foot and pastern. The knee joints can also be affected.

Not absolutely clear, but lack of room in the uterus causing a lack of movement of the joints has an influence on the development of the condition.

■ Most cases cure themselves as the foal gains in strength and starts to

Symptoms = 👁 Cause/diagnosis = 🦴 Treatment = 📖

exercise himself, but physiotherapy in the form of five or ten minutes every day spent straightening the joint will speed recovery.

■ More serious cases will benefit if the limb is splinted in an extended position. The splint needs to be in place for two weeks and good padding is essential to prevent any pressure sores developing.

■ It is debatable whether the extreme cases – those where the flexion cannot be reduced manually – should be treated, as it is unlikely that a return to full athletic ability will ever be reached.

Acquired flexural deformities
Synonym: contracted tendons
Most common in the older foal; the condition is typified by a gradual knuckling over of the foot of either the front or the hind limbs; this is due to an inability to extend the coffin joint.

Occurs in foals between 6 weeks and 6 months of age and starts when the foot begins to knuckle over, with weight taken at the toe. As the foot becomes more upright the toe wears and the foot becomes boxy. In some foals the wear is extensive enough to cause bruising, and the foot then becomes painful so the foal stands in a non-weight-bearing manner which causes even more flexion of the coffin joint.

As with so many diseases that affect our modern foals, the overriding cause is the pressure of the market. The showing, racing and equestrian sport industries demand over-topped, overgrown, early developing youngsters, and this insistence on fast growth allows the long bones of the lower limb to outstrip the ability of the flexor tendons to accommodate this growth. The result is a bowing of the limb accentuated at the weak point, the coffin joint.

■ Mild cases or those caught early can be arrested by modifying the diet to cut down the growth rate, and by applying a shoe with a toe extension. The extra leverage this causes will straighten out the defect. If a toe extension is put on the foot, remember to keep the foal on a hard surface to ensure that maximum leverage is applied.

■ More serious cases can be treated by tendon resection which allows the 'string' of the bow apparatus to catch up with the growing bones, the 'bow' in our example.

Hyperextension of the fetlock
(illus p122)
This condition is seen in the new-born foal and affects the fetlock joints of both front and hind limbs. Oversized weak foals are commonly affected.

The foal is born with fetlock joints in full extension and walks on its heels. In severe cases the back of the fetlock joint and pastern might touch the ground.

A temporary imbalance between the group of muscles which extends and that which flexes the lower leg.

■ Usually all that needs to be done is to protect the fetlock joint and pastern from damage whilst the foal gets stronger and the condition rights itself.

■ Refractory cases respond to a heel extension which is best applied using one of the new plastic glue-on shoes.

LYME DISEASE

Synonym: *Lyme borreliosis*
Disease caused by the bacteria *Borrelia burgdorferi* which affects man and other animal species including the horse. It has a wide distribution throughout the northern hemisphere and has been reported as causing disease in Europe, Great Britain, America, Russia and many other countries.

Indefinite, but most suggested cases are reported as having a fever; also joint swelling and pain, reluctance to move, poor appetite and lethargy. Sometimes there is brain involvement which might give rise to neurological signs.

Infection with the bacterium *Borrelia burgdorferi*. This organism is carried by the common tick and is transmitted from one horse to another when the larval stages feed.

The antibiotic tetracycline; also synthetic penicillins.

LYMPHANGITIS (illus p89)

An infection of the subcutaneous tissues and lymph vessels of the lower limbs. Can be confused with filled legs, but actually it is a more serious condition which often complicates the long-standing case of filled legs.

Starts with an often unnoticed infected wound of the lower leg. The infection spreads rapidly up the lymphatic vessels of the leg causing a hot painful swelling which involves the whole limb. Lymph glands and vessels are particularly swollen and serous fluid oozes from the skin. The horse is acutely lame and obviously ill with a high temperature. More commonly affects the hind legs.

When a cut becomes infected, or as a complication to mud fever. Horses that habitually suffer from the filled leg syndrome are especially prone.

■ High doses of antibiotics to control the infection; these should be given immediately.
■ Phenylbutazone and diuretics to reduce the inflammation and swelling. Inadequately treated cases will become chronic, leaving a thickened, scarred leg.

MALABSORPTION SYNDROME

An inability of essential nutrients to pass through the intestinal mucosa; more common in the elderly horse.

Chronic diarrhoea, associated with a gradual weight loss. The appetite remains normal. In the later stages ventral oedema develops.

Characterised by a chronic inflammation of the small intestine, the wall of which becomes thickened and unable to absorb essential food material. The cause of the inflammation is unknown, but avian tuberculosis and intestinal histoplasmosis have been incriminated.

None successful. Supportive nursing and strict attention to a highly digestible ration might stabilise the condition.

MALIGNANT OEDEMA

Synonym: gas gangrene

Rapid swelling of the area around a wound. The skin becomes hot and painful and gas is often present in the subcutaneous tissues. The discharge from the wound becomes frothy and foetid in nature. Affected horses quickly become dull and depressed and death follows rapidly. On the rare occasions when treatment is successful the affected area becomes necrotic and sloughs away, leaving a large wound.

Infection of a wound with bacteria of the Clostridial family. Malignant oedema often follows wounds caused by penetrating spikes of wood, following unhygienic castration or after a difficult birth.

Rarely successful.
■ Large doses of a suitable antibiotic such as intravenous penicillin given early in the course of the disease might arrest the condition.
■ Treatment for shock, such as intravenous fluids and non-steroidal anti-inflammatory drugs will also help.

MASTITIS (illus p100)

An infection of the mammary glands; a rare condition in the mare. It is often confused with the swelling and pain that occurs in these glands when the foal is ill and not sucking, or with the natural swelling that follows weaning.

The gland or glands become hot, hard and very swollen. The swelling often spreads forwards along the ventral body floor and upwards between the hind legs. The whole area becomes very painful and the mare resents any interference, either by the handler or the foal. The affected mare has a temperature and looks depressed and ill, and due to the pain and swelling she often moves in a stiff, unwilling way. All appetite is lost and the milk soon becomes clotted and discoloured.

Infection of the mammary gland with bacteria of the streptococcal species; often develops at or around weaning or just before foaling. Cases also occur during the summer, especially when the mammary glands are stimulated by the natural oestrogenic hormones present in some pasture plants. In these cases fly contamination and damage are a contributing factor. Severe mastitis often occurs as a complication of strangles (see p197).

■ Parental antibacterial, together with local application of an intramammary antibiotic preparation.
■ Local treatment of the mammary gland with hot water applications will ease the pain and might make it easier to introduce the intramammary preparation, often a difficult job as the teat orifices are very small and the gland very painful.

MECONIUM, RETAINED (illus p123)

The faeces which collect in the foal's rectum during pregnancy are called meconium. Blue-black in colour and fairly hard in consistency. Normally passed in the first twelve hours of life, followed by the yellow-orange, normally pasty faeces of the young foal.

Initially general discomfort. The tail starts twitching, and the foal spends more and more time lying down, looking around at his flank and straining. Often found lying in an awkward position on his back with forelegs folded over his head, or standing with legs and feet all together, back and tail up, trying to pass the nodules of meconium.

Foals, and especially large weak colts, can find it difficult to pass this material, because the diameter of the balls of meconium is often larger than that of the pelvic girdle.

■ Liquid paraffin by mouth, or given as an enema.
■ As a last resort, surgical removal.

MELANOMA (illus pp59 & 114)

Tumours of the melanin-producing cells of the skin. Found in all horses, occurring first in middle age; extremely common in grey horses.

First seen as small, firm black lumps in the substance of the skin; frequently multiple. Common sites are in the skin of the perineum especially around the anus, in the area around the eyes, sometimes in the eye itself, and in the glands of the neck. Grow slowly, especially in the grey horse, but occasionally they become aggressive and start growing rapidly and spreading to other parts of the body.

■ Surgery, but melanoma do tend to spread after apparent removal and it is often best to leave those that are causing no problems well alone!
■ New anti-carcinogenic drugs developed for use in humans have been used with success, although the cost tends to be prohibitive.

MUD FEVER (illus p117)

Mud fever, cracked heels and greasy heel: all conditions common in the horse wintered outside whose legs are continually wet.

Greasy heel and cracked heel: the skin below the fetlock and between the heels becomes red and inflamed; this exudes matter and a crusty lesion appears. These lesions can appear in summer and winter and are associated with wet skin and possibly an allergic factor (see p143).
Mud fever: occurs mainly in the winter and can affect the leg up to the knee

and hock. The initial lesions are much the same but spread rapidly up the leg, matting the hair into clumps. The legs swell up and become very painful, and the horse becomes lame and sometimes quite ill.

Cold wet skin is abraded by mud particles and becomes infected by the organism *Dermatophilus congolensis*.

■ Gentle bathing to remove all the scabs is essential.
■ The legs must be kept dry and clean.
■ Local or parental antibiotics might be necessary.

MYOGLOBINURIA

Synonyms: atypical azoturia, atypical myoglobinuria

Affects horses at pasture, all types, of all age groups, and it has a high mortality rate. Although it has been recorded since the thirties, the first major outbreak was reported in Scotland in 1985. Other outbreaks have occurred in Great Britain since this time, and reports of the condition have appeared in international literature.

Generally affects more than one horse in a group: they are first seen lying down, disinclined to move, and frequently unable to rise from lateral recumbency to sternal recumbency. If they are standing, the head hangs and the horse appears very lethargic and disinclined to move. Appetite is often normal as long as food can be reached.

Blood tests show a marked rise in the muscle enzymes CK and AST, signifying severe muscle damage.

The urine is coffee-coloured due to the presence of myoglobin and other muscle-breakdown products.

Unknown at the moment; the only common factor seems to be that most outbreaks are associated with a period of bad weather that occurred shortly before the outbreak.

■ Supportive: large quantities of fluids given intravenously. Also anti-inflammatory drugs and vitamin preparations, calcium and steroids.

Unfortunately in spite of treatment a high proportion of cases slip into a coma and die, probably as a result of heart failure caused by the damage that can occur to the myocardium (heart muscle).

MYOPATHIES

A group of diseases that can be defined as those that affect only the muscle, generally the major muscles of locomotion and whose effects are caused by inadequacies of the apparatus of muscle metabolism. The most common of this group is Azoturia (see page 135). Other myopathies have been recognised in recent years, none common and mostly affecting heavily muscled breeds such as the Quarter horse.

These conditions are:
1 Equine polysaccharide storage myopathy (p152)
2 Hyperkalaemic periodic paralysis (p161)
3 Glycogen branching enzyme deficiency (p157)

NASAL POLYPS (illus p85)

Soft, pedunculated growths that are found growing from the surface of the nasal chamber.

In the early stages there is little sign that a polyp exists, except that breathing might become slightly noisy, but as the polyp grows, the surface of the growth becomes damaged and diseased. The increasing bulk can cause obstruction to the free passage of air, and a noise to be made with each breath. The degenerating areas begin to smell, causing foetid breath and a dirty nasal discharge. Bleeding from the nose sometimes occurs.

Radical surgery is the only cure. The prognosis is poor.

NAVEL ILL

An infection of the navel cord stump, found in foals in their first month of life.

The navel cord becomes hot and swollen and the foal runs a temperature. Generally appetite is lost, and the foal becomes depressed. As the infection develops, a discharging abscess forms in the navel cord; this weakens the body wall and frequently an umbilical hernia develops at a later date.

Joint ill is a common complication and often follows navel ill. It is a sensible policy to monitor foals with navel ill for any signs of joint involvement.

■ Treat the navel cord with an antiseptic as soon after birth as possible to prevent any infection entering.
■ Once navel ill is present, the navel should be bathed with hot water frequently throughout the day to encourage the abscess to form and burst.
■ Systemic antibiotic treatment, prescribed by your veterinary surgeon.

NAVICULAR DISEASE

A degenerative disease occurring in the navicular bone of one or both front feet. (This is the tiny bone at the back of the coffin joint, deep in, just above the bulbs of the heels; it acts as a pulley over which the deep flexor tendon runs as it passes across the joint.) Common in the hunter, warmblood and hack types, but rare in the Arab and in pony breeds.

Navicular disease develops gradually, and although the case is often presented as sudden lameness, a careful look at the horse's history will show that the gait has been altering for some time. One affected foot is often pointed forwards at rest; if both are affected, the horse may not be obviously lame but moves in a pottery manner. A nerve block done on one foot will then demonstrate the lameness in the other. Loss of confidence in jumping and a developing tendency to trip up are common findings.

In long-established cases the lack of wear to the frog and heels of the foot leads to overgrowth and contraction of the

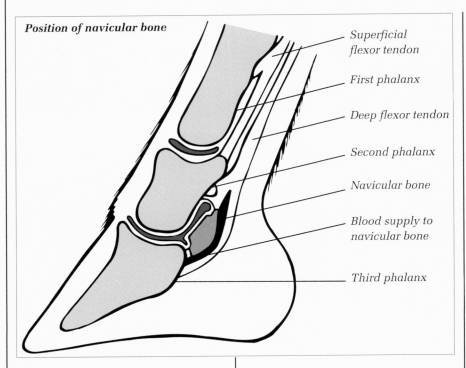

Position of navicular bone

Superficial flexor tendon

First phalanx

Deep flexor tendon

Second phalanx

Navicular bone

Blood supply to navicular bone

Third phalanx

heels, and the foot becomes boxy in appearance.

There are three theories:

1 Physical trauma to the bone: that the commonly found long toe, low heel conformation of the Thoroughbred foot increases the forces that act on the navicular bone, which leads to damage to areas of the bone.

2 That changes to the arterial blood supply to this region, and a loss of blood supply to the navicular bone cause the damage.

3 Degenerative change is responsible.

As research progresses we will probably find that all the theories will connect and that navicular disease is a syndrome caused by many interacting factors.

■ Radical attention to the shape of the foot is essential, and the correct hoof/pastern axis must be returned. The foot, and especially the heels, must be given a chance to expand, and must be adequately supported. Ideally an egg-bar shoe with rolled toes should be fitted.

■ Drugs which act on the circulation to increase the blood flow to the navicular bone, for example warfarin, which acts as an anti-clotting agent. It is considered to aid the development of a secondary blood supply in cases where the primary arteries have been damaged and blocked by thrombus (clot) formation. Warfarin is a toxic drug and only to be used under expert supervision.

■ Isoxsuprine hydrochloride dilates the peripheral blood vessels, lessens the viscosity of the blood and improves the blood supply to the navicular bone. A regime of corrective foot care and a course of isoxsuprine for at least three weeks has produced good results. The only disadvantage is the cost.

■ A new treatment has been described by continental workers. The drug Tiludronate, one of a group of drugs active at normalising bone metabolism by inhibiting bone reabsorbtion, seems to have a positive effect. Horses that received the drug showed long-term improvement in their attitude and soundness.

■ Surgical: (i) neurectomy – the sectioning of the nerves supplying that area of the foot – has been used for some time, but the severe complications that sometimes occur limit its usefulness.

(ii) Sectioning of the collateral navicular suspensory ligaments; this is a new method and seems more promising. These ligaments keep the joint capsule under tension; cutting them releases the tension and allows a better blood supply to develop.

■ Anti-inflammatory agents can be used to control pain, but should be considered a short-term measure.

NEONATAL MALADJUSTMENT DISEASE (illus p123)

Synonyms: barker foal, dummy foal, wanderer foal

Affects the new-born foal, and is generally associated with complications at or soon after birth.

Vary tremendously from subtle nervous signs such as a slight vagueness or a staring attitude, and a slight twitching of limbs and head, to a completely uncontrolled seizure and even constant fits – but all affected foals show some behaviour change and all generally lose the ability to suckle the mare. In between fits the foal might be comatose, or it might wander aimlessly round making strange barking sounds, or it might stand with its head pressed up against a wall or the floor. Although the suckling reflex is generally absent, it might be able to suck from a bottle even if in a manic way.

The most significant is trauma during birth. The resulting brain damage can cause circulatory and respiratory disturbance and a lack of oxygen to the brain, which in its own right causes further brain damage. This cycle must be arrested otherwise it rapidly leads to in death.

Concentrates on stabilising the foal so that the original damage can heal and the foal return to normal function.

■ The nervous signs, if severe, can be controlled with anti-convulsant drugs such as Diazapam™, or if necessary by light anaesthesia.

■ Some foals might only need supervision to prevent them wandering into harmful situations. Food should be administered by stomach tube if the suck reflex is absent, and some more severely affected foals might need fluid therapy.

■ As a general rule, all but the mildest cases need the attention of a specialist centre in order to cope with the many complications that this syndrome

Symptoms =   Cause/diagnosis =   Treatment =

presents. On the happy side, however, if the condition is treated quickly and the foal stabilised, then most cases recover to lead a completely normal life.

NEPHRITIS

An infection of the kidneys; rare in the adult horse.

In the initial stages possibly a high temperature; pain and swelling of the affected kidneys might be found on rectal palpation. Laboratory examination of the urine may demonstrate blood and pus, but this should be distinguished from that found due to **cystitis** (see p145).

In more chronic cases, examination of blood will show changes in the levels of serum protein, urea and creatinine.

An ascending infection from the bladder. A common complication of septicaemia (see p193).

An extended course of potentiated sulphonamides or antibiotic.

NETTLE RASH (illus p112)

Can be recognised by large areas of raised hair over the affected part of the body. The skin in these areas is hot and painful. Also profound nervous signs. Horses become unsteady on their feet (ataxic) and abruptly demonstrate signs of acute pain, frequently throwing themselves on the ground or striking out with all four legs. Care should be taken when handling horses in this condition as they seem to be completely unaware of their surroundings. These alarming symptoms regress over a few hours, although the horse can be depressed for up to 36 hours. The condition has caused fatalities, especially in the older horse.

Thought to be a hypersensitive reaction to nettle stings. Cases are associated with horses grazing pastures with large stands of mature nettles, and the condition occurs more often in horses that are hot and whose skin is wet.

Normally resolves in a few hours. Treatment with painkillers and anti-inflammatory agents should be attempted on humane grounds.

NODULAR SKIN DISEASE
(illus p61 & p114)

Synonym: collagen disease

The sudden appearance of firm, painless nodules varying in size from a grain of rice to a pea in the skin of the neck or back.

Thought to be an allergic reaction: possibly to migrating parasitic larvae, occurring when these larvae are killed by the effect of a wormer; or a hypersensitive reaction to insect bites.

Generally resolves over a period of time. Individual lumps, especially those in positions where they might interfere with articles of tack, can be removed surgically.

OESTROUS CYCLE

The oestrous cycle of the mare starts at puberty and carries on throughout the rest of her life until old age. The cycle varies between 18 and 22 days in length and is separated into a period when she is receptive to the stallion (oestrus) which lasts 4 to 6 days, and a quiescent period (dioestrus, the period between each oestrus) which lasts 16 days. Oestrus itself shows considerable variation in both intensity and duration, especially at the beginning and end of the breeding season.

The average mare shows that she is in oestrus by changes in her behaviour. She spends frequent periods crouching as if about to urinate, but only passing small amounts of urine. She is attracted to a stallion or gelding and shows this attraction by again crouching and assuming a position and attitude of docility. She raises her tail to one side, and contracts and expands the vulva and everts the clitoris, an action called 'winking'. There is often a character change: the normally placid mare becomes irritable, and the highly strung mare quiet and manageable. There is also often a change in the performance of the athletic mare during oestrus, most performing less well.

The oestrous cycle is orchestrated by a group of chemicals called hormones which act and react with the reproductive organs in the body to produce the changes which happen during the cycle.

The cycles start early in the spring when an organ in the brain called the *hypothalamus* reacts to increasing periods of daylight, higher temperatures and better food and starts to secrete a group of hormones: these act on a small gland tucked under the brain called the *pituitary gland*, and persuade it to secrete increasing amounts of a hormone called *follicle stimulating hormone* (FSH).

FSH in its turn acts on the ovaries, and stimulates the growth of under-developed follicles. These small, fluid-filled sacs each contain an egg or ovum, and as they develop they secrete another hormone called *oestrogen*; oestrogen is responsible for the physical signs of heat.

The pituitary gland is constantly checking on the level of oestrogen in the blood, and once a certain concentration has been reached, it acts again by secreting a further hormone called *luteinising hormone* (LH). LH first reduces the production of FSH and then, acting on the ovary, accelerates the development of one follicle, causing its eventual rupture and the release of the ovum. This process is called *ovulation* and it occurs about 24 hours before the end of oestrus.

Once ovulation has occurred, the level of oestrogen produced by the follicle falls rapidly and the mare goes out of season.

The collapsed follicle develops into a specialised gland called the corpus luteum, which secretes yet another hormone named *progesterone*. The progesterone effect is directed mainly at the uterus: it prepares this organ for the implantation of the fertilised ovum, ensuring that its lining is ready to maintain early pregnancy. It also reduces the amount of FSH secreted from the pituitary gland, thus slowing down the development of new follicles.

The control of the cycle now passes to the uterus. If fertilisation has not taken place and implantation has not occurred, the hormone *prostaglandin* is produced in the uterus. This destroys the corpus luteum in the ovary, and the level of progesterone produced by this gland falls rapidly.

The pituitary gland, the overall coordinator, senses this drop and, in reply, increases the amount of FSH hormone which acts on the ovary, stimulating the growth of the next crop of follicles. So the cycle repeats itself.

The oestrous cycle can be manipulated by the use of drugs and by altering the environment of the mare:
■ Repeated injections of the gonadotrophin-releasing hormone (GnRH), a hormone secreted by the hypothalamus and one of whose functions is to stimulate the production of FSH and LH, can be used to advance the onset of the mare's oestrous cycles.

■ Increasing the daytime period with the use of artificial light, and increasing body condition and warmth, will also bring forward the onset of oestrous periods.
■ The dates of actual oestrus can be changed with the use of the hormone prostaglandin (Pg). As already stated, this hormone removes the corpus luteum and restarts the cycle, and mares in the dioestrous phase of the cycle will come into heat 3–8 days after the use of a prostaglandin injection.
■ Orally active, synthetic progesterone such as Regumate™ can also be used to regulate the cycle. Oestrus is suppressed whilst the mare is under the influence of these progesterones; once the influence is removed – ie Regumate™ supplementation ceases – oestrus returns in 3 to 5 days. This effect can be used to treat those mares that do not cycle well in the early part of the breeding season, and also to synchronise mares that are going into an artificial insemination programme.

OESTROUS CYCLE, TRANSITIONAL

The period in the early spring when the mare is changing from the normal winter anoestrous state towards full reproductive activity. The start and length of the period varies according to managerial factors and the physical condition of the mare.

Irregular reproductive activity varying from long periods of apparent heat to short heats at irregular intervals. Ovarian activity might occur with no observable heat, or observable oestrus with little ovarian activity.

The transitional period is a normal phase in the yearly cyclic behaviour of the mare. It starts when the environmental threshold – in this case comprised of increasing body condition, longer daylight hours and improving weather – tip the anoestrous mare into the beginnings of oestrous activity; and it lasts until the threshold is powerful enough to stimulate the start of full ovarian activity.

Normally one should not need to treat mares in the transitional period, but modern stud practice often insists that mares must breed early so that foals will

As spring advances

Increasing light and warmth

Increasing food   Gaining condition

stimulates the

Hypothalmus

to produce releasing hormone which in turn stimulates the

Pituitary gland

To increase the secretion of follicle stimulating hormone (FSH) and decrease the level of progesterone secretion

Failing conception causes a secretion of prostaglandin from the uterus which destroys the CL. This lowers progesterone levels in the blood and allows the influence of FSH to start a new cycle

This stimulates the growth of follicles

The CL produces progesterone. Increasing blood levels of this hormone further depresses FSH and causes changes in the uterus readying it for implantation

One of these developing follicles becomes the 'chosen one' and rapidly matures releasing increased amounts of oestrogen

In turn increasing levels of LH cause the maturation of the follicle, ovulation and the development of a corpus luteum (CL)

The increasing levels of oestrogen circulating in the blood cause changes in behaviour and changes in the reproductive tract ie the mare comes on heat

The high levels of circulating oestrogen and FSH together depress FSH production and increase that of luteal hormone (LH) from the pituitary gland

Symptoms = 👁️   Cause/diagnosis = 🦴   Treatment = 💊

reach their maximum size for the sales. With this in view, it is often desirable to stabilise the cyclic behaviour of the mare in the transitional period thus:
■ The hormone preparation Regumate™ acts by halting the oestrous cycle; when treatment ceases, the oestrous cycle resumes with extra force, and a normal cycle with a successful ovulation occurs.
■ The hormone prostaglandin can also help, because it removes the active corpus luteum which might be interfering with the development of a normal cycle. Ovulation occurs 3 to 5 days following the removal of the corpus luteum.

ONCHOCERIASIS (illus p118)

Onchocerca cervicalis is a filariad worm with a worldwide distribution.

The migrating larvae cause patches of scaly dermatitis to develop along the mid-line, the face, withers and chest. These might develop into crusty lesions. A lesion characterised by alopecia and depigmentation often found around the eye is thought to be due to a hypersensitive reaction to dying larvae. Eye lesions, especially **recurrent uveitis** (periodic ophthalmia) (see p189), have been associated with the migration of the larvae through the eye.

The adult worm lives in the *ligamentum nuchae*, the large ligament that runs from poll to withers, and seems to cause very little trouble. Microfilariae produced by the females migrate to the skin where they infect biting insects. After completing a stage of development they are introduced back into the horse via the insect bites.

Any preparation containing the anthelmintic drug ivermectin will kill the microfilariae, and the lesions should resolve in two weeks.

ORCHITIS

Infection of the testicle or its associated structures; rare in the stallion.

Swelling of one or both testicles, which become hot and painful to the touch. The affected stallion might walk stiffly, and

will generally refuse to cover mares. In the early stages there will be a rise in body temperature and loss of appetite.

Usually infection or trauma.

■ Large doses of antibiotics to control the infection quickly.
■ In chronic cases affecting one testicle, unilateral castration might be necessary.

ORPHAN FOAL

The hand-rearing of an orphan foal is a demanding, full-time job, but if done properly, it is very rewarding. It must be remembered, however, that a strong bond rapidly develops between foal and the handler, and it is very easy to allow the foal to become extremely spoilt – this will only do it a great disservice because it is bound to experience severe emotional problems later in its life. At all times handle the foal gently but firmly, and introduce it to other young foals as soon as possible; hopefully it will then grow into a well adjusted yearling.

Foals are generally orphaned at birth due to the death of the dam during or after parturition. A foal might have to be orphaned because of the mare's lack of milk, or as a result of rejection by the mother.

The orphan foal should be given about one litre of colostrum as soon after birth as possible; this is to ensure that it starts life with adequate protection against all the diseases with which it will come into contact. It can either be reared by the bottle/bucket method, or fostered onto a foster mother.

Foster method
If a suitable mare can be found, this is a very successful method of rearing an orphan foal.
■ The mare should be kept with her dead foal until she is settled, then the foster foal should be introduced to the mare, preferably dressed in the skin of the mare's own foal or with plenty of foetal fluids rubbed into its coat.
■ With the mare held firmly, an attempt

should be made to suckle the foal. If this succeeds, then the mare and new foal can be left to complete the bonding process, though they should still be observed to be sure that the mare has wholly accepted the foal and does not harm it. More often, however, quite a few attempts at introducing the new foal and mare, together with suckling sessions, are needed before the two confirm a bond together. Sometimes a nervous mare might need twitching or sedating before she will accept the foal. The dead skin can be removed in 24 to 36 hours, and the mare and foal should be kept under observation for at least two days.

Bottle- or bucket-rearing
■ If at all possible, bottle-rearing should be avoided: it is very time-consuming, and it is extremely difficult to avoid humanising the foal.
■ Using a bucket and teat is a much more practical method. Patience is needed to teach the foal to suck from the teat, although most, if they are hungry, learn to do this quite quickly. In the early stages of a foal's life feeding intervals should be at least every two hours, but as the weeks progress this can be lengthened.
■ The most convenient milk substitutes are the specially formulated, mare's milk powders. Goat's milk can be used with great success, and some foals can even be persuaded to suckle the nanny as long as she is placed up on a stand. Cow's milk is the least successful, and should be low fat with extra sugar and calcium added.
■ Creep feed, such as milk pellets, calf creep, or commercial foal creep, should be introduced from 10 days onwards; it should be offered in small quantities and replaced daily.
■ Good quality hay can be given as the foal gets older.
■ Foals can be weaned from about 16 weeks onwards.

OTITIS EXTERNA

Inflammation of the external ear canal.

Excessive rubbing of the affected ear and shaking of the head, which might be tilted to that side. The ear is extremely painful and there might be a purulent discharge from the ear canal.

A foreign body, such as a grass seed, might be lodged in the ear canal; or there might be bacterial or fungal infection.

■ A thorough examination of the ear canal with an auroscope should be arranged with your veterinary surgeon and any foreign bodies removed. Most horses will need sedating, or a twitch must be used, to enable this to be done.
■ The ear canal should then be cleansed gently, and antibiotic, anti-fungal, anti-inflammatory ear drops administered.

OVER-REACH (illus p60)

Synonym: forging

The heel area of a fore foot is struck into by the toe of a hind foot, generally the one on the same side. Wounds of varying severity can occur but the most common outcome is that the fore shoe is pulled off as the hind shoe catches its heels.

Faulty conformation or bad trimming and shoeing cause a late break-over of the front feet; this increases the chance of the hind feet interfering with the fore.
Fatigue leading to poor co-ordination also increases the chance of interference.

Correct trimming and shoeing – ensure that the toe is short enough and that the shoe is rolled – speeds up break-over and so helps remove the front foot from danger.

PARASITES

Bots (illus pp41 & 93)
The bot is a large, noisy, hovering fly often seen annoying the horse in late summer, when it lays yellow or orange-coloured eggs on the horse's legs and lower abdomen.

It is not known how much trouble the bot larvae cause while in the stomach, but in the healthy adult horse it is probably not great. However, large accumulations of bots might cause unthriftiness in the late winter/early spring.

Eggs are laid by the fly on the legs and lower abdomen of the horse throughout the late summer and autumn. The horse's licking and grooming actions stimulate the eggs to hatch in a week and the larvae pass via the mouth through the tissues to the stomach. Here they develop for up to ten months before detaching from the lining of the stomach and passing out onto the pasture in the faeces. The adult flies hatch out in the late spring ready to mate and renew the cycle in midsummer.

■ Eggs should be removed by grooming with a bot knife every day, thus reducing the number eaten by the horse.
■ A wormer effective against bots such as ivermectin, or an organo-phosphate based preparation, should be given once all the egg-laying adult flies have been killed by frost.

Ear mites
Mites of the *Psoroptes* family are known to have caused otitis in horses, and are suspected of being one of the causes of head shaking.

Acute irritation of one or both ears. Rubbing the head against any available object, head shaking and scratching the ears with the hind feet should suggest that something is causing a problem in the ear. This could be due to the presence of ear mites.

Daily application of an antiparasitic ear preparation of the type used to cure parasitic otitis in dogs or cats.

Lice (illus p117)
There are biting and sucking types, and both are small, active creatures about

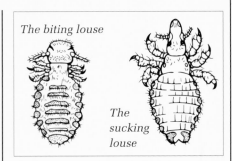

The biting louse

The sucking louse

2mm (^{1}/$_{16}$in) long which breed in the long winter coat and feed from skin debris and body fluids. Biting lice are found mainly in the body coat; sucking lice live in the hair of the mane and tail.

The coat becomes dull and hair is lost from the neck and shoulders; the mane and tail become matted, and altogether the affected horse assumes a moth-eaten appearance. Infected horses itch and rub and bite the skin to relieve the irritation. Severe infestations can cause loss of condition and anaemia, especially in young horses or those with a concurrent worm infestation. In good light conditions, lice can be seen on the skin surface.

Horses are more susceptible when they are in poor condition and are kept in large numbers. The eggs – or nits as they are commonly known – are laid on the hair and hatch out in ten days.
Lice enjoy the comfort of warm long hair and their numbers build up during the winter and are at their highest in the early spring. The effects on body and coat condition are seen from January onwards. In the summer when the hair is short the numbers of lice are low.

■ If possible the coat should be clipped out.
■ To break the life cycle, treatment should be at two-week intervals, either by washing the coat with a residual insecticidal medication, or by dusting with a suitable louse powder.
■ Administer ivermectin worm doser: these have the useful side-action of killing lice.

Symptoms = 👁   Cause/diagnosis = 💥   Treatment = 💊

Liver fluke

A disease primarily of sheep and cattle, but cases of chronic liver disease caused by liver fluke have been recorded in horses.

The same as those shown by any agent that causes chronic liver disease (see p92).

Grazing wet pastures infested by the liver fluke parasite.

Most of the agents used to treat liver fluke in cattle can be used. The drug Triclabendazole, although not licensed for use in horses, has a useful activity against fluke.

Mange (illus p118)

Three types of mange mite affect horses, all rarely seen nowadays:

Chorioptes equi

Infects the back of the fetlock area in horses with heavy feather. Affected horses spend their time stamping the ground in an attempt to get some relief. There will be scabbing, and signs of an intense itch.

The mites which live in and on the skin.

Psoroptes equi

Moist, bloody patches develop at the base of mane and tail.
Can cause a severe **otitis externa** (see p173) with a purulent discharge, also **head shaking** (see p159).

Psoroptic mange mites, which live on the skin or in the ear canal and feed on the skin surface.

Sarcoptes scabei (syn. scabies)

Small hairless patches exuding serum. These tend to be clustered around the head, neck and shoulder region. Intense itching.

Very infectious, and like all manges, it is spread by direct contact, or from shared tack or grooming utensils. The mange mite burrows into the skin and causes an intense puritis. Sarcoptic mange is a notifiable disease.

■ All mange mites can be treated with weekly washes of an acaricide.
■ Ivermectins are a successful method of treatment.

Mites (syn. bracken bugs, chiggers, harvest mites, orange tawneys)

A free-living mite called *Trombicula autumnalis* living in long grass, hay and straw.

An intensely itching rash appears on the lower legs of thin-skinned horses. Most prevalent during the late summer.

The bite of the young larvae which move on to the legs when the horse is in contact with long grass or straw.

■ Twice-weekly washes with an effective insecticide.
■ Anti-inflammatory ointments applied to the affected areas.

Roundworms

Dictyocaulus arnfieldi (syn. lungworm)

The normal host of the lungworm is the donkey, in which they live and breed without causing much disease. They lay large numbers of eggs which contaminate the pasture for many years, often long after the donkeys have moved on. Similarly the eggs that horses eat while grazing hatch out in the intestine and the larvae migrate to the lungs – but here they remain as immature worms, unable to complete their life cycle, but able to cause disease.

A chronic, irritating cough that alters very little, with no nasal discharge and little effect on appetite or condition.

Lungworm infection: this affliction should be suspected in any horse that has

a chronic cough present both at rest and when exercising, and that grazes in company with donkeys or in a field in which donkeys have grazed.

■ All donkeys should be wormed regularly with a wormer that is effective against lungworm.
■ Any horse that has a chronic cough out at pasture should also receive an effective worming dose.
Effective wormers are Eqvalan, Equitac or Systamex, or large doses of Panacur.

Oxyuris equi (syn. pinworm, thread-worm)

The adult is a slender worm about 7cm (3in) long which lives in the large intestine. The female moves to the anus to lay eggs, which appear as yellow/white masses stuck to the perineal region. Animals are re-infected by eating or drinking contaminated food and water.

An intense irritation caused by the presence of the eggs and the activities of the female worm. Hair is lost from the head of the tail and the skin may be damaged from rubbing.

All modern wormers are effective at removing this parasite.

Parascaris equorum (syn. whiteworm) (illus p93)

A large white worm, up to 20cm (8in) long, which lives in the foal's small intestines. Numbers are at their peak during the first nine months of a foal's life; thereafter they decrease almost to zero.

Life cycle: Adult worms lay large numbers of infective eggs which are climatically resistant and can contaminate the pasture for years. Very high worm burdens in susceptible foals are possible. Eggs are eaten by the foal and reach the intestine, where the larvae hatch out and pass through the wall to the liver; here they spend a few days before migrating to the lungs to be coughed up and swallowed again. The larvae develop in the forepart of the small intestine for 8 to 10 weeks until they reach maturity; they then begin to lay eggs which pass onto the pasture ready to infect further foals.

 Foals with large numbers of worms developing in the small intestine become dull and lethargic and lose their appetite. If this number becomes extreme, their physical presence can cause impaction in the intestines or even rupture. Their migration through the foal's lungs might cause a dirty nose and a cough.

■ The dam should be wormed two weeks before foaling to reduce the risk of infection early in the foal's life, and her hindquarters and udder should be washed after foaling.
■ The foal should be treated regularly, every 6 weeks up to 9 months of age.
■ The anthelmintics citrazine and ivermectin, given by mouth, are effective against both adult and larval forms.

Strongyles

The strongyles can be divided into two groups: the large strongyles, which can be subdivided into three types; and the small strongyles.

Together they are considered to be the major intestinal parasites of the horse, although the importance of the large strongyles as pathogens has decreased since the introduction of effective larvicidal wormers.

Large Strongyles
The three types are:
1 *Strongylus vulgaris* (syn. redworm) (illus p40)
The most common and dangerous worm of the three types.
Life cycle: The adult worms live in the large intestine, and here the female lays eggs which pass out on to the pasture. In 1 to 2 weeks the larvae hatch and become infective. Eaten by the horse and entering its digestive system, they burrow through the intestinal wall and migrate along tiny arteries towards the main arteries of the intestine. For 3 to 4 months they remain buried in the artery walls undergoing further development. They then make a further migration to the large intestine, where they burrow into the wall and hibernate for six weeks.

When they emerge as adults, they start feeding on the lining of the large gut, where they damage considerable areas of mucosa and blood vessels.

2 *Strongylus edentatus*
This species is uncommon.
Life cycle: A longer but less damaging migratory phase, with the larvae passing from the gut into the liver and, after further development, to the lining of the abdominal cavity and then the large intestine where they finally mature.
3 *Strongylus equinus*
Seldom found in Britain; its life cycle is much like that of *S. edentatus*.

 The symptoms of all three groups are much the same and can be taken together: thus, the larvae of the redworm block arteries, depriving areas of the body of blood and causing local damage and death of tissue. When it occurs in the gut, this type of damage is one cause of spasmodic colic. *S. edentatus* larvae can damage the liver as they pass through it. The symptoms resulting from both types of damage include rapid weight loss, depression and fever.

In comparison, adult worms are less dangerous. However, in large numbers they can cause chronic anaemia, especially in young horses, and the damage they do to the intestinal mucosa upsets the body's fluid balance, causing diarrhoea.

■ Regular preventive treatment is necessary.
■ Preparations containing ivermectins, and those containing oxfendazole are effective against both adult worms and larvae and are recommended to be given every six weeks.
■ Most other preparations are effective against adult worms only and are recommended to be given on a monthly basis.

Small strongyles (**syn**. cyathostomes, triconemes, whip worm) (illus pp40 & 93)
Now known as *cyathostomes*, and occur in significant numbers in the large gut; although once thought to cause little harm, they are now known to cause serious illness under certain conditions.
Life cycle: Eggs are laid throughout the year. They hatch out in the faecal material, and in warm, wet conditions the larvae spread into the adjacent foliage and reach an infective stage within a week. Cold, dry conditions slow down this stage, and this graduated development ensures that the maximum number of infective larvae are present when conditions favour their survival. Once in the horse they burrow into the wall of the large intestine and undergo further development for a variable period.

They then emerge from their cysts and gradually mature into adults in the lumen of the large intestine. In situations where there are already numbers of adults in the gut, or perhaps where the horse has developed a partial immunity, large numbers of larvae enter the lining of the gut and remain encysted for months in an inhibited state. Normally these leave the gut wall in the early spring.

 Encysted larvae in large numbers damage the glands of the large intestine and interfere with its motility. This can predispose towards colic, and can cause loss of weight and lethargy in the late autumn. In spring, the encysted larvae may leave the gut wall in numbers large enough to cause an intense reaction which, if severe enough, results in a condition called 'larval cyathostomiasis'. The latter can also be triggered following a routine worming; presumably the removal of all adult worms stimulates a release of the larvae. This syndrome can occur any time between November and May.

The horse suffers acute diarrhoea and rapid weight loss, usually has a temperature, loses its appetite and appears very depressed; without rapid, effective treatment, the prognosis is bad.

■ Adult worms are removed following treatment with any of the three main groups of wormers. These are the benzimidazole group (Thiobendazole and Panacur), tetrahydropyrimidines (Strongid-P) and the macrocyclic lactones (abamectin, ivermectin and moxidectin). Unfortunately it has been discovered that cyathostomins have developed a resistance to the first two groups of anthelmintics, and special regimes need to be set up to deal with this problem (see p177 above).
■ Cases of larval cyathastomiasis need intensive fluid replacement. Steroids have been used and proved effective in increasing the survival rate of horses suffering this serious condition.
■ All the usual wormers will effectively remove adult worms.

■ Encysted larvae are resistant to most wormers; however, Panacur (fenbendazole) given as a single dose of 60mg/kg, or daily for 5 days at the normal dose rate of 7.5mg/kg, or any of the ML group (eg ivermectin, moxidectin or avamectin) at normal dose rates given three times at weekly intervals, will remove nearly all larvae. Worming using this regime is recommended in November if encysted larvae are suspected.

Strongyloides westeri (syn. threadworm)
A small worm common in the small intestine of foals.

Life history: Not completely understood. Very young foals are certainly infected by larvae present in the mare's udder and excreted in the milk. These can infect the foal via the milk as soon as 4 days from birth, and will develop full patency during the next 2 weeks.

Eggs can be demonstrated in the faeces from 2 weeks post birth, coming to a peak at 2 to 3 months of age and disappearing at 6 to 9 months when a self-cure occurs. In favourable conditions larvae can infect the foal through the skin. This is also probably the source of larvae in the udder of the mare.

Apart from a transient scour this worm causes very little trouble; heavy infections, however, can cause a chronic diarrhoea and loss of weight.

The anthelmintics thiabendazole (Thiabenzole) or ivermectin (Eqvalan) are very successful at eradicating the worm.

Tapeworms (illus pp40 & 93)
Anoplocephela perfoliata, the tapeworm of the horse, lives at the junction of the small and large intestines; a flat worm 8–10cm (3–4in) long, 1cm (⅜in) wide.

Life cycle: The adult tapeworm sheds segments of its body which contain eggs and are passed out in the droppings. These segments soon break down and release the eggs on to the pasture where they are consumed by small mites called orbital mites which live in the base of the turf. Here they develop for 4 months; they find their way inside the horse when the mites are taken in with a mouthful of grass.

Acute attacks of colic occur if large numbers damage and interfere with the efficient working of the ileo-caecal valve. As the damage becomes chronic, unthriftiness, diarrhoea and weight loss, with sporadic cases of colic might be seen.

Twice yearly preventative treatment with a double dose of Strongid-P: this should remove a high percentage of tapeworms present in the caecum. The first dose should be given 6 to 8 weeks after the horse is turned out in the spring, and the second in the autumn.

Ticks
Many species of tick feed on horses, but the main importance of tick infestation is its role in the transference of other diseases.

A heavy burden of ticks causes anaemia and loss of condition. Tick bites can become infected and cause multiple skin abscesses.

■ Prevent horses from grazing rough ground; this will reduce the chance of infestation.
■ Wipe-on or spray acaracides will kill ticks found on the body of the horse.

Warbles
The campaign initiated by the Ministry of Agriculture, Fisheries and Food (now DEFRA) to eradicate the warble fly from the cattle population has reduced the number drastically and the condition is now rare in the horse. The warble larva is unable to complete its development in the horse and generally dies in the skin.

A hard lump develops on the horse's back, often in the saddle area, caused by the body's reaction to the dying larva; it often has a breathing hole on the dorsal surface.

The warble fly lays its eggs on the horse's legs, where they hatch out and burrow through the skin. Once under the skin they migrate up the legs to the back where they develop for a time, but then die.

Sometimes the undeveloped larvae can be removed manually or by poulticing, but more often the lump has to be removed surgically.

PARROT MOUTH (illus p46)
Synonym: overshot jaw

The upper jaw, the maxilla, protrudes beyond the lower jaw, similar to a parrot's beak.

A congenital fault.

■ If the displacement is minimal no treatment is necessary.
■ More severe displacements will need regular dental care in adult life due to the lack of wear of the first upper premolars and last lower molars.

PATENT URACHUS

Urine seeps continually from the stump of the navel cord of a new-born foal. Urination becomes difficult and the flow from the umbilicus increases as the foal strains. The soiled area becomes necrotic and infected.

During the inter-uterine period of the foal's life the urine that is produced by the kidneys is drained through a tube called the urachus into the allantoic space. Sometimes this tube does not close as it should in the first few hours after birth and urine is allowed to escape through the urachus and umbilical cord.

■ Thorough cleaning and cautery of the umbilicus is necessary to encourage healing.
■ Those which do not heal will require surgery.
■ Antibiotic treatment should be administered for 5 days.

PEDAL BONE FRACTURE

 Sudden onset of a severe lameness, generally in a front foot, and almost always when being worked on rough ground. Acute pain is shown when pressure is applied to the foot. X-ray will show a fracture line through the pedal bone; several views at different angles might be necessary before the fracture can be demonstrated.

Severe localised trauma such as occurs when the foot strikes a stone at high speed.

■ Fractures that do not involve the joint space can be treated conservatively. Fitting a bar shoe with good side clips will help immobilise the fracture site and healing should take place. A period of 9 to 12 months is necessary.
■ Fractures that involve the coffin joint are best dealt with surgically. A bone screw is used to compress the two fragments together.
The prognosis is good for fractures not involving the coffin joint, but less so if the fracture runs into the joint surface.

PEDAL-OSTITIS

An inflammatory condition of the pedal bone.

Low-grade, shifting lameness in the front feet and a pottery action. On X-ray, characterised by a thinning of the bone at the anterior edge and a roughening of the bottom margin of the pedal bone. However, care should be taken in the diagnosis of pedal-ostitis as there is so much variation in the appearance of the bone on X-ray that it is difficult to judge what is normal or abnormal.

Severe bruising of the sole of the foot and repeated low-grade trauma such as occurs with a high workload on a hard surface.
The flat, Thoroughbred-type foot is considered at risk.

Seldom successful.
■ Non-steroidal anti-inflammatory drugs may help in the short term.
■ Protective pads used under the shoes may be the most helpful, and a bar applying pressure across the frog is valuable to improve circulation.

PELVIC INJURIES (illus p111)

Pelvic fracture

 Clinical signs vary tremendously depending upon which part of the pelvis is fractured. Thus, fractures involving the hip joint result in a total lameness, whilst a fracture of the ileum with little displacement can cause minimal lameness even at the trot.
Equally, fractures of the pelvis can be visually obvious, as is a fracture of the *tuber coxae* (pin bone), but clinically of little consequence.

Severe trauma. A common sequel to a heavy fall or after a road traffic accident. Horses which habitually rush in and out of stable doors risk fractured pin bones.

Surgery can help in some pelvic fractures, such as those involving the pin bones.
■ Fractures of the body of the pelvis are best treated by a long period of box-rest and a wait-and-see policy.

Pelvic strain

A common injury in the competitive horse, normally of the sacro-iliac region.

The most common is a disinclination to move forwards freely. Sometimes the hindquarters feel stiff and 'held in' on exercise. Horses that normally jump well and with enthusiasm will show that they are not enjoying it.

Strain to the sacro-iliac ligaments which join the pelvis to the sacrum.

■ Anti-inflammatory agents.
■ A long period of rest.

■ The application of heat with a heat pad reduces the pain and speeds up repair.

PERIDONTITIS (illus p83)

A disease of the structures around the teeth; seen predominantly in aged horses.

Foetid breath due to the trapped, decaying food material; a tendency to salivate while chewing. Affected horses take a long time to eat their hard food, and lose condition. Poorly digested grain might be found in the faeces.

Predisposing factors are poorly apposed teeth and abnormal mastication. Pockets of infection occur on the gum/tooth margin, which becomes impacted with food material. This leads to even more infection, which in turn loosens the tooth in its socket and causes infection and eventual death of the pulp cavity of the tooth.

Regular dental care will prevent the cycle from starting.

PERITONITIS

An infection of the peritoneum, the lining of the abdominal cavity. This is a serious disease in the horse.

Severe abdominal discomfort with tense, painful abdominal muscles. The horse is reluctant to lie down; when it does so, or when it moves, a respiratory grunt is evident. Severe depression, loss of appetite and rapid weight loss.

Common sequel to a penetrating wound of the abdominal wall or, more seriously, following rupture of the uterus during foaling or covering. Can also occur following a rupture of the intestine or a penetrating ulcer of the stomach wall.

Peritonitis due to the latter causes is almost always fatal due to the acute shock that follows the introduction of intestinal contents into the peritoneal cavity. Prompt treatment by your veterinary surgeon for shock and aggressive antibiotic therapy sometimes cures peritonitis resulting from penetrating wounds of the abdomen.

PHOTOSENSITIVITY (illus p112)

An increased sensitivity of the skin to sunlight.

The skin, especially white or hairless areas, reacts to sunlight and becomes reddened, thickened and inflamed. As it dies, it becomes hard and wrinkled and eventually sloughs off, leaving a granulating bed which heals slowly, generally leaving an ugly scar.

A condition that affects skin which contains photosensitive agents. These agents can be ingested in the food – an example is the weed known as St John's Wort – or may build up in the skin as a result of liver dysfunction.

They increase the sensitivity of the skin to sunlight, basically causing a very severe sunburn.

■ Prompt removal to a darkened box is essential in order to prevent further damage.
■ Cortisone and antihistamine injections will reduce the skin damage. The areas of affected skin should be treated with antiseptic ointments.

PIG MOUTH

Synonyms: undershot jaw

The lower jaw, known as the mandible, protrudes beyond the upper jaw, the maxilla, similar to a pig's mouth.

Often the maxillary bones are deformed as well as shortened and the mandibles are twisted.

A congenital/developmental fault.

■ If the abnormality is minimal, no treatment is necessary.
■ More severe displacements will interfere with the ability of the foal to suckle and euthanasia should be considered.

PIROPLASMOSIS

Synonyms: babesiosis, equine bilary fever, equine piroplasmosis, horse tick fever

A tick-borne disease of horses caused by the protozoan blood parasites *Babesia equi* and *Babesia caballi*. It is present in tropical and subtropical areas such as South America, the Caribbean, southern Europe, parts of Africa, Asia and the Middle East. The state of Florida underwent a severe outbreak in 1960, although this was due to the import of horses from Cuba and has since been eradicated. The disease has recently assumed more prominence due to the increase in movement of horses from tropical/subtropical regions to temperate regions with suitable tick vectors. The danger of introducing babesiosis into these susceptible areas gives cause for concern. At the present time the USA requires negative serology before allowing the import of horses.

Clinical signs are variable. Horses that contract the disease for the first time as adults are more seriously affected. Fever, depression and weakness are common signs. The mucous membranes become yellow as icterus develops, and petechael haemorrhages (blood splotches) appear on the gums, conjunctiva and vulva. Oedema of the dependent areas might develop and bloody urine is occasionally passed. Most horses recover from the acute stage to develop an immunity and become carriers of the parasite.

In those areas where the disease is endemic, foals are born with a passive immunity which largely protects them from the acute disease. However, they inevitably become subclinically infected and enter the carrier state.

The carrier animal remains in normal health unless stress, either of travel or competition type, causes a resurgence of the acute disease.

The blood-born protozoa can be demonstrated inside the red blood cells by microscopic examination of suitably stained blood films. Carrier animals also demonstrate a positive complement fixation test.

■ In acute cases the goal is to reduce the fever and prevent any further destruction of red blood cells. There are several anti-protozoan drugs that can be used for this purpose.
■ It is more difficult to eradicate babesia completely from the system in the chronic carrier case. However, in the last few years, new treatment regimes using the drug Imidocarb have been developed that will achieve clearance in over 90 per cent of cases.

PLACENTA, RETAINED (illus p100)

A long rope of placenta is seen hanging from the vulva. The mare normally expels the placenta within a few hours of birth, and retention beyond this period increases the risk of an acute metritis and laminitis.

Not known. A mare having once retained a placenta, often does so again in succeeding years.

There are no guidelines as to how long you should wait before action must be taken to remove a retained placenta, although 12 hours is the accepted period. You should then contact your veterinary surgeon.
■ He might attempt to remove the placenta manually.
■ A more usual method nowadays is to give the mare an intravenous injection of normal saline and a hormone called oxytocin; this causes the uterus to contract and to expel the membranes. This method has the advantage that the microscopic attachments between placenta and uterus are expelled as well, thus reducing the risk of an infection developing.

PLEURISY

The pleura is the lining that covers the lungs and the inside of the chest cavity. 'Pleurisy' describes an inflammation of this lining.

Inappetance; fever; lethargy. The painful chest causes rapid, shallow respiration together with a reluctance to move and to lie down. A soft, short cough is generally present. A rasping sound, rather like crunching up brown paper, can be heard if you listen with your ear at the chest wall.

Later on in the course of the disease the pleurisy might become exudative. The excessive fluid produced causes a fluid line in the chest that can be demonstrated by tapping the chest wall: once below the line the sound becomes dull and indistinct.

Ultrasound examination demonstrates pleural effusions well, and is an essential diagnostic tool.

Pleurisy is normally associated with pneumonia; in fact the condition should more accurately be called pleuro-pneumonia.

■ Call your vet quickly, as early treatment with antibiotics and NSAIDs (non-steroidal anti-inflammatory drugs) is essential if a complete cure is to be obtained.
■ X-rays can be used to define the presence of a fluid line. Draining the fluid from the chest might be a necessary adjunct to drug therapy.
Horses that recover well are likely to resume an active athletic career, but secondary complications such as abscess formation or fibrous adhesions between lung and pleura are common, and will jeopardise a complete recovery.

PNEUMONIA

An infection of the lung tissue. Uncommon in the horse, and most cases are seen in the young foal or the old, debilitated animal. Many agents can cause such an infection, most of them as a secondary development to another disease. The pneumonia which sometimes follows strangles or influenza is a good example.

Very much the same as with pleurisy: rapid respiration, inappetance, high temperature. The horse generally has a cough and a nasal discharge, and is often seen standing, reluctant to move or lie down, with an anxious expression on its face.

Any infective agent can cause pneumonia. The respiratory viruses are commonly involved, especially in stressed horses. The streptococcal bacteria are common pathogens. Horses that travel for long periods in poorly ventilated lorries or planes are especially at risk and should be monitored carefully after such journeys. Daily monitoring of their temperature is a good precaution.

■ The prompt attention of your veterinary surgeon is needed, as any delay increases the chance of permanent lung damage.
■ A long course of a suitable antibiotic is necessary, together with a broncholytic agent such as Sputolosin®.
■ Bronchodilators such as clenbuterol will also help.

PNEUMONIA, FOAL

Synonym: the rattles

A particular form of pneumonia, common in dry dusty conditions and associated with a high stocking density, caused by the bacteria *Rhodococcus equi*. It can cause a particularly nasty chronic pneumonia in foals.

Foals may be affected up to 6 months of age, but most become infected in the first few months. The disease is insidious in nature, and by the time the foal appears ill, considerable lung damage has occurred. The infected foal gradually loses condition and a chronic cough develops. Frequently it appears quite well until just before death.

A nasal discharge is sometimes present, and the foal has a variable appetite. Temperature is always elevated and the resting respiratory rate higher than normal.

A positive diagnosis is difficult to make, and depends upon isolating the bacteria from a bronchial wash and demonstrating lung abscessation with X-ray.

The organism is found in soil, and infection seems to be caused by inhalation of contaminated dust. The condition is common in the hot, dry conditions such as are found on Australian and Californian stud farms. Perhaps our nor-

mal high rainfall, wet summers and lack of dust is the reason why the disease is comparatively rare in the UK.

■ Twice-weekly examination of all foals will make it easier to recognise and treat the disease earlier.
■ A long course – at least 4 weeks – of a combination of the antibiotics erythromycin and rifampin is most effective.
■ Reducing the population density of groups of mares and foals, and taking management steps to reduce the level of dust, will reduce the incidence of the disease.

POISONING

Poisonous plants

Horses are selective grazing animals and therefore plant poisoning is relatively uncommon. If poisoning does occur, it is when horses are grazing poor pasture with little grass or when they are first introduced into a new field.

There are few specific treatments for plant poisoning and symptomatic care is generally all that can be done. It is essential to keep poisoned horses as warm and comfortable as possible. Large quantities of liquid paraffin by mouth will help remove any remaining toxins in the gut, whilst activated charcoal absorbs organic toxins to itself. Intravenous fluids will help to combat shock.

Acorns

Do not usually cause poisoning in horses as it is rare that they are on the ground in large enough numbers to cause problems. However, they are toxic and occasionally a high wind together with a heavily fruited tree will deposit enough to poison.

Constipation, abdominal pain and blood in the urine. Severe kidney damage can occur which can cause nervous symptoms such as head pressing, circling and so on. Milder cases might show obstructive colic.

Ingestion of oak leaves or acorns.

None specific. Large quantities of liquid paraffin will help.

Symptoms =   Cause/diagnosis =   Treatment =

Algae
Toxic algae bloom following a spell of hot weather, in water that has high nitrate and phosphate levels.

Acute: Increased sensitivity, muscle tremors, followed quickly by ataxia and recumbency. Death can occur in a few hours.
Chronic: Liver damage leads to jaundice and photosensitivity.

Drinking water from ponds or lakes that have experienced an algae bloom.

Sodium nitrite and sodium thiosulphate given intravenously may help.

Autumn crocus (**syn**. meadow saffron)
Flowers in the autumn; the leaves appear in late spring. Grows in permanent pasture; the toxic principle, colchicine, is found in the seeds produced in the spring and in the fleshy corm.

Profuse salivation, gut pain and diarrhoea occur early on. Later, colic and frequent passing of urine might be present. Large doses cause intense gut pain, staggering and death.

Ingestion of the leaves and seedheads in the spring and the flowers in the autumn. Poisoning is rare in the horse.

None specific.

Bracken (illus p80)
An upland fern found throughout the temperate zones of the world.

Gradually increasing inco-ordination, muscle tremors, loss of condition followed by recumbency and death.

 Bracken contains an enzyme, thiamase, which destroys the thiamine (Vitamin B₁) in the body, and the symptoms shown are the result of thiamine deficiency. However, horses find bracken unpalatable and do not usually graze it in

enough quantity to cause symptoms. Nevertheless, in drought conditions on mountain pastures it can be the only food available, and in these situations poisoning can occur. Moreover, some horses can develop a craving for bracken and will seek it out in preference to other fodder; obviously, these horses are at risk.

Thiamine, 100mg a day by injection until better.

Briony
A climbing plant common in hedgerows throughout temperate climates. Berries and roots are the most toxic parts.

An unknown toxin causes polyuria, increased sweating, diarrhoea and also convulsions.

Ingestion of the plant is rare, but berries and roots might be eaten by an inquisitive youngster.

None specific; symptomatic therapy might help in mild cases.

Dandelion weed
A plant that grows in Australia; considered to be the cause of **Australian stringhalt** (see p198).

Deadly nightshade
Atropa belladonna contains an atropine-like substance which is very toxic. However, poisoning is rare because the plant is unpalatable in the fresh state, and its natural habitat renders it unlikely to be found in conserved crops.

Dry mouth, mydriasis (dilated pupils), irregular heartbeat, blindness, nervousness and muscle tremors. Convulsions might develop, followed by coma and death.

Neostigmine methylsulphate, with sedatives to control the convulsions.

Equisetum (**syn**. mare's tail, horse tail)
Commonly known as mare's tail. A spiky plant found in damp soil conditions.

 Contains the same enzyme, thiaminase, that is found in bracken. Signs of poisoning are therefore the same as bracken poisoning.

The growing plant is rarely eaten, and cases are associated with eating the plant in fodder.

As for bracken poisoning.

Foxglove
This common wild plant is rarely grazed fresh due to its bitter taste. As 100–200g is a toxic dose, and foxgloves are palatable when dried in hay, it can be a cause of poisoning in the horse.

 The active principle (digitalis) is used clinically to slow and to increase the force of the heartbeat. At toxic levels digitalis causes a quickening and weakening of the heartbeat, and eventually leads to heart failure. Profuse salivation is common, as is abdominal discomfort and colic.

None.

Hemlock
Common throughout the temperate zones of the world; although unpalatable to the horse, it can cause poisoning, especially in the spring when the foliage is green and normal fodder might be scarce. Even so, the horse is relatively resistant to the effects of hemlock poisoning, and poisoning from this plant is relatively uncommon.

The toxic alkaloid conine causes progressive paralysis. The pupils are dilated, and the muscle masses, especially the hindquarters, become weak and tremble. Eventually the horse might become comatose, and in severe cases death results from respiratory collapse.

■ Stimulants such as atropine and strychnine will counteract the depressant effect of conine.
■ Tannic acid will neutralise the active principle.

■ Large doses of liquid paraffin will remove the plant material from the intestinal tract.

Laurel

A common hedging shrub not often eaten due to its bitter taste and leathery leaves. It and the chokecherry, a cherry found in the USA, together with other less common shrubs, have leaves which under certain circumstances can release enough hydrogen cyanide to kill.

 Hydrogen cyanide combines with oxygenated haemoglobin and prevents the oxygen being given up to the cells. The heart muscle is especially prone to poisoning.

Death results quickly from cardiac and respiratory failure.

 The cyanogenic compounds and the enzymes needed to produce free hydrogen cyanide are mixed together when chewed and can then release cyanide.

 Artificial respiration using high concentrations of oxygen might help. Normally, however, the horse is either dead or recovering by the time anything can be done.

Locoweeds

Belong to the *Astragalus* and *Oxytropis* species. They grow throughout the Western States of America and when consumed in large quantities can cause severe nervous signs in the horse.

 Visual impairment, inco-ordination and exaggerated movements of the hind legs are common.

Recovery is often only partial, and many horses die from paralysis, weakness and starvation.

 Many members of these plant species contain locoine, an alkaloid which causes the nervous symptoms. Other members of the family have the ability to concentrate selenium and can contain enough of this chemical to cause selenium toxicity.

 None. Those horses that might recover tend to have irreversible brain damage.

Oleander

This scrub is found growing wild throughout the southern United States and many members of the family are grown as garden scrubs throughout the world. The toxic principle has a similar action to digitoxin.

 Acute depression and profuse diarrhoea occur soon after eating any part of the scrub. As with foxglove poisoning the heart becomes weak and arrhythmic, and death from heart failure follows within a few hours.

 The plant is naturally unpalatable and poisoning normally occurs when clippings are left where they can be eaten by horses. Small quantities of leaves, up to 200g, are fatal.

 None effective.

Ragwort (illus p80)

A weed, which together with stinking willie and common groundsel is a member of the Senecio family. Found throughout the temperate zones of the world, and together with other members of the family, contains pyrrolizidine alkaloids which will kill liver cells. The plants are seldom eaten in a fresh state as they are extremely unpalatable, but they are potent poisons when they contaminate hay or silage.

 The most important and most toxic of the Senecio family, with an accumulative effect on the liver. The liver cells are destroyed gradually and by the time symptoms of chronic liver failure are seen (see p160) it is too late to effect a cure generally, and death usually occurs in a few weeks.

 Normally supportive and symptomatic. However, by the time symptoms are seen it is generally too late for effective treatment.

Rhododendron

Common garden shrubs throughout the world, and have become a problem weed in neglected woodlands.

 Initial salivation, followed by abdominal pain, staggering gait, collapse and death in a few days.

 As with so many garden plants, prunings are the most usual source of poisoning, although horses breaking into gardens or grazing in woodlands might eat the shrub.

 Symptomatic, with mineral oil.

Solanine-containing plants

Nightshade (woody, black and garden), green potatoes and tomatoes all contain the poisonous alkaloid solanine; the most dangerous are the black berries of black nightshade.

 Initial salivation and acute diarrhoea, followed by increasing depression, weakness, and finally prostration and death.

 Black nightshade is a common wild plant throughout the temperate zones and is especially dangerous in the autumn when the berries are ripe and natural fodder scarce.

Green potatoes and tomatoes which have been tipped out into fields where horses are grazing, and horses which have been turned into old potato and tomato fields, are both scenarios that could lead to poisoning.

 Symptomatic treatment with stimulants and mineral oil.

Sorghum

Sorghum species are used as forage crops throughout the world but have the disadvantage that under certain conditions, they release cyanide in the same manner and cause the same acute toxicity as laurel and chokecherry. A chronic toxicity **equine sorghum cystitis** has also been reported in the south-western United States.

Symptoms =   Cause/diagnosis =   Treatment =

Weakness of the hind limbs and a characteristic stringhalt-like action which is more pronounced at the trot or when moving off or backed. A large percentage also show urinary incontinence and cystitis. Urine scalds are found on the skin of the hindlegs.

Cases occur in horses which are put out to graze sorghum pastures, and are thought to be due to exposure to low levels of cyanide.

None specific.

St John's wort
A common member of the *Hypericum* family; contains one of the agents that causes the skin to react to sunlight (photosensitivity – see p179).

Water hemlock (**syn**. cowbane)
Grows in ditches and boggy areas and has a wide distribution. The toxic principle is a resin called cicutoxin.

The toxin has an immediate effect on nerve cells and causes central nervous stimulation. The pupils dilate and the major muscle masses start to twitch. Major contractions of these muscles cause loss of balance and unsteady gait, followed by recumbency and death from respiratory paralysis.

The fleshy roots are the most toxic portion of the plant, and most cases of poisoning occur after land reclamation or clearing out ditches when the exposed roots might be eaten by an inquisitive horse.

Anticonvulsive drugs will help to control the spasms in less acute cases. Those horses that survive six to eight hours will often recover.

Yellow star thistle
Yellow star thistle and Russian knapweed, both members of the Centaurea family, grow in California and other western states of America. At dry times of the year they can be the only pasture plant available for horses.

Develop quickly in horses that have been eating large quantities of these plants for at least thirty days: affected animals are unable to eat or drink due to a facial paralysis, and are to be found with heads down attempting to forage. Swelling of the head due to oedema is common.

Poisoning occurs more often in the autumn when yellow star thistle may be the most common plant in the pasture. Young horses are particularly at risk.

No cure; affected horses die within a short time.

Yew (illus p80)
Commonly found in churchyards, and extremely poisonous. A chemical called taxin found in the leaves and fruit has an effect on the heart, stopping it from beating.

Sudden death: horses poisoned with yew can be found dead with sprigs of yew still in their mouths.

Yew trees do not normally grow where horses graze, and because most horse owners are aware of the yew's extreme toxicity, poisoning is rare. Occasionally, yew prunings are thrown over a fence where horses can get at them, and then cases of poisoning may occur.

Poisonous chemicals
Aflatoxins
Toxins produced by the fungus *aspergillus flavus* which can contaminate various foodstuffs.

Acute: severe depression, nosebleeds, ataxia and convulsions.
Chronic: weight loss, anaemia, jaundice, bloody diarrhoea, and formation of haematomas under the skin.

The toxin is present in feeds contaminated by the fungus *aspergillus flavus*. Feeds usually incriminated are sorghum, rice, maize, groundnut, cotton seed and mixes containing them.

None specific.
■ Activated charcoal in the early stages will remove some of the toxin.
■ Increasing zinc and selenium content of the diet might help in chronic stages.

Arsenic
The present-day danger is definitely industrial waste, but old weedkillers, wood preservatives and fruit-tree sprays can contain significant amounts of arsenic.

Acute: severe abdominal pain, inco-ordination, weakness and trembling leading to collapse and death.
Chronic: blindness and paralysis occur.

Horses which are grazing on old industrial waste ground might take in enough to become chronically affected. Acute poisoning is rare.

10–20 per cent solution of sodium thiosulphate, 10g given intravenously followed by 20–30g given by mouth.

Calciferol
The active ingredient of some rat poisons.

Loss of appetite, loss of weight, breathlessness, and also increased water consumption together with the increased production of urine.

Contamination of hard food with rat poison containing calciferol.

Restrict calcium intake.

Lead
Uncommon in the horse; most cases of poisoning occur when horses graze on pastures contaminated with industrial waste. Acute toxicity following large doses of lead can occur, but horses usually suffer from chronic poisoning following continual ingestion of small amounts of lead over a period of weeks.

Lead interferes with the normal function of the peripheral nerves and causes general weakness characterised by unsteadiness and knuckling over of the fetlocks. A serious complication occurs when the recurrent laryngeal nerve is damaged and a pharyngeal and laryngeal paralysis occurs; this can cause respiratory distress and death from lack of oxygen. Anaemia also contributes to the increasing weakness, and chronic lead poisoning can be associated with a developing blindness.

 ■ Successful if the condition is recognised in time. The chemical calcium disodium edetate given intravenously for 4 to 5 days removes lead from the body.

Monensin
A growth stimulant often included in ruminant rations; when fed to horses it can cause a fatal illness. Very toxic.

 Acute depression develops quickly, together with a lack of appetite. Affected horses become recumbent and soon die.

Accidental feeding of beef rations containing monensin to horses.

None specific.

Organo-phosphates
Were a common component of many insecticides and pesticides, but because of the long-term hazards associated with these products they have been banned in many countries and poisoning of horses is no longer common. However, there is still a stockpile hidden away in many barns and outhouses, and poisoning from this group of compounds is still possible.

Nervous symptoms, muscle tremors, breathlessness due to respiratory collapse, and diarrhoea. Excessive salivation, and colic followed by collapse and death in untreated cases.

Accidental use of a concentrated solution as an insecticide wash; also overdosing with wormers containing organo-phosphates.

Prompt treatment with atropine sulphate at a dose rate of 1mg/kg will effect a cure in less acute cases.

Selenium
A natural component of the soils in the mid-west states of America and other areas of the world; in these areas chronic toxicity is common. Has also occurred following accidental contamination of feed supplements.

Acute: Nervous symptoms, a progressive mania and blindness, depression, laboured breathing, collapse and death from respiratory failure.
Chronic: Loss of weight, loss of hair from mane and tail, and a change in coat colour. Serious foot lesions also occur: the coronary band develops a break which, as it grows down the foot, causes separation of the hoof wall. The quality of hoof also becomes very poor.

Many plants growing in these soils – locoweed, vetch, woody aster, goldenweed and other species – have the ability to concentrate selenium and are the usual source of selenium toxicity. They are poisonous in both the fresh state, or dormant, or when they are included in conserved forage.
Contaminated water supplies can also cause chronic poisoning.

 None specific.

Strychnine
A potent poison traditionally used as a rodenticide; nowadays it is used under licence to control moles.

Small doses cause quivering of the eyelids which are often drawn back, rolling of the eyeballs, and quivering of the main muscle masses. Larger doses cause periods of intense muscular contractions and general convulsions separated by periods of quiet. Similar to the convulsions which are caused by tetanus.

 Accidental ingestion of the poison.

Administer general anaesthesia until the effects of the poison have worn off.

Warfarin
The active ingredient of many rat poisons. It acts by neutralising vitamin K which is an essential part of the clotting mechanism of the blood. It is also used therapeutically in the treatment of navicular disease.

Horses poisoned with warfarin haemorrhage both internally and externally: nosebleeds, blood in the faeces and urine, and subcutaneous haemorrhage especially over bony prominences are usual. Blood tests will show a grave anaemia and the horse appears pale and is often lame, the latter symptom caused by intra-articular bleeding. Massive bleeding into the chest or abdomen can cause sudden death.

Accidental contamination of foodstuffs with rat poison; or inappropriate treatment for navicular disease.

■ Blood transfusions, and vitamin K at 1mg/kg given immediately.
■ Supportive treatment with vitamin B12 and iron preparations will help.

Poisonous insects and reptiles
Blister beetle
This pest contains a powerful poison called cantharidin and is found throughout the United States. The adult females lay eggs in late summer which hatch out into larvae in a few weeks. The larvae feed on caterpillar eggs through the autumn then hibernate in winter. The adults hatch the next spring and commonly feed on the flowers of alfalfa and other crops. The problem occurs when the crop is cut and the beetles are killed in the crop. The cantharidin poison is very stable and remains in the crop to cause illness to horses that eat the contaminated portion of alfalfa, either fresh or as dried forage.

Cantharides cause intense irritation to the stomach and intestinal lining and as

Symptoms = ◉ Cause/diagnosis = ✖ Treatment = 🗎

excreted through the kidneys, damage to the whole urinary tract, causing frequent attempts to urinate. Affected horses may have blistered mouths, often play with water (probably to sooth the mouth), frequently show signs of colic, and develop diarrhoea.

Eating contaminated alfalfa. First crop alflafa is less likely to be contaminated as the beetle tends to congregate on flowering crops or crops with flowering weeds present. Avoiding machines that crimp or damage the crop whilst harvesting will allow the beetles to escape before being killed.

No specific treatment. Affected animals need prompt supportive measures which include fluids to dilute and flush out the poison, and gastrointestinal sedatives.

Snake bite
Uncommon in Europe as there are few venomous snakes. In the Americas, Australia and South Africa, or anywhere where there is a concentration of both snakes and horses, the number of snake strikes increases.

Most snake bites occur on the head or the lower legs: the latter rarely cause much trouble as the tough skin and lack of soft tissue minimise the concentration of venom in these sites; however, strikes to the muzzle and nose are more serious, and most cases cause severe swelling of the whole head and neck. Breathing can become very difficult and an emergency tracheotomy might be necessary.

Most cases of snake bite survive, but the tissue damage and long period of recovery can cause secondary problems. Care in choosing suitable horse pastures will minimise the contact between horse and snake.

■ Prompt treatment with corticosteroids and antibiotics will help to reduce the intense reaction to the bite and to counter the inevitable shock.
■ If the type of snake is known, the use of specific anti-venom will help.
■ If possible, a tourniquet put above the wound and suction applied to the wound will prevent the venom spreading.

POLL EVIL

Infection of the sinus that lies in the area between and a little behind the ears.

Swelling, heat and pain in the poll area; inability to bend the head; later on the development of infected tracts which exude pus.

Probably trauma to the area followed by infection, the consequence of rearing up and striking the poll on beams, rearing and falling over. A bone chip from the back of the skull or the atlas that has become separated will always cause sinus infection and is probably the most common cause.

■ Antibiotic cover, poulticing and NSAIDs in the early stages.
■ Surgical exploration and opening up of the sinuses so that they can drain will be needed to cure long-standing poll evil.

POTOMAC HORSE FEVER

Synonyms: equine ehrlichial abortion, equine ehrlichial colitis, equine monocytic ehrlichiosis

First discovered along the Potomac river, but is now recognised as causing disease in the eastern states of America.

Two distinct syndromes:
■ *Equine ehrlichial colitis* (EEC) is the more common, when horses have a fever, are depressed and always have a degree of colitis. Some diarrhoea is common, secondary laminitis less so but is seen in up to 40 per cent of cases.
■ *Equine ehrlichial abortion* (EEA) occurs less frequently. Pregnant mares affected with EEA appear to recover normally but some weeks later abort because of subsequent infection and death of the foetus.

The pathogen *Ehrlichia risticii*. Method of spread is at the moment unknown. Other Ehrlichial diseases spread by tick vectors, but this is not the case with Potomac fever. Dung beetles and some parasitic worms might be involved in the transmission of the disease.

A course of the antibiotic oxytetracycline, given intravenously.

PREGNANCY DIAGNOSIS (illus p97)

There are four methods used to determine pregnancy:

1 Hormonal tests

Performed upon samples of blood or urine, and rely on the fact that the hormone levels circulating through the body during pregnancy are different from those found in an empty cycling mare. Three hormones are used:

Equine chorionic gonadotrophin (eCG) is produced by specialised groups of cells present in the placenta. The hormone, known by the initials eCG or PMSG, starts to appear in the blood by 40 days post service, and usually persists for a further 60 days. A blood sample taken from the mare during this period can be tested by your veterinary surgeon for the presence of this hormone. High circulating levels are a good indication that the mare is pregnant.

Progesterone is a normal hormonal component of the oestrus cycle, and levels of circulating progesterone are at their lowest at 18 to 20 days post service, just before the next heat. If the mare is pregnant, however, the persistent corpus luteum of pregnancy maintains a high level of circulating progesterone. A blood test taken at this time and showing a high level of progesterone indicates pregnancy. Unfortunately the test is inaccurate, as high progesterone levels can be due to factors other than pregnancy, ie during prolonged dioestrus or following early foetal death, and also due to a mis-timing of the sampling date.

Oestrogens are produced in large quantities by the placenta and the foetal gonads. They start to increase by day 60 of pregnancy and are at their peak at 210 days. The Cuboni test can demonstrate the presence of this hormone in a sample of the mare's urine, and other tests can demonstrate the level of oestrogen in the mare's blood. These tests can be done 90 days into pregnancy and if they are positive, pregnancy can be assumed with a high degree of accuracy.

2 Manual diagnosis

Rectal palpation is the traditional method of pregnancy diagnosis: your veterinary surgeon will gently introduce his hand into the rectum and palpate the uterus; depending upon its shape and consistency he can determine whether your mare is pregnant. The earliest this can be done is at about 21 days, but a more accurate decision can be made at the more usual time of 42 days.

As with all gynaecological examinations the mare must be safely restrained, both for her own and for the veterinary surgeon's protection.

3 Oestrous behaviour

A mare normally returns to oestrus 18–21 days from the start of the last heat. Observing her behaviour towards the stallion (teasing) from day 14–23 post service is the traditional way of determining pregnancy. If the mare resents the stallion she is assumed in foal.

Because many mares with foals at foot are wary of the stallion (foal shy) or have entered prolonged dioestrus or lactation anoestrus, this method is fundamentally inaccurate.

4 Ultrasonic examination
(illus p99)

Enables your veterinary surgeon to make an early, accurate diagnosis of pregnancy: it can be demonstrated from 14 days with a high degree of accuracy, and more importantly, twins can be detected at an early stage, thus allowing more time for corrective measures to be taken before it becomes too late.

The machine uses a pulse of high frequency sound to contrast the organs of the abdomen and to show them on a screen. The sound pulses are generated from a probe which is placed in the mare's rectum and the fluid-filled conceptus shows up in the uterus. However, it should be realised that this tool is only as good as its operator: thus the head of the probe must be correctly positioned, and the beam of ultrasound must be pointed in the right direction to obtain results that can be interpreted correctly.

It is essential to perform more than one examination as the older mare often has one or more cysts present in the wall of the uterus, which in an early scan can be mistaken for a conceptus. A second scan performed one or two weeks later will differentiate between the two, as the cyst will be the same size whilst the conceptus will have grown considerably.

Multiple scans are also useful in deciding if the conceptus is developing normally.

PREGNANCY, NORMAL (illus p98)

It starts when the ovum is fertilised and ends when the new foal is born: the period when the ovum differentiates from its initial single cell state into two groups of cells, one to form the foetal membranes and the other that will become the new foal. During this period of differentiation the latter group is known as an embryo, and it starts developing from the moment of fertilisation, which in the mare occurs 4 to 6 hours after service. Fertilisation takes place in the fallopian tube which lies between ovary and uterus, and it must occur within approximately four hours as the unfertilised ovum has a limited life-span.

The arrival and penetration of the sperm into the ovum stimulates the first cell divisions. These continue until, at about 14 days post-fertilisation, the mass of cells has reached a size of about 1.5mm in diameter; it is now called a blastocyst and appears as a pear-shaped sac. A group of cells, the beginning of the embryo, can be seen at the broad end.

By day 21 the sac (by now called a yolk sac) has reached a size of 34mm in diameter (1¼in) and the mass of cells at the blunt end can be recognised as an embryo, surrounded by a membrane, the amnion, and connected to the yolk sac by the umbilical cord. Over the next 20 days further development takes place, and by 40 days the yolk sac has developed into the true foetal membranes and the attachments between membrane and endometrium have started to form. The foetal membranes or placenta consist of two layers, the chorio-allantoic membrane which lies next to the uterus, and the allanto-amnion membrane or amnion which surrounds the foetus.

Specialised cells rapidly develop on the outside of the chorio-allantoic membrane and invade the surface of the uterus. A close contact between uterus and placenta is necessary if the large amounts of nutrients and oxygen that the growing foetus needs are to pass to it from the mare's blood supply.

The umbilical cord connects the embryo to the placenta. It can be divided into two portions, an amniotic length and an allantoic portion. Within its structure lie the arteries and vein which connect the placental net of blood vessels to the developing blood system within the foetus. A tube (the urachus) also passes through the umbilicus; this drains urine from the foetus into the allantoic space.

By this time the major organs of the embryo have differentiated into their primitive selves and the embryo can now be called a foetus, which at this stage weighs about 20g and has a crown-to-rump length of 2.5cm (1in). The eyes and eyelids, the small limb buds and the ears are recognisable, and over the next 20 days the lips, nose and feet develop. By 90 days the shape of the hooves can be seen, and the sex of the embryo can be determined by ultrasound examination.

At 120 days the weight of the embryo has increased to 1kg (2.2lb), and fine hair starts to appear on the lips, the nose and eyelids. This has spread to the tail and mane, the back and the lower legs by day 240, by which time the foetus weighs about 15kg (33lb). The covering of hair is complete by day 320, and the physically perfect new foal grows rapidly to its birth weight of about 45kg (100lb).

There is little change in the outside appearance of the mare during the early stages of gestation. However, as her pregnancy develops, her abdomen gets larger and she becomes slow and clumsy. Some mares develop a finicky appetite, or even lose it completely as termination approaches. The udder becomes swollen and hard during the last month of pregnancy.

Internally the uterus undergoes a whole series of changes as pregnancy advances. It must grow in size to accommodate the developing foetus, whilst still retain enough strength to contain the weight of foetus and foetal membranes, and also a perfect seal at the cervix.

It somehow must learn to recognise the foreign placental cells that invade its internal surface: normally this invasion would provoke an intense reaction as the host body tries to reject the invader, but during pregnancy this does not happen.

The first signs of change occur at about 15 days post service, the pregnant uterus becomes turgid and a more narrow shape. A small swelling in the pregnant horn can be palpated at 21 days, and by 90 days the whole uterus

Symptoms = 👁 Cause/diagnosis = 🔪 Treatment = 📋

is filled by the conceptus and it has spread from the pelvic area forwards into the abdomen.

From 200 days on the foetus can be detected per rectum, and when the mare is quiet, can sometimes be seen moving in the flanks.

PREMATURE FOAL

The mare has such a varied gestation length, from 320 to 355 days, that it is difficult to know when a foal is premature or not. Generally those born over 300 days but before 320 days are considered premature.

It can be recognised by virtue of its small bodyweight, the average birthweight of the Thoroughbred being in the region of 49kg (110lb). It is generally weak and does not stand well; has difficulty in suckling and in keeping warm; and has a thin, scrawny look. The hair and skin feel silky to the touch and the mucous membranes and tongue are often brick-red in colour.

The inability of the mare to sustain pregnancy due to disease of the placenta or hormonal imbalances.

Successfully rearing the premature foal is a very rewarding job; however, it may equally be full of disappointment, as the foal born before its time is extremely vulnerable to a wide variety of diseases and more often than not succumbs to one or other of them.

■ It is essential to make sure that an adequate supply of colostrum is fed within the first few hours of birth.

■ The foal must be kept warm at all times, as premature foals seem unable to maintain their body temperature.

■ Feeds must be kept small and frequent, both day and night. A stronger foal might do this naturally and will only need supervision, but a weaker foal might need bottle feeding.

■ Milk and fluids might have to be administered through a nasogastric tube, a job for a specialist hospital.

■ Preventative antibiotic cover should be provided in an attempt to prevent a septicaemia developing.

PRICKED FOOT (illus p103)

When a nail is driven close to, or into, the sensitive area of the hoof wall during shoeing.

Evidence of pain while the nail is being driven home. Blood might be present at the nail-hole.

Incorrect angle of entry of horseshoe nail. Sudden movement of horse whilst nail is being driven home.

■ Prompt removal of nail and dressing of nail-hole with an antiseptic.
■ Tetanus antitoxin and antibiotic treatment might be needed.

PROLAPSE OF VAGINA, UTERUS

These two conditions are rare, but they constitute a surgical emergency and if treatment is to be successful they must receive veterinary attention.

The first visual signs of a prolapsed vagina are the appearance of a pink, grapefruit-sized swelling protruding from the vulva. The mare usually strains, and as time progresses the prolapsed vagina becomes larger, more congested and oedematous.

A prolapsed uterus is always associated with foaling. Often the inside-out uterus still covered with the placenta follows immediately behind the foal, but more usually the uterus everts during the third stage of labour (see page 156). Compared with the prolapsed vagina this is a much larger, more flaccid structure.

A **vaginal prolapse** often follows a mismatched or brutal covering where the vagina has been damaged; it occurs more commonly in poorly conditioned mares.

Uterine prolapse is commonly associated with a foaling were the foetus is relatively oversized, causing strain and over-relaxation of the uterine ligaments. The condition is also associated with maternal weakness, or age, or a long and difficult second stage of parturition.

■ It is important that the prolapsed organs are replaced as soon as possible. As long as this can be done before they become damaged by trauma and oedema and whilst they are of a relatively normal size, the chances of a successful outcome are good.

■ The prolapsed organs should be wrapped in a wet sheet to protect them until professional help arrives. Keep the mare warm as loss of body heat and shock are a great danger.

■ Your veterinary surgeon will probably sedate the patient, and with the help of epidural anaesthesia, replace the prolapsed vagina or uterus. Antibiotic cover and fluid therapy will also be necessary as part of the treatment.

PROLONGED DIOESTRUS

The period between each oestrus, which is usually 14 to 16 days, is extended for longer than normal.

An absence of oestrus cycles. This can occur after a period of normal oestrus cycles and is relatively common. Often confused with pregnancy.

The presence of a persistent corpus luteum and therefore high circulating levels of progesterone which block the oestrus cycle. The condition is almost impossible to diagnose by manual examination as the corpus luteum of the mare spends most of its allotted span deep in the substance of the ovary and is impossible to palpate. However, an ultrasound examination will demonstrate the presence of a persistent corpus luteum. The presence of high levels of the hormone progesterone in the circulating blood supply also indicates a persistent corpus luteum.

Depends upon getting rid of, or 'lysing', the corpus luteum: the progesterone levels then start to drop, and FSH levels to rise, instigating the development of a normal heat.

■ The injection of prostaglandin will lyse the persistent CL and allow a normal heat to develop. Oestrus normally occurs in 3 to 5 days, and ovulation 7 to 10 days after treatment.

PUNCTURE WOUNDS (illus p108)

By their nature such wounds are deep, with a small entry hole; they should not be taken lightly. Common in the foot where they cause immediate lameness but often few external signs; likewise wounds that occur elsewhere on the body are often missed – all that you might see is a small hole in the skin, with little haemorrhage and no evidence of a deep wound.

Because they are often deep and with little drainage, infection develops in most of these wounds; the area then becomes swollen, hot and painful and a small purulent discharge seeps from the hole.

Puncture wounds to the foot by nails and glass, which can often be found still stuck in the foot. These, especially if they occur in the frog region, are serious as there is a great danger that the coffin joint or navicular bursa might well be damaged. Wounds of this type should be treated aggressively.

Also commonly caused by broken fence rails and farm machinery.

■ Immediate treatment is necessary: if in the foot, the wound should be trimmed out and thoroughly cleaned.
■ Other wounds should be flushed with water twice a day to allow the deeper areas to heal before the surface puncture.
■ A course of antibiotics should be started.
■ If the wound becomes infected, the area should be poulticed or bathed in hot water as frequently as possible and the wound checked to ensure that it can drain.
■ Tetanus can follow this type of injury, so if the horse is not vaccinated, immediate protection should be administered.

PUS IN THE FOOT (illus p103)

Acute lameness, so bad that it is often assumed that the horse has broken a bone in its leg: it is reluctant to move, and stands with the affected leg raised with the toe just touching the ground. The foot becomes hot, and the blood vessels entering the foot are enlarged; a definite pulse can be felt at mid-pastern, and some swelling might develop higher up the leg. At a later date, pus appears at the coronary band, generally above the initial entry site.

Infection can develop following a penetrating wound, or from a bruised foot or corn. Small particles of dirt can track up a defect in the hoof, generally at the white line, and start an infection. Pus takes about five days to build up to a pressure that, within the rigid foot, causes the considerable pain exhibited.

■ The sole should be thoroughly cleaned, and any sign of a tract explored until the abscess is found and drained.
■ In early diagnosed cases, hot water tubbing and poulticing will help to mature the abscess in situations where it cannot be found on the first examination, and ensure that the infection is eliminated completely when an abscess is eventually found.
■ Once the infection has been drained, antibiotic treatment is helpful.

QUITTOR (illus p104)

A chronic infection of the lateral cartilage of the foot. Traditionally quittor was seen in the heavy draught horse, but is now a relatively uncommon condition.

Pain, swelling and heat at the heel of the hoof. Multiple sinuses appear at the coronary band; these discharge pus, and a suppurating mass soon develops which often dries up, only to reappear at later intervals.

Various forms of local trauma to the lateral cartilage, followed by infection and death of parts of it. Also commonly penetrating wounds in the heel region, over-reach and foreign bodies.

■ Initially antibiotic therapy, but this is generally unrewarding and many cases re-occur.
■ Radical surgery to remove all the dead infected cartilage offers a better result, but even then some cases prove refractory to long-term cure.

RABIES

A viral disease that affects the nervous tissue of all warm-blooded species. Found throughout the world, but especially common in South and Central America. Great Britain, Australia, New Zealand and some scattered islands are at the moment free from rabies. The horse is particularly susceptible to its effects.

Pictured as causing furious, aggressive behaviour as in folklore tales of mad dogs foaming at the mouth. Although horses can behave like this, it is more common to find the less violent paralytic form where the affected horse has a temperature, is dull and often shows a degree of hypersensitivity. A progressive paralysis develops, starting at the hindquarters and ending with complete paralysis. Death almost always occurs from respiratory or cardiac arrest in 4 or 5 days.

Transmitted by the bite of an affected animal. In Europe and Canada the fox is the most common factor, in the USA the skunk and racoon, and in South America the bat. Once introduced into the body the virus spends a variable length of time, up to three months, in the muscles local to the bite before moving up the nerves to the brain and spinal cord.

■ None. In most countries it is a notifiable disease, and suspected cases should be reported to the authorities.
■ Vaccines against rabies are available and should be used in countries where rabies is endemic.

Symptoms = 👁   Cause/diagnosis = ✂   Treatment = 🧴

RAGWORT POISONING

(See p182)

RAIN SCALD (illus pp61 & 117)

A similar condition to mud fever, but affecting the skin of the back, flanks and hindquarters.

The skin along the back and on each side of the neck develops scabby, crusty lesions. Under the crusts the skin is moist, red and inflamed. The extreme irritation makes the horse very uncomfortable and the loss of condition can be marked. Occurs most frequently in those horses which are turned out unrugged and whose skin is permanently wet. Thin-skinned youngstock are also very susceptible. Horses which are allowed to grow a thick ungroomed coat with all the protective natural oils in place have more resistance.

Dermatophilus congolensis is the primary organism associated with this condition, although other bacteria can become secondary contaminants. Constant rain washes out the protective skin oils, softens the skin and allows the organism a chance to invade.

■ Caught in time, the condition can be cleared up by keeping the skin dry and by gentle grooming to stimulate the body's natural defence mechanism.
■ If neglected, then more rigorous treatment is needed: the skin should be shampooed with a medicated wash and the crusts removed, and the uncovered sores treated with an antibiotic ointment; this procedure must be repeated until all affected areas have been treated. Systemic antibiotics will probably have to be used.

RECTO-VAGINAL FISTULA/TEAR
(illus p96)

A fistula is a hole which connects the rectum with the vagina; a tear is when the tissues between the anus and the vulva are torn, leaving an opening connecting vagina and rectum.

Faecal material passes out through both anus and vagina.

Tears occur as a complication of foaling, normally due to foetal oversize. Fistulas are generally caused by a foal's foot passing through the upper vagina wall into the rectum during the birth process; this is most likely if the foal is delivered with one or both front legs hooked behind its neck.

Both injuries respond well to surgery, but this is best done either immediately the damage is done, or preferably when the damage is healed. The amount of reconstructive surgery necessary to effect a repair can be more accurately assessed when primary repair is complete.

RECURRENT AIRWAY OBSTRUCTION

See **Chronic obstructive pulmonary disease,** p140

RECURRENT UVEITIS (illus p84)

Synonyms: moon blindness, periodic ophthalmia

Acute pain in the eye, with gross pathological change to the structures of the anterior and posterior chambers. The pupil constricts and the horse becomes photophobic (sensitive to light); the eyelids remain tightly shut and tears often run down the cheeks.

The conjunctiva and iris are red and inflamed, and the fluid in the anterior chamber, the aqueous humour, reflects the light, causing a flare. The reaction within the eye might cause the iris to stick to the lens. The posterior portion of the eye becomes filled with a grey inflammatory exudate.

Recurrent attacks at indeterminate intervals occur, each attack causing increasingly diminished sight until complete blindness results.

An inflammation of the ciliary body and the iris, the structures which support the lens; this condition is thought to be due to an exaggerated immune response to a wide range of organisms.

The bacteria *Leptospira pomona* and the larval form of the worm *onchocerca cervicalis* (see p173) are likely culprits.

■ Immediate veterinary help is needed.
■ Long and vigorous treatment with parental NSAIDs is necessary to control the inflammation. Antibiotic treatment might be considered if a bacterial cause is suspected. Corticosteroids and atropine applied to the eye are also essential.

RHINOVIRUS (illus p75)

Belongs to the same family of viruses as the human cold virus. Three types of virus commonly affect horses.

A short-lived temperature rise with a runny nose, sore throat and cough. A short span, and affected horses are generally back to normal in a week.

The behaviour of this virus is very similar to the human cold: it frequently attacks young horses that are exposed to the virus for the first time, for example when brought together at weaning time or taken to shows or sales.

■ Good nursing is generally all that is needed.
■ Antibiotic treatment if serious secondary infection develops.

RINGBONE (illus p104)

Synonym: phalangeal exostoses

Bony swellings that develop on the front and sides of the first and second phalanx and the top of the third phalanx.

When the bony swelling involves the coffin joint it is called a **low ringbone**: this area is hidden inside the hoof, and unless the bony swelling becomes large enough to distort the hoof capsule it remains unseen by the naked eye and can only be demonstrated by X-ray.

When ringbone involves the first and second phalanx it can be seen as a swelling involving the lower end of the pastern and is known as **high ringbone**.

Ringbone can be further divided into bony swellings that involve the joint – **articular ringbone** – or swellings that involve the areas outside the joint capsule – **periarticular ringbone**.

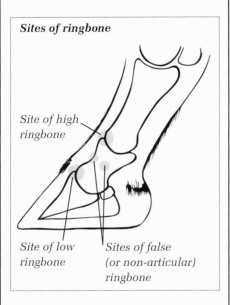

Normally a chronic condition in which a low-grade lameness, more often in a front foot, becomes apparent. A hard swelling above the coronary band generally develops. X-rays will show new bone

Sites of ringbone

Site of high ringbone

Site of low ringbone

Sites of false (or non-articular) ringbone

formation in cases that have been ongoing for some time.

Trauma to the pastern area causes a more acute condition, a typical injury being that which results from a hard blow to the front of the foot. In these cases the initial lameness is marked, but becomes chronic as the lesion organises.

Trauma to the bones of the pastern or strain of the ligaments connecting the joints can cause new bone formation.

Conformational faults such as toe in or out, base wide, or narrow or upright pastern will almost certainly predispose to the development of ringbone, as will long periods of work on a hard surface.

■ Acute injuries benefit from rest and treatment with anti-inflammatory agents.
■ Ringbone involving the joint surfaces

has a poor long-term prognosis. Surgery to fuse the joint might give some relief.
■ Ringbone not involving the joint also responds to rest and anti-inflammatory drugs and generally resolves given time.

RINGWORM (illus pp61 & 117)

An important and highly contagious skin disease of man, companion and farm animals, and also the horse. It causes skin disease wherever horses are kept.

Produces characteristic lesions. A single, round, crusty scab appears on the skin, generally in the area under the edge of clothing or where the tack rubs. This single lesion grows in size and in number until large areas of skin become involved. The lesions are initially hairless but soon develop small papules which burst, causing a scabby appearance.

Two groups of fungi, *Trichophyton* and *Microsporum*. The infection spreads either from direct contact with another horse, or from contaminated tack, blankets or brushes.

■ A course of the antibiotic griseofulvin, administered in the feed every day for one week: this works well against the *Trichophyton* type of ringworm, less well against *Microsporum*. Griseofulvin is concentrated in the skin and prevents the fungus from growing.
■ The antibiotic natamycin, used as a topical wash; the whole body should be covered so that any unseen lesions are treated. The wash must be repeated every fourth day for at least three times.

ROTOVIRUS (illus p77)

A highly infectious virus which can cause diarrhoea in the young of all mammalian species. In the horse it can cause outbreaks of foal diarrhoea which spread rapidly throughout the foal population. However, with suitable nursing and treatment, few become seriously ill.

Foals from 2 days to 6 months may be affected. The first signs include a full udder in the mare, this signifying a diminished

suckling response from the foal, together with a foul-smelling diarrhoea; this can range from watery to semi-solid and from bright yellow to grey-green in colour. Affected foals are dull and depressed but have a normal temperature; young foals can easily become dehydrated and even more depressed, with sunken eyes and tight skin.

Once ingested, rotovirus multiplies enormously in the cells of the duodenum and small intestine, destroying large numbers of the cells that are responsible for the absorption of fluids and nutrients. The resulting diarrhoea contains millions of viral particles which contaminate the foaling box and provide a potent source of infection for the next foal that uses the box. The damage done to the intestinal lining is quickly repaired and the diarrhoea is normally over in 3 to 4 days.

■ Antibiotic treatment is not indicated in this condition.
■ Strict attention to the hydration state of the foal. Electrolytes should be given by mouth or by intravenous infusion if the clinical condition suggests a need for more aggressive treatment.
■ Absorbent drugs such as kaolin preparations and lactobacillus-rich foods such as natural yoghurt, help to ensure a swift return to normal.

RUPTURED BLADDER

Uncommon; seen in 2- to 3-day-old foals, normally following a difficult birth.

A foal with a ruptured bladder behaves as if suffering from **retained meconium** (see p168): it strains in an attempt to pass the urine trapped in the abdominal cavity and tends to roll and lie in abnormal positions. The abdomen becomes distended with fluid, and except where the tear is very small, urine is passed in small quantities.

The condition is diagnosed by performing a paracentesis, a procedure involving the tapping of fluid in the abdomen; the presence of urine can be recognised by its smell and chemical constitution. Ultrasound examination will also demonstrate the quantity of fluid in the abdomen.

Symptoms = ◎   Cause/diagnosis = ✂   Treatment = ▤

Excessive pressure exerted on the foal's abdomen during birth. A defect occurs in the wall of the bladder, and urine escapes into the abdominal cavity.

■ Surgery to repair the defect, and it should be performed as soon as possible once the condition has been diagnosed. The outcome is generally good.

RYE GRASS STAGGERS

Belongs to a group of diseases caused by eating contaminated grass or hay made from one particular strain of this grass. The disease is well known in Australia, New Zealand and America.

Affected horses become increasingly ataxic (unsteady), and some become completely paralysed.

Certain species of rye grass grown in Australia and New Zealand are infected with an endophyte, a parasitic fungus which produces an alkaloid toxin: when eaten by horses or other herbivores, this alkaloid causes the symptoms described above.

Until recently, grasses grown in the UK did not harbour the fungus but unfortunately a type of rye grass called yatsyn, which does carry it, has been imported into this country. Cases of rye grass staggers in horses fed hay from this type of grass have been recognised in the UK, and we must now include this disease as another of the type that causes nervous symptoms.

None specific.

SADDLE SORES

Develop as a result of pressure or excessive friction between saddle and back.

Loss of hair at the point of friction. Untreated, the skin becomes broken and sores develop. Common sites are to each side of the withers and on the loins, generally at a point under the pin bones of the rider.

Almost always an ill-fitting, or badly stuffed saddle. Endurance horses are especially at risk due to the long hours they are at work. Carelessness when fitting a saddle cloth – ie allowing wrinkles between saddle and skin – and dirty numnahs predispose to saddle galls.

Poor riding technique or rider fatigue: both can cause unequal weight distribution, hence increased local pressure leading to saddle sores.

■ Once developed, saddle sores will not heal if the horse is kept in work: rest is imperative.
■ Any healing ointment: zinc oxide cream is cheap and good.
■ If the sores are hot and inflamed and obviously infected, then consult your veterinary surgeon as there is a considerable risk that fistulous withers (see p154) will develop.
■ Constant attention should be paid to the fit of the saddle, especially in relation to the changing weight and shape of a horse as it gets fit.

SALMONELLOSIS (illus p91)

Salmonella infection is becoming one of the most common causes of acute diarrhoea in adult horses. Although it more often follows a stressful occurrence such as concurrent treatment with antibiotic, it can also cause primary disease.

Initially acute diarrhoea, colic and discomfort. A fever of 104–106°F, and the heart and respiratory rates rise.

As the disease progresses the horse becomes weak and very depressed; the release of endotoxins into the system through the damaged mucosa cause profound shock; septicaemia might also develop. This cascade of events, together with increasing dehydration and circulatory collapse, can cause a rapidly terminal condition.

Infection by members of the *Salmonella* family of bacteria: in the horse, *Salmonella typhimurium* is the most common. Stress is also involved in the development of the disease, and diarrhoea is common following the stress of surgery or after a long journey.

Salmonella bacteria are capable of living in the gut of apparently normal horses and are excreted in the faeces of these horses. Companion horses can become infected through eating contaminated feed or bedding.

■ Prompt administration of intravenous fluids to correct the dehydration and developing shock is essential.
■ Antibiotic treatment is questionable as it is possible that it might encourage the carrier state and lead to populations of *Salmonella* that are resistant to the antibiotic used.
■ Anti-inflammatory drugs such as phenylbutazone or flunexin will help to reduce the body temperature and minimise the associated shock.
■ Good nursing and attention to hygiene is essential.

SANDCRACKS (illus p105)

Synonyms: hoof-cracks, grass-cracks

Vertical cracks that develop in the hoof wall.

Sandcracks either start at ground level and extend upwards to the coronary band, or, more seriously, start at the coronary band and grow downwards towards the bearing surface of the hoof wall.

Many horses develop superficial sandcracks and never become lame. However, sandcracks can reach into the sensitive layers of the hoof wall or extend into the coronary band, and in these more serious cases, infection can develop, resulting in acute lameness.

Full thickness quarter cracks, occurring generally on the lateral quarter of the hoof wall, weaken the structural integrity of the hoof. Movement between the two sections of hoof causes pain and inflammation of that foot.

Sandcracks that originate from the coronary band are generally caused by a defect in the band which results from a wound to that point – the quality of hoof produced at this site is poor, and when this grows down the hoof a vertical crack is formed.

Large wounds, bruises or infection breaking out at the coronary band cause a horizontal crack which extends part-way round the circumference of the hoof wall. These rarely cause any trouble until they grow down to near the ground surface, when the section of hoof below the crack may break off. This can cause shoeing problems until the defect has grown out.

Cracks that extend from the ground surface upwards are caused by an unbalanced or overgrown foot. The unequal forces acting on the foot cause separation of the horn tubules, which extends up the foot until the bond between tubules is stronger than the separating force.

■ An infected sandcrack must be trimmed out, and all evidence of infection removed.
■ Antibiotic treatment, both local and systemic, will probably be needed, together with daily dressing.
■ Once the horse is sound, the defect can be stabilised by filling the trimmed-out crack with a synthetic resin and fixing it with staples or wire lacing.
■ Another method of fixation is to build up a fibreglass pad over the filled crack. Small screws are used to secure the pad to the hoof wall on each side of the crack.
■ Sandcracks originating from the ground surface generally respond to regular foot trimming and balancing.

SARCOIDS (illus pp59 & 115)

Locally invasive, non-spreading tumour of the skin. There are six types:

■ *Occult sarcoids:* common on hairless parts of the body. They appear as round swellings in the skin with a grey scaly surface and if left undisturbed remain unchanged for many years.
■ *Verrucose sarcoids:* have a warty appearance and often develop into flat thickened growths in the skin; they are slow-growing but if disturbed by injury or surgery can become aggressive and locally invasive.
■ *Fibroblastic sarcoids:* involve both the dermal and sub-dermal layers of the skin and extend much further than is apparent. They have a fleshy, aggressive appearance, which rapidly becomes ulcerated, and are often associated with surgical or accidental wounds.
■ *Malevolent sarcoids:* are particularly aggressive and spread along the local lymphatic channels causing large ulcerative masses commonly found on the face and the internal thigh. These sarcoids have a very poor prognosis.
■ *Nodular sarcoids:* appear to be entirely under the skin, are round and have a well-defined border. The overlying skin is often thin and shiny.
■ *Mixed sarcoids:* are common. They have components of the occult, verrucose and nodular types.

Thought to be a virus, and thought to be the result either of an earlier non-productive infection with the virus that causes juvenile warts, or infection with that which causes warts in cattle. Can occur anywhere on the body, either singly or at multiple sites, and seldom undergo spontaneous remission.

Notoriously problematic as they often appear at difficult surgical sites such as around the eye or in the ear. They also have a tendency to re-occur when removed by surgery.
■ Where the site allows, surgical removal is the easiest method, although up to 50 per cent of sarcoids re-occur later.
■ Cryo-surgery, a method where the tumour is frozen with a liquid nitrogen spray or probe, is more successful. The frozen tumour sloughs away and healing takes place over a period of three to eight weeks.
■ Radiation techniques are used at several specialist centres. Radio-active materials are implanted into the tumour mass and over the next six to twelve months the tumour gradually disappears. This method of treatment is especially valuable for tumours around the eye.
■ Cytotoxic ointments: these contain extremely toxic chemicals that poison the sarcoid cells more easily than healthy skin cells. Used with care, this method can be very successful.

SEBORRHOEA (illus p115)

A disease of the skin characterised by excessive scurf formation, accompanied sometimes by marked grease production. The condition is generally considered to be secondary to other skin disorders. Primary idiopathic seborrhoea is considered rare in the horse.

The hair becomes greasy and clogged with large amounts of scurf and scale.

Generally secondary to mange or lice infestations, or any generalised skin complaint such as **rain scald** (see p189) or **folliculitis** (see p156).

First identify and treat the primary cause. The seborrhoea will then often disappear by itself, but if not, bathing with sulphur and coal tar shampoos will help.

SEEDY TOE (illus p105)

The hoof wall at the toe separates from the pedal bone.

A gap filled with soft crumbly material or impacted mud or air develops at the toe. This can extend a varying amount up the front of the foot; it can be demonstrated by a lateral X-ray of the foot. Chronic lameness is generally present.

The damage that chronic laminitis causes to the bond between hoof wall and pedal bone. Also trauma to the sole at the front of the foot can also develop into seedy toe.

■ The whole of the front of the hoof must be removed so that the cavity is completely exposed. All diseased hoof should be removed.
■ The exposed area should be treated with a mixture of eucalyptus oil and formalin or iodoform.

Symptoms =   Cause/diagnosis =   Treatment =

SEPTICAEMIA

Synonym: sleepy foal disease

An acute and rapidly fatal disease of the young foal which is caused by a variety of organisms that infect it in the first few hours of life.

The immediate signs include loss of appetite, fever, and a rapidly increasing depression which culminates in a coma. In the early stages the foal can be roused from this coma and may even be tempted to suckle, but it very quickly sinks back into it. The temperature can reach 41°C (105.8°F), but often falls as the condition worsens.

The infection can enter the foal from the mother's bloodstream via the placenta or afterbirth or through the stump of the navel cord. Once there, it spreads rapidly through the foal's blood system to affect all the major organs. Most new-born foals are exposed to potential pathogens, but whether septicaemia develops depends upon their ability to withstand infection, and the level of immunity they have acquired from the first drink of colostrum – again stressing the importance of that first suckle.

■ Must be immediate, because even if the organisms responsible don't kill the foal, they can soon cause lesions in the joints and other organs which are much more difficult to cure.
■ Suitable antibiotic preparations should be given at regular intervals through the day.
■ Some intravenous fluid will probably be necessary.
■ Good nursing is essential. The foal should be kept warm; if collapsed, it should be checked regularly for pressure sores and be frequently repositioned. Massage of protruding areas such as hips, hocks and elbows will help to prevent sores developing.
The routine testing of foals for antibody levels helps pick out those that are at risk: for these, a course of antibiotics for the first three days after birth will help to prevent septicaemia.
■ Septicaemia can also be prevented by prompt dressing of the umbilical stump with an antiseptic solution. Foaling boxes should be thoroughly cleansed and disinfected after each foaling.

SEPTIC ARTHRITIS (illus p124)

Synonym: joint ill

Also common in the young foal. It can occur at any time between birth and three months of age and is a common sequel to septicaemia.

First, lameness. The affected joint or joints become hot and painful, the body temperature rises to between 38.5°C and 41°C, and the foal stops sucking. All too often the infection overcomes the local defences and the joint becomes very swollen, and an abscess forms in the joint cavity. The joint surfaces and surrounding bone quickly become irreparably damaged.

The causal organism generally enters the body through the umbilical cord, where it causes an abscess (see **navel ill** p169). From this reservoir of infection, or following septicaemia, the bacteria spread to and localise in one or more joint or tendon sheaths.

It is essential to start the treatment of joint ill immediately, as any delay will mean that the damage done to the joint surfaces and the bone will be irreparable.
■ A long course of an effective systemic antibiotic must be started as soon as the condition is noticed.
■ The joint should be catheterised or opened, and the joint cavity flushed with saline to remove the inflammatory products and antibiotics introduced into the joint capsule.

Unfortunately even with aggressive, immediate treatment the prognosis must always be guarded, as many cases end up chronically lame.

SESAMOIDITIS

When the two sesamoid bones become inflamed or damaged. These bones lie at the back of the fetlock where they act as pulleys for the flexor tendons; they are enclosed by the suspensory ligaments and they form an important and integral part of fetlock joint function.

Acute lameness of moderate to serious intensity. Swelling of the fetlock joint might not be marked, but pain can usually be demonstrated over one or both sesamoids. In the more chronic case the swelling will be hard and painless. X-rays of the sesamoids are essential to demonstrate the bony changes that occur in the chronic case.

Abnormal stresses can cause ligaments to tear from the surface of the sesamoid bone, or for the bone itself to split in half. Direct trauma can also bruise or split the bone. A long, sloping pastern which increases the strain on the sesamoid bones is a conformational fault that can predispose to sesamoid damage.

■ Immediate immobilisation in a cast will provide relief from pain and support the injury. Even relatively minor damage needs a long period of rest, up to 12 months.
■ A fractured sesamoid can be treated by surgery if the fragments are large enough; the two pieces are screwed together and the leg supported by casting.

SHEARED HEELS (illus p105)

A condition of the foot that is commonly seen where the standard of farriery is not what it should be. Describes a foot where one heel is shorter than the other. This can best be observed when the foot is viewed from behind.

In the early stages sheared heels can be recognised when one heel, generally the inner heel, appears shorter and more compressed than the other. As the condition progresses the wall on the affected side becomes more upright, or might even curl under the centre of gravity. A crack might develop between each heel and eventually the heels separate and begin to move independently of each other.

Most commonly the uneven trimming of the foot. This imbalance leads to a distortion of the hoof capsule as the area transferring the greatest weight becomes compressed and grows more upright whilst the opposite side becomes flared. Large studs worn constantly on one side of the shoe will, over a period of time, have the same effect.

 ■ In the early stages accurate trimming to arrive at a balanced foot will correct the problem.
■ More serious cases will need a bar shoe fitted.

SHIVERING

With a few exceptions, it affects the hind legs only. When the horse is startled or a leg is touched, as during bandaging, it is flexed in an exaggerated way and at the same time starts to shiver. The horse leans over the weight-bearing leg while this is going on, sometimes so much that he falls over. In extreme cases the tail, forelegs, eyes and ears might shiver as well.

There is no known cause.

None. Horses that demonstrate mild symptoms can, with care, lead an almost normal life, but euthanasia should be considered in horses that show severe symptoms.

SIDEBONE

The laying down of calcium (ossification) in the cartilage wings of the pedal bone. Seen in the heavy draft type of horse, and rare in the light sports' horse.

The horse may or may not be lame in one or both front feet; if lame, there is generally heat and swelling over the quarters of the foot. Pain might be evident when the heels are compressed, and a loss of elasticity can be appreciated when ossification is advanced.

X-rays will aid in the diagnosis of sidebone, and will demonstrate the degree of ossification.

Any factors that increase the concussive forces acting on the back of the pedal bone will predispose to sidebone formation: poor or delayed shoeing; shoeing with large calkins; long periods of work on hard surfaces.

■ If sidebone is the cause of lameness – and it rarely is the primary cause – grooving the hoof will allow the foot to expand and relieve the pain.
■ Rest and treatment with NSAIDs is probably the best course of action.

SINUSITIS

Infection of the frontal and/or maxillary sinus of the horse: a relatively uncommon disease, especially when one considers the high incidence of respiratory disease affecting stabled horses.

Normally unilateral, but usually affects both the frontal and the maxillary sinuses. A thick, creamy nasal discharge is generally present. The normal hollow sound that one hears when the sinus is tapped becomes dull, especially when the sinus is full of pus. The eye on the affected side might have a discharge, and the area below the eye might be swollen.

X-rays of the head can show the fluid line of pus as it lies in the sinus. The general attitude of the horse suggests that his head hurts.

Primary sinusitis follows a respiratory infection, especially when the horse is kept in badly ventilated, restricted stables.

Secondary sinusitis is caused by dental disease: the sinus becomes infected from an infected tooth root.

■ Early cases of sinusitis can be treated with a course of antibiotic and mucolytic drugs such as sputolosin.
■ The horse should be turned out as much as possible and all food fed from the ground: the head-down posture facilitates drainage from the affected sinus.
■ In long-standing cases, surgery might be needed to cure the condition. Infected

teeth will have to be removed if they are the cause. The usual surgical procedure is to make holes into the sinus, a technique known as trephining, and to irrigate the sinus with an antiseptic solution until the infection has gone.

SOFT PALATE DISLOCATION

The soft palate of the horse is a long, mobile continuation of the hard palate which divides the mouth from the nose. Its function is to interact with the walls of the pharynx and structures of the larynx during the swallowing reflex to prevent food material entering the windpipe. In some horses this interaction goes wrong and the soft palate becomes hooked up on the entrance of the larynx, ie dorsally displaced.

A loud gurgling, choking sound suddenly occurs as the soft palate interferes with breathing and the horse abruptly stops running; in racing parlance he is said to have 'swallowed his tongue'. Normally a temporary condition, seen most often in racehorses during the final stages of a race.

Not clear, as the displacement and symptoms disappear once the horse is at rest. However, it is probably connected with the size of the epiglottis and the action of muscles in the throat.

More about the dynamic functioning of the structures of the pharynx is being found out now that video endoscopic examination on the treadmill is possible.

■ A tongue-strap used to tie the tongue down during exercise, or the use of a straight bit, both prevent the condition in some horses.
■ Surgical intervention to correct the condition is possible.

SORE SHINS

Synonyms: metacarpal periostitis, bucked shins.

A condition found in young racing Thoroughbreds during their first season of work. It generally manifests itself in the front limbs, and is another example of the over-excessive demands of the racing industry. On the rare occasion that it occurs in an adult horse the cause is generally direct trauma.

A swelling appears along the front of one or both fore cannons; in the early stages this is warm and painful to pressure. If the condition is unilateral, or worse on one side, the horse is lame, but sore shins of equal severity cause a shortening of the stride, especially the forward-going phase. This gets worse the more the workload is increased, and at rest the horse shifts his weight from one leg to the other.

In the young racing Thoroughbred, excessive force applied to the front of the leg to bones that are still soft and immature causes the periosteum to tear off the front of the cannon. Obviously this results in considerable pain and reaction. Training and racing immature horses on hard ground provides the type of force that leads to sore shins.

■ Many cases can be prevented by adopting more sensible training methods, that minimise the concussive forces acting on the shins.
■ Good farriery and a decent track surface will also help to cut down the numbers of young horses affected. Rest and treatment with anti-inflammatory drugs will bring most young Thoroughbreds back to normality.

SPAVIN

Disease of the hock joint, popularly divided into two conditions:

Bog spavin (illus p108)
A swelling of the joint capsule of the hock. It rarely causes any lameness and is of cosmetic importance only.

A soft, fluctuant swelling is seen high on the outside and low on the inside of the joint; occasionally a third swelling is present on the inside of the joint. These swellings are the result of an out-pushing of the enlarged joint capsule between the ligaments and tendons of the hock joint.

There is rarely any associated heat or discomfort, and the horse is seldom lame.

Probably a combination of poor conformation and strain.

■ Immobilisation, cold hosing and rest might help in the early stages of the condition.
■ Your veterinary surgeon might consider sedating the horse and draining the fluid from the joint. Then intra-articular injections of corticosteroid drugs might prevent the capsule filling again.

Bone spavin (illus p108)
An arthritis of the lower, immobile bones of the hock joint. Said to be characterised by a bony swelling on the lower inner side of the hock joint, but actually most cases show no external signs.

Initially an indefinite hind-limb lameness; this might appear to be in one leg only, but careful examination will show that it is actually bilateral. Early on in the course of the disease the affected horse is accused of showing a loss of impulsion or being awkward in his flat-work, or not enjoying his jumping any longer, and the condition may be confused with a back problem.

Other fairly constant signs of spavin are a reduced flexion of the hock, a shortening of hind-limb stride, and a corresponding wear of the hind toes.

Arthritic changes occur in the joint spaces, and new bone might appear on the medial aspect of the joint. These changes can be shown on good quality X-rays. Once the new bone has formed and the joint becomes completely fused, the horse might become sound.

In occult spavin, all the changes occur within the joint. Carefully directed X-rays and intra-articular anaesthesia are necessary to demonstrate its presence.

Most likely is constant strain to the hock; this might explain the higher incidence of spavin in trotters. Conformation of the hock is thought to be of significance, with spavin believed to be more common in horses with sickle or cow hocks.

Relies upon speeding up the changes within the joints so that they fuse completely. Once inter-articular movement is impossible, the pain disappears and the horse becomes sound.
■ This can be done surgically by drilling out the joint surfaces and relying on the healing process to fuse the bones together.
■ Another method is to control the pain with NSAIDs and to work the horse until fusion occurs. Obviously this will only be possible where the discomfort is controlled by such drugs.
■ A third method, in its infancy yet, relies on the destructive properties of sodium monoiodoacetic acid (MIA), which is injected into the affected joints under general anaesthesia. After a short period of intense reaction and discomfort, controlled with analgesic medication and local anaesthesia, the horse can be worked. This speeds up the fusion of the affected tarsal bones and a return to soundness. The initial trial results are apparently encouraging.

SPLINT (illus pp61 & 108)

A hard, bony swelling that appears on the cannon bone generally of young horses.

Occurs most frequently on the inside of the front cannons, although can occur on a hind leg and on the outside of the cannon. In the early stages of development splints are often warm and painful when palpated and can cause a degree of lameness; as they mature they become cold and hard, and generally reduce in size. Unless the splint is high enough to interfere with the knee, or behind enough to react with the suspensory ligament, they cause no lameness; however, they do constitute a conformational blemish which will affect showing prospects.

Excessive concussion to immature bones. The short interosseous ligaments which bind the splint bones to the cannon become bruised and strained and as a result, first fibrous tissue and then new bone are laid down. Splints normally occur in young horses just coming into work, but are also found in yearlings, probably as a result of strenuous play on hard ground. Splints can also appear in mature horses, the nature of whose work has suddenly changed; horses brought into endurance work are a good example.

Splint-like lesions can follow a blow to the splint bone, generally caused by brushing or forging by another hoof. X-rays might be necessary to differentiate between a fracture of the splint bone and a normal splint. Removal of the bone fragment will be necessary if a fracture is demonstrated.

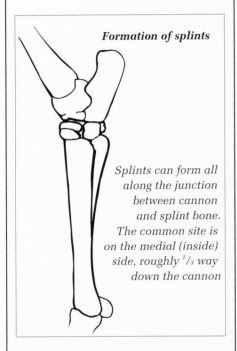

Formation of splints

Splints can form all along the junction between cannon and splint bone. The common site is on the medial (inside) side, roughly $^1/_3$ way down the cannon

Conservative treatment is generally all that is necessary:
■ Anti-inflammatory lotions might reduce the swelling in the early stages.
■ Rest and developing maturity will reduce the bony lump.
■ Large splints, or those that are cosmetically important, can be removed by surgery, but often the residual scar is more obvious than the splint.

SPONDYLITIS

Inflammation and new bone formation of the vertebrae of the thoracic and lumber spine. Long-standing inflammation of the interosseous ligament joining the dorsal spines of the vertebrae can cause new bone formation to such an extent

that the dorsal spines touch and grate upon each other. This condition is known as 'kissing spines', and can sometimes be palpated or demonstrated by a sky-line X-ray.

Equally the new bone can form on the underside of the vertebrae and develop spurs which eventually touch and then fuse together, a condition known as 'anky-losing spondylitis'. Both of these conditions are very painful when forming, but become less so once they are fused.

Increasing signs of back pain, for example irritability and abnormal sensitivity during saddling and mounting – but beware of the horse that just does not like being saddled. Increasing tendency to refuse jumps that were no problem, or

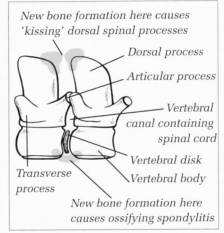

New bone formation here causes 'kissing' dorsal spinal processes

Dorsal process

Articular process

Vertebral canal containing spinal cord

Vertebral disk

Vertebral body

Transverse process

New bone formation here causes ossifying spondylitis

a decreasing ability to move in an athletic way. Also a clumsy or unco-ordinated way of moving behind.

Usually repeated trauma such as follows a badly fitting saddle and/or a heavy rider who sits too far back.

■ In the early stages a period of rest will give immediate relief, but the problem often returns once the horse is ridden again.
■ The condition called 'kissing spines' can be treated surgically: the bony spurs are removed and many cases respond well.

STALLION, INJURIES TO

Infection of sheath (illus p94)
Serious infections are rare and normally

asymptomatic. If infection with venereal organisms is present it is normally discovered following routine pre- and mid-season swabbing. The types of organism causing infection and the steps taken to eradicate it and prevent transmission to susceptible mares is covered on p202 and in Appendix A. However, older stallions and geldings can suffer from an infection of the sheath which can cause considerable irritation and discomfort if left untreated.

The sheath becomes swollen and oedematous, a foul-smelling discharge is sometimes present, and urination is often difficult. The lining of the prepuce and the epithelium of the penis appear red and inflamed, and the smegma, the normally cheesy material found in the folds of the prepuce and at the base of the penis, generally becomes more strong-smelling.

Infection of the prepuce become more common as age increases, and damage to the lining of the prepuce or to the penis can lead to infection. Constant cleaning of the sheath, especially if disinfectants are used, usually leads to drying and cracking of the epithelium which increases the chance of infection. The normal non-pathogenic bacterial population contained in the smegma is an essential component of the protective mechanism of the sheath, and should be protected.

■ The penis should be exteriorised and the lining of the prepuce washed and cleaned with warm, soapy water.
■ Antibiotic ointment should be applied daily. If this treatment has to be extended for more than a few days then the prepuce should be seeded with a soup of smegma obtained from a healthy male.

Injuries to penis
The erect penis of a stallion is prone to injury because of its shape and size, especially during mating or while posturing over a fence at other horses.

The most common injury is bruising and rupture of the extensive blood

Symptoms = 👁 Cause/diagnosis = 🦴 Treatment = 💊

system of the penis. The first signs are rapid swelling of the prepuce and penis due to haematoma formation: the prepuce becomes thickened and discoloured, and the penis grossly enlarged and dependent. Secondary bruising and cuts are common due to the large size and weight of the penis.

Kicks during teasing and mating; damage to the penis during mating due to mare positioning, or to stitches left in after a Caslick's operation; jumping over fences to get to mares; and fighting.

Immediate and aggressive treatment is necessary to restore the penis to its normal size and function. All too often the end result is a paralysed penis and the possibility of amputation.
■ Prompt support of the heavy, dependent penis is essential, to prevent further damage and minimise the risk of further bleeding. This can be done by enclosing the penis in the prepuce if the swelling is minor, or by using a sling arrangement if it is considerable.
■ Cold water hosing and ice packs are essential, to reduce the swelling and inflammation.
■ Antibiotic treatment, both systemic and local, should be started promptly.

Paralysis of penis

The use of certain tranquillising drugs such as Acepromazine causes paralysis of the retractor penis muscle and consequently an inability to withdraw the penis. Occasionally this can result in paraphimosis (swelling of the penis) and then permanent paralysis.

Paralysis of the penis. If the condition is ignored the penis can become oedematous and swollen.

A relatively uncommon side effect following the use of the promazine group of tranquillisers.

Prompt support of the penis and manual compression of the penis might reduce the swelling. If paralysis remains, then amputation might be necessary.

STRANGLES (illus pp56 & 78)

Primarily a disease of the upper respiratory tract. It has a worldwide distribution, and is a disease of considerable antiquity, since descriptions exist from the twelfth century and earlier.

Has an incubation period of between 3 and 10 days. The first signs are an increasing depression, high temperature (in excess of 39°C), and the development of a slight cough. A mucoid nasal discharge rapidly becomes mucopurulent, then purulent. The glands behind the ears and in the angle of the jaw and between the arms of the lower jaw become swollen and tender, and the horse often stands with head outstretched and rigid. Frequently unwilling to eat, coupled with an inability to swallow due to the pain of the swollen glands. Pressure on the larynx and pharynx from the rapidly swelling retropharyngeal lymph glands will cause a degree of respiratory noise. Respiratory distress might necessitate a tracheotomy to allow the horse to breathe.

One or more glands continue to swell and in a few days burst, releasing quantities of pus. The glands between the arms of the lower jaw are most often involved.

Once the strangles abscesses have matured and burst, most cases rapidly improve. However, in the very young or the old horse, complications can occur and the organism can spread from its upper respiratory tract location and cause abscess formation in the lungs and brain or in the lymph nodes of the abdomen. This complication is called bastard strangles, and carries a poor prognosis. In a few horses, between 1 and 2 per cent, a condition called *purpura hemorrhagica* develops a few weeks after the horse has apparently recovered.

Infection with the bacterium *Streptococcus equi*. It is extremely contagious and is spread by direct contact with the pus and nasal discharges that occur so readily with this disease. Contaminated tack, feeding utensils, water troughs and bedding are all potent sources of infection.

The organism gains entry to the body at the back of the throat and rapidly settles in the tonsils and adjacent lymph nodes. From here it spreads to the lymph glands of the head and neck, and causes the swelling and abscess formation so typical of the disease. Rarely does it spread any further. Most horses recover with no complications, and some 70 per cent develop a life-long immunity. It is thought that the remainder could form a carrier population able to perpetuate the disease.

Prevention is possible, and should be attempted, in spite of the contagious nature of the disease.
■ In a closed herd situation, new arrivals should be isolated for 2 weeks.
■ Affected horses should also be put into isolation quarters with separate food and containers, grooming kit and if possible, handler. Everything that has been in contact with the affected horses should be washed and cleaned, especially hands and boots. All contaminated bedding and clothing should be burnt, and buildings should be thoroughly cleaned and steam-sterilised.
■ Careful nursing: the swelling abscesses should be encouraged to mature and burst by constant application of heat, either by bathing with hot water or using one of the heat pads that are commercially available.
■ Steam inhalation, with or without Vick, to help the breathing.
■ Food should be soft and palatable.
■ Antibiotic treatment is not indicated in the uncomplicated case. There is now evidence that its use in fact serves to prolong the development and maturation of the abscesses, a situation which might even increase the chance of bastard strangles developing.
■ Commercial vaccines against strangles are available in the US.

STRINGHALT

Exaggerated movement affecting one or both hind legs, observed when in action.

As the horse moves, the affected hind leg is drawn sharply forwards and upwards, sometimes with so much force that the front of the fetlock hits the belly. After a short pause, when the foot remains motionless, the leg is brought sharply down. The degree of exaggerated movement varies from case to case. Some horses exhibit stringhalt with every stride, others only show it when backed or turned.

Of common stringhalt: unknown. Australian stringhalt, found in Australia and New Zealand and recently reported in the USA, shows identical symptoms and seems to be due to the continual ingestion of the dandelion weed which is a common pasture contaminant in parts of these countries.

■ The muscle relaxant Mephanesin helps some cases.
■ Surgical, in which a part of the lateral digital extensor tendon and muscle are removed under general anaesthesia. (The traditional remedy.)
■ Cases of Australian stringhalt tend to recover spontaneously when removed from pasture contamination.

SUNBURN (illus p115)

True sunburn is unusual in the horse, although many agents can make the skin more sensitive to the effects of sunlight (see **Photosensitivity** p179). However, some thin-skinned horses do seem to get sunburn on any white areas of the nose and muzzle.

A reddening of the skin of any white or hairless areas of the nose or muzzle. Blisters and scabs form a crusty, cracked skin which is obviously sore.

Extra-sensitive skin which is burnt by the effects of sunlight. Photosensitive agents may be involved.

■ Remove the horse from the direct effects of sunlight by keeping it under cover by day, and use sun-blocking creams on the affected areas.

SWEET ITCH (illus p113)

Synonyms: Dhobie itch, kasen, *Lichen tropicus*, Queensland itch, summer sores

A severe and disfiguring dermatitis

affecting horses from all over the world. As with many other diseases which are widely distributed and highly resistant to treatment, a multitude of causes and treatments have been put forward. All types and colours of horses can be affected, but in Great Britain the cob and pony breeds seem to have a higher incidence. A family background suggests that an hereditary factor is involved.

The national incidence of the disease in the UK is between 3 and 6 per cent and it first appears in ponies of about three years of age. Once it has established itself it occurs each summer, the first lesions appearing once the temperature rises, only to regress again with the first frosts of winter. In the warmer south the lesions reach two peaks of severity, in June and September; further north, the worst period seems to be July.

A localised dermatitis affecting the mane and poll and the root of the tail, and in severe cases perhaps the neck, shoulder area and hindquarters as well.

In the early stages the skin becomes very thickened and oedematous because the intense irritation causes the animal to rub on any convenient rubbing post, rail or tree. The hair in these areas quickly becomes thin and tufted and many papules develop, oozing small blobs of serum on to the surface.

As the itch becomes worse and the rubbing constant, the hair of the mane and tail is completely lost and the skin develops a corrugated appearance, becoming ridged and scaly. Long-standing cases develop skin sores and ulcers that are impossible to heal.

Reputedly many: allergies to grass proteins, sensitivity to sunlight, reaction to filariad worm larvae as they move through the skin, and allergy to the bite of the midge. Work by researchers in Australia and in Ireland in the 1970s and 1980s identified a probable allergic reaction to the biting midge, *Culicoides*. More recently, workers in Ireland have investigated the landing and feeding habits of midges, and the reaction of susceptible horses to bites of a whole range of insects, and in Ireland at least it seems that *Culicoides pulicaris* is not the only species of midge involved, since other

members of the midge family were found feeding on the predilection sites. However, they found that the reaction to the bites of the *Culicoides* species was consistently higher than that to other biting flies.

In conclusion, it is now thought that sweet itch is probably an immediate hypersensitive reaction to the saliva of midges of the Culicoides group.

The general conclusion is that prevention is better than cure, and that local treatment of the lesions is of little value. First, treatments used to control the damage done to the skin:
■ Corticosteroids and antihistamine preparations: the most widely used. Their disadvantages are that they need frequent application, and they are costly. Long-acting corticosteroid injections are the most useful for controlling the intense reactions present.
■ Other lotions and remedies have been used: Benzyl Benzoate, Caladryl, coal-tar lotions and even sump oil all have their advocates. Whether their action depends upon some local effect, or is due to an inherent anti-midge quality, is difficult to judge, but they all suffer from the same drawback – their effect is temporary, and daily application is necessary. Moreover unless some effort is made to prevent the midges biting, all these local and parental treatments will continue to be of limited use.
■ The only successful control is to prevent the midge biting, by stabling the susceptible pony and preventing the midges from entering the stable by the use of screens and insecticide strips. A partial solution is to stable the pony during the time of most risk, ie from late afternoon until the next morning.
■ Another solution is to use one of the new synthetic pyrethrum insecticides and kill the midges before they feed: spray the whole surface of the pony with a solution of the insecticide at least once a fortnight, and in wet weather once a week.
■ Various neck straps and head-collar strips or tags, impregnated with pyrethrum, have recently become available.

To be effective, any method has to kill the midge before it feeds. As the products mentioned above last all summer they are worth a try; and if their effect is

Symptoms = 👁   Cause/diagnosis = 💥   Treatment = 💊

not good enough, then sweet itch lesions will soon appear and weekly spraying will have to be resumed.

■ The most exciting cure – and it will be a cure – is borrowed from human medicine, where great advances have been made in the blocking of the agents causing allergy. If we can identify the exact chemical that causes sweet itch it should be possible to produce blocking agents, and these administered as a vaccine would prevent the allergen starting its allergic reaction.

TENDON STRAIN (illus p109)

Synonyms: bowed tendon, broken down

Tendon is a tough fibrous tissue that connects muscle to bone, and transmits the locomotive power that the muscles impart to the skeleton. It consists of many fibrils grouped together to form a rope-like structure; the whole is encased in a sheath of fibrous tissue. Strain can occur in any tendon, but most commonly it is in the flexor tendons that run down the back of the fore- and hind limbs between the knee or hock and the fetlock and onto the foot; these are the superficial and deep flexor tendons, together with the check ligament and the suspensory ligaments.

The racehorse, and especially the 'chaser, is most at risk because of the tremendous strain that these tendons have to withstand as the horse lands at speed over the large fences. Also the event horse as he tackles the cross-country phase, and the endurance horse, although in this discipline it is not force that does the damage, but fatigue – towards the end of a 100-mile race the tendons can be so tired that even relatively minor strains can cause extensive damage.

A varying degree of lameness, depending upon the amount of damage sustained to the tendon. In severe cases the foot is held raised, with maybe a little

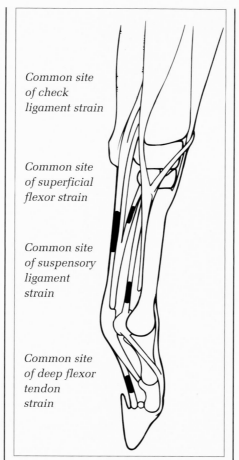

Common site of check ligament strain

Common site of superficial flexor strain

Common site of suspensory ligament strain

Common site of deep flexor tendon strain

weight taken on the toe; other horses are almost sound although the leg shows a fair degree of swelling. The damaged area swells rapidly as the torn and broken fibrils provoke a severe inflammatory reaction; fluid floods into the area and compounds the damage by forcing damaged and normal fibrils apart; heat and pain are evident.

The swelling can be so marked that without an ultrasound scan it is difficult to assess the extent of the damage. Ultrasound images are therefore essential if a meaningful prognosis is to be made (illus p109).

Strain occurs when the natural ability of the tendon to stretch and rebound to normal is exceeded, and is common in horses that compete in speed events.

The immediate application of cold to the area is essential to reduce the amount of blood and fluid pouring into and between the damaged fibrils. The

most practical method is some form of ice pack, secured by a firm bandage; this will help support the leg, as will a heel block taped to the bottom of the foot.

■ Anti-inflammatory drugs injected into the damaged area, or given intravenously, again to help reduce inflammation.

■ Later treatment consists of immobilising the leg in a cast until the pain and inflammation have subsided, followed by box rest until the horse is sound.

■ Then controlled, graduated exercise is necessary to encourage the fibrils to heal along the lines of force.

■ The drug Adequan® during the recovery phase also helps to improve the quality of the repair process.

This convalescent period should take nine to twelve months. The use of the drug Adequan® during the recovery phase also helps to improve the quality of the repair process. Recent work by Dr Virginia Reef of the New Bolton Centre has shown that the injection of a drug called BAPN-F into the tendon has significantly increased the quality of healing of the injured tendon.

Surgical methods of treatment, in which various implants are inserted into the tendon in an attempt to provide a scaffold, have been tried, but none has been any more successful than a long period of rest. However, new materials are constantly being assessed and eventually one will be found that does help the successful repair of badly damaged tendons.

The traditional method of treating tendon strain has been firing, but fortunately many surveys have proved that firing is of no benefit in healing whatsoever, and holds no place in the modern treatment of this type of injury.

TETANUS (illus p79)

Synonym: lockjaw

The bacterium *Clostridium tetani* can live in soil as highly resistant spores for several years; it causes disease in horses when it gains entry to a wound and starts to multiply and produce toxin. The wound can be the obvious external one, or it may be in the intestinal tract, which is why so many cases of tetanus are not associated with a visible external wound.

The toxins cause a type of paralysis in which the muscles become stiff and hard, unable to relax or contract.

The most consistent early sign is a closing of the third eyelid across the eye, and the more excited the horse the more marked this closure is. Raising the head by placing a hand under the muzzle and lifting is a good way of demonstrating this characteristic movement.

The ears remain pricked because the muscles at their base become paralysed, and for the same reason the dock is slightly raised. The gait becomes slightly stilted at this stage as the main muscles of locomotion are affected. The horse has an anxious expression, probably because the muscles at the corners of the lips become paralysed and are drawn back into a worried smile.

At this stage the condition can frequently be treated successfully, but then the horse deteriorates rapidly and the prospects of recovery become increasingly bleak. The legs become progressively paralysed so that the gait becomes stilted, and finally the horse develops a trestle-like appearance, unable to move its legs at all; if pushed it will fall with its legs still extended. Once recumbent, treatment is hopeless and paralysis of the respiratory muscles and death soon occur.

Tetanus spores are anaerobes, that is they prefer an environment with no oxygen in it. So when they establish themselves in a deep wound such as that caused by a nail in the foot or a stab wound caused by a branch, or under a burn scab, they start to multiply and produce toxin, which travels along nerves to the spinal cord and then to the brain; only at this point are clinical signs seen. The length of time between the injury and the development of these signs depends therefore upon the distance from the original wound to the brain. A wound in the head will only take a week or so to produce signs, whereas in the foot it might take three weeks or longer.

■ Tetanus demands extremely good nursing. Because of the increasing muscle paralysis, eating and drinking become more difficult, and both might have to be offered by hand or in extreme cases by stomach tube or intravenous drip.
■ Warmth and a quiet stress-free environment are essential, as any stimulus, whether it is noise or activity, can cause

further muscle spasm and paralysis. This is best achieved by placing the horse alone in a darkened loose-box, keeping noise to a minimum, and visiting it as little as possible. These precautions may have to be continued for days, or even weeks.
■ Medical treatment follows three lines:
1 To destroy the tetanus organism and prevent any further toxin production by thoroughly cleaning and aerating the wound wherever possible, and by using a suitable antibiotic parentally.
2 To neutralise the toxin that has been formed and is acting on the nervous system, by treating the horse with large doses of a concentrated tetanus antitoxin. This can be given daily by intravenous injection, but the best results are obtained when the antitoxin is introduced into the spinal canal so that it can reach and neutralise the toxin as soon as possible.
3 To sedate and relax the horse as much as possible so that the spasmed muscles have a chance to relax and the horse has a chance to eat and drink a little. The tranquilliser acepromazine hydrochloride (ACE) is very efficient at this job, and injected every three to six hours each day will provide good relaxation. Food and drink should be offered 15 to 30 minutes after treatment during the period of maximum relaxation.

It is during this time that expert nursing and feeding is necessary, but it should be realised that, if the disease is caught in time and treated in this way, up to 60 per cent of horses will recover.

Tetanus is a highly distressing disease for both horse and owner, and it is so much better to plan ahead and avoid the risk altogether by instigating a vaccination policy (see p36).

THOROUGHPIN

Soft swelling of the joint capsule which occurs just above and behind the hock joints.

Present in many hard-working horses: they often reduce in size during work and reappear after a period of rest.

Probably poor conformation of the hock.

Usually unsuccessful, and since these blemishes are rarely significant,

apart from being unsightly, none is therefore needed. Draining the thoroughpin and injecting with cortisone sometimes works, in the early stages.

THRUSH

An infection which develops in the sulci, the grooves lying on each side of the frog.

A black tarry discharge develops in the overgrown sulci of the frog. As the infection develops, the frog separates from the underlying structures and the whole area becomes soft, cheesy and foul-smelling. At this stage the lesion causes irritation and pain.

Wet and dirty conditions underfoot encourage the development of thrush. Stables where the horse spends long periods of time standing in dung and urine, or foul muddy yards predispose to the condition. Poor foot hygiene or neglected feet, where the frog is allowed to overgrow thus trapping decayed material, can also cause thrush.

■ Extensive paring of the foot to remove all diseased tissue is essential.
■ Once the sulci are pared out and all the under-run areas exposed, antibiotics, iodoform or formalin should be painted on to the infected areas. The cleaning and treating should be repeated twice a day until the area has healed. Neglected cases can prove very refractory to treatment.

TUMOURS (illus p115)

Not common in the horse, apart from sarcoids and melanoma; can be divided in a practical sense into those that are visible or cause recognisable changes in behaviour, and those that develop inside the horse and are only discovered during an exploratory operation or post mortem.

TWINNING (illus p98)

A common reason for non-infective abortion. The mare's placenta is designed to support one foetus and finds it rather difficult to share this support between twins. All too often one of the pair finds that the division of resources is unequal

Symptoms = 👁   Cause/diagnosis = 🦴   Treatment = 💊

and its share of the essential nutrients is not sufficient to support growth: at some time the smaller twin gives up the unequal struggle and dies. The other more fortunate twin carries on for a little time, sometimes to full term, but more often it also dies and both are aborted. The early diagnosis of twinning is obviously important, as 65 per cent of twins are aborted at around the eight-month period and the mortality rate in those that survive to full term is calculated to be about 50 per cent – not a very economical proposition. Also, any manipulation has to be achieved before the endometrial cups start to produce eCG at about 40 days, because after this period an aborted mare will not breed again for several months. Luckily the mare has her own method of reabsorbing the smaller twin so often only one embryo is left to complete its development. If twins are diagnosed then the most practical method is probably to abort both and start again.

TYSSER'S DISEASE

An uncommon, rapidly fatal disease affecting the liver of young foals.

The disease is very acute, and affected foals die after a short illness or are found dead. Those that are observed ill have a high body temperature, are depressed, and soon collapse and die.

The organism *Bacillus piliformis*: it causes an acute hepatitis, and post-mortem examination will show large areas of damage to the liver.

None.

ULCERS

Stomach and duodenal ulcers were considered uncommon in the adult horse but since endoscopic examination of the stomach has been possible it has become apparent that the condition is often seen in highly stressed competition horses kept stabled for most of the year. Several studies have demonstrated the high incidence of adult stomach and duodenal ulcers in this class of horse and interestingly have shown that the condition disappears when the affected horse is allowed to live a more normal life and spends adequate time at pasture.

Ulcers are also seen in the foal, especially following long-term illness or stress. An extended period of diarrhoea or treatment with NSAIDs also predisposes to gastroduodenal ulceration.

Adults and foals with ulcers *look* as if they have stomach pain. Foals suck half-heartedly, grind their teeth and frequently chew on straw. Adults also show stomach pain but also look strained and permanently uncomfortable. The mental state of affected horses changes for the worse, they become irritable and depressed. The overall discomfort is more marked after feeding.

Untreated ulcers can perforate, and if this occurs the foal becomes extremely depressed. Collapse and death follow soon after.

As with ulcers in humans, the exact cause of gastroduodenal ulcers is not known, but stress causing excess acid formation is one of the major reasons.

■ Prompt treatment with antacids and human gastric ulcer drugs such as Zantac™ or Tagamet™ will control the condition.
■ To assure a complete cure it is necessary to remove the underlying cause.

UPWARD FIXATION OF THE PATELLA (illus p109)

Synonym: luxating patella, straw cramp

Looks most alarming, but in fact is a slight abnormality of the normal stay mechanism of the hind legs. The horse uses the stay mechanism to lock one or other of the hind legs in order to rest.

When the leg is in full extension the ligaments holding the knee cap to the tibia get hooked over the medial condyle of the femur, rather like the leg of a person riding side saddle. When the horse wants to release the leg, the quadriceps muscle contracts to lift the patella free of the condyle, and then relaxes to let the patella slide down the stifle and free the hind leg. Horses that fix the patella find it difficult to free it from the medial condyle.

The hind leg is locked in place in full extension and cannot be drawn forwards; the affected leg is dragged along behind the horse with each stride. The locked phase might last for only half a stride, or for several minutes. The release, when it happens, is accompanied by a loud crack or snap.

This characteristic movement generally occurs when the horse first moves off or when it comes out of the stable in the morning after a night's rest. It is difficult to reproduce the movement in horses that lock up sporadically. Backing the horse, stopping and starting it, or turning are probably the best ways of demonstrating the condition.

It is thought that horses with straight stifles are more prone to this condition, which might explain why it can be common in certain families, ie those with a similar familial conformation.

The most common reason, however, is sudden loss of condition. Whether the cause in these cases is loss of the strength needed to lift the patella over the medial condyle or whether the loss of fat in the joint allows the patella to fit more snugly over the condyle, is not clear. In any case, the condition disappears as body condition improves.

It is also possible that young horses which develop upward fixation might do so because of poor co-ordination between the muscles that flex and extend the stifle joint. Certainly these cases improve dramatically as they come into training.

■ Many cases improve with time. As the young horse improves in condition and co-ordination the upward fixation occurs less and less. Increasing periods of controlled exercise, especially trotting in a straight line up an incline, also helps.
■ In cases where improvement in

bodyweight or fitness makes no difference, three other options can be used:

1 Injection of an irritant, normally containing iodine, into the median patella ligament causes inflammation and thickening of the ligament. This prevents the ligament from being hooked up.
2 The same effect can be obtained from surgery. Under general anaesthesia the medial patella ligament is split at the upper end. As the ligament heals it also thickens and prevents upward fixation.
3 An operation which has been used for many years – carried out under local anaesthesia – involves the medial ligament of the patella being sectioned, thus preventing the locking that occurs in this condition.
All these methods will cure upward fixation of the patella; however, all can cause long-term damage to the patella and future chronic hind-limb lameness.

URTICARIA (illus p113)

Synonym: nettle rash
Characterised by the sudden appearance of skin weals.

Skin weals commonly develop on the neck and flanks, and are associated with swelling of the muzzle, ears, vulva and legs; causes intense irritation, and considerable self-mutilation often occurs. These lesions frequently occur along the belly following the attentions of various biting flies.

Can be a symptom of a systemic reaction, often associated with a sudden change in the food, such as new spring grass. Equally severe urticaria can follow the attention of biting flies such as horse flies, horn flies and midges.

■ Prompt use of antihistamine preparations by intravenous injection will result in a quick recovery in cases of urticaria caused by systemic agents.
■ Regular applications of persistent pyrethrum skin washes; if started early in the season and used on all the local horse population, will prevent the severe urticaria due to insect bites by reducing numbers.

UTERINE CYSTS

Found in the lining of the uterus, the endometrium, in older mares. Until the advent of ultrasound examination of the uterus they remained unnoticed.

Large, thin-walled cysts up to 3cm (1in) in size, protrude into the lumen of the uterus. They start to appear in mares over ten years of age and are filled with lymph. Unless present in large numbers they cause no direct harm, but they are important in that they make the early diagnosis of pregnancy by ultrasound scanning more difficult.

Probably part of the normal ageing process of the uterus.

Normally cysts are left alone, but if they are present in large numbers and are suspected of causing infertility, they can be removed by laser or by direct puncture with the biopsy attachment of an endoscope.

VENEREAL DISEASE

Can occur in both stallion and mare. Normally the stallion catches the infection from a symptomless infected mare and then passes it on to other mares as he completes his book. Unfortunately, with the exception of coital exanthema, the stallion does not show many signs of venereal infection and it is not until covered mares start returning to service or themselves show signs of disease that a problem is suspected.

These depend upon the causal organism. Equine herpes virus causes papules which rupture and become pussy sores on the penis of the stallion and the external genitalia of the mare

(see p140). Infection with the bacteria that cause venereal infection might cause a transient discharge from the sheath of the stallion and a slight inflammation of the penis and lining of the sheath, but often infection is unnoticed. In the mare the usual signs are a persistent discharge from the vulva and a vaginitis which starts a few days after service. Venereal diseases caused by a virus, such as equine viral arteritis (see p152), generally cause a systemic illness in both mare and stallion.

Five agents are considered to be capable of causing venereal infection: three bacterial, and two viral in origin. The **bacterial** causes are:

1 *Taylorella equigenitalis*, the organism that causes CEM (contagious equine metritis): these bacteria are the most important of this group and have been described earlier (see p142).
2 *Klebsiella pneumoniae* capsule types 1 and 5 cause a less dramatic infection, and fewer mares are usually infected, although it might be more difficult to clear up the infection in those that are.
3 *Pseudomonas aeruginosa* causes a low-grade infection that often reappears after apparently successful treatment. It becomes endemic on stud farms and causes an overall depression of fertility. New arrivals to the stud farm and aged mares are the most at risk.

The two **viral** diseases are:

1 Coital exanthema, an acute disease that affects the external genitalia of mare and stallion, as described earlier (see p140). It does not appear to cause infertility, although soreness might prevent covering and cause problems in a busy stud.
2 EVA (equine viral arteritis): considered to be a significant threat because of its ability to cause a symptomless chronic infection in stallions which then transmit the disease via infected semen by natural service or artificial insemination. For further information, see p152.

■ The best course of action is to prevent veneral disease from entering a stud. This can be done by ensuring that

Symptoms = 👁 Cause/diagnosis = 🔧 Treatment = 💊

standing stallions are free from infection, and that all visiting mares are certified free before service. The procedures are covered in Appendix A, and visiting mares should have at least one negative clitoral swab before covering. Stallions should be checked before the covering season by examining washings taken from the prepuce and from samples from the urethral fossa. The routine checking of mares and stallions in this way has markedly reduced the incidence of the disease.

■ In the stallion, local treatment of the sheath and penis is generally sufficient. The penis and sheath should be washed with soft soap and water, dried and anointed with an effective antibiotic cream. This régime should be carried out daily for five days. Cases of coital exanthema can be treated above, but the disease is generally self-limiting, lasting from 10 days to 3 weeks.

■ Treatment of acute infectious endometritis consists of irrigating the uterus with a suitable antibiotic – ie to which the organism is sensitive – for a period of 7 to 10 days. The use of a plastic indwelling uterine catheter is a very convenient method of delivering the daily dose of antibiotic. The springy coiled arms, looking very like 'ram's horns', are straightened out inside an applicator, then introduced into the lumen of the uterus. Once free of the applicator the arms spring back to their coiled position and hold the device within the uterus. The applicator can then be withdrawn leaving the coiled tubes and catheter in place. The end of the flexible catheter is generally sutured or superglued to the perineal region to anchor it in place. The advantage of this method is that the treatment can be administered by the owner with very little fuss and negligible stress for the mare.

■ Some of the pathogenic strains associated with venereal disease, especially the *Klebsiella* strains and *Pseudomonas aeruginosa* are particularly resistant to most disinfectants and antibiotics. They also make life very difficult for those investigating an outbreak of venereal disease as they often cause no clinical signs in the stallion. The only practical method of preventing cross-infection in these cases is the use of artificial insemination.

■ In the face of an outbreak of venereally transmitted endometritis, it is essential to sterilise all those objects that might transmit the organism between mares. Pathological strains of *Klebsiella aerogens* are particularly resistant to chemical methods of sterilisation, so a bucket of disinfectant is not adequate, and the use of disposable gloves and heat-resistant, reusable instruments is necessary.

VENEZUELAN ENCEPHALOMYELITIS

A viral disease of the brain and spinal cord occurring in South America and the southern states of America (see p153 equine viral encephalomyelitis).

VESICULAR STOMATITIS

Synonyms: mal de terra, red nose
A viral disease affecting horses, cattle, pigs and occasionally humans, and characterised by the appearance of blisters in the mouth and on the skin of the coronary band on the feet. A disease of the Americas, as its distribution extends from the northern parts of southern America to the southern states of the USA.

Normally affects single horses, although epidemics can occur. The disease is characterised by a high fever and the development of vesicles on the tongue, lips and buccal mucosa. These burst rapidly, and large ulcerated areas develop. The coronary band can also be affected, leading to hoof cracking and lameness. In severe cases hoof separation can occur. The fever is short-lived and the lesions generally heal in 1 to 2 weeks, although cases affecting the coronary band can lead to long-term lameness.

Three strains of the virus exist, of which the New Jersey strain is the most virulent. The exact mode of transport is unknown but probably virus-infected insects play an important role.

No specific cure, but suitable nursing is indicated and most cases self-cure in 2 to 3 weeks.

VULVAL ASPIRATION

Synonyms: windsucking, pneumovagina
See **Endometritis** p147

WARTS (illus p115)

Caused by the equine papilloma virus.

Small groups of lumps appear in the skin of young horses, the soft skin of the muzzle, around the eyes or the area under the tail being common sites. These first appear as small grey swellings 1 to 2mm ($\frac{1}{16}$ to $\frac{1}{8}$in) in size, slowly growing to between 5 and 7mm ($\frac{1}{4}$ and $\frac{3}{8}$in) and changing colour to a pinky grey.

The equine *papilloma* virus probably gets into the skin through insignificant abrasions. The young horse's habit of nuzzling various objects could result in small skin wounds which, in turn, could lead to infection and explain the high incidence of warts on the muzzle.

The practice of grouping foals at weaning time or before the sales provides a perfect environment for the spread from one to another, and explains the sometimes explosive nature of the disease.

Warts are self-limiting; they have an incubation period of about 2 to 3 months, and grow to maturity and disappear over a further 3- to 4-month period. Many different methods, ranging from cryosurgery to heat treatment and autogenous vaccines have been used to remove warts, but it should always be remembered that warts are self-curing.

WEAVING

Considered to be one of the more serious behavioural vices (see p21) to which stabled horses are prone.

The horse rocks from side to side, swinging his head and alternating his weight from one foreleg to the other in time with the swing. This generally takes place through an open half door, but is sometimes seen within the stable. The intensity of weaving often increases as certain activities, such as the start of feeding, happen on the yard.

Like most vices, there is a danger that other horses will copy the action.

Probably a reaction to long periods of boredom.

■ Anti-weaving bars fitted to the front of the box will prevent sideways movement (illus p22). However, all too often the weaver then retreats to the interior of the box to resume his replacement therapy out of sight.
■ Relieve the boredom by turning the horse out: this is one method that will nearly always work.

WESTERN ENCEPHALOMYELITIS

A viral disease of the brain and spinal cord occurring in the western states of America: (see p153 equine viral encephalomyelitis).

WEST NILE FEVER

West Nile Virus (WNV) is a member of the Japanese encephalitis complex of flaviviruses and belongs to the equine viral encephalomyelitis group of illnesses. The earliest isolations of WN virus from humans were taken in Uganda in 1937 and then in Egypt during the 1950s: hence the name West Nile. The disease first occurred in America in New York State during the summer of 1999. Since then it has spread to most of the states of mainland America and Canada; it has also caused disease in southern Europe, eastern Europe, Russia, Africa, Egypt and Israel. WNV can infect humans and horses but both are dead-end hosts: the primary hosts are mosquitoes and birds.

WNV causes encephalitis (inflammation and swelling of the brain and spinal cord). The incubation period is between 5 and 15 days from the time that the horse is bitten by an infected mosquito. Common signs are an increasing weakness and inco-ordination, muscle tremors, loss of appetite, head pressing, aimless wandering and apparent loss of vision. Severe cases develop hyper-excitability, eventual coma and death. Between 30 to 40% of horses die after infection.

These symptoms are mirrored by many other diseases that affect the brain such as equine viral encephalomyelitis (p153), rabies (p188), and equine protozoal myeloencephalitis (p152) so expert help could be needed to make a diagnosis.

WNV develops when a horse is bitten by an infected mosquito. Mosquitoes are infected when they feed from birds carrying the virus and they, the mosquitoes, can pass on the infection when they feed on humans and horses. It is important to realise than once a horse is infected the virus cannot be passed back to uninfected mosquitoes. Active transmission is from bird to bird or from bird to mosquito to bird, and infected mosquitoes can pass infection on to their offspring.

■ Supportive treatment is the only treatment available.
■ A vaccine produced by Fort Dodge has been available for some time, and a new vaccine developed by Meriel has just come on the market. Both vaccines require two primary shots given 4 weeks apart and then boosters every 6 months.
■ Control of the disease in both humans and equines can be obtained by cutting down on the numbers of mosquitoes breeding by removing or treating stagnant water. Local authorities in affected areas can advise on how best to do this.

WHITE LINE DISEASE

Synonyms: onychomycosis, hollow hoof

A fungal infection of the hoof. It was first recognised in the southern states of America, particularly Florida, but is now considered a problem wherever horses are kept indoors. The condition is now considered to occur secondary to a primary hoof problem such as laminitis, long toe/low heel conformation, foot imbalance or any condition which leads to hoof separation.

The condition is first seen as a cavity or crack which appears between the white line and the surface of the hoof. This cavity gradually increases in size and becomes filled with a foul-smelling, crumbly material. Lameness is not a factor in the early stages of the disease, but becomes a problem when the integrity of the hoof wall is weakened to such an extent that it is impossible to keep a shoe on the foot.

Advanced cases involve the white line and cause under-running of large areas of the hoof wall. The lesion usually develops at the toe or quarters of the foot; both front and hind feet can be infected.

Uncertain, but it seems likely that the fungi and yeast species found in the lesions enter through defects due to poor conformation, and in suitable conditions become established and begin to break down the structure of the hoof wall.

Seems to be more prevalent in horses that are stabled in hot, damp conditions.

■ The most successful involves correcting the original conformational fault followed by debridement of the whole area and treating the exposed surface with a tincture of merthiolate or iodine.
■ In those cases where extensive areas of hoof wall have to be removed, the foot should be supported with egg-bar shoes.

WINDGALL (illus pp61 & 110)

A windgall is a soft swelling of the joint capsule which occurs just above and behind the fetlock.

Present in many horses that have had a hard working life; often reduce in size during work and reappear after a period of rest.

Poor conformation of the fetlock is said to be the most likely cause, but the general wear and tear of hard work or slight fetlock strain are the more likely.

Symptoms = 👁   Cause/diagnosis = 🩻   Treatment = 🧴

Usually unsuccessful, and as these blemishes are rarely significant apart from being unsightly, none is needed. Intra-lesional injection of cortisone may work.

WINDSUCKING

See **Crib-biting**, p144

WOBBLER DISEASE (CERVICAL VERTEBRAL STENOTIC MYELOPATHY) (CVSM)

CVSM is a condition of 1- to 2-year-old male Thoroughbreds. Rare in other breeds. Characterised by a gradually increasing inco-ordination of the hindquarters.

Loss of control of the hindquarters; worse at the walk and when turning. A gradual onset, in which the colt might reach a level of instability that remains static, or which could develop to a state where the ability to remain upright is almost lost. Severe cases are a danger to themselves and handlers as they blunder about, crashing into walls and doors, completely unable to control themselves.

A narrowing of the spinal canal in the neck which causes a constriction in the spinal cord. The nervous messages that control the hindquarters are interfered with to an extent that the horse cannot control his movements.

Other conditions such as **equine protozoal myeloencephalitis** (see p152) can cause very similar symptoms, and should be eliminated as a cause before a diagnosis of wobbler disease is made.

Surgical or medical.
■ Medical: consists of reducing oedema and swelling with non-steroidal, anti-inflammatory drugs; in young animals strict attention to the diet might help. If the growth rate can be slowed down, then the spinal canal might increase in size.
■ Surgical: carries a risk of severe complications but techniques have been developed that decompress the spinal cord and relieve the symptoms.

WOLF TEETH

Vestigial premolars which appear in the gum immediately in front of the upper cheek teeth.

Cause no health problems to the horse, but are often blamed as the cause of fighting the bit. Certainly many horses seem to accept the bit more readily once the offending teeth have been removed.

Your veterinary surgeon will be able to remove the tooth with little or no discomfort.

WRY NOSE (illus p124)

Synonym: squiffy face
A congenital fault that affects the bones of the nose and maxilla.

Affected foals are born with a twisted nose. The abnormality can be so slight that breathing and eating are hardly affected, but more often the malformation is so great that normal functions are severely restricted.

Most likely a malposition of the foetus in the uterus leading to undue pressure being applied to the developing head. This is borne out by the fact that in one survey 80 per cent of such foals were born to primiparous mares.

Surgery offers the only hope. In the most severe cases, humane destruction is the only option.

APPENDIX A

The information provided in this appendix *is based on* the Codes of Practice as drawn up by the Horserace Betting Levy Board (HBLB) in the year 2004.

Codes of Practice on:
◆ Contagious Equine Metritis (CEM), Klebsiella pneumoniae, Pseudomonas aeruginosa, Equine viral arteritis (EVA)
◆ Equine herpesvirus (EHV)

Guidelines on:
· Strangles
  Isolation
  Transport

CONTENTS

GLOSSARY OF TERMS

Aerobically In the presence of oxygen
Antibody Protective protein produced by the body in response to the presence of a virus or bacteria
Antigen Substance or organism which may be recognised by the body as being foreign to it, eg part of a virus or bacteria
Cervix Neck of the uterus opening into the vagina
Clitoral Relating to the clitoris
Clitoris A body of tissue found just inside the vulva
EDTA Blood sample which has been prevented from clotting by the addition of ethylenediamine tetra-acetic acid (EDTA)
Endometrial Tissue that forms a lining inside the uterus
Genitalia Genital (ie reproductive) organs
Guttural pouch Two large sacs connected to the tube (eustachian) between the ear and throat
Heparinised blood Blood sample which has been prevented from clotting by the addition of heparin
Immunofluorescence A test that uses a specific antibody and a fluorescent compound to detect a specific organism
Jaundice Condition in which a yellow colour can be seen in the mouth, eye and vagina
Lethargy Dullness or drowsiness

Microaerophilically In the virtual absence of oxygen (10% of carbon dioxide)
Nasopharyngeal swab Swab taken from the nose and throat
Oestrus/oestrous period In heat or in season
Pathogenic Capable of causing disease
Placenta Membrane which surrounds the foetus in the uterus
Scrotum Pouch containing the testicles
Seroconversion Change from being seronegative to seropositive
Serological test Testing of a blood sample by a laboratory to look for antibodies to a virus
Seronegative No evidence of infection in a blood test
Seropositive Past or existing infection indicated in a blood test
Serum Clear fluid which separates from solid materials of blood after clotting
Urethra Tube through which urine is discharged from the bladder
Uterus Womb
Venereal disease A sexually transmitted disease
Vulva External opening of the vagina

INTRODUCTION

THIS APPENDIX CONTAINS 3 CODES OF PRACTICE ON:

* The recommendations within the Codes of Practice are common to France, Germany, Ireland, Italy and the United Kingdom.

* These Codes of Practice are published by:
Horserace Betting Levy Board
52 Grosvenor Gardens
London
SW1W 0AU
Tel: 020 7333 0043
Fax: 020 7333 0041
e-mail: hblb@hblb.org.uk

The Codes and list of Approved Laboratories may be found on our website at www.hblb.org.uk
Select 'Veterinary Science and Education', then 'Codes of Practice' or 'Laboratory Approval Scheme' This booklet is available from the HBLB, Thoroughbred Breeders' Association and the Welfare Department of the British Horse Society.

REMEMBER:

◆ Venereally transmitted bacterial diseases caused by the contagious equine metritis organism, *Klebsiella pneumoniae* and *Pseudomonas aeruginosa*
◆ Equine Viral Arteritis (EVA)
◆ Equine herpesvirus (EHV)
It also contains guidelines on *Streptococcus equi* (strangles).

The Codes aim to help breeders minimise the risk of venereal disease in the horse population by making recommendations for disease prevention and control during the breeding season. Breeders should implement these minimum recommendations – and any additional precautions – in consultation with their veterinary surgeon.

There is a serious risk of widespread disease problems if breeders ignore the Codes. Outbreaks of reproductive disease can have severe economic and other consequences for breeding in the Thoroughbred and non-Thoroughbred sectors alike. EVA and EHV can also be transmitted by routes other than breeding and so can have severe consequences outside the breeding sector, ultimately for all branches of the horse and pony population.

Precautions are as important when using Artificial Insemination (AI) as they are for natural mating. Breeders using AI should also refer to the Code of Practice on AI published by the British Equine Veterinary Association (BEVA). The Codes are reviewed annually by a Sub-Committee of the Veterinary Advisory Committee of the Horserace Betting Levy Board. They are agreed with representatives of the other participating countries.

The Codes do not imply any liability by the Horserace Betting Levy Board or the Veterinary Advisory Committee nor its Sub-Committees in the implementation of, nor responsibility for enforcement of, the Codes.

◆ Breeders are responsible for implementing the Codes
◆ Ignoring the Codes may jeopardise your horse(s) and those of others
◆ The Codes make **minimum** recommendations for disease prevention and control
◆ If using AI, refer to the BEVA Code of Practice as well
Throughout the Codes, the term 'horse' includes mares and stallions of any breed of horse or pony; 'stallion' includes stallions of any breed to be used for natural mating, teasing or semen collection for AI; 'breeding activity' includes natural mating, teasing and collection and insemination of semen.

Strangles: As well as CEM, EVA and EHV, a number of other diseases may affect studs during the breeding season. In this context, strangles is of particular concern at present; new guidelines for this disease have therefore been developed (see page 225). These guidelines are for Britain; they have not been agreed with France, Germany, Ireland or Italy.

IMPORTED HORSES

In recent years, there has been a significant increase in the level of international movements of horses for breeding and sporting purposes. The attention of breeders and owners is therefore drawn to the importance of obtaining disease clearances for imported animals.

This applies to those diseases covered by these Codes of Practice, as well as to other diseases which may be present in other countries. For further advice, refer to your veterinary surgeon.

COMMON CODE OF PRACTICE FOR
CEM, KLEBSIELLA PNEUMONIAE AND PSEUDOMONAS AERUGINOSA

1. What Causes these Diseases?

Three species of bacteria are recognised as liable to cause outbreaks of infectious reproductive disease in the horse:
- *Taylorella equigenitalis* (CEM Organism, or CEMO)
- *Klebsiella pneumoniae*
- *Pseudomonas aeruginosa*

2. How Does Infection Spread?

Infection with these bacteria can be highly contagious.

Infection spreads through direct transmission of bacteria from mare to stallion or teaser, or from stallion or teaser to mare at the time of mating or teasing.
It is also transmitted to mares if semen used in AI comes from infected stallions.
Indirect infection also occurs, for example:
- through contaminated water, utensils and instruments
- on the hands of staff and veterinary surgeons who handle the tail and genital area of the mare or the penis of the stallion or teaser
- genital to genital or nose to genital contact between stallions/teasers and mares

Indirect infection is a significant risk for the transmission of *Klebsiella pneumoniae* and *Pseudomonas aeruginosa* between horses.

3. What Are the Symptoms?

In the **mare**, the severity of infection with CEMO varies. The main outward clinical sign is a discharge from the vulva, resulting from inflammation of the uterus. There are 3 states of infection:
- In the **acute** state, there is active inflammation and obvious discharge
- In the **chronic** state, the signs may be less obvious but the infection is often deep seated and may be difficult to clear
- There is also the **carrier** state. There are no outward signs of infection. However, the mare is still infectious because the bacteria are established on the surface of the clitoris, the clitoral fossa and sinuses and, in the case of *K. pneumoniae* and *P. aeruginosa*, sometimes in the urethra and bladder.
Infected **stallions, teasers** and **stallions used for AI** are usually passive carriers, meaning that they do not show clinical signs of infection but

have the bacteria present on their penis, sheath and, in the case of *K. pneumoniae* and *P. aeruginosa*, sometimes in the urethra and bladder. Stallions pass the bacteria on to mares during mating. Bacteria may also pass to mares, directly or indirectly, from infected teasers. Although internal spread in the male is rare, the bacteria may occasionally invade the sex glands, causing pus and bacteria to contaminate the semen.

4. How is Infection Prevented and Controlled?

The main ways of preventing infection are:

♦ check stallions and mares for infection before they are mated: this is done through swabbing

♦ checking that horses remain free from infection during breeding activities;

♦ always exercise strict hygiene measures when handling mares and stallions

The main ways of stopping the spread of infection if it does occur are to:

♦ stop mating by the infected horse(s)

♦ treat the infection, and re-swab to check that the infection has cleared up before resuming mating

♦ exercise strict hygiene measures when handling the horses involved

5. CEMO is a Notifiable Disease

In the UK, isolation of CEMO is notifiable by law, meaning that a suspicion or isolation of the organism must be reported to a Divisional Veterinary Manager (DVM) of the Department for Environment, Food and Rural Affairs (Defra) who will investigate all cases.

6. Hygiene

Owing to the risk of indirect infection, stud staff should be made aware that CEMO, *Klebsiella pneumoniae* and *Pseudomonas aeruginosa* can be highly contagious. Staff should wear disposable gloves at all times when handling the tail or genitalia of mares and stallions, and should change gloves between each horse.

Separate sterile and, where appropriate, disposable equipment and clean water should always be used for each horse.

If mares are infected when pregnant or foaling, hygiene is very important to prevent the transmission of infection through contaminated utensils or discharges from the mare.

7. Swabbing

Swabbing requirements are different for the stallion and mare.

For mares there are 2 types of swab:

♦ 'Endometrial swab': a swab taken during early oestrus from the lining of the uterus via the open cervix to demonstrate whether the uterus is free from infection.

♦ 'Clitoral swab': taken at any point during the reproductive cycle to demonstrate whether the clitoral fossa and sinuses are free from infection. In the case of pregnant mares, these swabs may be taken before or after foaling.

For stallions and teasers 'a set of swabs' includes samples from the urethra, urethral fossa and penile sheath, plus pre-ejaculatory fluid when possible and cultured aerobically and microaerophilically in all circumstances.

Swabs from mares, stallions and teasers should be taken each year after 1st January. The swabs should be labelled clearly to show the date and time they were taken, the horse's name and the site of swabbing; and sent to an Approved Laboratory (see page 213) to arrive within 48 hours of being taken. Indicate clearly whether aerobic, microaerophilic or both cultures are required.

Swabs should be fully submerged in Amies Charcoal Transport Medium to protect them from the damaging effects of light, which will readily kill any CEMO, *K. pneumoniae* or *P. aeruginosa* present;. Veterinary Surgeons submitting samples by routine postal services are advised not to swab mares on Fridays, Saturdays or Sundays as this usually leads to transit delays.

The Approved Laboratory will culture all swabs either aerobically or microaerophilically or both to screen for CEMO, *Klebsiella pneumoniae* (capsule types 1, 2 and 5) and *Pseudomonas aeruginosa*. The results will be returned on an official Laboratory Certificate. When planning the timing of breeding activities, breeders and veterinary surgeons should be aware that the results of microaerophilic cultures will not be available for at least seven days. The immunofluorescence test may be used in addition to culture, but this is only available in France at present.

8. 'High Risk' and 'Low Risk' Mares

'High risk' mares are:
a. mares from which the CEMO, *K. pneumoniae* (capsule types 1, 2 or 5) or *P. aeruginosa* has been isolated. The 'high risk' status will remain until three sets of negative swabs have been taken at three different oestrous periods in each of two years;
b. mares which have visited any premises on which the CEMO, *K. pneumoniae* (capsule types 1, 2 or 5) or *P. aeruginosa* has been isolated within the previous 12 months;
c. mares arriving from Canada, France, Germany, Ireland, Italy, the UK and the USA which have been mated during the last breeding season with stallions resident outside these countries;
d. all mares who have been in countries other than Canada, France, Germany, Ireland, Italy, the UK and the USA within the last 12 months.
'Low risk' mares are any mares not defined as 'high risk'.

9. Preventing Infection – Recommendations

A. Stallions and Teasers
After 1st January and before a stallion is used for mating/teasing/semen collection, stallion and boarding studs should ascertain whether the stallion is 'high risk' or 'low risk' by:
◆ Taking 2 sets of swabs, at an interval of no less than 7 days; these should be cultured aerobically and microaerophilically.
NB: Do not mate or tease until **ALL** the swab results are available.

'High risk' stallions and any other stallion standing on a stud for the first time warrant additional precautions. The first four mares mated with them should be screened for the CEMO, *K. pneumoniae* (capsule types 1, 2 and 5) and *P. aeruginosa* by taking a clitoral swab two days after mating. If the mare subsequently returns to oestrus, an endometrial swab should be taken at that time. These swabs should always be cultured aerobically and microaerophilically.

Stallion and boarding studs should receive, for each mare booked in, a Mare Certificate and Laboratory Certificate(s) before the mare arrives. Advance Laboratory Certificate requirements are detailed in Section B below.
NB: It should be noted that, in stallions, bacterial growth of the CEMO is generally more easily recoverable after mating. Swabbing of all stallions after their first few matings in any season should therefore be considered in consultation with the attending veterinary surgeon. In addition, mid-season swabbing should be considered for all stallions and teasers. These swabs may be examined for the presence of the CEMO only.

B. Mares

Before mares are moved to the stallion or boarding stud, owners should classify them as 'high risk' or 'low risk', then:

◆ Complete a Mare Certificate (available from the Horserace Betting Levy Board)

◆ Carry out any swabbing to be done at the home premises and await the Laboratory Certificate

◆ Send the Mare Certificate and any Laboratory Certificate to the stallion and/or boarding stud. Ensure that certification is received there before the mare arrives

◆ Request a Laboratory Certificate confirming the stallion's disease-free status in the current breeding season

Swabbing requirements are as follows:

'Low risk' mares – resident at stallion stud
Before first mating:

◆ Clitoral swab on arrival at stallion stud. Aerobic and microaerophilic cultures*

◆ Endometrial swab during oestrus at stallion stud. Aerobic culture
Mating in subsequent oestrous periods:

◆ Repeat endometrial swab as above

'High risk' mares – resident at stallion stud
Before first mating:

◆ Clitoral swab before arrival at stallion stud. Aerobic and microaerophilic*

◆ Clitoral swab on arrival at stallion stud. Aerobic and microaerophilic

◆ Endometrial swab during oestrus at stallion stud. Aerobic and microaerophilic
Mating in subsequent oestrous periods:

◆ Repeat endometrial swab as above
NB: Do not mate until **ALL** the swab results are available.

'Low risk' mares – walking in
Before the mare is first walked in:

◆ Clitoral swab. Aerobic and microaerophilic*

◆ Endometrial swab during oestrus. Aerobic and microaerophilic*
Walkings in during subsequent oestrous periods:

◆ Repeat endometrial swab as above

'High risk' mares – walking in
Before the mare is first walked in:

◆ Clitoral swab before arrival at boarding stud. Aerobic and microaerophilic*

◆ Clitoral swab during the next consecutive oestrus period on arrival at boarding stud. Aerobic and microaerophilic*

◆ Endometrial swab during oestrus at boarding stud. Aerobic and microaerophilic·
Walkings in during subsequent oestrous periods:

◆ Repeat endometrial swab as above
Laboratory Certificates from all swabs should be sent to the stallion stud before the mare is walked in.
NB: Do not mate until **ALL** the swab results are available.

* This swab may be taken at the home premises by agreement with the stallion stud. The Laboratory Certificate must be sent to the stallion stud before the mare arrives.

* The Laboratory Certificate must be sent to the stallion stud before the mare arrives.

* The Laboratory Certificates must be sent to the stallion stud before the mare is walked in.

* Laboratory Certificate from first clitoral swab – send to the boarding stud before the mare arrives.

Mare owners/managers should not accept semen for AI without obtaining evidence that the donor stallion was free from infection when the semen was collected. In the UK, this evidence would be provided by a Laboratory Certificate confirming the stallion's disease free status in the current breeding season. When importing semen, it should be accompanied by documentary evidence of freedom from infection with all three bacteria.

Important Notes on Swabs

Results of swabs:
Clitoral swabs: in the case of pregnant mares, these swabs may be taken before or after foaling.
Endometrial swabs: a negative result remains valid during the oestrous period in which the mare is mated and subsequently if she is not mated. If she does not conceive on first mating, a repeat swab should be taken during all subsequent oestrous periods prior to further mating.

Abnormal Return to Service (All Mares)

If mares come back into season at unusual times, a full set of swabs must be taken and cultured under aerobic and microaerophilic conditions.

Boarding of 'High Risk' Mares

High risk walking-in mares should be boarded at a farm which is under control by, or meets full approval of, the stallion stud. If the CEMO is confirmed on a boarding farm where a 'high risk' mare resides or at a stallion stud she has visited, no mares should be moved from the boarding farm until all have been swabbed with negative results.

Foaling of 'High Risk' Mares

Mares infected with the CEMO must be foaled in isolation. The placenta must be incinerated. Foals born to known infected mares should be swabbed 3 times, at intervals of not less than 7 days, before 3 months of age. The swabs should be cultured aerobically and microaerophilically:
◆ Filly foals: swab the clitoral fossa
◆ Colt foals: swab inside the penile sheath and around the tip of the penis

When infection is suspected or confirmed, mating must cease until treatment has taken place under veterinary direction and subsequent swabbing has proved that the infection has cleared up. The first swabs should be taken 7 or more days after the treatment has ended. Repeat clitoral and penile swabs should subsequently be taken at intervals of 7 or more days. Thereafter, the first three mares mated or inseminated by the stallion should have clitoral swabs taken 3 times at intervals of at least 7 days, starting 2 days after mating or insemination. Repeat endometrial swabs should ideally be collected during the next 3 oestrous periods.

10. Controlling Infection – Recommendations

If the CEMO, *K. pneumoniae* (capsule types 1, 2 or 5) or *P. aeruginosa* is subsequently isolated from any mare, stallion or teaser:
a. Stop mating, teasing and collection and insemination of semen immediately;
b. Seek veterinary advice immediately;
c. Isolate and treat the infected horse(s) as advised by the attending veterinary surgeon. In the case of the CEMO, the laboratory will have notified Defra, who may give directions which must be followed;
d. Arrange swabbing of any at-risk horses, as advised by the attending veterinary surgeon or by Defra;
e. Inform all owners of mares booked to the stallion, including any which have already left the premises;

f. Inform people to whom semen from the stallion has been sent;

g. Inform the relevant breeders' association;

h. Arrange for one straw from every ejaculate of stored semen from infected and at risk stallions to be tested by a laboratory. If a straw from any ejaculate is infected, all straws from that ejaculate should be destroyed;

i. Do not resume any breeding activity until freedom from disease has been confirmed in all infected horses (see below). The approval of the attending veterinary surgeon or, in the case of CEM, of the DVM of Defra, should be obtained before resumption of breeding activity.

11. Export Certification (UK)

Swabs taken for examination for the CEMO from horses in the United Kingdom for the purpose of official export health certification must be sent to the designated laboratories within the Veterinary Laboratories Agency (VLA) of Defra. These are the VLA Regional Laboratory, Bury St Edmunds for samples from England and Wales, and the VLA Regional Laboratory, Lasswade for samples from Scotland. In the case of horses that are to be exported from Northern Ireland, swabs should be sent to the Veterinary Science Division Laboratory, Belfast.

12. *Klebsiella Pneumoniae* and *Pseudomonas Aeruginosa*

The means of spread of infection and the signs and stages of infection with *Klebsiella pneumoniae* and *Pseudomonas aeruginosa* are similar to those described for CEMO in Sections 2 and 3 above, but infection may also become established in the bladder and urinary system.

Infection by these bacteria can be prevented by implementing the same measures as for CEMO (Sections 4, 6, 7 and 9 above). All swabs should therefore be screened for these bacteria as well as for CEMO. The veterinary surgeon should advise on the resumption of mating in all cases.

There are many different capsule types of *K. pneumoniae*, most of which are not considered to be pathogenic in the true venereal sense. However, types 1, 2 and 5 (venereal types) are considered to be pathogenic and may be sexually transmitted. Therefore, when *K. pneumoniae* is identified from mares, stallions or teasers, the tests necessary to determine which capsule type(s) is (are) present must be undertaken and then advice from a specialist laboratory and/or veterinary surgeon must be sought.

There are a number of strains of *P. aeruginosa*, not all of which cause true venereal disease and there is, as yet, no reliable laboratory test to differentiate between the strains. All isolates must therefore be considered as potential venereal pathogens. When transmitted to the stallion's penis, *P. aeruginosa* can be extremely difficult to eradicate.

Approved Laboratories

A list of laboratories in Britain approved by the Horserace Betting Levy Board for the purposes of testing for the CEMO, *K. pneumoniae* and *P. aeruginosa* is published each December in the Veterinary Record and is available from www.hblb.org.uk.

Reminder: 'High Risk' Mares

Information on the risk status of mares from France, Germany, Ireland, Italy, and the UK is also available from your appropriate breeders association.

COMMON CODE OF PRACTICE FOR EQUINE VIRAL ARTERITIS

1. What is EVA?

Equine viral arteritis (EVA) is a contagious disease caused by the equine arteritis virus (EAV). The virus occurs worldwide and is present in the United Kingdom, Ireland and every mainland European country.

The virus may cause abortion or pregnancy failure in mares.

EVA may be fatal.

2. How Does the Infection Spread?

A. Routes of infection

Infection spreads through transmission of the virus between horses:

◆ direct transmission during mating;
◆ direct or indirect transmission during teasing;
◆ artificially inseminating mares with semen from infected stallions, or which has been contaminated during semen collection or processing. The virus can survive in chilled and frozen semen and is not affected by the antibiotics added;
◆ contact with aborted foetuses or other products of parturition;
◆ via the respiratory route (eg via droplets from coughing and snorting).

B. The shedder stallion

The stallion is a very important source of the virus. On infection, the virus localises in his accessory sex glands and he will shed the virus in his semen for several weeks afterwards, or for many months or years and possibly for life. After recovery from acute illness, his fertility is not affected and he will show no further clinical signs of infection even though he may still be infectious. Shedder stallions will infect susceptible mares during mating and these mares may, in turn, infect in-contact animals via the respiratory route.

It is important to note that the shedder stallion is always seropositive (ie past or existing infection is indicated in a blood test) but that a seropositive stallion is not necessarily a shedder.

C. Mares

Present available evidence indicates that the 'carrier' state does not occur in mares.

3. What are the Symptoms of EVA?

The variety and severity of clinical signs of EVA vary widely. Infection may be obvious or there may be no signs at all. Even when there are no signs, infection can still be transmitted and stallions might still become shedders.

The main signs that are seen include fever, lethargy, depression, swelling of the lower legs, conjunctivitis ('pink eye'), swelling around the eye socket, nasal discharge, 'nettle rash', and swelling of the scrotum and mammary gland. In pregnant mares, abortion may occur.

4. How is the Disease Diagnosed?

Because of the variability or the possible absence of symptoms, clinical diagnosis is not always possible. Laboratory diagnosis is therefore essential. This requires one or more of the following: nasopharyngeal swabs, heparinised or EDTA blood, semen and, possibly, urine to be taken by a veterinary surgeon and sent to a specialist laboratory.

In blood samples, laboratories look for antibodies to the virus (serological test); in other samples, they look for the virus itself (virus isolation test).

Where abortion may be EVA-related, detailed clinical information must be sent to the laboratory with the foetus and its membranes (see page 217).

5. How is EVA Treated?

There is no treatment available for EVA itself, although there may be treatments to alleviate some of its symptoms.

6. How can EVA be Avoided?

The main ways of preventing EVA are to establish freedom from infection before breeding activities commence and to vaccinate stallions and teasers.

7. EVA is a Notifiable Disease

In the UK, EVA is notifiable by law under the Equine Viral Arteritis Order 1995. Under the Order, anyone who owns, manages, inspects or examines a horse must notify a Divisional Veterinary Manager (DVM) when:

◆ they suspect the disease in a stallion, either on the basis of clinical signs or following blood or semen testing,

◆ they suspect disease, either on the basis of clinical signs or following blood testing, in a mare that has been mated or artificially inseminated within the past 14 days.

DVMs are based in the Animal Health Divisional Offices of Defra.

Under the Order, Defra may:

◆ serve notices prohibiting the use for breeding of the suspect stallion and any semen obtained from it unless permitted under licence by a DVM of Defra;

◆ take samples or obtain information in order to establish whether the disease is present and, if so, the extent to which it has spread.

Under confirmation of disease, Ministers will publish this fact and the name and location of the stallion concerned, followed by similar publicity when the disease has been eradicated

8. Preventing Infection – Recommendations

A. Imported horses

Where it is intended to import horses, semen or embryos, veterinary or other specialist advice should be taken on the incidence of EVA in the exporting country. As a general guide, the importer should take the following precautions if the horse is imported from a country where EVA is known or suspected to occur.

Mares

◆ Ensure that the mare is blood tested within 28 days before import and proceed only on the basis of a seronegative result or, if seropositive, of stable or declining antibody levels in at least one further test at an interval of not less than 14 days;

◆ Immediately on arrival, place the mare in isolation for at least 21 days. Blood tests should be done immediately and repeated at least 14 days later. If the results are seronegative, or seropositive with stable or declining antibody levels, breeding activities may begin. If the results are unexpectedly seropositive, or the antibody level is rising, keep the mare in isolation, do not use her for breeding activities and consult a veterinary surgeon about the next steps.

Stallions

The following applies to import of stallions normally resident overseas, returning shuttle stallions and stallions who are normally resident in the UK when they have been overseas for non-breeding purposes but will be used for breeding activities upon return to this country.

In the UK, the law does not require any official testing of stallions for EVA before importation from EU member states so voluntary testing to establish their EVA status should be undertaken. Official testing requirements exist for imported stallions from non-EU countries.

◆ Ensure that the horse is blood tested no more than 28 days before import, and since he was last used for mating. If the result is seronegative, importation may proceed. If the result is seropositive, seek veterinary advice before proceeding.

◆ Immediately on arrival, place the stallion in isolation for at least 21 days. Two blood samples should be taken, one immediately and the second at least 14 days later. They should both be sent to the same laboratory. If the results are seronegative, breeding activities may commence. If any result is seropositive, notify the DVM of Defra immediately, and keep the stallion in isolation while steps are taken to determine whether he is shedding the virus in his semen (see page 219). The stallion must not be used for mating, teasing or semen collection during this time.

Sport Horse Stallions

Where stallions are imported into the UK for competition purposes, their EVA status should be established if it is decided, after their arrival, to use them for mating or semen collection while they are in the country. The stallion should be isolated for at least 21 days, and blood tested immediately and again at least 14 days later, using the same laboratory each time.

If the results are seronegative, breeding activities may commence.

If any result is seropositive, notify the DVM of Defra immediately, keep the stallion in isolation and consult a veterinary surgeon about the next steps. The stallion must not be used for mating, teasing or semen collection during this time.

Artificial Insemination

◆ When importing semen for use in AI, establish the status of the donor stallion at the time when the semen was collected. If the stallion was seropositive, the semen should not be used unless it can be proved that he was not a shedder.

◆ Under EU law, import of semen from shedder stallions is not permitted. Mare owners planning to use semen from overseas stallions should check the EVA status first. Semen should be accompanied by documentation certifying that the stallion or the semen was tested negative for EVA shortly after the semen was collected in the country of origin. Frozen semen should additionally be tested on arrival in the UK. It is only necessary to test one straw from each ejaculate. If the result is negative, the semen may be used. If it is positive, all straws from that ejaculate should be destroyed. For practical reasons it is not possible to test chilled semen on arrival. Appropriate testing in the exporting country is, therefore, essential.

Embryo Transfer

◆ When importing embryos, establish the status of both the stallion and mare at the time of conception. For mares, seronegative status, or seropositive status with stable or declining EAV antibody levels, is required. For stallions, seronegative status, or seropositive status with proof that they are not shedders, is required.

B. Stallions

After 1st January in any year, all **unvaccinated stallions and teasers** should be serologically tested. Do not use them for mating until the results are available.

If the stallion or teaser is seronegative, mating or teasing may begin.

If the stallion or teaser is seropositive, he must not be used for mating, AI or teasing during this time.

If he proves to be a shedder, he must not be used for breeding activities during this time. If he proves not to be a shedder, he may be used for breeding activities as long as any advice from the veterinary surgeon, and any conditions laid down by the DVM of Defra, are implemented. If he proves to be a shedder, he must remain in isolation until his future is decided. None of his semen should be allowed off the premises and previously released semen should be traced and the recipients notified.

Vaccinated stallions and teasers may be seropositive or seronegative, depending on when the last course of vaccine was given and on whether the horse might have become infected since the effect of the vaccine wore off. These horses should be blood tested after 1st January. Do not use them for mating until the results are available. If the stallion or teaser is seronegative, mating may begin. If he is seropositive, his history in the past 12 months – including dates of EVA vaccinations, results of pre-vaccination blood testing and contacts with other horses since the last vaccination – should be reviewed.

If there is any possibility that his seropositive status is the result of infection rather than vaccination, he should be isolated and further tested to determine whether he is shedding virus in his semen – see page 219 for test methods – and the DVM of Defra notified immediately. He must not be used for mating, AI or teasing during this time.

C. Mares

The risk associated with any mare can vary. Decisions regarding the testing of mares visiting stallions should therefore be made at local level, in consultation with the veterinary surgeon, according to the circumstances of individual studfarms and the mare's history and contacts with other horses in the past year. In any breeding season, the safest way to avoid risk is to blood test all mares within 4 weeks before mating. Foster mares should also be tested. Do not mate the mare until the results are available.

If a mare is seronegative, mating may begin. If she is seropositive, she must be isolated – preferably off the stallion stud – until her EAV antibody levels are stable or declining. Repeat blood samples should be taken at intervals of at least 14 days and sent to the laboratory that tested the first sample. In-contacts should be isolated and screened for EAV. Foster mares should also be tested.

If a mare was seropositive in a previous year and her current test returns seropositive, breeding activities may begin if the antibody level in the current sample is stable or declining compared to the level in her last test (ideally, the laboratory that tested the previous sample should test the current sample). If there is any doubt about the comparison of results, a second test should be done at least 14 days after the first, using the same laboratory. If the antibody level is stable or declining, breeding activities may commence. If it has increased, isolate the mare and consult a veterinary surgeon immediately.

D. Foaling – seropositive mares

Any pregnant seropositive mares should be foaled in isolation unless the vaccination or infection which caused seropositivity occurred before the pregnancy. If in any doubt, consult the veterinary surgeon.

E. Abortion and newborn foal death

Where abortion or newborn foal death may be EVA-related, a detailed clinical history of the mare must be sent to the laboratory immediately, together with blood samples from the mare, samples of the placenta and the fetus or carcase for specific examination for the EAV.

F. Artificial Insemination

The EVA virus survives in chilled and frozen semen and is not affected by the antibiotics added to semen. Donor stallions must therefore be checked according to section B above.

The stallion stud must record the dates of movement of the stallion on and off the premises, collection and movement of semen and insemination of mares at the stallion's premises.

G. EVA vaccine

One vaccine (Artervac, Fort Dodge) is available for use in all horses in the UK. Its use is recommended particularly for stallions. Horses that were seronegative before vaccination will become seropositive afterwards. This positive status cannot be differentiated from positive status caused by infection. It is essential, therefore, for breeding and export purposes, to be able to demonstrate that the horse is positive because of vaccination and not infection.

This is done by blood testing before vaccination to show that the horse was previously seronegative and keeping a record of the test result, certified by a veterinary surgeon, preferably in the horse's passport. The vaccine should not be administered until the blood test result is available. All vaccinations (primary course and booster doses) should be recorded, preferably in the horse's passport, by the veterinary surgeon who administered the vaccine.

Details should include the date and place where the vaccine was given, and the name and batch number of the vaccine.

VACCINATION IS NOT AN ALTERNATIVE TO GOOD MANAGEMENT

THE CODE OF PRACTICE REMAINS ESSENTIAL TO PREVENT EVA

9. Controlling Infection – Recommendations

If EVA occurs:
a. Seek veterinary advice and notify the DVM of Defra IMMEDIATELY.
b. Stop movement on/off the premises.

c. Stop mating and teasing.

d. Stop semen collection for AI; check stored semen (one dose of each batch to be tested by a competent laboratory).

e. Isolate and treat clinical cases as advised by the attending veterinary surgeon and/or DVM.

f. Group the in-contacts away from other horses on the premises and ask the attending veterinary surgeon to take samples for virus detection. When the results are available, separate any healthy horses which have tested negative away from those which have tested positive. Horses which have tested positive should be treated as advised by the attending veterinary surgeon and DVM, and kept in isolation until freedom from active infection is confirmed.

g. Ask the attending veterinary surgeon to screen all other horses at the premises by blood testing. If any of these return positive results, they should be separated from those with negative results, and be treated as advised by the veterinary surgeon and the Defra DVM. They should be kept in isolation until freedom from active infection is confirmed.

h. Notify:
◆ owners of horses at and due to arrive at the premises
◆ owners of horses which have left the premises
◆ recipients of semen from the premises
◆ your breeders' association

i. Arrange for the attending veterinary surgeon to repeat the blood testing after 14 days and again every 14 days until freedom from active infection is confirmed. Use the same laboratory for repeat samples as for the first samples. If any of the previously healthy or seronegative horses become ill or seropositive, they should be moved into the appropriate group and treated as advised by the veterinary surgeon and DVM. Testing of these horses should continue until freedom from active infection is confirmed. Seropositive stallions and teasers must be investigated to determine whether they are shedders. Those which prove to be shedders must be kept in strict isolation until their future is decided and must not be used for breeding activities during this time.

j. Clean and disinfect stables and vehicles used for horse transport.

k. Good hygiene must be exercised. If possible, separate staff should be used for the different groups of horses.

l. Breeding and movement should only be resumed with the approval of the attending veterinary surgeon and the DVM.

m. Pregnant mares must be isolated for at least one month after leaving the premises. Those remaining on the premises should be kept in isolation for at least one month after active infection has stopped.

Identifying Shedder Stallions: When a seropositive stallion is identified, it is vital to establish whether he is shedding EAV in his semen. If so, he is a primary source of infection.

The stallion must be kept in strict isolation for at least 28 days while the following methods are used under the direction of the attending veterinary surgeon and the Defra DVM to determine whether he is a shedder:

1. Virus Isolation
Collect 2 whole ejaculates of semen at intervals of at least 7 days and send them to a competent laboratory. Transport requirements (eg. cooling)

should be arranged with the laboratory.

If EAV is detected in either sample, the stallion is a shedder. He must be kept in isolation and not used for any breeding activities while he is still shedding, unless permitted under an official licence from Defra. In the event of negative results for both semen samples, experience has shown that it is advisable to confirm these results by test mating.

2. Test Mating

This must be done only in strict isolation and under veterinary supervision. The stallion and mares must be kept away from all contact with other horses.

Apply the following procedure:

◆ Identify at least 2 seronegative mares
◆ Take and store blood samples from each, then isolate the mares. Consult the testing laboratory about storage conditions.
◆ Mate each mare twice a day with the stallion on 2 consecutive days
◆ Keep the mares in isolation
◆ After 28 days, take blood samples and send them, with the pre-isolation samples, to a competent laboratory for a virus isolation test.

If the mares remain seronegative, the stallion is unlikely to be a shedder and can be released after a clinical examination.

If one or more mares becomes seropositive, the stallion is a shedder and must be kept in isolation. He must not be used for mating or AI as long as he is still shedding unless this is permitted specifically under an official licence issued by Defra. Seropositive mares must remain in isolation until they are no longer infectious or until they have a stable or declining antibody level in two sequential blood tests taken at an interval of at least 14 days.

CODE OF PRACTICE FOR EQUINE HERPESVIRUS

1. What is EHV?

Equine herpesvirus is a common virus that occurs in horse populations worldwide. The two most common strains are EHV-1 which causes abortion, respiratory disease and paralysis; and EHV-4 which usually causes respiratory disease only but can occasionally cause abortion. Although EHV-1 causes outbreaks of abortion, EHV-4 has only been associated with single incidents and is not considered a risk for contagious abortions.

2. How Does Infection Occur?

All classes of horses and ponies can be a source of EHV. Pregnant mares should therefore be kept separate from all other stock to avoid infection which may lead to abortion and to disease in live foals.

The virus usually spreads via the respiratory tract, but aborted foetuses, foetal membranes and fluids are a particularly dangerous source of infection. All aborted foetuses and carcases from newborn foal deaths must therefore be handled hygienically and sent to a competent laboratory for examination.

Infected foals can pass on infection via the respiratory route and by shedding virus into the environment to healthy mares, other foals and other in-contacts.

Mares which have aborted or whose foal has died are a source of infection to other foals and horses, also via the respiratory route. Disease can be transmitted to healthy foals from any infected horse as well as infected mares and foals.

All horses can be 'carriers' of the virus, meaning that they may transmit infection without showing signs of illness themselves. Illness may become apparent in carriers from time to time, especially after stress or after suffering another disease. The virus is always contagious at this time.

The virus can survive in the environment for several weeks; indirect infection is therefore possible.

3. When Does Abortion Occur?

Abortion usually occurs in late pregnancy (8–11 months) but can be as early as 4 months. Following infection, abortion can happen from 2 weeks to several months later.

Prolonged transport and other types of stress during late pregnancy may increase the risk of infection of the foetus.

4. What about Live Infected Foals?

Foals infected *in utero* are usually abnormal from birth, showing weakness, jaundice, difficulty in breathing and occasionally nervous symptoms. They usually die within 3 days.

These foals are highly contagious through direct contact via the respiratory route and through shedding the virus into the environment. All horses can become infected but mares which have recently foaled are probably at greatest risk.

5. What about Respiratory Disease?

EHV usually causes respiratory disease in weaned foals and yearlings, most often in autumn and winter. However, older animals can succumb. These are more likely than the younger animals to transmit the virus without showing signs of infection. The signs that are seen are mild fever, coughing, and discharge from the nose.

6. How is EHV Diagnosed?

The presence of EHV can only be diagnosed in a laboratory. For abortion and newborn foal death, the laboratory requires the foetus or foal carcase.

Members of the Thoroughbred Breeders' Association in Great Britain are reminded that a contribution may be available towards laboratory costs for aborted foetuses or foals which die within 14 days of birth. Further details are available from the TBA.

For confirmation of EHV as the cause of respiratory disease or paralysis, blood samples and swabs from the throat are required. In the event of death from paralysis the whole carcase should be submitted (if this is not possible, contact the laboratory to agree appropriate post-mortem materials). Blood samples should be treated with heparin or EDTA to prevent clotting.

7. Is EHV Notifiable?

There are no legal notification requirements for EHV in the UK. However, because the disease is spread easily between horses and can have severe consequences, it is **very important** to alert owners of horses which might be at risk of infection or might spread infection away from your premises following an outbreak at your premises. These owners can then arrange to take their own precautions against the spread of infection at their premises. Recommendations for reporting are given in section 9 below.

On no account should any horse known or suspected to have disease caused by EHV be sent, during the breeding season, to a stallion stud or to other premises where there are pregnant mares or brood mares.

8. Preventing EHV – Recommendations

A. Management

Pregnant mares should be kept separate from all other stock. Where possible, mares should foal at home and go to the stallion with a healthy foal at foot. Where this is not possible, pregnant mares should arrive at the stallion stud ideally one month before foaling is due. They should be put in isolated groups with other healthy pregnant mares; these groups should be as small as possible. Mares in late pregnancy and those from sales yards and abroad are a particular risk and should be isolated alone.

The isolated groups and individuals should be separated as far as possible from weaned foals, yearlings, horses out of training and competition horses. Fillies out of training are a particular risk to pregnant mares. Mares in late pregnancy should not travel with other stock, particularly mares which have aborted recently. If a foster mare is brought to the stud, she should be isolated – particularly from pregnant mares – until it has been proved that her own foal's death was not caused by EHV. Stallions should ideally be housed in premises separate to the mare operations.

B. Hygiene

EHV is destroyed readily by heat and disinfectants. Stables and and equipment and vehicles for horse transport should therefore be cleaned and disinfected regularly as a matter of routine, using approved disinfectants and steam cleaning. If cleaning and disinfection are inadequate, the virus may survive in the environment for several weeks.

Ideally, separate staff should deal with separate groups of mares. If this is not possible, pregnant mares should be handled first each day. Separate equipment and clean water should be used for each horse or group of horses, and staff should wear a new pair of disposable gloves each time they foal a mare and dispose of them safely.

C. Vaccination

The vaccine Duvaxyn EHV 1,4 (Fort Dodge) is licensed in the UK for use as an aid in the prevention of abortion and respiratory disease caused by EHV-1 and EHV-4.

Vaccination of all breeding stock, under veterinary direction, raises the level of protection against EHV and is believed to be particularly advantageous in preventing abortion storms. However, vaccination will not necessarily provide total protection. Veterinary advice should be sought on vaccination timings and administration.

VACCINATION IS NOT AN ALTERNATIVE TO GOOD MANAGEMENT

THE CODE OF PRACTICE REMAINS ESSENTIAL TO PREVENT EHV

9. Controlling EHV – Recommendations

A. If:
- abortion occurs
- a foal is born dead
- a foal is born ill
- a foal becomes ill within 14 days of birth

a. Seek veterinary advice immediately.

b. For abortions, stillborn foals and newborn foal deaths.
- place the mare in strict isolation
- send the foetus and its membranes or the foal carcase to a competent laboratory for examination as instructed by the veterinary surgeon; use leakproof containers. These materials must be handled under strict hygienic conditions; ensure that the attendant has no contact with pregnant mares.

c. For sick live foals:
- place the mare and foal in strict isolation
- send samples (usually nasopharyngeal swabs and heparinised or EDTA blood) to a competent laboratory for examination as instructed by the veterinary surgeon; use leakproof containers.
- the attendant should have no contact with pregnant mares

d. Stop movement off the stud. Do not allow any pregnant mare on to the stud until EHV has been excluded as the cause of the abortion, still-birth, foal death or illness.

e. Notify owners due to send mares to the stud.

f. Disinfect and destroy bedding; clean and disinfect premises, equipment and vehicles used for horse transport under veterinary supervision.

g. If preliminary laboratory results indicate EHV, divide pregnant mares in the contact group into even smaller groups to minimise the spread of any infection (NB: some may still abort). Any non-pregnant mares, with which the infected mare had contact, should be segregated from pregnant mares.

B. If EHV is confirmed:

a. Maintain isolation and movement restrictions and hygiene measures.

b. Notify:
- Your breeders' association
  (i) by telephone
  (ii) in writing
- Owners (or their agents) of:
  (i) mares at the stud
  (ii) mares due to be sent to the stud
- Others:
  (i) Those responsible for the management of premises to which any horses from the stud are to be sent;
  (ii) Those responsible for the management of premises to which any horses have been sent in the previous 28 days, with the condition that owners of those horses must be informed immediately;
  (iii) Those responsible for the management of premises to which any pregnant mares (that have been in-contact after the first 3 months of pregnancy) have been sent, with the condition that owners of those mares must be informed immediately.

C. After EHV abortion at a stallion stud:

Notification is extremely important. Failure to notify the disease can contribute to the spread of infection to the detriment of all owners and their horses, particularly mare owners.

* It may be possible, under the direction of the attending veterinary surgeon, to move them earlier than 28 days if: they have been isolated from pregnant mares and handled by separate staff; testing of blood samples taken immediately and again 14 days later indicates that they are not infected; there is no other evidence of spread of infection.

a. *The stud can accept barren mares, maiden mares and mares which have produced healthy foals at home, providing there is no sign of infection at the home premises but must be kept separate from pregnant mares.*
b. *Non-pregnant mares which have been on the stud can visit other premises after one month from the date of the last abortion, providing they can be isolated from all pregnant mares for at least 2 months at the premises they are visiting.* *
c. *Pregnant mares due to foal in the current season must stay at the stud until they foal.*
d. *Mares which have aborted must be kept in isolation from mares in late pregnancy for 8 weeks after abortion. Present evidence indicates low risk of spread of infection if mares are mated on the second heat cycle after abortion.*
e. *Mares that returned home pregnant from studs where abortion occurred the previous season should foal in isolation at home. Where this is not possible, the stud to which the mare is to be sent in the current season must be informed so that precautions can be taken.*

D. Walking-in mares:
Providing the stallion unit is separated geographically from the pregnant mares, and is attended by separate staff, walking in can be permitted. Following mating, the mare(s) involved should be isolated from any pregnant mares for at least 56 days.

E. If paralytic EHV is suspected in any horse:
a. *Seek veterinary advice immediately.*
b. *Stop mating and teasing.*
c. *Stop all movement on and off the stud for at least one month.*
d. *Send samples as directed by the veterinary surgeon to a competent laboratory for examination; use leakproof containers.*
e. *Divide horses into small groups, keeping pregnant mares separate from all others.*
f. *Do not allow any pregnant mare on to the premises until EHV has been excluded as the cause of the paralysis.*
g. *Implement Ae, Af and B above.*

F. If paralytic EHV is confirmed, policy should be decided with the veterinary surgeon. This should include screening and clearance of each group before individuals in the group return home. Individuals should then be isolated at home, especially pregnant mares until after foaling.

G. Confirmation of freedom from disease:
EHV is, to a certain extent, endemic among the horse population in the UK. Total freedom from disease can never be confirmed and vigilance is therefore important in the management of breeding stock, particularly pregnant mares.

H. Export:
EHV is not notifiable by law. However, no horse with clinical signs or recent contact with the disease should be exported.

STRANGLES, ISOLATION, TRANSPORT

1. What is Strangles?

STRANGLES

Strangles is caused by the bacterium *Streptococcus equi*. Affected horses, typically, have a high temperature, cough, poor appetite, nasal discharge and swollen and abscessed lymph nodes of the head. These can appear as open sores. The disease may be fatal if the bacterium spreads to other parts of the body. However, a nasal discharge without glandular swelling is often all that is seen, and the carrier state without any obvious clinical signs is also possible.

The incubation period is usually about one week but may be longer. The organism is shed from draining abscesses and the nose, and it survives in the environment and water troughs.

Other than direct contact with infected horses, poor hygiene among handlers is the most important means of transmitting the disease.

Infection can be controlled through the isolation of infected horses and shedders until they are free from infection. Shedding usually ends rapidly after recovery and this can be detected by culture of nasopharyngeal swabs. However, shedding may be intermittent. Therefore, before any convalescent horse or any in-contacts of any infected horse can be considered likely to be free from infection, a series of three negative swabs over a 2-week period are needed.

It is particularly important that nasopharyngeal swabs sample the back of the pharynx adequately. Swabs with extra long shafts and an enlarged absorbent head can be obtained from the Animal Health Trust, Lanwades Park, Kentford, Newmarket, Suffolk CB8 7UU (01638 552993).

2. Disease Prevention

All horses entering a stud should be monitored closely for at least 2 weeks.

All horses that develop a nasal discharge should be segregated and swabbed by a veterinary surgeon for the presence of *S. equi*.

3. Disease Control

The spread of strangles can be limited by the early detection of shedders among newly affected horses and their in-contacts. Any suspected cases should be segregated immediately. Three nasopharyngeal swabs should be taken at 5–7 day intervals over a 2 week period and cultured for *S. equi*. Young horses are most susceptible to infection and should be monitored.

All infected horses and their in-contacts should be placed under veterinary supervision in strict isolation with the highest possible standards of hygiene. When strict isolation fails to prevent the spread of infection, this is usually due to a breakdown in hygiene standards.

Horses should not enter an affected stud unless they can be kept in strict isolation from all sources of infection.

No infected or in-contact animal should be released from isolation or veterinary supervision unless 3 consecutive negative swabs have been taken over a 2-week period.

Recovered cases may retain potential for carrier status in spite of undergoing three negative swab tests and it is recommended that the guttural pouch, sinus openings and trachea are examined carefully with particular reference to carrier status.

The carrier state may be diagnosed by sequential nasopharyngeal swabs or, preferably, endoscopic examination of the guttural pouches and bacteriological examination of guttural pouch washes.

4. Disease Notification

There are no legal notification requirements for strangles in the UK although it is advisable to inform the relevant breeders' association if infection occurs.

ISOLATION
The Codes of Practice often refer to the isolation of horses. These notes offer guidance on isolation. In its most rigorous sense, 'isolation' means a separate facility with separate staff, separate protective clothing, separate utensils/equipment, and thorough steam cleaning and disinfection of stables between each occupant. The following guidelines, at least, should be adhered to:

Premises
1. The isolation premises must be a separate, enclosed building of sound, permanent construction, capable of being effectively cleansed and disinfected.
2. It must not be possible for other horses to approach within 100 metres of the isolation premises while they are in use.
3. An adequate supply of fresh, clean water must be available at all times for the isolated horses and for cleaning purposes.
4. Adequate supplies of food and bedding material for the whole of the isolation period must be made available and stored within the isolation premises before isolation commences.
5. Equipment and utensils used for feeding, grooming and cleansing must be used only in the isolation premises during the isolation period.
6. Protective clothing to be used exclusively in the isolation premises must be available at the entrance to the isolation premises and not be taken outside this facility.
7. A separate muck heap should be used within the isolation facility.

Procedures
1. Before use, all fixed and movable equipment and utensils for feeding, grooming and cleaning within the isolation premises must be disinfected using an approved disinfectant. A list of these is provided on the Defra website (www.defra.gov.uk).
2. Attendants of the isolated horses must have no contact with any other horses during the isolation period.
3. The isolation period for all isolated horses shall be deemed to start from the time of entry of the last horse.
4. No person may enter the isolation premises unless specifically authorised to do so.
5. When no attendants are on duty, the premises must be locked securely to prevent the entry of unauthorised persons.

If such strict measures are not possible in practice, studs should devise their own isolation programme and procedures in consultation with the veterinary surgeon. These should include, for example:

♦ The designation of a yard and associated paddock as an isolation area in a geographically separate area of the stud.

♦ The designation of individual staff to work in the isolation facility with separate protective clothing and recognised disinfectants as and when required. These individuals should either not be involved with work on the rest of the stud farm during periods of isolation, or they should work in the isolation area only after they have finished the rest of the stud. They should not return to other areas of the premises thereafter.

♦ The establishment, for use when required, of 'standard procedures', the precise details of which might be varied with the disease condition in question, following consultation between the stud manager and the attending veterinary surgeon.

TRANSPORT

There is potential for transmission of infectious diseases during transport.

Cleanliness and hygiene on board all forms of transport is the responsibility of the vehicle owner in private transport and the vehicle operator in contracted transport. The following notes are for guidance in either case:

♦ Vehicles should be cleaned and disinfected frequently and regularly, using approved disinfectants capable of killing bacteria and viruses. A list of these is provided on the Defra website (www.defra.gov.uk).

♦ Vehicles should be cleaned before horses are loaded.

♦ Prior vaccination of horses may reduce the risk of disease transmission during transport. Ideally, these should be booster vaccinations but if horses have not been vaccinated previously, then sufficient time should be allowed before transport for both primary and secondary vaccinations to produce adequate immunity.

♦ When mixed loads (eg breeding and competition horses; pregnant and non-pregnant mares) are unavoidable, give careful consideration to the categories of horses which are transported together so as to minimise the disease risk (eg risk to pregnant mares of EHV infection, risk of spread of EVA infection).

♦ Horses should only travel if they are considered fit to do so by a veterinary surgeon.

♦ Sick animals should not be transported except when they are travelling, under veterinary supervision, to obtain veterinary treatment. Where transport of such horses is unavoidable, they must not be put in mixed loads without the consent of other owners (or their agents) of horses in that load. Veterinary advice may be needed.

♦ If horses or their in-contacts are ill on or shortly after arrival at their destination, inform the transport operator at once. The operator should inform other clients with animals in the same load. Take veterinary advice on the sick horses, isolating them if necessary.

♦ Facilities should, if needed, be made available for cleaning/mucking out of lorries at premises where loading/unloading stops are made.

APPENDIX B

CONTENTS

THE HORSE PASSPORTS (ENGLAND) REGULATIONS 2003

Made 4th November 2003
Laid before Parliament 4th November 2003
Coming into force 30th November 2003

The Secretary of State for Environment, Food and Rural Affairs, being designated[1] for the purposes of section 2(2) of the European Communities Act 1972[2] in relation to the common agricultural policy of the European Community, in exercise of the powers conferred on her by that section hereby makes the following Regulations.

[1] 1972/1811
[2] 1972 c. 68

INTRODUCTION

Following epidemics such as the foot and mouth outbreak in the UK in 2001 and other contagious diseases there is a general move among authorities worldwide to improve controls of identification and movement of animals. Although the horse population is considered part of the food chain in some parts of the world it is not in others, and the argument that a system of recording the drugs administered to equines will prevent these reaching the plate does not endear the passport policy to most horse owners. However better controls will help reduce the risk of problems that affect the sport horse world, such as EVA or influenza, as well as helping identify the total horse population. A further negative side of the introduction of horse passports for many people is the additional cost for something they may not consider of personal significance, while the co-ordination of different methods of obtaining passports is another symptom of the problems of a fragmented horse industry. The following are the regulations governing the equine passport system in England.

The following document is published by The Stationery Office Limited as The Horse Passports (England) Regulations 2003, ISBN 0110481925. It may be purchased by contacting TSO Customer Services on 0870 600 5522. A full listings of recognised organisations permitted to issue passports is also available from this source and from the DEFRA website at www.defra.gov.uk/animalh/tracing/horses/horses_index.htm

THE HORSE PASSPORTS (ENGLAND) REGULATIONS 2003

TITLE, COMMENCEMENT AND APPLICATION

1. These Regulations, which shall apply in England, may be cited as the Horse Passports (England) Regulations 2003 and shall come into force on 30th November 2003.[3]

INTERPRETATION

2. (1) In these Regulations

'horse' means a domestic animal of the equine or asinine species or cross-breeds of those species;

'keeper' means a person who is not the owner of a horse but is appointed by the owner to have day to day charge of that horse;

'passport' means an identification document which has been issued for a horse by a recognised organisation and which is completed appropriately and is in conformity with the provisions of the Schedule to these Regulations;

'recognised organisation' means an organisation
a. recognised by the Secretary of State for Environment, Food and Rural Affairs under Regulation 3 of the Horses (Zootechnical Standards) Regulations 1992[4] or
b. recognised by any other authority in the United Kingdom competent to recognise such organisation; or
c. recognised by any other authority in another Member State competent to recognise such organisations; or
d. an international association or organisation registered under regulation 3 or registered under equivalent statutory provision in any other part of the United Kingdom; or
e. Fédération Equestre Internationale;

'studbook' means any book, register, file or data medium
a. which is maintained by a recognised organisation, and
b. in which particulars of horses are entered or registered with mention of all their known ascendants.

(2) For the purposes of the passport 'the competent authority' is the recognised organisation as defined in paragraph (1) above.

HORSES FOR COMPETITION AND RACING

3. (1) Any international association or organisation which manages horses for competition or racing in England and at the date of the coming into force of these Regulations is registered with the Secretary of State for Environment, Food and Rural Affairs under Article 4 of the Horse Passports Order 1997[5], shall continue to be registered for the purposes of these Regulations.

[3] Following concern that the original date would be impossible to meet, the British government extended the deadline for passport application to 30 June 2004

[4] S.I. 1992/3045

[5] S.I. 1997/2789

2. Any international association or organisation not operating in England at the date of the coming into force of these Regulations but which intends to manage horses for competition or racing in England shall register with the Secretary of State for Environment, Food and Rural Affairs before it does so.

3. Any international association or organisation registered under an equivalent statutory provision to these Regulations in force in any other part of the United Kingdom shall be exempt from the requirement in paragraph (2) to register with the Secretary of State.

ISSUE OF A PASSPORT FOR HORSES REGISTERED BEFORE 30TH NOVEMBER 2003

4. (1) The owner of a horse, with the exception of the owner of a horse as referred to in regulations 6, 7 and 8, whose horse was, prior to 30th November 2003, either registered or eligible for entry in a studbook of a recognised organisation and which does not have a passport issued by a recognised organisation, shall on or before 30th June 2004

a. obtain from a recognised organisation a passport for that horse which is in conformity with the provisions of the Schedule; and

b. where they have already been issued with a passport by a recognised organisation which is not in conformity with the Schedule, ensure that they obtain the appropriate extra pages from the recognised organisation.

(2) On application in accordance with regulation 4(1)(a) or 4(1)(b) and on compliance by the owner with any requirements of the recognised organisation, the recognised organisation shall issue to the owner a passport or appropriate extra pages, as the case may be, in conformity with the provisions of the Schedule.

ISSUE OF A PASSPORT FOR HORSES NOT REGISTERED BEFORE 30TH NOVEMBER 2003

5. (1) The owner of a horse not registered prior to 30th November 2003, with the exception of the owner of a horse referred to in regulations 6, 7 and 8, shall on or before 30th June 2004, obtain from a recognised organisation a passport for that horse.

(2) On application in accordance with paragraph (1) and on compliance by the owner with the requirements of the recognised organisation, the recognised organisation shall issue to the owner a passport in conformity with at least sections I, II, III, IV and IX of the Schedule.

HORSES ENTERING ENGLAND

6. (1) The owner of a horse entering England without a passport issued by a recognised organisation shall, within 30 days of so entering, apply to a recognised organisation for a passport in conformity with the provisions of the Schedule.

(2) A passport issued under paragraph (1) shall state that the horse is not intended for human consumption.

HORSES ENTERED IN THE LISTS OF THE NEW FOREST VERDERERS, OR DARTMOOR COMMONERS COUNCIL	**7.**	(1) Where a horse is entered in the lists kept by the New Forest Verderers, or Dartmoor Commoners Council, a passport shall only be required when the horse is moved from the area in which its owner has grazing rights for equines granted by those bodies. (2) An owner who has been granted grazing rights for equines in the New Forest or Dartmoor shall a. ensure that all such equines are individually identified and entered in the lists kept by the New Forest Verderers or the Dartmoor Commoners Council; or b. shall obtain a passport from a recognised organisation.
PASSPORTS FOR YOUNG HORSES	**8.**	A horse is required to have a passport a. by 31st December of the year of its birth; or b. by six months after its birth, whichever is the longer; or c. if, before then, it leaves the premises on which its dam is normally kept for a continuous period of two weeks or more.
REQUIREMENTS OF OWNERS AND KEEPERS OF HORSES AS TO DECLARATION ON HUMAN CONSUMPTION	**9.**	(1) The owner or keeper of a horse, on receipt of a passport or appropriate extra pages issued by a recognised organisation, shall sign the declaration in section IX, Part II or III-A, as to whether or not the horse is intended for human consumption. (2) If the declaration referred to in paragraph (1) above is signed by the owner or keeper of a horse confirming that the horse is not intended for human consumption, then that declaration cannot be changed by any subsequent owner or keeper. (3) Subject to regulation 9 (2) if the declaration in Part II has been made, it shall be reconfirmed on each subsequent change of ownership of the horse by the signature of the new owner.
WHEREABOUTS OF PASSPORTS	**10.**	(1) The owner of a horse shall ensure that the passport is held by the keeper of the horse. (2) If the keeper changes, the previous keeper shall give the passport to the new keeper. (3) The owner or keeper of a horse shall ensure that the horse is accompanied by its passport when it is moved (a) into or out of Great Britain; (b) to other premises for competition purposes; (c) to other premises to receive veterinary treatment; (d) to the premises of a new keeper; (e) to a slaughterhouse for slaughter; (f) for the purpose of sale; or (g) for breeding purposes.
REQUIREMENTS OF VETERINARY SURGEONS	**11.**	(1) Where veterinary treatment is to be administered to a horse, the owner or keeper shall show the passport to the veterinary surgeon who is to administer such treatment.

(2) The veterinary surgeon shall

a. satisfy himself that the horse is the one described in the passport;

b. record in the passport the treatments administered to the horse as required in sections V and VI of the passport; and

c. if the owner or keeper of the horse has signed the declaration contained in section IX, Part III-A of the passport that the horse is intended for human consumption

(i) refrain from administering any of the drugs listed in Annex IV of Council Regulation 2377/90/EEC [6]; and

(ii) enter in section IX, Part III-B of the passport the date of the last treatment administered to the horse with a medicinal product containing substances not included in Annex I, II, III or IV of Council Regulation 2377/90/EEC.

(3) If the veterinary surgeon is not able to satisfy himself as provided in paragraph 2, he shall refrain from administering any of the drugs listed in Annex IV of Council Regulation 2377/90/EEC.

[6] OJ No. L224, 18.8.90, p. 1

LIFE NUMBER

12. The recognised organisation when issuing a passport or appropriate extra pages shall

a. identify that horse by a number which has not been used for any other horse;

b. record that number in section II and section IX of the passport or appropriate extra pages issued in respect of that horse; and

c. provide the number in accordance with any codes which may be issued from time to time by the Secretary of State for Environment, Food and Rural Affairs.

LANGUAGE OF PASSPORTS

13. All passports and extra pages issued in England shall be in English and French, but may in addition contain a translation (either of the whole passport or of part of it) into such other language or languages as the recognised organisation thinks fit, except that section IX may be in English only.

PROHIBITION

14. No person shall

a. amend sections I to IV of a passport unless he is a person authorised by the recognised organisation which issues it;

b. hold more than one passport for any horse at the same time;

c. change the name of a horse as stated in its passport unless the passport has previously been amended by the recognised authority to show the new name whilst retaining an indication of the previous name or names;

d. retain a passport unless he is the owner or keeper of the horse; or

e. apply for a passport for a horse for which a passport has already been issued.

SALE OR DEATH OF A HORSE

15. (1) On the sale of a horse, the seller shall give the passport to the buyer or, at auction sales, the auctioneer shall give the passport to the buyer.

(2) The buyer shall send the details of the new owner to the recognised organisation of issue within 28 days of the purchase of the horse.

(3) If a horse dies in a slaughterhouse, the slaughterhouse shall retain its passport for one year.

(4) If a horse dies in a place other than a slaughterhouse, the owner or keeper shall return the passport to the recognised organisation with an indication of the date and circumstances of death and the recognised organisation shall amend their records accordingly.

REPLACEMENT OF A LOST OR DAMAGED PASSPORT

16. (1) Where a passport has been lost or damaged the owner of a horse in respect of which that passport has been issued shall apply for a replacement passport for that horse
a. where the recognised organisation of issue is known to him, to that organisation for a replacement passport for that horse; or
b. where the recognised organisation of issue is not known, to any recognised organisation.

(2) The recognised organisation applied to in accordance with paragraph (1) shall issue a replacement passport marked with the word 'Duplicate' and including, in the case of a passport which
a. Is lost or is damaged so that the original declaration as to fitness for human consumption is not legible, a declaration that the horse is not fit for human consumption; or
b. Is damaged but the original declaration as to fitness for human consumption is still legible, a declaration which is the same as the original.

TIME LIMITS FOR APPLICATION

17. Where the owner of a horse makes an application for a passport for that horse outside the time limits provided for in these Regulations, the owner shall be issued with a passport indicating that the horse is not intended for human consumption.

POWER AND DUTIES OF RECOGNIZED ORGANISATIONS

18. (1) A recognised organisation may cancel a passport issued by it under these Regulations if it is satisfied that the provisions of these Regulations have not been or are not being complied with or that the passport has not been properly completed or has been falsified in any way.

(2) A recognised organisation may require any person in possession of a passport which it issued to produce it on reasonable demand and surrender it on demand.

(3) A recognised organisation in England shall
a. supply to the Secretary of State information contained in applications for passports and appropriate extra pages and notifications of deaths of horses in such form and in such frequency as she may from time to time require;
b. require in application forms for passports and appropriate extra pages an indication of the intended declaration as to whether or not the horse is intended for human consumption and sign the passports or appropriate extra pages accordingly;
c. keep records of such information and of the issue of passports and appropriate extra pages and of deaths of horses notified to it.

WITHDRAWAL OF RECOGNITION   **19.** The Secretary of State for Environment, Food and Rural Affairs may withdraw recognition from any recognised organisation or registered organisation that issues a passport which does not comply with the provisions of regulations 4(1), 5(2) and 12 and the Schedule and may withdraw any such passport.

OFFENCES   **20.** It shall be an offence for any person or organisation to fail to comply with the provisions of these Regulations.

POWERS OF ENTRY   **21.** (1) An inspector appointed by a local authority or the Secretary of State for Environment, Food and Rural Affairs for the enforcement of these Regulations shall, on producing some duly authenticated document showing his authority, have a right at all reasonable hours, to enter any premises (excluding any premises not containing any horse and used only as a dwelling) for the purpose of administering and enforcing these Regulations; and in this regulation 'premises' includes any vehicle or container.

(2) An inspector so appointed may
a. carry out any inquiries;
b. have access to, and inspect and copy any records (in whatever form they are held) kept under these Regulations;
c. remove such records to enable them to be copied;
d. have access to, inspect and check the operation of any computer and any associated apparatus or material which is or has been in use in connection with the records; and for this purpose may require any person having charge of, or otherwise concerned with the operation of, the computer, apparatus or material to afford him such assistance as he may reasonably require and, where a record is kept by means of a computer, may require the records to be produced in a form in which they may be taken away;
e. mark any animal or other thing for identification purposes; and
f. take with him
(i) such other persons as he considers necessary; and
(ii) any representative of the European Commission properly interested in the administration of these Regulations.

(3) Any person who defaces, obliterates or removes any mark applied under paragraph (2) shall be guilty of an offence.

(4) If such an inspector enters any unoccupied premises he shall leave them as effectively secured against unauthorised entry as he found them.

OBSTRUCTION   **22.** (1) No person shall
a. intentionally obstruct any person acting in the execution of these Regulations;
b. without reasonable cause, fail to give to any person acting in the execution of these Regulations any assistance or information which that person may reasonably require of him for the performance of his functions under these Regulations;
c. furnish to any person acting in the execution of these Regulations any information which he knows to be false or misleading; or
d. fail to produce a record when required to do so to any person acting in the execution of these Regulations.

(2) Nothing in paragraph (1)(b) shall be construed as requiring any person to answer any question if to do so might incriminate him.

PENALTIES 23. (1) A person guilty of an offence under these Regulations shall be liable
a. on summary conviction, to a fine not exceeding the statutory maximum or to imprisonment for a term not exceeding three months or both; or
b. on conviction on indictment, to a fine or to imprisonment for a term not exceeding two years or both.

(2) Where a body corporate is guilty of an offence under these Regulations, and that offence is proved to have been committed with the consent or connivance of, or to have been attributable to any neglect on the part of
a. any director, manager, secretary or other similar person of the body corporate, or
b. any person who was purporting to act in any such capacity, he, as well as the body corporate, shall be guilty of the offence and shall be liable to be proceeded against and punished accordingly.

(3) For the purposes of paragraph (2) above, 'director', in relation to a body corporate whose affairs are managed by its members, means a member of the body corporate.

ENFORCEMENT 24. (1) These Regulations shall be enforced by the local authority.

(2) The Secretary of State may direct, in relation to cases of a particular description or any particular case, that an enforcement duty imposed on a local authority under this regulation shall be discharged by the Secretary of State and not by the local authority.

REVOCATIONS 25. The Passports Order 1997[7] and the Passports (Amendment) Order 1998[8] are hereby revoked insofar as they relate to England.

[7] S.I. 1997/2789
[8] S.I. 1998/2637

ALUN MICHAEL
Minister of State Department for Environment, Food and Rural Affairs
4th November 2003

SCHEDULE

Identification document for registered equidae

PASSPORT

GENERAL INSTRUCTIONS

I. Passports must contain all instructions needed for their use and the details of the competent authority which issued them.

II. II. Information shown on passports

A. Passports must contain the following information

1. Section I: Owner
The name of the owner or his agent must be stated

2. Sections II and III: Identification
The equid must be identified by the competent authority

3. Section IV: Recording of identity checks
Whenever laws and regulations so require, checks conducted on the identity of the equid must be recorded by the competent authority

2.

4. Sections V and VI: Vaccination record
All vaccinations must be recorded in Section V (equine influenza only) and in Section VI (all other vaccinations)

5. Section VII: Laboratory health tests
The results of all tests carried out to detect transmissible diseases must be recorded

6. Section IX: Medicinal Treatment

3. Part I and Part II or Part III of this Section must be duly completed in accordance with the instructions provided for in this Section

B. Passports may contain the following information

Section VIII: Basic health requirements

Section VIII states the basic health requirements
It lists the diseases which must be noted on the health certificate

DISEASES FOR WHICH AN ENDORSEMENT MUST BE MADE ON THE HEALTH CERTIFICTE ATTACHED TO THE PASSPORT

1. African horse sickness
2. Vesicular stomatitis
3. Dourine
4. Glanders
5. Equine encephalomyelitis (all types)
6. Infectious anaemia
7. Rabies
8. Anthrax

APPENDIX C
NATURAL HOOF CARE

The conventionally accepted need for horse shoeing is discussed in Part 1. However, there is now also an extensive movement that contends that horses should not be shod at all, and another that promotes a radically different form of shoeing. Both of these movements have developed from studies of horses 'in the wild'. While the studies have produced much valuable information on the natural form and function of the equine foot, the conclusions of the various researchers are open to interpretation and so far lack statistically proven and scientifically supported evidence. There is still much disagreement and controversy. For example, traditional theory suggests that the frog and sole have little to do with weight bearing, while proponents of 'natural hoof care' suggest that they are very important.

NATURAL BALANCE SHOEING

'Four-point' theory was developed by American farrier Gene Ovnicek, who studied various groups of wild horses that were being managed by the Bureau of Land Management in Montana, taking photographs and making impressions of their hoofprints while the horses were captured as part of a horse adoption scheme. The method of shoeing horses developed from this study, initially called 'four-point shoeing' was widely taken up, but unfortunately often without proper understanding of the theory, resulting in a bad reputation for the method. Ovnicek discarded the name and now calls his method 'natural balance' shoeing. He went on to successfully develop the 'World Racing Plate', a special shoe that applies his findings to the racing industry, followed by a special shoe for laminitis. The work of Ovnicek and his colleagues has been scientifically acknowledged by publication of the paper 'Natural Balance Trimming and Shoeing: Its Theory and Application' (Ovnicek, Page and Trotter: Veterinary Clinics of North America: Equine Practice, August 2003).

THE BAREFOOT HORSE

The barefoot movement first gained momentum through the work of Dr Hiltrud Strasser, a German veterinarian who developed her 'barefoot trim' over a period of 20 years' study. She has attracted both high praise and strong criticism over her approach to promoting her methods – through a system of 'certified' practitioners and encouraging horse owners to learn to trim their own horses' feet – as much as the methods themselves. In Britain, unlike many other countries, it is illegal for an unqualified person to shoe a horse, though not to trim it unless for the purpose of shoeing, and at the end of 2001, the British Equine Veterinary Association (BEVA) issued a position statement on Strasser Hoof Care, published in the *Equine Veterinary Journal*, stating *inter alia*:

> It is not illegal for an owner to trim a horse's foot, provided it is not subsequently going to be shod. This is to enable owners to carry out regular maintenance of unshod hooves but not to allow major alteration of their horses' feet. BEVA fully supports the statement issued by the Worshipful Company of Farriers and The Farriers Registration Council that horsowners should involve a registered farrier for routine hoof care and especially when considering reshaping the feet. Furthermore, a veterinary surgeon should always be consulted for the diagnosis and management of lameness, as this can be due to a variety of causes, some of which may be exacerbated by Dr Strasser's methods.

The same issue carried an open letter to veterinarians by W. Robert Cook, FRCVS, PhD, Professor of Surgery Emeritus of Tufts University School of Veterinary Medicine, Massachusetts, supporting her work: 'Dr. Hiltrud Strasser of Tuebingen, Germany, has studied the horse's hoof for the last 20 years. Through her clinical work and publications she has demonstrated that the horseshoe is an unnecessary evil.'

This is the problem at the centre of the controversy. Few would argue that in ideal conditions the barefoot horse maintains a comfortable and healthy foot. Research so far has shown ideal conditions to include primarily 24-hour turnout with the possibility for the horse to cover 20 to 30km per day on natural, preferably mainly dry and hard terrain. In this environment, feet will wear to the shape that is most comfortable, healthy and appropriate for the horse, avoiding such problems as navicular disease, pedal bone rotation, separation of the laminae, laminitis, concussion problems and tendon strain. The feet will be neither upright and boxy (which seems to be the major problem of domestic horses in dryer climates), nor low and flat with long toes and under-run heels (which persists in wetter climates with soft ground and in breeds such as the Thoroughbred). Strasser also maintains that hooves need regular daily soaking to remain supple and healthy, although there is disagreement on this point from other barefoot proponents.

BAREFOOT FOR THE PERFORMANCE HORSE?

Unfortunately, the modern domesticated horse seldom has the opportunity to live in the ideal conditions mentioned above. Restricted movement in stables or small paddocks, soft grassy loam, clay or sand underfoot, constant standing in wet conditions in winter all mean that the horse, even if left barefoot, cannot maintain a healthy foot without human intervention.

From this develops the question, can the modern horse be kept barefoot and still perform as required? The evidence so far, from the limited amount of information available, shows that it *is* possible to keep a horse barefoot and still compete successfully even in 160km endurance rides. However, the problem, at present, is that those who have succeeded in this experiment have put an enormous amount of time and effort into maintaining their horses barefoot and the information available is not widespread enough to know how much horses can adapt to varying conditions. If they are trained on one type of terrain, for example, how do they adapt if transported to completely different conditions? Even barefoot enthusiasts accept the need to use hoof boots to protect the horse's foot, firstly during the period of adaptation after removing the shoes, and then when working on unfamiliar terrain. Trimming has to be carried out meticulously, with understanding of the mechanism and anatomy of the horse's foot, and also frequently – usually every three weeks when the horse is established

as barefoot. So while some impressive results have been obtained, a much greater body of proof is needed before we can say that barefoot should be the norm.

The Strasser technique, which has received criticism for being too aggressive in its approach, is not the only type of barefoot trim in use. In America, developed from the work of Gene Ovnicek and former farrier Jaime Jackson, who also studied wild horses, among others, the use of the 'wild horse trim' is becoming more widespread. This is a method designed to rehabilitate the horse more slowly and to keep it as much as possible in work and sound, while the transition from shod horse to barefoot takes place. The basic aim is to achieve a hoof shape that works as nature intended, with the pedal (coffin) bone parallel to the ground and the white line (where the laminae join) healthy and tight.

For those interested in further study, there is a growing body of literature, books, videos and information available on the internet.

CONCLUSION

While it is undoubtedly true that a healthy barefoot hoof is best, we are a long way from having a straightforward and practical method of achieving that goal, and despite the criticisms of shoeing by some barefoot supporters, there is no scientific proof that shoeing in itself is harmful. For an explanation of the function of the foot and how it is affected by shoeing, see 'Form and Function of the Equine Digit' Andrew Parks, The Veterinary Clinics of North America, Equine Practice 2003. Thousands of horses have been shod and lived long and successful lives, while in the wild it is probable that only those horses with good conformation, that predisposed to healthy feet to start with, survived! And the average life expectancy of a truly wild horse is nowhere near as long as that of the well cared for domestic horse.

Of course poor farriery is harmful and, although there are many excellent practitioners, it still seems that worldwide there is a paucity of well qualified farriers willing or able to work in a modern, interactive way with clients and their veterinary surgeons to achieve the best for their horses. Nothing is more vital in the horse owner's quest to have a happy, healthy horse, successfully performing in a chosen discipline, than healthy, durable feet, and it is only frustration with the service on offer that turns most horse owners to seek an alternative solution. Against diehard traditionalism, a practical approach to barefoot may well be the better choice.

INDEX OF SYNONYMS

GENERAL INDEX

Italic page numbers refer to illustrations

The authors wish to thank the Horse Race Betting Levy Board for
permission to reproduce Appendix A.

PHOTOGRAPH ACKNOWLEDGEMENTS

The authors and publishers would like to thank the following people for
   supplying photographs for this book:

Dr D.C. Knottenbelt, University of Liverpool Department of Veterinary
   Clinical Science and Animal Husbandry, pp40 (all), 41 (top left), 77
   (all), 83 (top left), 84 (top left, btm right), 85 (both), 87 (top & btm left),
   91 (both), 93 (mid top, mid left, btm left & right), 100 (left & right), 104
   (right), 105 (right), 111 (left), 117 (mid right), 120 (mid right);
Haydn Price DipWCF, p45 (all);
Dr A.G. Matthews, p84 (btm left);
Dr J.K. O'Brien, University of Bristol, Langford, p90 (right);
Mark Caldwell FWCF, p103 (top left & right);
Dr D.L. Doxey, Department of Veterinary Clinical Studies, University of
   Edinburgh, p119 (right).
All other photographs were taken by Tony or Marcy Pavord.
Black-and-white and colour illustrations in Parts I and III by Visual Image,
   except p54 (Sally Alexander) and p67 (Eva Melhuish)

A DAVID & CHARLES BOOK

David & Charles is a subsidiary of F&W (UK) Ltd.,
an F&W Publications Inc. company

Hardback first published in the UK in 1997
Reprinted in 1998, 1999 (twice), 2000, 2001, 2002 (twice)
Paperback first published in the UK in 2002
Reprinted 2003, 2004
New edition 2004

Distributed in North America
by F&W Publications, Inc.
4700 East Galbraith Road
Cincinnati, OH 45236
1-800-289-0963

A catalogue record for this book is available from the British Library.

ISBN 0 7153 1883 7 (paperback)
ISBN 0 7153 1884 5 (hardback US only)

Book design by Visual Image

Printed in Singapore by KHL Printing Co Pte Ltd
for David & Charles
Brunel House   Newton Abbot   Devon

Visit our website at www.davidandcharles.co.uk

David & Charles books are available from all good bookshops; alternatively you can
contact our Orderline on (0)1626 334555 or write to us at FREEPOST EX2110,
David & Charles Direct, Newton Abbot, TQ12 4ZZ (no stamp required UK mainland).